RECONSTRUCTING SPACE: ARCHITECTURE IN RECENT GERMAN PHOTOGRAPHY

Edited by Michael Mack
Architectural Association

Reconstructing Space: Architecture in Recent German Photography
Editor Michael Mack
Design Jason Beard at Barnbrook
Print Steidl Verlag, Germany

Reconstructing Space has been produced to accompany an exhibition held at the Architectural Association from 19 April to 22 May 1999. The AA is grateful to the German Embassy and the Goethe Institut in London for their support of the exhibition and related lecture series.

AA Publications are intitiated by the Chairman of the Architectural Association, Mohsen Mostafavi.

AA Publications
Editor Pamela Johnston
Editorial Assistants
Clare Barrett and Mark Rappolt

AA Exhibitions Organizer
Andrew Mackenzie

ISBN 1 870890 98 1

AA Publications
36 Bedford Square
London WC1B 3ES
Telephone 0171 887 4021
Fax 0171 414 0782
E-mail publications@arch-assoc.org.uk

Front cover Heidi Specker, *Alexanderplatz, Berlin, 1995* (detail)
Back cover Christine Erhard, *Visitors in front of Curtain Blinds, 1998* (detail)

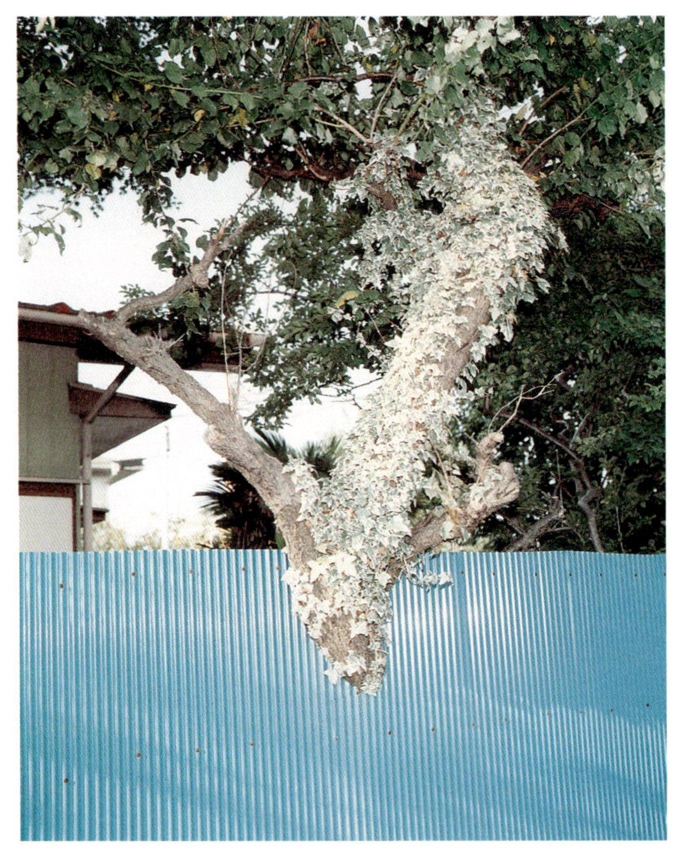
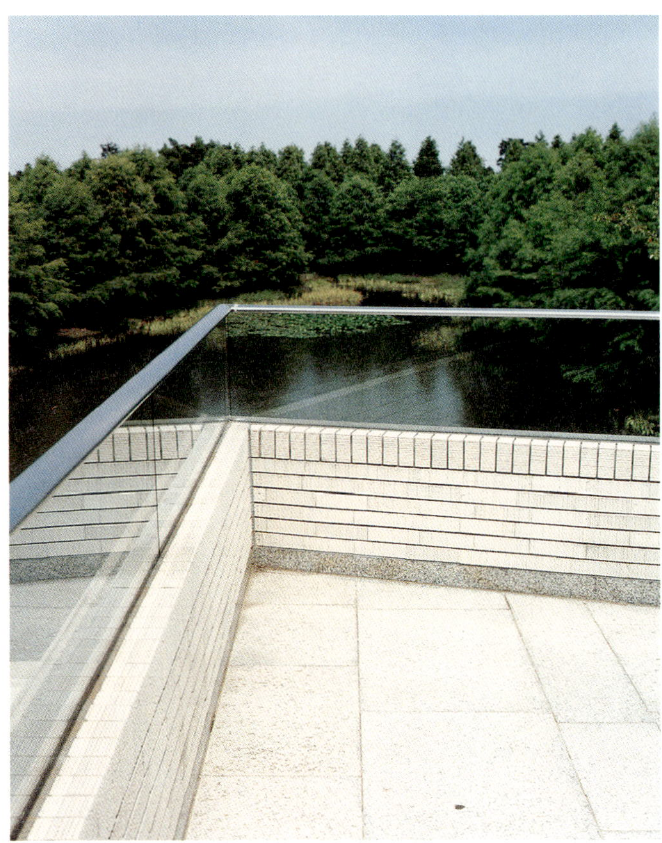
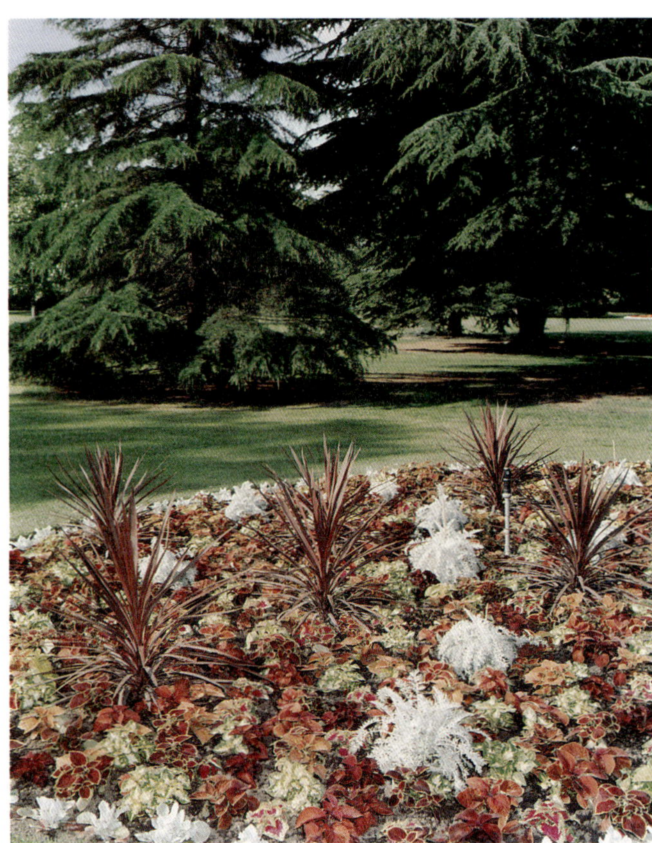
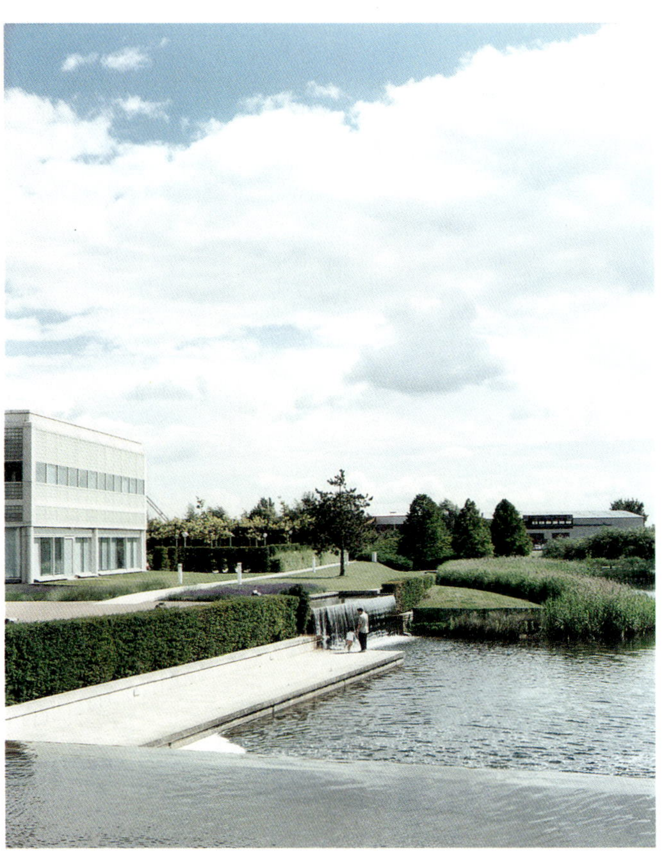

A Sense of Space

Michael Mack

If we judge the work of an architect according to what Adorno described as 'the ability to articulate space purposefully', then photographs have become the measure of that ability. Architecture and photography have been inextricably linked ever since this medium, so perfectly adapted to the two-dimensional representation of static space, came into existence. Architecture has colluded with the camera's ability to manipulate our sense of space, while photography has been obsessively applied to the documentation and interpretation of architecture as a manifestation of culture.

In Germany the entanglement of architecture and photography is reflected in the fascination of modernist architects with the aesthetic of industrial design. Functionalism influenced not only early twentieth-century architecture but has also played an instinctive part in post-industrial architecture. The largely theoretical postmodern break with technological utopianism has now been bridged, with a return to constructions based on transparency and universal design principles. The role of the functionalist aesthetic, and the impact of realism and objectivity as a product of the machine age, can be traced from early twentieth-century photography through to the practice of many of the artists whose work is included here.

All of these artists are involved in some level of construction or fabrication, distinct from the realist and objective position which is usually attributed to the medium. Some create documentary records of environments, then institute a process of cataloguing and exhibiting the photographs, of archiving them in typological systems and series. Other artists view photography as just one element of the creative process: they are paper architects who do not simply represent the space before them, but construct a whole environment for the camera.

The intense engagement of contemporary German artists with the built environment through the medium of photography forms the focus of this project. Comprising a range of diverse essays and photographs, it represents an attempt to consider particular architectures, histories and philosophies which have informed the present scene.

← Michael Danner,
Delocalizer, 1997/1999

Architecture, Industry and Photography: Excavating German Identity

Michael Mack

Many of the artists in this publication investigate architecture because they see it as a reflection of the economic and cultural history of their society. An excavation of that history – of particular movements and significant moments in the development of German identity and nationhood – will illuminate their work.

Industrial Unification & Cultural Pessimism

The German Confederation emerged from the Napoleonic Wars in 1815 as a disparate array of feudal states[1] – a battleground for the Austrian Habsburgs and Prussian Hohenzollerns, far removed from traditional concepts of nationhood.[2] Although the works of Goethe and Schiller had laid the foundations of a German literary culture, cultural identity generally remained tied to the local community – the home town or *Heimat*.

It was only in the mid nineteenth century, with the advent of industrialization and improved education for all levels of society, that the concept of a national culture became relevant to the majority of Germans. In 1866 the Prussian Otto von Bismarck began a military campaign to secure political unification, and success in wars against Austria and France led to the King of Prussia being proclaimed German Emperor in 1870. The celebration of new-found nationhood foreshadowed the euphoria of reunification one hundred and twenty years later.

Before 1870, German industrial development was some way behind that of Britain and France, and certainly lacked the orientation towards mechanical production that characterized the American economy. After 1870, an ambitious strategy of industrialization was funded by French war reparations[3] and fuelled by the abundant coal deposits of the Ruhr. Over the last decades of the nineteenth century the country was transformed from a predominantly rural and agrarian society into an urban industrial economy.

Germany became the powerhouse of Europe by means of a rapid and thorough appropriation of new technology. But while the nation's industry underwent a dynamic modernization, its 'cultural furniture'[4] remained archaic. Among the population at large, the 'shock of the new' raised extreme, irrational fears about the erosion of inherited cultural and moral values by the increasingly powerful – secularizing – forces of liberalism and technology. At the same time Bismarck's new empire, in failing to establish harmony, fell short of the Utopian dreams of a nation-state. A spirit of cultural pessimism and social resentment prevailed, encouraged by the alienating effects of population displacement and urban upheaval.[5] A conservative revolt against this spiritual impoverishment led to a growth in romantic notions of rural nostalgia and pantheism, linked to *völkisch* ideals. With hindsight, this period of German history has been referred to as the source of a developing 'Caesarism' – a desire for some Hegelian hero – in the fabric of the culture. The events of 1914 created the opportunity to identify with a national cause.

Industry & Functionalism

The impact of industrialization upon the landscape was immense. Large swathes of land in the Ruhr, the Saar and Upper Silesia were quickly colonized by the iron and steel industries; brown-coal-burning power stations, engineering plants, chemical works and textile factories were all built in large numbers in the years up to 1918. These production houses, machine rooms and industrial plants were on the whole constructed with reference to pre-industrial architectural styles. The new barons of industry – true to the reactionary tastes of the bourgeoisie – embraced the historicism that dominated European architecture of the time.[6] Buildings modelled on medieval fortresses, gothic castles and baroque palaces were thought to be appropriate to the economic stature of the companies. Such styles articulated the entrepreneurs' desire to appropriate the feudal heritage of the aristocracy; they also served to hide the working operations of the structures – in the hope of avoiding accusations of blight from conservative commentators and the press.

For many years historicism was commonplace in industrial (and particularly mining) structures, which were mostly designed by employees of the industries concerned. In the late nineteenth century, however, a new tendency arose. The possibilities of new construction materials – such as reinforced concrete, steel and glass – placed engineers at the forefront of industrial design. Engineers were hailed as 'the creators of the new architecture',[7] and from around 1900 the possibilities of functional form began to be explored.

It was a collaboration between an engineer and an architect which created one of the most iconic of early German industrial structures – the Zeche Zollern complex of the Gelsenkirchen Mining Company, built between 1898 and 1904 on a site in Böringhausen, west of Dortmund. The first half of the development was completed to designs by Paul Knobbe and included housing for workers. In an effort to raise the company's profile and share-value its owner, Emil Kirkdorf, then commissioned an engineer, Reinhold Krohn, and the most famous *Jugendstil* architect of the day, Bruno Möhring, to produce a machine room to house the first electrically powered winding and pumping gear in a German mine. The hundred-metre-long glass, redbrick and steel building featured an oval entrance portal which has become synonymous with *Jugendstil*. The mine was decommissioned in 1955 and was set to be demolished fourteen years later: the successful public battle to save it marks the moment which coalesced the German industrial preservation movement and led to the founding, throughout the country, of a series of museums and institutes devoted to industrial archaeology.[8]

A significant contribution to the Zeche Zollern history was a 1977 publication, subtitled 'The Beginning of Modern Industrial Architecture', which included one hundred and forty-two photographs taken by Bernd and Hilla Becher in 1971, detailing the interior and exterior of the machine hall, the exterior of the outbuildings, and Knobbe's 'company' homes,[9] each captioned with its address and an indication of the number of families it was designed to house.

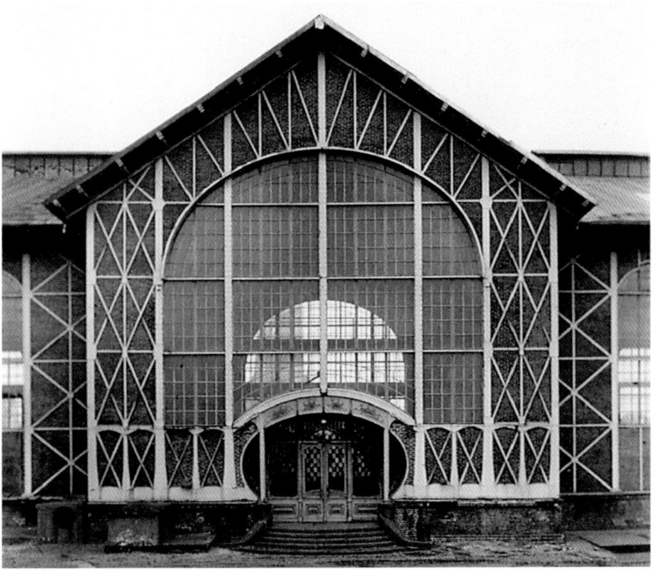

Bernd & Hilla Becher, Zeche Zollern II, Dortmund, Germany 1971

In the early 1900s the *Lebensreformbewegung* (Movement for the Reform of Life) became firmly established among many middle-class groups and associations, paving the way for the emergence of the *Heimatschutz* and *Deutscher Werkbund*. The two movements were strongly linked, particularly as policy was formulated by individuals common to them both. They shared an antipathy towards historicist architecture and supported the production of functional buildings, designed collaboratively by architects and engineers. Both also promoted notions of design imbued with simplicity and honesty, and promoted a social policy grounded in improving the industrial workplace.

Eventually, however, the open membership of the *Heimatschutz* movement became ideologically removed from the elitist *Werkbund*. The *Heimatschutz* (Protection of the Homeland) was not only populist, but had strong links with the aristocracy which helped it bring about legislation against the 'disfigurement' of the landscape by industrialization. It championed traditional building techniques and the Biedermeier architecture of the early nineteenth century, as opposed to classical models.

The *Werkbund* sought to create a national art without any stylistic imitation. Its ideals were typified by the work of one of its early members, Peter Behrens, during his seven-year tenure as artistic director of the AEG Company. Behrens's AEG Turbine Factory (1909)[10] is one of the landmarks of twentieth-century architecture, yet his influence derives mainly from the fact that he employed Walter Gropius, Mies van der Rohe and Le Corbusier in his Neubabelsberg studio prior to the First World War.

Walter Gropius was intimately involved in the output of the *Werkbund*. He lectured at its annual meetings, wrote for its Yearbook (*Jahrbuch*), and curated exhibitions. In 1914, with Adolf Meyer, he designed the facades of the Fagus factory in Alfeld. The impact of such functionalist structures was presciently described by Hermann Muthesius in a lecture at the *Werkbund's* Conference in Cologne that same year:

> with the internationalization of our lives, a certain uniformity in architectural forms across the globe will become manifest... those forms which have been developed in the German movement for... industrial, commercial and transport buildings will also become the world forms.[11]

(Muthesius may not, however, have anticipated the extreme forms of functionalism in late capitalism – the blind corrugated boxes which blandly dominate today's industrial estates.)

The Werkbund was instrumental in the development of a modern industrial architecture in Germany – and one of the means it used to achieve this was photography. At a meeting of the *Werkbund's* steering committee in Würzburg in February 1909, it was agreed to gather a collection of photographs of exemplary factories for an exhibition at the annual conference in Frankfurt later that year. The archive was subsequently stored and developed as a holding of the German Museum of Art in Trade and Commerce in Hagen, Westphalia. By 1910 the collection included forty thousand prints and formed a resource for the *Werkbund* magazine (*Der Industriebau*) and Yearbook, as well as for local exhibits and international touring shows.[12]

Gropius was given the task of co-ordinating the material, and used it as the basis for his 1912 exhibition, *Industriebauten*, and for some of his influential lectures and essays of the period.[13] He also added photographs to the collection, notably of massive grain silos, which he described in the 1913 Yearbook as being 'almost as impressive in their monumental power as the buildings of ancient Egypt'.[14] In the same volume silos were included in Muthesius's list of structures appropriate to the modern age,[15] and they have since reappeared as icons of modernist design in many publications,[16] not least in the first volume of the Bechers' own work.[17]

Weimar: Anonymity & Objectivity

Founded in the aftermath of war and revolution, the Weimar Republic had one of the most completely democratic paper constitutions ever written. Its cultural movements reflected this spirit, placing great emphasis upon honesty, realism and fact.

Architects of the *Heimatschutz* and *Werkbund* played a major role in the country's reconstruction in the immediate post-war period (though the *Heimatschutz* was eventually discredited by its role in the corruption of *völkisch* principles). A politicized concept of architecture prevailed as a vehicle for revolutionary social transformation. Yet the ideals of expressionism remained largely unrealized, as the paper architectures of Bruno Taut, Mies van der Rohe and Erich Mendelsohn make clear. The Treaty of Versailles, which required Germany to agree 'to the direct application of her economic resources to reparation',[18] thrust the country into another period of economic upheaval. Political romanticism grew amongst a populace resentful of military defeat and the terms of the Treaty; the seeds of National Socialism were sown.

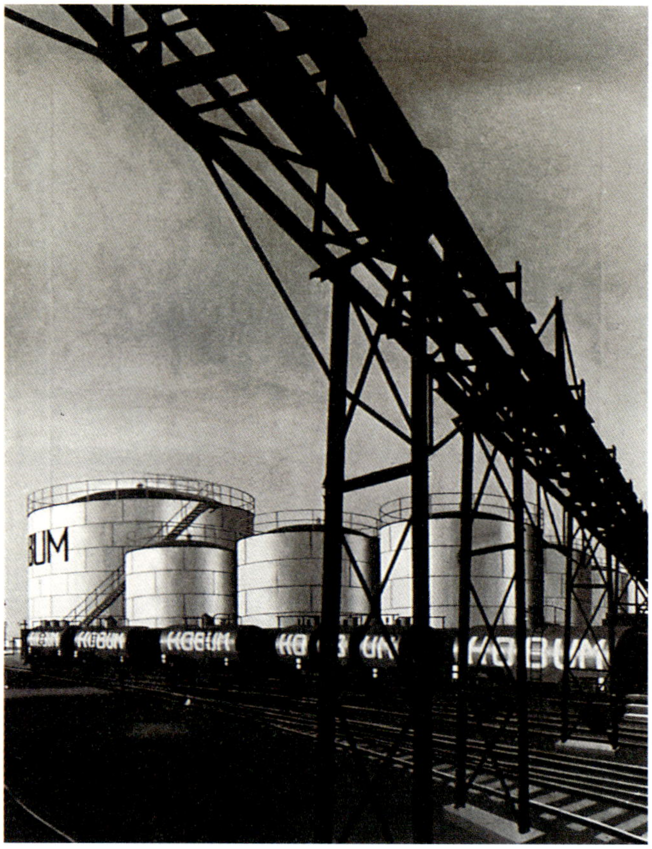

→ George Grossberg, Oil Tanks, 1933

A brief economic stability was achieved in 1924 with the implementation of the Dawes Plan.[19] The influx of venture capital (mainly from America) stimulated a number of disparate movements that had existed in a vacuum since the war. The various strands of German Dada, which had replaced expressionism, coalesced into the *Neue Sachlichkeit* (New Objectivity). The latter began as a critical description of social realist painting,[20] but expanded to include manifestations of the same spirit in other arts (unadorned design, functional architecture, the utilitarian music of Hindemith and Weill, and Brecht's matter-of-fact verse).[21]

In the early years of the twentieth century Hermann Muthesius had applied the concept of *Sachlichkeit* to design theory as a strategy for achieving a synthesis of art and culture. His project was part of a broader movement of social reform founded upon the revolutionary changes unleashed by new technology and industrial production, and it was governed by principles of pragmatism:

> The goal remains sincerity, straightforwardness and a purity of artistic sensibility, qualities that avoid all secondary considerations and superficialities, so that one can be fully dedicated to the great problem of the time.[22]

In the Weimar period this social responsibility matured into a diminishment of the artist's personality in favour of a new concern for the collective – reflected in Mies's requirement that architecture should amount to the 'will of the age':

> The decisive achievements in all areas are objective in nature, and their originators are usually unknown. They are part of the trend of our time toward anonymity. Our engineering structures are typical examples: gigantic dams, huge industrial installations and important bridges... Our utilitarian buildings will mature into architecture only if they interpret their time through their perfect functional expression.[23]

This emphasis on utility and fact manifested itself in the widespread application of the camera in reportage and documentary pursuits. A cool, detached and positivistic manner was developed under numerous guises. At the Bauhaus under Lászlo Moholy-Nagy, the ideology of functionalism led photographers to establish a 'new vision' that went beyond 'the prevailing concepts of artistic reproduction' (which were limited by the 'rules of perspective') to explore the medium's 'own laws' and 'inherent possibilities'.[24] A number of photographers pursued these possibilities with decidedly more emphasis on straightforwardness than was the

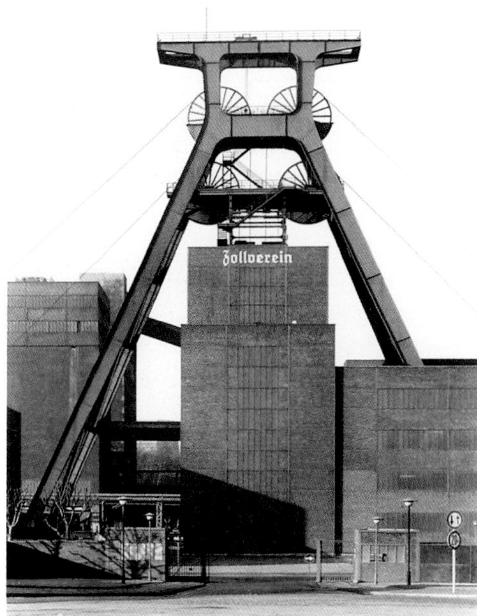

Bernd & Hilla Becher, Zeche Zollverein, Essen, Ruhrgebiet, 1973

case with Moholy-Nagy's constructivist-influenced experimentation. Two publications of 1928 firmly entrenched photography in *Neue Sachlichkeit*: Albert Renger-Patzsch's *The World is Beautiful* showed the application of the camera to 'capture the magic of material things',[25] while Karl Blossfeldt's *Urformen der Kunst* contained detailed and abstract studies of plants which revealed in plant existence 'a totally unexpected treasure of analogies and forms'.[26]

Another photographer of the Weimar period, August Sander, is often cited as the significant influence for many German artists using photography today. Sander's project involved the systematic documentation and categorization of all classes and professions within German society. He framed his work in terms of the camera's capacity to extract patterns and types and thereby increase our understanding of reality:

> Nothing seems better suited than photography to give an absolutely faithful historical picture of our time ...let me honestly tell the truth about our age and people.[27]

Sander also used photography as a means of preserving buildings for posterity. Before the Second World War he created a catalogue of Cologne's landmark structures which became a record of the city's grandeur before its destruction by bombing – and a valuable guide for its reconstruction. Preservation, by means of documentation, has been a driving force behind much photography of architecture in Germany.

Between the wars the culture of collecting was reinforced by the systems of rationalization applied to industry and economics. The archival model was adopted by *Neue Sachlichkeit* photography (in the work of Karl Blossfeldt, for example). It also figured in the writings of intellectuals such as Walter Benjamin, whose enormous collection of notes and images of nineteenth-century Parisian culture formed the foundations of a 'materialist' reading of history.[28] The materials in question were the industrial fossils of modernity – buildings, technologies and commodities – and it was with the effects of industrialization that Benjamin was engaged.

In a similar vein, Louis Aragon equated the inter-war fascination with technology with a sacred 'mythology of the modern' and proposed a reading of the 'concrete forms... external symbols... and the painted or sculpted representations of its divinities'.[29] Among the deities of this religion were the enormous oil and gas tanks at petrol stations, emblazoned with the corporate logos of Texaco, Esso and Shell. Aragon paid them irreverent homage:

> Here are the great red gods, the great yellow gods, the great green gods... A strange statuary presides over the birth of these simulacra. Hardly ever before have human beings submitted themselves to so barbarous a view of destiny and force... anonymous sculptors... constructed these metallic phantoms... These idols bear a family resemblance that renders them awesome.[30]

During the Weimar years industry became a common subject matter for artists – the almost photo-realist paintings of George Grossberg being just one example. At the same time German industrial architecture adapted to American systems of rationalization.[31] (The Chrysler plant in Berlin (1927) and Coca-Cola plant in Essen (1929) provided firsthand experience of these methods.) Plants were modernized. The expressionistic bias of the pre-war *Werkbund* was adjusted to fit industrial mass production and machine standardization, and building construction was made to respond to new systems of labour management.

In this boom-before-bust economy, the threat of inflation and speculation resulted in the creation of conglomerates. For one of these – the biggest coal and steel company in Europe, Vereinigte Stahlwerke AG – the Ruhr architects Fritz Schupp and Martin Kremmer designed a grandiose corporate symbol incorporating the ideals of functionalism and *Sachlichkeit*. Shown left, the Zollverein Pit No. XII in Essen was built between 1927 and 1932. It remained in operation until 1987, and on its closure was made the subject of a preservation order.

Reconstruction

Following the Second World War Germany was again battle-scarred, burdened by enormous reparation obligations, and subject to control by external forces. The country was partitioned – contrary to the Allies' original intention – and was treated as a buffer zone during the Cold War. The Potsdam Agreement called for the dismantling of large elements of German heavy industry, primarily out of a desire to destroy any capacity for rearmament,[32] but also as a form of reparation. The Soviet zone was at first subject to the wholesale removal of industrial plants for reconstruction on sites in Russia, but this proved impracticable and occupation by Soviet companies became a preferred alternative.[33] In the West, on the other hand, the process of dismantling was scaled down as the Allies came to realize the essential role of German industry in the rebuilding of the European economy as a whole.

The process of reconstruction was aided by many who saw it as a new beginning. Economic migrants boosted the population beyond pre-war figures, and machinery removed from plants was often replaced by the most modern equipment. Reconstruction overtook reparation in an attempt to reduce the costs of occupation. As the economy began to regenerate, the concept of reconstruction (*Wiederaufbau*) was replaced by 'new building' (*Aufbau* or *Neubau*).[34] As in the Weimar period, the post-war struggle to regain stability resulted in a boom which stimulated the reconstruction of the country's cities and industrial base.

In 1952 the German Federal Republic became a founder member of the European Coal and Steel Community, the forerunner of the EC. By 1957 the country had regained its position as a world economic power: the *Wirtschaftswunder* had been achieved. As traditional industries were displaced, the electrical engineering and information sectors expanded to fill the void.[35] During the ambitious period of reconstruction in the 1960s, ecological concepts of preservation gained strength and *Industriekultur* developed. In the following decade, conservation laws were extended to cover the industrial landscape, as a testimony to man's interaction with nature.[36]

Both Bernd Becher and August Sander are from the Siegerland, to the east of Cologne, where their fathers were employed in the mining industry. Becher began to make drawings of the mining and heavy industrial structures in the region around the same time that the coal industry entered a crisis provoked by competition from alternative sources of fuel. He also collected early photographs that documented the history of the local culture, taking particular interest in the work of the amateur photographer Peter Weller. Part of this collection was included in *Documenta 6* at Kassel.[37]

Weller had built up an extended record of the late-nineteenth-century development of the region, photographing people at home, occupied in leisure pursuits, and at work, as well as documenting the mines and other industrial buildings where most of them were employed.[38] As part of their research the Bechers have returned to many of Weller's sites in order to update the catalogue of industrial culture begun by him (and continued by the likes of Sander and Renger-Patzsch). The Bechers' own work has played a significant role in the developing industrial preservation movement, and their teaching at the Düsseldorf Art Academy has instilled in the generation of artists now dominating European art a subtle sensibility of photography and its possibilities in the excavation of man-made landscapes.[39]

Reunification

In the German Democratic Republic the creation of a communist state formed the basis for physical and ideological reconstruction. Subservience to the state was justified by relating the atrocities of the Third Reich to the worst excesses of capitalist imperialism, and the country took up a new mission to propagate Marxism.[40] Communist reconstruction also sustained economic recovery throughout the 1960s, and in the mid 1970s international recognition of GDR statehood appeared to confirm the long-term division of Germany. However, communist values began to be eroded by the intrusion of Western mass media and, during the 1980s, disillusionment with the worsening economic situation rekindled the old desire for German unity. Around this time, the governments of East and West Germany began to join forces to oppose Russian and American military sites. On the 3rd of October 1990 reunification was finally achieved.

{ Bernd & Hilla Becher, Grube San Fernando, Herdorf, Siegerland, 1963

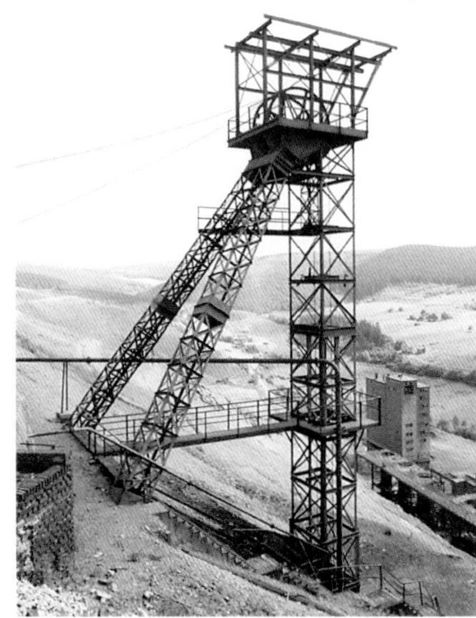

Germany has come full circle: from feudal fragmentation to a unity destroyed by two world wars; from the divisions of mid-twentieth-century ideology to a nation reconstituted from the ashes of xenophobia. The final irony is that Germany's fractured histories appear to be appropriate experience for a country now leading the harmonization process in the build-up to a supranational European state.

Within a few years of reunification a major photographic archive of architectural sites in the former GDR was established. The collection was funded by the newly privatized gas utility company of Leipzig, the Verbundnetz Gas AG, and was first put on show at the company's stand at a trade fair. The subtitle of a catalogue published in 1994 refers to the basis of the project - 'A Collection of Topographic East German Photography'.[41] Described as an 'archive of reality', it is intended to preserve architectures which are representative of a culture undergoing structural change in the tide of post-reunification reconstruction. The archive initially consisted of the work of four photographers in and around Leipzig, but it has expanded rapidly, with the addition of work by photographers from the former GDR who have documented post-war built landscapes in the East.[42]

Conclusion

The map of Germany has been shaped by the fluctuating fortunes of war, reparation, unification and reconstruction. An investigation of that history – as revealed by the changing fabric of the built environment – is the basis for much of the work included here. Many of the artists explore the economic, functional and cultural aspects of architecture as well as the social conditions which have given rise to particular kinds of buildings. Their subjects include the post-industrial sites of consumerism, the growth of radical new process technologies, research and service-based industries. The work is invariably in the form of a series of images which establish a narrative of socio-historical reality, based on photography's potential to retain some indexical trace of its subject.

Over the course of this century photographic archives have come to be used as storehouses of history. Photography has acquired the power to influence our perception of the world around us. August Sander referred to this in a radio broadcast in 1931, when he elaborated the programme that has driven much of the German photography of architecture of our time:

> We can see the human spirit of a particular age expressed in the landscape, and we can comprehend it with the camera. It is the same for architecture and industry and all other large and small works. The landscape within a particular boundary expresses the historic physiognomic image of a nation.[43]

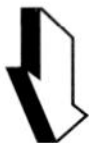

1 The Congress of Vienna (1815) resulted in the formation of a Confederation (*Bund*) of thirty-nine German states out of the medieval patchwork of three hundred and sixty states.
2 The Austrian House of Habsburg held the office of Holy Roman Emperor and opposed the claims of the Prussian Hohenzollern dynasty.
3 The reparations amounted to five billion francs (plus interest) and the cession of Alsace and Lorraine (with their highly developed textile industries and rich deposits of iron ore and potash). So began a cycle of reparations that defined the fluctuations of Germany's borders during the first half of the twentieth century.
4 Thorstein Veblen, *Imperial Germany and the Industrial Revolution* (1915) (University of Michigan Press, 1966) p. 86.
5 See Fritz Stern, *The Politics of Cultural Despair: A Study in the Rise of the Germanic Ideology* (Los Angeles: University of California Press, 1961) and George L. Mosse, *The Crisis of German Ideology* (London: Weidenfeld and Nicholson, 1964).
6 For an excellent and detailed analysis of German industrial architecture in this period see Matthew Jeffries, *Politics and Culture in Wilhelmine Germany: The Case of Industrial Architecture* (Oxford/Washington, DC: Berg, 1995).
7 Henri van de Velde, *Die Rolle der Ingeniere in der modernen Architektur [1899]*, in Sigfried Giedion *Space, Time and Architecture: The Charles Eliot Norton Lectures for 1938-1939* (Berkeley: Yale University Press, 1966; first edition 1941) p. 217.
8 See Jeffries (1995) pp. 33-9.
9 Bernd and Hilla Becher, Hans Günther Conrad, Eberhard G. Neumann, *Zeche Zollern 2: Aufbruch zur Modernen Industriearchitektur und Technik* (Munich: Prestel, 1977).
10 See Jeffries (1995) p. 126.
11 Hermann Muthesius, *Die Werkbund-Arbeit der Zukunft* (1914) p. 46. Quoted in Jeffries (1995) p. 177 (translation Jeffries).
12 The photography collection of the German Museum of Trade and Industry is now split between the Werkbund-Archive, Berlin, the Kaiser Wilhelm Museum, Krefeld, and the Karl Ernst Osthaus-Museum, Hagen.
13 Jeffries (1995) pp. 106-9.
14 Walter Gropius 'Die Kunst in Industrie und Handel' in *Jahrbuch des Deutsches Werkbundes* (Jena 1913) pp. 21-2. Quoted in Giedion (1966) p. 343.
15 *Jahrbuch des Deutsches Werkbundes* (Jena, 1913) p. 30.
16 For example, see Walter Benjamin, *Gesammelte Schriften*: 1, edited by Rolf Tiedemann and Hermann Schweppenhaüser with Theodor W. Adorno and Gershom Scholem (Frankfurt am Main: Suhrkamp, 1982) and Le Corbusier, *Towards a New Architecture* (1923) (London: Architectural Press, 1946) pp. 21-31.
Le Corbusier's book includes strangely retouched illustrations of silos, some of which were in the Werkbund collection. In one example, captioned 'Canadian Grain Store' (although, according to *Werkbund* records, it is in Buenos Aires), the gabled adornment has been removed to better illustrate the functionalist creed. Compare *Moderne Baukunst 1900-1914* (Krefelder Kunstmuseen, 1993) p. 205, plate 270 (the Werkbund photograph) and Le Corbusier (1946) p. 27 (the manipulated version).
17 Bernhard and Hilla Becher, *Anonyme Sculpturen: Eine Typologie Technischer Bauten* (Düsseldorf: Art Press, 1970).
18 This included the payment of 20,000 million gold marks, the cession of Alsace and Lorraine to France, and the surrender of all Germany's overseas possessions. *The Treaty of Peace Between the Allied and Associated Powers and Germany* (London: HMSO, 1919).
19 In 1923 Germany's inability to meet its reparation payments resulted in the occupation by France and Belgium of the Ruhr. The Dawes Plan involved a 200 million dollar loan that enabled Germany to meet its outstanding reparation debts and begin a five-year period of relative peace and industrial growth.
20 Although the 1925 Mannheim exhibition of the same name did include certain of Munich's 'Magic Realists'.
21 On the Weimar period in general see John Willett, *The New Sobriety 1917-1933* (London: Thames and Hudson, 1978).
22 Hermann Muthesius, *Style-Architecture and Building Art: Transformations of Architecture in the Nineteenth Century and its Present Condition* (1902) (Santa Monica, CA: Getty Centre, 1994) trans. Stanford Anderson, p. 100.
23 Ludwig Mies van der Rohe, 'Architecture and the Will of the Age' (from *Der Querschnitt*, 4 (1924) pp. 31-2), in Anton Kaes, Martin Jay, Edward Dimenberg, eds., *The Weimar Republic Sourcebook* (Berkeley: University of California Press, 1994) pp. 438-9.
24 László Moholy-Nagy, *Painting Photography Film* (1925) (London, 1969) pp. 27 and 35.
25 'The secret of a good photograph … resides in its realism. For rendering our impressions of nature, of plants, animals, the works of architects and sculptors, and the creations of engineers, photography offers us a most reliable tool', Albert Renger-Patzsch, 'Aims' in *Das Deutsche Lichtbild* (1927) p. xviii, trans. Joel Agee, in *Photography in the Modern Era: European Documents and Critical Writings, 1913-1940*, Christopher Phillips, ed. (New York: Metropolitan Museum of Art/Aperture) p. 105.
26 Quoted in Susan Buck-Morss *The Dialectics of Seeing: Walter Benjamin and the Arcades Project* (Cambridge, MA: MIT Press, 1991) p. 158.
27 August Sander, 'Remarks on my Exhibition at the Cologne Art Union November 1927', in Kaes, Jay and Dimenberg (1994) pp. 645-6.
28 Published in Benjamin, *Gesammelte Schriften*: V. See also Buck-Morss (1991).
29 Louis Aragon *Le Paysan de Paris* (Paris: Gallimard, 1926) p. 145, trans. Simon Watson Taylor, *Aragon: Paris Peasant* (London: Jonathan Cape, 1971) pp. 130-1.
30 Louis Aragon (1926) pp. 146-7. My translation relies, in part, on that by Watson Taylor (1971) pp. 131-2, and Buck-Morss (1991) p. 257.
31 See Otto Bauer, 'Rationalisation and the Social Order' (1931), in Kaes, Jay and Dimenberg (1994) pp. 410-11.
32 The Allies had become aware of how the National Socialists had re-armed Germany during the Weimar period with the collaboration of industry, despite the limitations imposed at Versailles in 1918. See the images by Johannes Bruns on pp. 42-47 which relate to aircraft hangars built secretly in the late 1920s and early 1930s for use by the Luftwaffe.
33 See Roy E. H. Mellor, *The Two Germanies: A Modern Geography* (London: Harper and Row, 1978) pp. 144-6.
34 See Jeffrey M. Diefendorf, *In the Wake of War: The Reconstruction of German Cities after World War II* (New York and Oxford: Oxford University Press, 1993).
35 See Trevor Wild and Philip Jones, eds., *De-Industrialisation and New Industrialisation in Britain and Germany* (London: Anglo-German Foundation, 1991).
36 The period saw the institutionalization of industrial history with the establishment of the Museum of Technical and Cultural Monuments in Hagen (1973), the Bochum Mining Museum (1975) and the Rhein and Westphalia Industrial Museum (1979). In 1977 the Bechers' *Zeche Zollern II* was published, followed by a book on the framework houses of the Siegenland, reflecting not only Bernd's personal relation to the region but also the strong opposition in the mid 1970s to the demolition of workers' housing estates linked to mines, for example in Eisenheim, Ückendorf and Homberg.
37 Documenta 6, vol. 2, *Fotografie Film Video* (Kassel, 1977) p. 82. The eight images from the Bechers' collection were exhibited in a section entitled 'Industry and Technology', alongside works by Germaine Krull, Werner Manz, Renger-Patzsch and Charles Sheeler. See also Wend Fischer, *Industriebauten 1830-1930: Eine fotografische Dokumentation von Bernd und Hilla Becher* (Munich: Staatliches Museum für Angewandte Kunst, 1967).
38 See Winfried Ranke and Gottfried Korff, *Hauberg und Eisen Landwirtschaft und Industrie im Siegerland um 1900: Photographie von Peter Weller* (Munich: Schirmer Mosel, 1980).
39 The photographers who studied under Bernd Becher at the Düsseldorf Art Academy between 1976 and 1997, and who are included in this volume are: Laurenz Berges, Johannes Bruns, Andreas Gursky, Candida Höfer, Thomas Ruff, Heiner Schilling, Thomas Struth and Petra Wunderlich.
40 Karl Gernot Kuehn *Caught: The Art of Photography in the German Democratic Republic* (Berkeley/Los Angeles: University of California Press, 1997) pp. 27 and 29.
41 Rolf Sachsse, *VorOrt: Eine Sammlung Topografischer: Fotografien Ostdeutschlands* (Leipzig: VNG, 1994). The four photographers were Max Baumann, Farnk-Heinrich Müller, Matthias Hoch (see pp. 80-85) and Thomas Wolf.
42 A second, far more substantial, private catalogue was published in 1997. A further four photographers were added, including Ulrich Wüst, see pp. 64-71.
43 August Sander, 'Photography: A Universal Language', Lecture 5, 1931. Broadcast on West German Radio (WDR), Cologne. Cited in *August Sander, Photographs of An Epoch 1904–1959* (Philadelphia: Aperture, 1980) p. 94.

Walter Benjamin, Mimesis and the Dreamworld of Photography

Neil Leach

Walter Benjamin wrote extensively on photography. Aside from his 'A Small History of Photography', there are references to photography throughout his works. Much of his famous essay, 'The Work of Art in the Age of Mechanical Reproduction', is devoted to film and photography. Indeed, for Benjamin, photography captures the very essence of the age of mechanical reproduction, even if, as he acknowledges, film is better suited to grasp its transitory, fleeting character. Moreover, Benjamin's writings are peppered with photographic allusions. Not only do we find references to the 'snapshot' throughout his oeuvre — as in the piece, 'Surrealism: The Last Snapshot of the European Intelligentsia' — but the very flash of recognition that forms the core of the 'dialectics of seeing' seems to have been drawn as much from the burning magnesium powder of photography as from the lightning flash of nature.

It is as though human beings — in an age increasingly dominated by photography — have taken on the attributes of the camera. Just as workmen in the factory, as Benjamin observes, are conditioned by the jolting, jarring, repetitive actions of the machine, such that their own behaviour begins to replicate those actions, so too human beings in general have adapted to the world of the camera. We now see the world in terms of the 'snapshot', and according to the mechanism of the camera itself. Indeed Benjamin makes an explicit reference to the 'flash bulb' and the process of photographic exposure when describing the way that various architectural spaces are imprinted on to the mind:

> Anyone can observe that the duration for which we are exposed to impressions has no bearing on their fate in memory. Nothing prevents our keeping rooms in which we have spent twenty-four hours more or less clearly in our memory, and forgetting others in which we passed months. It is not, therefore, due to insufficient exposure time if no image appears on the plate of remembrance. More frequent, perhaps, are the cases when the half-light of habit denies the plate the necessary light for years, until one day from an alien source it flashes as if from burning magnesium powder, and now a snapshot transfixes the room's image on the plate. Nor is this very mysterious, since such moments of sudden illumination are at the same time moments when we are beside ourselves, and while our waking, habitual, everyday self is involved actively or passively in what is happening, our deeper self rests in another place and is touched by the shock, as is the little heap of magnesium powder by the flame of the match.[1]

The mind acts like a form of camera obscura: a provocative analogy that establishes a connection between the mind and the architectural environment via a form of 'photographic' image. And the image plays a vital role in Benjamin's way of thinking, especially in the two autobiographical pieces, 'A Berlin Childhood around 1900' and 'A Berlin Chronicle'.[2] Memories are constructed as images, and his whole recollection of childhood is presented in largely architectural vignettes — 'street images', as he terms them. Descriptions of buildings, such as his old school with its frosted glass and 'carved wooden battlements over the doors', are presented as brief verbal portraits that develop a form of 'unconscious optics', highlighting often overlooked features with their close-up details.[3] These are snapshots of the physical fabric of Berlin, on to which has been etched, as though through some photosensitive process, a deeply personal sense of meaning. Thus the classrooms are haunted by Benjamin's fear of the Abitur examination, and by 'dreamlike memories' of the damp odour of sweat caused by rushing up the stone steps into the school. Otherwise insignificant places have been charged with a special significance as part of a mental 'map', as Benjamin calls it, of his early childhood experiences in Berlin.[4]

If the mind stores these images as though in some photo album, to recollect one's youth is, as it were, to leaf through the pages of that album, which constitutes the visual archive of the mind. Each image is charged with the capacity to retrieve a past. Like Proust with his tale of the madeleine cakes, these snapshots trigger unconscious associations of a bygone world, and in the flash of recognition past and present are conjoined for a fleeting moment. But might not the corollary also hold true? If the mind acts, like some vast photographic album, as a repository of images of past events, might not actual photographs act as a register of potential events? In this sense the photographic image may have some privileged role in summoning up an entirely new world. In order to fully appreciate a photograph, the mind must work in creative and imaginative ways so as to engage *through the medium of the photograph* with the world that it represents. This article addresses this process. It does so in the context of Benjamin's autobiographical writings on Berlin and the insights they offer into how photographs can act as a form of window on to the architecture that they depict.

Benjamin and the Picture Postcard

Benjamin makes few references to actual photographs in his possession, but he does claim to have been an avid collector of picture postcards. In 'A Berlin Chronicle' he describes how as a young boy he started this collection, much of it supplied by his maternal grandmother, who was an inveterate traveller. These postcards had a magnetic effect on the young Benjamin. They seem to have had the capacity to transport him to the places they depicted, as though by some form of magic carpet:

> For I was there — in Tabarz, Brindisi, Madonna di Campiglio, Westerland, when I gazed, unable to tear myself away, at the wooded slope of Tabarz covered with glowing red berries, the yellow-and-white-daubed quays at Brindisi, the cupolas of Madonna di Campiglio printed bluish on blue, and the bows of the 'Westerland' slicing high through the waves.[5]

⟨ Martin Zeller, Eldenaer Straße 2, Berlin, 22.02.96

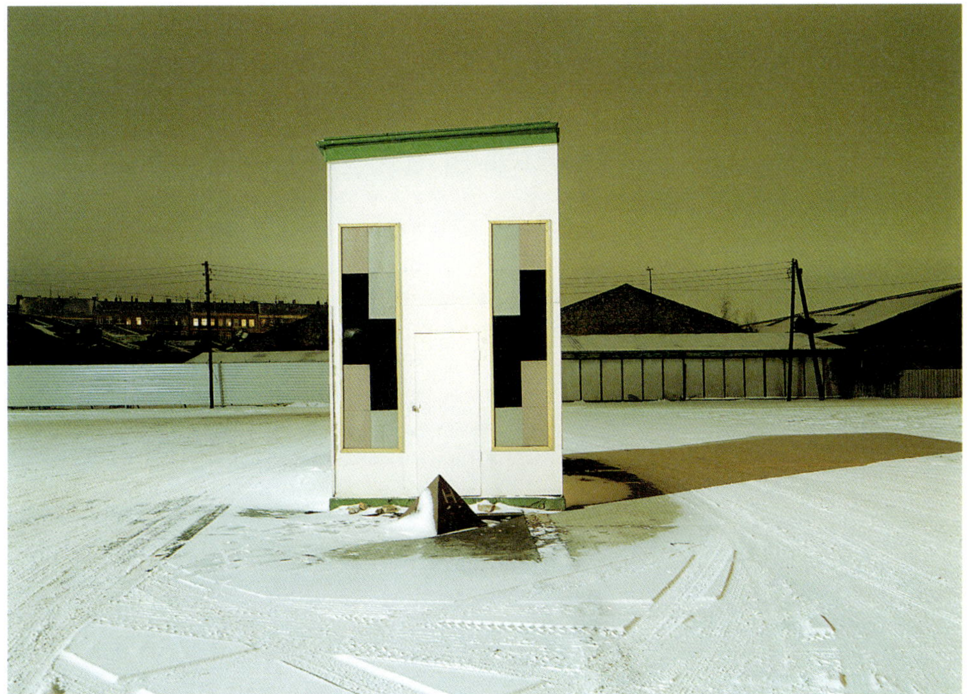

This seemingly throw-away comment — 'I was there ... when I gazed' — is one which merits further investigation. It is, arguably, part of a consistent and highly sophisticated theory of representation that adds a certain crucial gloss to Benjamin's aesthetic theory in general and to his approach towards photography in particular. Nor is the observation of this phenomenon an isolated, and therefore insignificant, remark by Benjamin. In the essay 'The Work of Art' there is a further enigmatic reference on a similar theme:

> A man who concentrates before a work of art is absorbed by it. He enters into this work of art the way that legend tells of the Chinese painter when he viewed his finished painting.[6]

This comment, seemingly overlooked by mainstream commentators on Benjamin, is explained by a fuller version contained in 'Die Mummerehlen', a fragment of 'A Berlin Childhood' which has yet to be published in English. This tells the tale of the young Benjamin being absorbed into the world depicted on a porcelain vase:

> [The story] comes from China and tells of an old painter who gave his newest painting to friends to look at. The painting was of a park, a narrow path along the water and through some foliage, ending at a small door offering entry in the back to a little house. The friends looked around for the painter, but he was gone and in the picture. He walked along the narrow path to the door, stopped in front of it, turned around, smiled, and disappeared through the crack. So was I, with my little bowls and brushes, suddenly in the picture. I became similar to the porcelain, into which I moved with a cloud of colour.[7]

The process by which Benjamin becomes absorbed either into the world of the porcelain vase or into the scenes depicted on the picture postcards can be explained, I would argue, by engaging with Benjamin's provocative theory of mimesis, which suggests a way in which children in particular have the ability to identify with and assimilate to another world. Moreover, once Benjamin's use of the concept of mimesis has been examined, and its relevance to the visual arts articulated, it can be recognized as possibly one of his most important contributions to aesthetic theory.

Benjamin and Mimesis

In *One-Way Street* Walter Benjamin offers a telling description of a child hiding:

> Standing behind the doorway curtain, the child becomes himself something floating and white, a ghost. The dining table under which he is crouching turns him into the wooden idol in a temple whose four pillars are the carved legs. And behind a door he is himself door, wears it as his heavy mask and as a shaman will bewitch all those who unsuspectingly enter. At no cost must he be found. When he pulls faces, he is told, the clock need only strike and he will remain so. The element of truth in this he finds out in his hiding place. Anyone who discovers him can petrify him as an idol under the table, weave him for ever as a

ghost into the curtain, banish him for life into the heavy door. And so, at the seeker's touch he drives out with a loud cry the demon who has so transformed him — indeed, without waiting for the moment of discovery, he grabs the hunter with a shout of self-deliverance.[8]

What is striking about this story is the way in which the child becomes so perfectly at one with the environment. Behind the curtain, the child turns into the curtain, 'floating and white', like a 'ghost'. Under the dining table the child becomes a wooden idol in a temple, and behind a door he is himself a door. Just as the child might carry the burden of the face he is pulling, if caught in that pose when the clock strikes, so he risks remaining camouflaged and absorbed into the environment. He needs to offer a shriek of self-deliverance to free himself from the spell which has made him identical to the interior landscape around him.

What Benjamin is alluding to here is the theory of mimesis which he developed in two short writings, 'Doctrine of the Similar' and 'On the Mimetic Faculty', the latter being a condensed reworking of the former.[9] Mimesis here should not be understood in the Platonic sense of simple 'imitation'. In Walter Benjamin's writings, as in Adorno's, mimesis is a psychoanalytic term — taken from Freud — that refers to a creative engagement with an object. Freud writes about the term in the context of jokes. Mimesis is ideational. It operates through the medium of the idea, and is what allows one to empathize with the subject of a joke. In listening to the tale about the unfortunate individual who slips on a banana skin, one puts oneself in the position of that individual and imagines oneself also slipping, drawing upon memories of similar experiences. But the implications of the term extend beyond empathizing with the subject of a joke. Mimesis is a term, as Freud himself predicted, of great potential significance for aesthetics.[10]

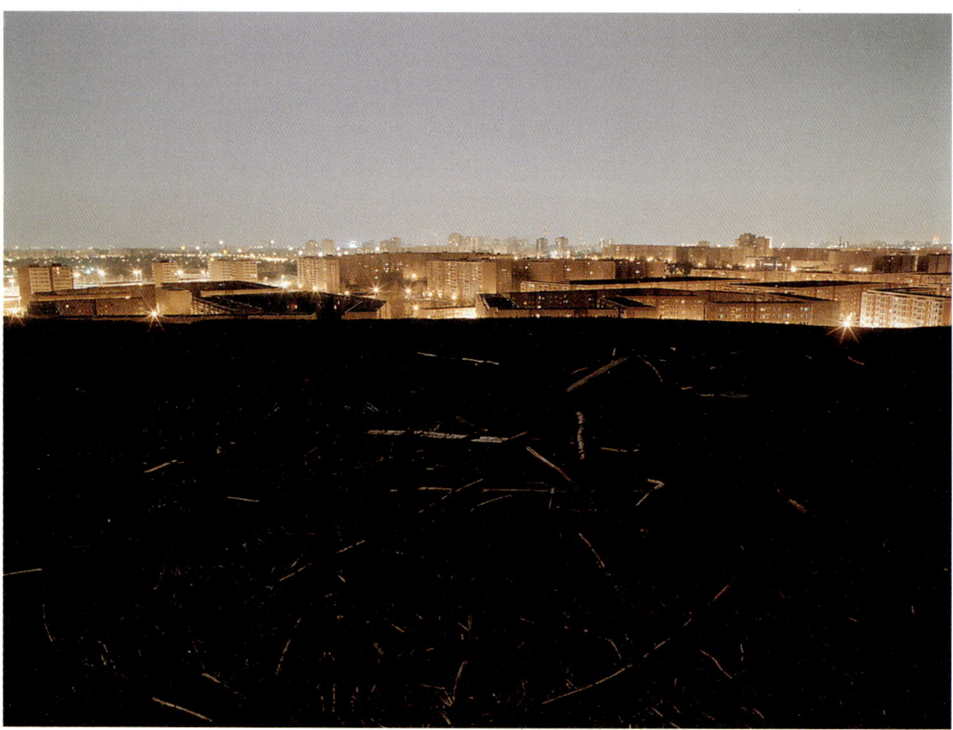

{} Martin Zeller, Ahrensfelder Berge, Berlin, 21.04.97

For Benjamin the concept of mimesis allows for an identification with the external world. It facilitates the possibility of forging a link between the self and the other. The principle behind mimesis is the urge to seek similarities as a means of relating to the world. 'Every day', Benjamin writes, 'the urge grows stronger to get hold of an object at very close range by way of its likeness, its reproduction.'[11] To understand the meaning of mimesis in Benjamin we must recognize its origin in the process of modelling, of 'making a copy of'. In essence it refers to an interpretative process that relates either to modelling oneself on an object, or to making a model of that object. Likewise mimesis may come into operation as a third party engages with that model, making it the vehicle for identifying with the original object. In each case the aim is to assimilate to the original object. Mimesis is therefore a form of imitation that can be evoked both by the artist who makes a work of art and by the person who views it.

Mimesis for Benjamin is a linguistic concept. It offers a way of finding meaning in the world, through the discovery of similarities. These similarities become absorbed and then rearticulated in language. As such, language becomes a repository of meaning, and writing becomes an activity which extends beyond itself, engaging writers in unconscious processes. Indeed, writing often reveals more than the writer is conscious of revealing. Likewise the reader must decode the words, resorting to the realm of the imagination which exceeds the purely rational. Thus the activity of reading also embodies the principles of mimesis, serving as the vehicle for some revelatory moment. For Benjamin the meaning becomes apparent in a constellatory flash, a dialectics of seeing, in which subject and object become one for a brief moment. Mimesis can also be observed, according to Benjamin, in dance movements. Here he opens up the possibility, which Adorno goes on to explore, that mimesis can extend to all forms of aesthetic expression, including photography and the visual arts.

The point here is that reproduction may step beyond mere imitation. Benjamin reverses the hierarchy of the object and its representation. He challenges the earlier Platonic notion of mimesis as an essentially compromised form of imitation that necessarily loses something of the original. For Benjamin mimesis alludes to a constructive reinterpretation of an original, which becomes a creative act in itself. Furthermore, it becomes a potential way of empathizing with the world, and it is through empathy that we can — if not fully understand the other — at least assimilate to the other. In mimesis imagination is at work, and serves to reconcile the subject with the object. This imagination operates at the level of fantasy, which mediates between the unconscious and the conscious, between dream and reality. Fantasy creates its own fictions not as a way of escaping reality, but as a way of accessing reality, a reality that is ontologically charged, and not constrained by an instrumentalized view of the world.

Children and Mimesis

The urge to seek similarities leads one to read similarities into the other and — ultimately — to read oneself into the other. Thus, for example, in 'A Berlin Childhood' Benjamin tells the story of a child trying to hunt a butterfly. The butterfly begins to take on human characteristics, while the child takes on characteristics of the butterfly:

> The old rules of hunting took over between us: the more my being, down to its very fibres, adapted to my prey (the more I got butterflies in my stomach), the more the butterfly took on in all it did (and didn't do) the colour of the human resolution, until finally it was as if capturing it was the price, was the only way I would regain my humanity.[12]

It is precisely through children's play, as Walter Benjamin has observed, that one can best see the principle of mimesis at work. For Benjamin 'play' is the 'school' of mimesis: 'Children's play is everywhere permeated by mimetic modes of behaviour, and its realm is by no means limited to what one person can imitate in another.'[13] The child therefore has a form of privileged access to mimetic processes. Much depends on the child's creative imagination, and it is this which allows the child to invest discarded objects with a special significance. As Benjamin observes:

> [In the child's bureau] drawers must become arsenal and zoo, crime museum and crypt. 'To tidy up' would be to demolish an edifice full of prickly chestnuts that are spiky clubs, tin foil that is hoarded silver, bricks that are coffins, cacti that are totem poles, and copper pennies that are shields.[14]

It is as though children's creative imagination — the capacity for indulging in make-believe — gives them a greater ability to assimilate. And if mimesis is the key to understanding the principle of representation in art, the play of children might offer us some insight into that question. This is precisely the viewpoint taken by Kendall Walton: 'In order to understand paintings, plays, films and novels, we must look first at dolls, hobbyhorses, toy trucks and teddy bears. The activities in which representational works of art are embedded and which give them their point are best seen as continuous with children's games of make-believe.'[15]

Mimesis involves the capacity to mimic and identify with not only the animate world, but also the inanimate. Benjamin notes that children may equally play at being inanimate objects. 'The child plays at being not only a shopkeeper or teacher but also a windmill and a train', he notes, as though the windmill or train has some animate life force that the child can appropriate.[16] The play between the animate and the inanimate, between life and death, is crucial to understanding the force of mimesis. The origins of this adaptation to the inanimate may be found in instinctual mechanisms of self-defence. Animals, when threatened with life-endangering situations, will often freeze so as to blend in with their environment and escape the gaze of the predator. These instincts may also be traced in human responses. But this 'surrendering' of life in the moment of becoming one with the inanimate world serves ultimately to reinforce life. These gestures of surrender are in fact predicated on survival.

It is this ability to assimilate to the inanimate world which makes Benjamin's observations so relevant to the question of architecture. It suggests a capacity to read oneself into the environment, and to see oneself reflected in that environment.[17] If, moreover, we are to understand mimesis as offering the possibility of assimilation not only by modelling oneself on an object, but also by engaging with the model of that object, we can see how photographic representation may provide that mechanism of identification. Photography becomes the model, and architecture the object of assimilation. Through the architectural photograph we may read ourselves into the architecture, just as the young Benjamin found himself within the scenes depicted in his picture postcards, as though transported there by some magic carpet.

Mimesis and Sympathetic Magic

But what exactly can one understand by the expression 'as though transported there by some magic carpet'? Can one make a direct comparison between mimesis and magic? Here we might reflect on the world of voodoo dolls, effigies, models and other types of representation which attempt to establish some link between an originary object and its miniaturized representation through a form of sympathetic magic.[18]

There are clear parallels between mimesis and magic. Both appear to operate within the same conceptual orbit, and both establish an ideational relationship between subject and object. In the context of architectural photography, the photograph's relation to the architecture that it depicts is not dissimilar to the figurine's relation to the originary object in sympathetic magic. Just as the viewer of a photograph may imagine him or herself within that scene, so too the primitive imagines a relationship between the voodoo doll or image and the intended victim. One might point also to a more direct connection between magical practices and the domain of art and architecture. Freud acknowledges the affinities between the world of art and sympathetic magic. Citing Reinach,

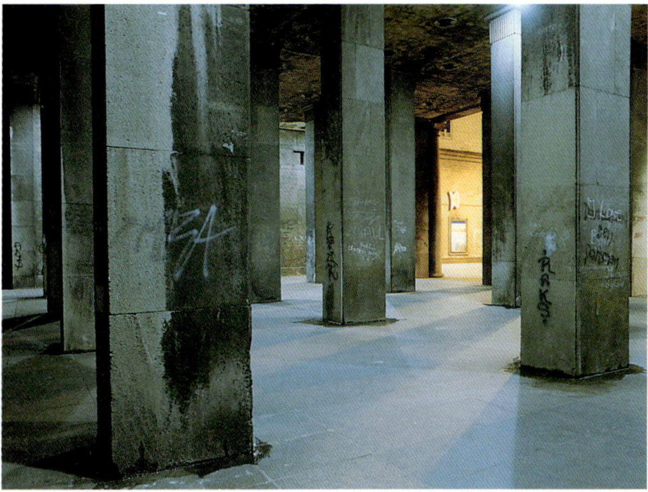

⇨ Martin Zeller, Frankfurter Tor, Berlin, 26.01.96

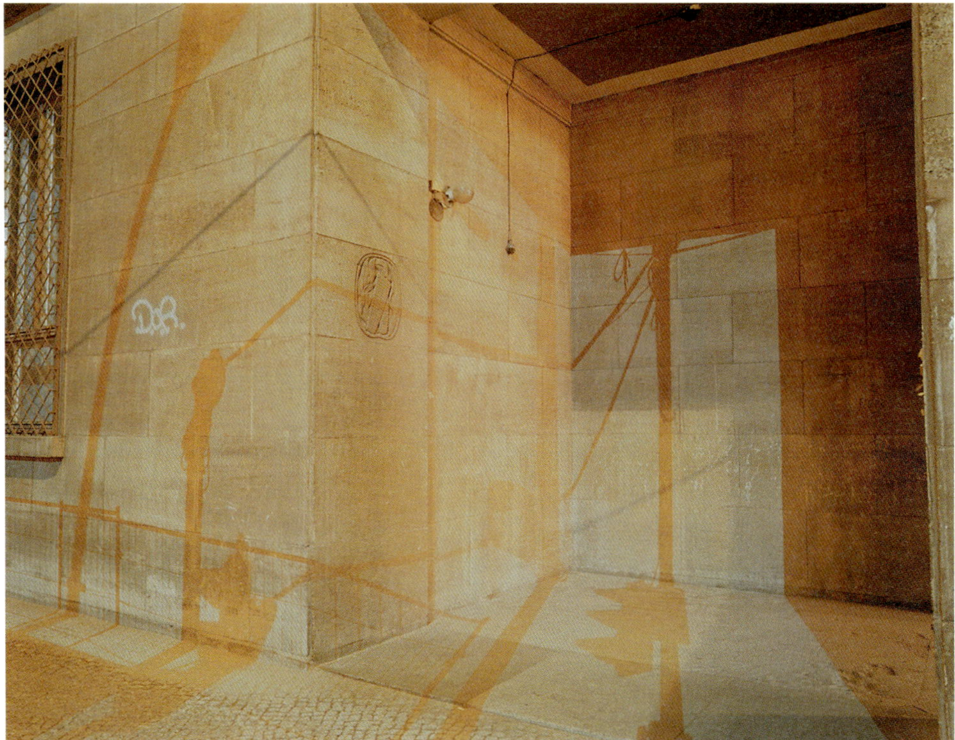

Martin Zeller, Französische Straße, Berlin, 23.08.94

who observes that the 'primitive artists who left behind the carvings and paintings in the French cave did not seek to "please" but to "evoke" and conjure up', he traces parallels between the two:

> In only a single field of civilization has the omnipotence of thoughts been retained, and that is in the field of art. Only in art does it still happen that a man who is consumed by desires performs something resembling the accomplishments of those desires and that what he does in play produces emotional effects — thanks to artistic illusion — just as though it were something real. People speak with justice of the 'magic of art' and compare artists to magicians. But the comparison is perhaps more significant than it claims to be. There can be no doubt that art did not begin as art for art's sake. It worked originally in the service of impulses which are for the most part extinct today. And among them we may suspect the presence of many magical processes.[19]

It would be wrong, however, to equate art — as a form of mimesis — with magic. Certainly, even if Freud is happy to bracket them together, Benjamin always resists this temptation. There is a clear genealogy to art. Benjamin acknowledges that at one stage pictures were indeed connected with magic: 'The elk portrayed by the man of the Stone Age on the walls of his cave was an instrument of magic.'[20] But equally he adds that there has been a shift, as the work of art later became recognized in its own right, and a further shift, within the age of mechanical reproduction, when the accent on 'cult value' has been replaced by one of 'exhibition value':

> With the different methods of technical reproduction of a work of art, its fitness for exhibition increased to such an extent that the quantitative shift between its two poles turned into a qualitative transformation of its nature. This is comparable to the situation of the work of art in prehistoric times when, by the absolute emphasis on its cult value, it was, first and foremost, an instrument of magic. Only later did it come to be recognized as a work of art. In the same way today, by the absolute emphasis on its exhibition value the work of art becomes a creation with entirely new functions, among which the one we are conscious of, the artistic function, later may be recognized as incidental.[21]

We can therefore detect in Benjamin's thought a sympathy for mimesis that extends to new forms of representation such as photography, but which distances itself increasingly from magic. As Susan Buck-Morss explains:

> [Benjamin] holds open the possibility of a future development of mimetic expression, the potentialities for which are far from exhausted. Nor are they limited to verbal language — as the new technologies of camera and film clearly demonstrate. These technologies provide human beings with unprecedented perceptual acuity, out of which, Benjamin believed, a less magical, more scientific form of the mimetic faculty was developing in his own era.[22]

Indeed Adorno, who subsequently develops Benjamin's thesis on mimesis, explicitly distances art from magic. While there is a certain affinity between the two — the artist exerts a form of 'organized control' that has parallels in the conjurer plotting a trick — art does not follow the same project as magic. Both are grounded in human imagination, but art operates in the domain of the 'as if', while magic claims to operate within the domain of the actual. 'Art', Adorno notes, 'is magic delivered from the lie of being truth.'[23]

None the less, through the process of mimesis — an imaginary identification with a representation of an object — the original object can be invoked. And the process applies equally to photography. Photographs can be seen in the same light as mimetic representations of actual buildings, which might 'conjure up' those buildings for the beholder. Photographs are therefore charged with the potential to open up a 'world'. Although the mimetic impulse should not be equated with sympathetic magic, there are clear affinities between the two. The photograph therefore plays out its role as an object of wish-fulfilment. It is as though we might entertain the wish of entering another world through the medium of the photograph itself, as though stepping through a window.

Conclusion

What then is the consequence of this? Above all it highlights an important aspect of what it is to be human. According to the film *Bladerunner* one of the features which distinguishes replicants from humans is a compulsion to acquire photographs. Without a natural memory (imprinted on to their minds as though on to some photographic plate, as Benjamin describes it), replicants need to construct an artificial memory for themselves through photographs of someone else's childhood.

Yet it could be argued that it is precisely the capacity to gaze at a photograph and to imagine oneself in the picture that marks out the very essence of what it is to be human. The capacity to recognize similarities is one of humankind's distinguishing features. As Benjamin comments: 'Nature creates similarities. One need only think of mimicry. The highest capacity for producing similarities, however, is man's.'[24] Moreover, on the subject of mimesis, Theodor Adorno once claimed, 'The human is indissolubly linked with imitation: a human being only becomes human at all by imitating other human beings.'[25] If we extend Adorno's comments from a mimesis of other individuals to a mimesis of architectural environments through representations of that environment, we might argue that what defines humankind as being human is the capacity to identify with those representations and through them to conjure up whole environments which they depict. And so it would appear that while we have adapted to the camera, and have assimilated to its technological mechanisms, such that we now read the world in terms of the snapshot, it is also *through* the camera — and the images it produces — that we can understand precisely what it is to be human.

What is crucial is the manner in which one gazes at these representations — photographic or otherwise. The action of mimesis is dependent upon a state of mind. One has to be receptive, alert to the possibilities of the creative imagination. And it is children above all who would appear to be the most receptive to images, the most capable of reading themselves into them, so as to imagine other possible worlds. The fantasy of the creative genius, as Freud himself observes, is born of the play and games of children.[26]

Perhaps, then, there is something to be said for viewing photographs with a certain childlike imagination, while not overlooking, of course, the negative side of childish behaviour — the threat of regression into some fascistic tantrum. To gaze with a childlike imagination at a photograph — or indeed at any pictorial image — is to be absorbed by it. It is to dream oneself into another place, like Benjamin being transported into his postcards, like the Chinese painter disappearing into his painting, or indeed like Alice stepping through the looking glass.

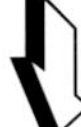

1 Walter Benjamin, *One-Way Street* (London: Verso, 1979) pp. 342-3.
2 'A Berlin Childhood around 1900' appears as 'Berliner Kindheit um Neunzehnhundert', in *Gesammelte Schriften*, IV: 1, but has yet to be published in English. 'A Berlin Chronicle' appears in Benjamin, *One-Way Street*, pp. 293-346.
3 For Benjamin 'unconscious optics' are the visual equivalent of the Freudian 'slip of the tongue'. 'By close-ups of the world around us,' Benjamin notes, 'by exploring commonplace milieux under the ingenious guidance of the camera, the film, on the one hand extends our comprehension of the necessities which rule our lives; on the other hand, it manages to assure us of an immense and unexpected field of action.' [Benjamin, *Illuminations*, trans. Harry Zohn, London: Fontana, 1973, p. 229.] Hence, Benjamin concludes, 'The camera introduces us to unconscious optics as does psychoanalysis to unconscious impulses.' [loc. cit., p. 230.]
4 Benjamin, *One-Way Street*, p. 295.
5 ibid., p. 328.
6 Benjamin, *Illuminations*, p. 232.
7 Benjamin, *Gesammelte Schriften*, IV:1, pp. 262-3, quoted in Gebauer and Wulf, *Mimesis*, p. 277.
8 Benjamin, *One-Way Street*, p. 74.
9 Benjamin, 'On the Mimetic Faculty', in *Reflections* (New York: Schocken, 1986) pp. 333-6.
10 'I believe that if ideational mimetics are followed up, they may be as useful in other branches of aesthetics...' Sigmund Freud, *Jokes and Their Relation to the Unconscious* (1905), trans. James Strachey (London: Routledge, 1960) p. 193. For further reading on mimesis, see Erich Auerbach, *Mimesis*, trans. Willard Trask (Princeton University Press, 1953); Michael Taussig, *Mimesis and Alterity* (London: Routledge, 1993); Gunter Gebauer and Christoph Wulf, *Mimesis: Culture, Art, Society*, trans. Don Reneau (Berkeley: University of California Press, 1995).
11 Benjamin, *Illuminations*, p. 217.
12 Benjamin, *Gesammelte Schriften*, IV: 1, pp. 262-3, quoted in Gebauer and Wulf, *Mimesis*, pp. 277-8.
13 Benjamin, *Reflections*, p. 333.
14 Benjamin, *One-Way Street*, p. 74, quoted in Buck-Morss, p. 263.
15 Kendall Walton, *Mimesis as Make-Believe* (Cambridge, MA: Harvard University Press, 1990) p. 11.
16 Benjamin, *Reflections*, p. 333.
17 Assimilation can therefore be seen as a narcissistic form of identification. Narcissistic identification with others has been examined by many theorists, including Laura Mulvey in the context of film theory, but the notion of identification with an inanimate object remains relatively unexplored.
18 These practices have fascinated anthropologists for some time. *The Golden Bough* by James George Frazer, for example, is full of such examples. 'When an Obejway Indian desires to work evil on any one,' writes Frazer, 'he makes a little wooden image of his enemy and runs a needle into its head or heart, or he shoots an arrow into it, believing that wherever the needle pierces or the arrow strikes the image, his foe will the same instant be seized with a sharp pain in the corresponding part of his body; but if he intends to kill the person outright, he burns or buries the puppet, uttering certain magic words as he does so.' [James George Frazer, *The Golden Bough* (1890), London: Penguin, 1996, p. 15.] Significantly, in terms of any discussion of photography, the representation of the victim need not be a three-dimensional model, but may equally be a two-dimensional drawing: 'Thus the North American Indians, we are told, believe that by drawing the figure of a person in sand, ashes, or clay, or by considering any object of his body, and then pricking it with a sharp stick or doing it any other injury, they inflict a corresponding injury on the person represented.' [loc. cit., p. 15.] Of course these gestures need not be malignant. Magic can also be used for more benign purposes such as medicine and hunting.
19 Freud, *The Origins of Religion*, pp. 148-9.
20 Benjamin, *Illuminations*, p. 218.
21 ibid., p. 219.
22 Susan Buck-Morss, *The Dialectics of Seeing: Walter Benjamin and the Arcades Project* (Cambridge, MA: MIT Press, 1989) p. 267.
23 Theodor Adorno, *Minima Moralia*, trans. Edmund Jephcott (London and New York: Verso, 1978) p. 222.
24 Benjamin, *Reflections*, p. 332.
25 Adorno, *Minima Moralia*, p. 154.
26 Freud, 'Creative Writers and Day-Dreaming' in *The Freud Reader*, Peter Gay, ed. (London: Vintage, 1995) p. 437.

Pictures of Paradox: The Photographs of Andreas Gursky

Gerda Breuer

→ Andreas Gursky, Düsseldorf, Airport II, 1994
↓ Caspar David Friedrich, The Monk on the Lake, 1808/1810

The German photographer Andreas Gursky has declared his love of paradox on more than one occasion.[1] When, for example, he adapts a romantic motif in order to comment on contemporary changes in the relationship between Man and Nature (as in *Düsseldorf, Airport II*, where he refers to Caspar David Friedrich's *The Monk on the Lake*[2]) he is also playing with a fundamental concept of romanticism itself. According to this concept the character of romantic art arises out of the conflict between the 'finite manifestation' and the 'infinite idea', which are polar opposites, locatable within the constellation of the 'paradoxical'. Friedrich Schlegel has described the important and illuminating function that paradox plays in romantic speculation: 'Paradoxicality is the *conditio sine qua non* for irony; its soul, source and fundamental constituent.'[3] It is, therefore, a necessary condition for the ironic conflict whereby a work of art relies upon the viewer's subjectivity to reveal it in its objective openness, and with all its possible interpretations. In fact one finds ironic twists, an undercurrent of humour and, above all, playfulness everywhere in Gursky's photographs, however classical they may appear at first glance.

Gursky lends his pictures this classical tone through the deployment of familiar views borrowed from art-historical sources. He has written, '...there appears to exist in the history of art a generally applicable wealth of forms, to which we are forever referring'.[4] Indeed in Gursky's photographs we see the layout of the *fenestra aperta* – a visual structure, organized along symmetrical axes, which simultaneously reduces the world to an object and elevates the viewer to master of all he surveys. This method of controlling the view directed the epistemology of art in the Renaissance and formed the foundation of its theory of mimesis. Crucially this theory insisted on an external reference, namely the world inhabited by the perceiving subject.

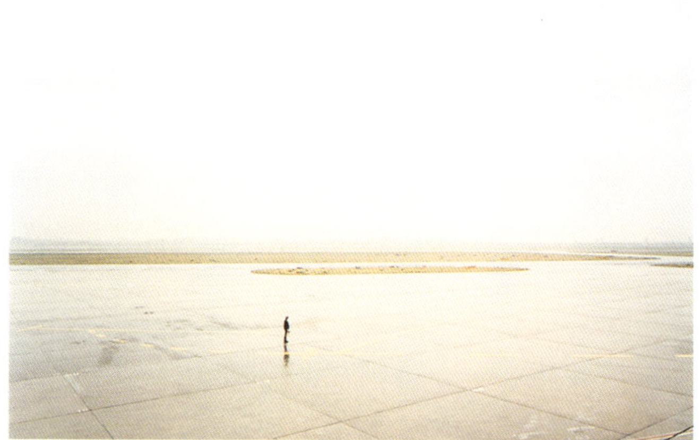

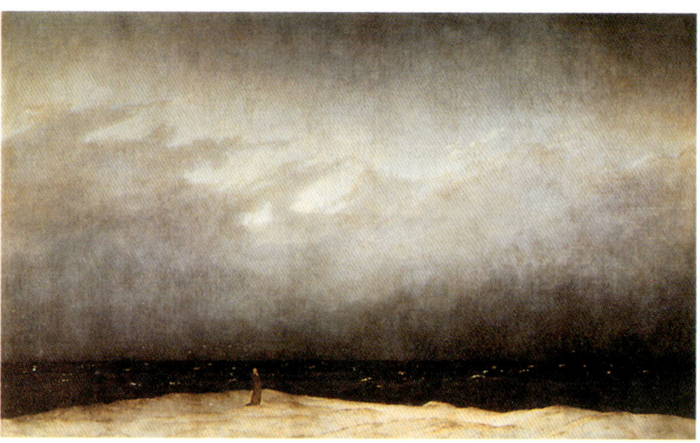

In subsequent eras the mimetic tradition was used to locate art in the context of new counter-arguments. Just as the recognizability of an increasingly abstract world became questionable, so too the perceiving subject began to explore new forms of individual certitude. The loss of faith in the very essence of mimesis threw both its objects and its subjects into doubt. This crisis in the history of ideas bore down upon artistic form, and culminated in art's preoccupation with its most introspective elements. Gursky appears to counter this, by reaching back to a traditional mode of art and a classical ascription of the function of photography – in short, to representation itself. And yet, in so doing, he unnerves the viewer.

When Gursky employs paradoxical strategies, he seems to be operating within the dialectical conflict of romantic irony. In *Düsseldorf, Airport II*, for example, he couples together traditional conceptions of art and photography; in other works he places them in opposition to one another. It is in this way that he opens them up for discussion.

The result of these couplings is friction – a fruitful awkwardness brought about by the act of viewing itself. Since Gursky's views are the familiar art-historically imparted types (such as Cartesian perspective, the nineteenth-century sublime and others that we will encounter further on), it is a straightforward matter for him to manipulate his pictures digitally, in order to focus on the elements of perception which interest him most. For example, to strengthen the impression of monumentality and seriality in *Prada II*, he adds one horizontal to the display case; in *Untitled V* (1997) he increases its size by a further two.[5] In other instances he tends more towards abstraction: in *Brasília, General Assembly I* (1994) (see p. 90) the ceiling lighting is represented as a pure diffusion of light. Yet even here a companion-piece, *Untitled VII* (1998), provokes a reference to art-historical tradition: its subject matter – clouds – forms the basis for numerous treatments by artists ranging from Alexander Cozens to Gerhard Richter. In this respect association and cross-reference play an essential role in Gursky's work.

That the 'reality' depicted by photography is extra-pictorial allows for a second paradox, that of 'fictitious reality'.[6] Whenever art has rejected its mimetic ambitions, photography has had to renounce, or at least vary, its representative function if it wished to qualify as art (as demonstrated, most extremely, in American modernism and the European movements of the 1960s). Gursky himself does not deny photography its representative character – on the contrary. But he does employ the representative as a dialectical element. He is always on the look-out for subjects that exemplify a 'contemporary phenomenon', or the modern world's 'aggregate state'.[7] By finding elements that stand in opposition to a preformed aesthetic perception, or by placing his subjects within a pictorial structure that intensifies them in a non-aesthetic, conventionalized viewing mode, Gursky imbues 'reality' with something resistant, drawing attention to the way in which, outside of art, reality has already fused with the modes of its perception.

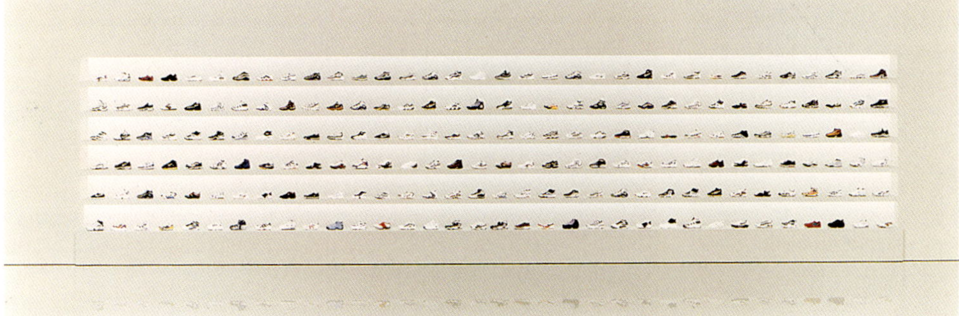

Andreas Gursky, Untitled VII, 1998
Andreas Gursky, Untitled V, 1997

Gursky once described his approach in the following terms:

> I sense that I am capable of picking out and holding in reserve 'valid' images from the tide with which we are inundated on a daily basis. I then intuitively combine these with immediate visual experiences in order to produce autonomous variants.[8]

On other occasions he has said, 'I subjugate the real situation to my artistic conception of pictorial strategy',[9] and 'the immediate visual experience should always be the trigger for a picture'.[10] Gursky works slowly, eliminating the elements of surprise from his photographs and carefully calculating their final effect:

> With this way of working I have always got the image before my eyes and approach the final result step by step, without letting myself be influenced by spontaneous flashes of inspiration.[11]

It is almost superfluous to mention that Andreas Gursky opposes the notion that documentary photography, as a medium, has a revelatory quality which predisposes it towards didacticism. All members of the so-called Becher School are opposed to this idea, and have developed a separate rhetoric of art photography (although it is not one that strictly follows the teaching of Bernd Becher).

The Becher Tradition

The objectifying photography advocated by Bernd and Hilla Becher may have influenced Gursky in his decision to move from the Folkwang-Hochschule[12] to Bernd Becher's class at Düsseldorf Art Academy, where he studied from 1981 to 1987. The Bechers have been photographing the monuments of the 'Industrial Revolution'[13] since the end of the 1950s, and their work has been published as a series of volumes, each focusing on a building type such as water towers, silos or blast furnaces. Bernd Becher originally worked as an artist, but he turned to 'pure' photography because he had come to believe that, 'with drawing, despite realistic reproduction, it is impossible to avoid a subjective view'.[14]

Initially, the Bechers took their photographs with an old 13 by 18 wooden plate-camera, relying on its precision mechanics to achieve an accurate and objective depiction of structures and

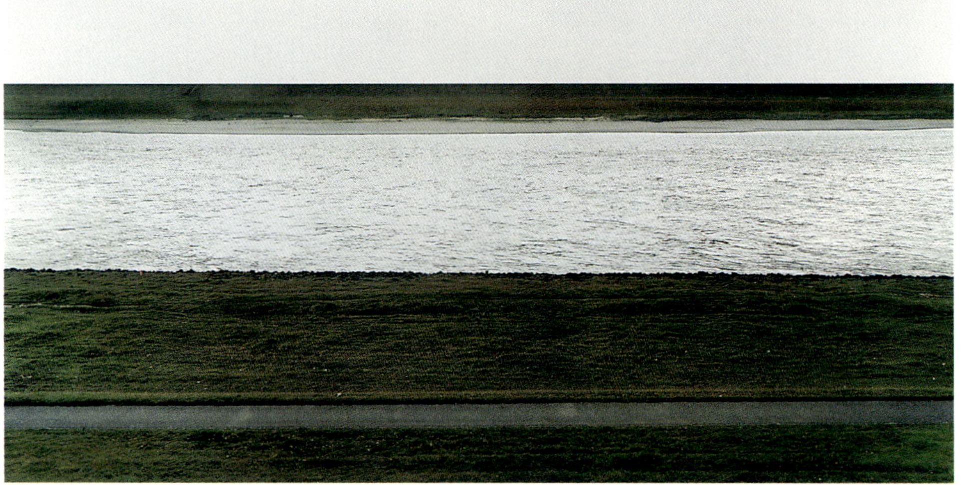

} Andreas Gursky, Rhein, 1996
{ Andreas Gursky, Schießer, 1991

buildings. Today they use modern large-format cameras, with fine-grain film which guarantees high resolution. By adjusting the lens- and film-holders they can ensure that all the lines on the plane of the photograph remain parallel with those of the edge of the image; they can also keep the vertical lines parallel (with smaller cameras these taper as they rise).

By means of these objectifying techniques, the Bechers have sought to oppose the staged photography of architecture that regularly uses unusual angles to control aesthetic effect. They often work from a slightly raised position that allows them to organize the construction of their pictures on symmetrical axes around a centrally located vanishing point: 'The view from medium height on to the object [results in] its standing before you without distortion, in its entirety.'[15] The Bechers also avoid 'incidental' atmospheric elements (the effects of weather, season or time of day), interpretative detail-enlargements and retouchings. Over the years they have built up an archive containing many thousands of photographs of industrial structures throughout the world.

Whilst Gursky refers to his teachers, he approaches his own photography in a very different way. Instead of using the camera to establish parallel lines to objectify the photograph, he emphasizes those lines as a compositional element. What is more, he manipulates his pictures digitally, as seen most vividly in *Rhein* (1996) and the diptych *Schießer* (1991). The lines of *Rhein* accentuate a modern phenomenon, namely the straightening of a river course; the lines of *Schießer* accentuate, in essentially the same manner, the rationalization process of assembly-line work that is a condition of modern architecture and technology.

Another slight variation of the Bechers' 'objectifying standpoint' was required to allow Gursky's subjects to slide into monumental and sublime modes. The formal outline of the excavations in *Thebes, West* (1993), for example, highlights the phenomenal scale of the archaeological site, but also draws attention to the photograph's apparently 'incidental' subject: namely that the historical monument has become a tourist site of pilgrimage. Such alternative photographic devices ensure that the perception of an object is in keeping with the age.[16]

Gursky points out these unfolding paradoxes with a delicate, ironic wit. The same is true of his treatment of those means of 'pure' photography which are in fact derived from the discourse of art history.

Illusionary Minimalism

In many cases it is the ideologies of modernism[17] that Gursky opens up for discussion. Here, too, we find a paradox in the fact that Gursky offers us a criticism of modernism whilst at the same time appropriating modernist pictorial strategies for his photographic works.

We can see this most clearly when he borrows from the artistic strategies of minimalism. Gursky has explicitly stated that he quotes directly from one representative of American minimal art – Dan Flavin.[18] Usually, however, the allusions are not attributable to any specific individual, but relate more generally to the minimalist ideology that became an enduring – and latterly controversial – preoccupation of art. Backed by critics and art historians such as Clement Greenberg in America and Werner Haftmann in Germany, minimalism was for a long time normative. By adopting the pictorial strategies of modernism, Gursky offers an implicit criticism of the movement's canonical conceptions, referring not only to the principal figures and ideology of American minimalism, but also to its enormous long-term impact. (Many subsequent

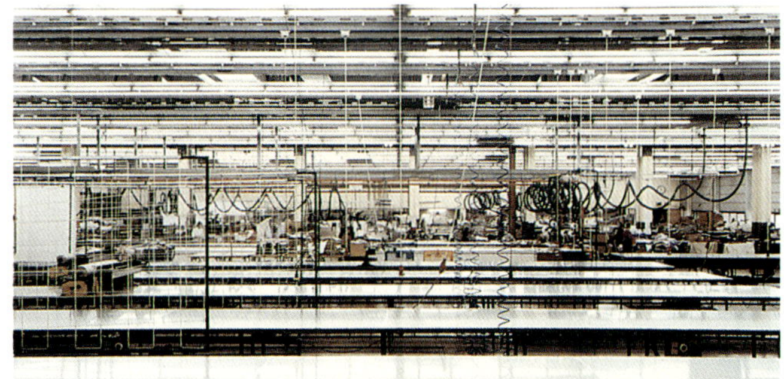

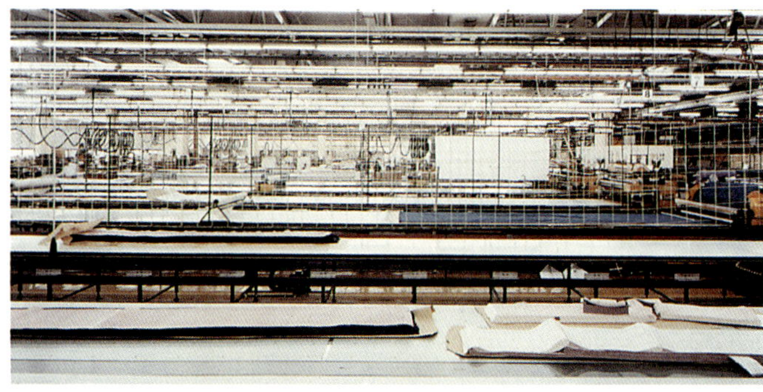

art movements have considered themselves 'beyond' minimalism, yet, paradoxically, those who have opposed the phenomenon have also contributed to its survival as a subject of aesthetic reflection.)

Gursky is playing with the fundamental concepts of minimalist ideology, including the ideal of purity which blocks out any detail or element of chance, and the reductive principle of self-referentiality whereby the highest attainment sought by works of art is 'their total identity as objects'.[19] Donald Judd's strategy of 'specific objects' (1965) provides a good example of this, presenting the pure materiality of the image in a literal manner – as pure form and pure colour. This is something that Jeff Koons emulated in a postmodern variation – a 'baptism in banality' – in *The New* (1981), when he displayed vacuum cleaners in a series of Plexiglas cases (which were meant to remind the viewer of Judd's cubes and Flavin's fluorescent spaces). His intention was to ridicule the concept of a purity that was bound up with expressions of pure form and pure colour. Here we can also find a connection between artlessness and purified vision, one that Dan Flavin formulated as follows: 'We are pressing downward toward no art – a mutual sense of psychologically indifferent decoration – a neutral pleasure of seeing known to everyone.'[20]

Andreas Gursky, Prada II, 1997
Dan Flavin, The Nominal Three (to William of Ockham), 1963

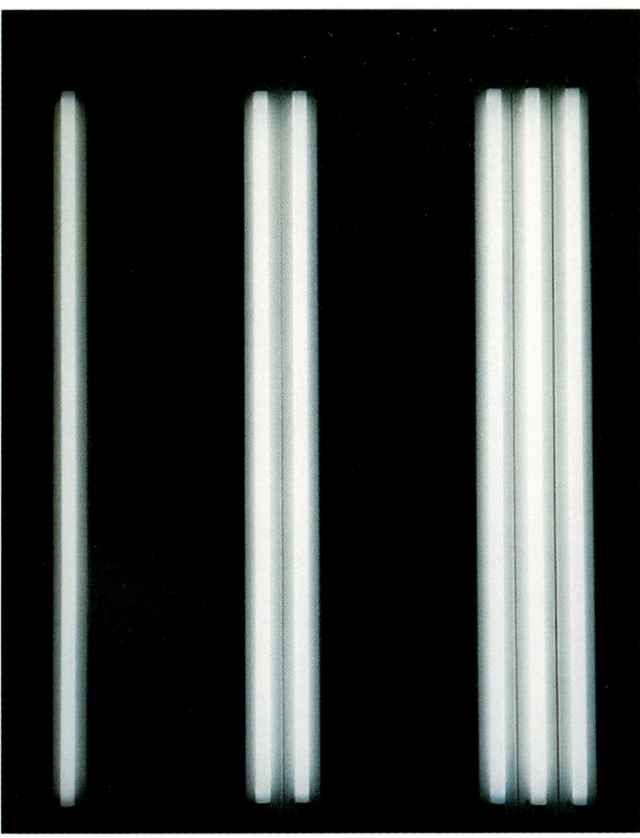

Gursky alludes to Dan Flavin's light boxes in his photograph of a large, illuminated display case – *Prada II* (1997). In other photographs such a case displays shoes (*Untitled V*, 1997; *Prada I*, 1996) or women's underwear (*Untitled IX*, 1998). He reinforces the allusion by repeating the rigorous stereometrical form of the case in the space that surrounds it.

However, all this merely constitutes one level of the picture's meaning. The display case also alludes to a well-known context-theory of art – the 'white cube'. According to this theory the *big pictures* of minimalist art, with their pure materiality (and consequent claim to artlessness), become magically charged in a white gallery space cleared of all extraneous items. Yet the emptying of the exhibition space produces precisely the situation that has been deemed unsatisfactory in the first place. The material context of a white exhibition room (which was meant to emphasize the pure presence of the *work* of art) *itself* becomes art. In the same way, the empty space within it becomes an alchemical medium that can transform even banalities into art.[21]

Gursky emptied out the display case in *Prada II* because he wished to point out that marketing managers also use such a technique – widely described as 'secular transubstantiation' – to transform everyday items into fetish objects. (The objects displayed in the cases of earlier works – the shoes and women's underwear – are those used by psychoanalysts to illustrate fetishism.) The effect is amplified by Gursky's emphatic use of a Cartesian perspective to add intensity to the subject by means of a fixed point of view (the *fenestra aperta*) reducing the world to a peep-show in which the consumer becomes the victim of his own autonomy.

The absolute exorcism of chance elements and extraneous details allows the viewer to see the 'meaninglessness' that the minimalists strove to achieve as an emphasis of the autonomy of their subjects. At the same time, no one could deny these pictures their classical beauty. Such a contradiction was revealed by Rosalind Krauss, when she noted the beauty of Donald Judd's 'specific objects' but also pointed out that the intended 'self-referentiality' was an illusion (since the identity gained 'its strength from a heightening of the illusion'). 'The illusory quality of the thing itself' had an unnerving effect, resulting in 'a heightening of the awareness in the viewer that he approaches objects to make meaning of them'.[22]

Allusion and Pure Vision

Gursky's choice of architectural subjects makes it apparent that perception can be inscribed in reality. *Paris, Montparnasse* (1993) is one of his largest pictures (180 cm by 300 cm). By means of a perspective laid out along symmetrical axes, the photograph

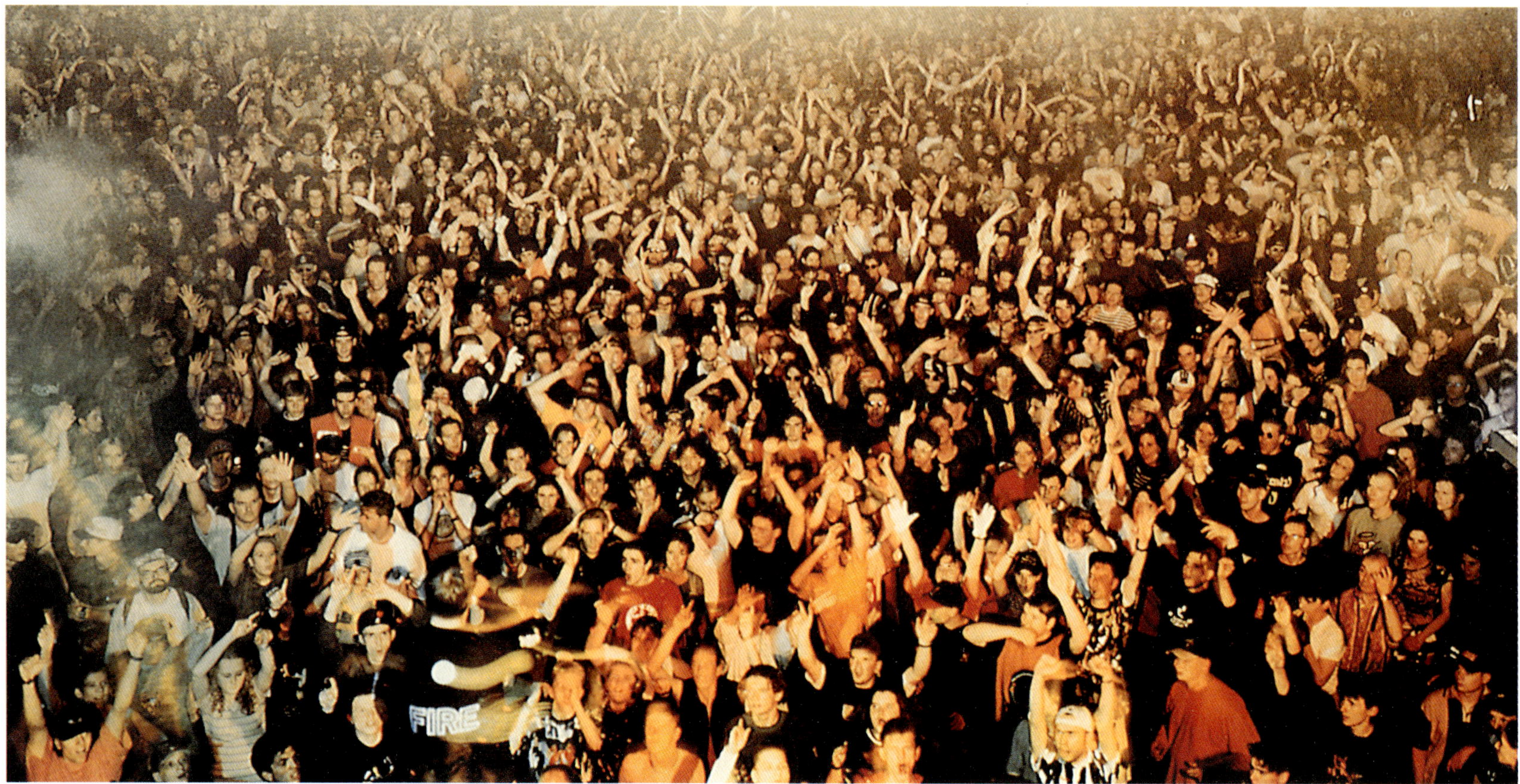

} Andreas Gursky, Union Rave, 1995

confronts the viewer with the grid-like structure of a monumental modern housing block. The building, designed in 1964 by Jean Dubuisson, embraces the precepts of Le Corbusier's Modulor and machine for living in. It accords precisely with the ideals of CIAM (Congrès Internationaux d'Architecture Moderne): 'a sense of order, a striving for unity, a sense of proportion – architecture is concerned with quantities'.[23] The strict rationality of geometry – and in particular the straight line – was intended to provide a structure for modern life. It suggested an order that underpinned individuality: unity within multiplicity.

At first glance one may wonder why Gursky chose as a subject of his photography the very type of building that is generally believed to have provoked the move towards postmodernism. The best-known promoter of postmodern architecture, Charles Jencks, chose a building scheme of similar type to symbolize the death of modernism. The Pruitt-Igoe housing project in St Louis was widely acclaimed upon its completion in 1955, yet, within twenty years, vandalism had rendered it unusable. For Jencks its demolition – in a series of dramatic explosions – was a vivid illustration of the rift between modernism's functionalist building goals and the ideal of buildings fit for human habitation. Paradoxically, Gursky's photographs of massive ordered structures, which prescribe a uniform, deindividualized way of life, provoke us into observing the detail in the individual box-like dwellings. Order is transformed into narrative: when the photograph *Paris, Montparnasse* was shown in Frankfurt in 1995, it was accompanied by a catalogue containing enlarged details of the homes and a commentary based on interviews with the residents.

A similar paradox can be seen in *Times Square* (1997) and *Atlanta* (1996). These show hotel interiors in which the serial structure of the individual floors around the atrium throws specific details into relief. Furthermore, the element of repetition imbues the structure with an ornamental quality – something hardly in keeping with the spirit of modernism. In both photographs the emphasis on the ordered structure of the hotel floors points back to the 'primary structures' of Donald Judd: symmetrically layered wall boxes based on modular structures, exemplified in *Stacks* (1966). Once again Gursky proceeds according to the visual principles of modernist art.

A further example might be added to this: in *Rhein*, Gursky undermines Barnett Newman's notion of a non-preconceived, apparently 'pure' vision. In this work the rectangle of the picture frame serves as the primary determinant of the picture's internal structure. The course of the river, its upper and its lower banks, are reduced to horizontal bands of colour. The formal components that contribute to the photograph's 'flatness' are digitally enhanced to amplify the horizontality of the picture or to express pictorial ideas that cannot be solved through perspective.[24]

This meta-dialogue with modern painting not only offers a critique of the perception that a photograph contains a specific tension between its formal and representative elements; it also attempts to be 'time-specific'. It does this by presenting the viewer with a modern – rationalized and straightened – variant of a river that is awash with historical associations: 'I was not

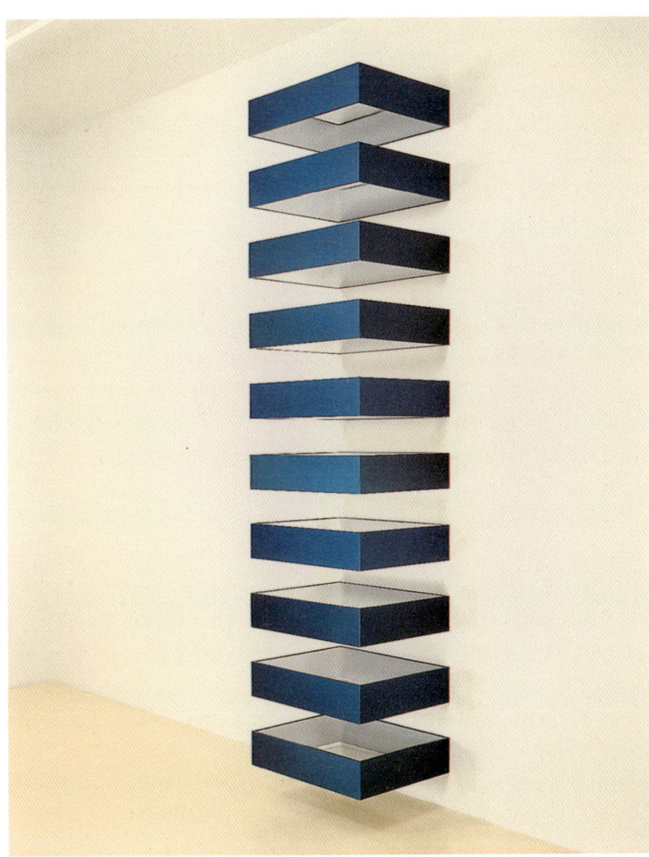

Donald Judd, Untitled, 1990

interested in an unusual, possibly picturesque part of the Rhine, but rather in the Rhine in its contemporary shape and form.'[25] Paradoxically a 'valid picture' of the Rhine cannot be captured by mere re-presentation: some form of reconstruction is required to achieve a faithful portrait of the modern river. The fictitious is made to represent reality – a protest against the 'flood' of pictures that overwhelms us today; a protest, in particular, against documentary photography, which lost its credibility when it turned reality into a commodity.

Formlessness as Form

In this context it is difficult to interpret recent photographs such as *Untitled VI* (1997) (of a painting by Pollock) and *Turner Collection* (1995) exclusively as homages to two visionary artists.[26] Both photographs play on the tension between the structureless (a central theme in both Pollock's and Turner's work) and the strictly structured order of the exhibition room. This tension is further increased by both the perspective and the size of the photographs. In the case of *Untitled VI*, the strictly composed order – with its delimitation of the painting area, linear repetition of light and shade, and combination of the linear features of the room with the rectangular edges of the photograph – is set against the artistic intentions of Pollock. The randomness of his 'drippings' – the trickling of paint on to a canvas lying on the floor – finds no counterpart in this new context. Yet the photograph, in a real sense, imitates the manner in which the painting has come to be received – as an icon of modernism. It expresses the paradoxical rhetoric of formlessness as a formal completion that is the essence of the 'drippings' in the 'all over'.

According to Clement Greenberg, purification reached its ultimate formal expression in 'flatness', an idea he illustrated primarily by reference to Pollock's method of painting.[27] Flatness was the term for a surface which no longer contained any meaning, which referred to nothing beyond itself. This resulted in the formal characteristics of modernist painting being fetishized and portrayed as an indispensable requirement of all serious art. Flatness became the unquestioned dogma of artists of the avant-garde and part of their revolt against the illusionistic representation of reality outside art.

Gursky reflects this fundamental principle of modernist art in his photographs of contemporary crowd-scenes – for example the financial markets in *Tokyo, Stock Exchange* (1990) and *Chicago, Board of Trade* (1997) (see p. 92), and the club scenes in *Union Rave* (1998) and *May Day I* (1997). The term 'flat' – in the sense of something lacking external references – could also be applied to these frenetic masses.

Siegfried Kracauer illustrated the concept of 'the mass ornament' with a serial presentation of the equivalent forms in 'distraction factories' (the legs of the Tiller Girls) and industrial factories (the hands of workers).[28] Kracauer related the entertainers to the Fordist principle of rationalized production through the linear repetition of standard operations and the production of standard parts. Today it

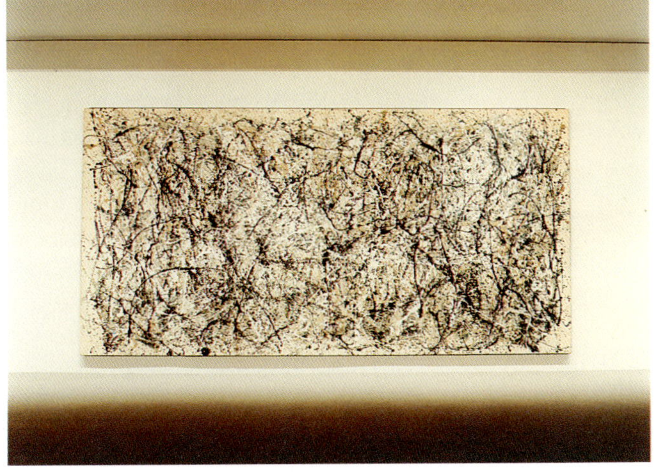

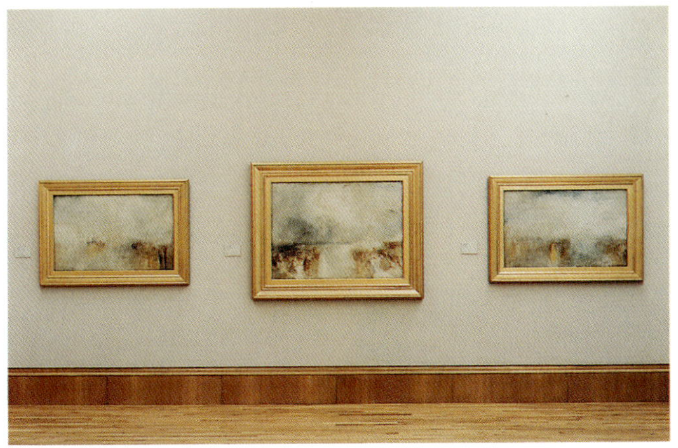

Andreas Gursky, Untitled VI, 1997
Andreas Gursky, Turner Collection, 1995

might be said that his formula has been given a new variant: the mass ornament assuming the form of a multipartite all-over. Gursky's own comparison, between the masses at contemporary events and modernist formal structures, imbues his montage with a distinctive brisance and sense of irony.

Conversely, Gursky acknowledges that real life does not always lend itself to such treatment and that Fordism is not always to be found where one might expect it.

> This phenomenon came to light... when I visited more than seventy world-renowned industrial plants. Most of them had a socially romantic facade that I had not expected. I had been looking for visual expressions of supposedly aseptic industrial environments. Any systematic documentation of these establishments would have given the impression of a world existing at the dawn of the industrial age. If it was not clear to me before I visited these places that one can no longer place trust in photography, then afterwards it certainly was. This experience made it much easier for me to justify digital picture-processing.[29]

In this context *Turner Collection* (1995) becomes even more striking. Turner's strategy of replacing mimetic revelation with a release of space, a dematerialization of the objective, and eventually an application of the pure resources of art – a pure orchestration of colours – is presented in its museological context, with the paintings mounted as a triptych. Furthermore, the sequence of paintings (as created by the limits of the photograph) mirrors the narrative of artistic development described above.

Whilst the established art of the mid nineteenth century remained bound by the framework of mimesis, a different tendency was developing in parallel. At first this took the form of an idealization of reality (as employed by classicism), but gradually the depiction of reality was abandoned altogether. Romanticism rejected the idea that there was an inherent harmony in mathematical rules. Opposed to any attempt to capture the world by realistic modes of depiction, romantic artists constructed their own universe of forms. Turner wanted to symbolize a reality beneath the surface of phenomena; at the same time, he opened up a free space for his own imagination. And yet, in Gursky's photographs, Turner's intentions appear to be tamed and regulated by their museological context.

Neues Sehen and Chaos

Among the most striking of Andreas Gursky's photographs is *Cairo, Diptych* (1992), which uses a visual layout favoured by the *Neues Sehen*. A busy traffic junction in Cairo is photographed twice from an extremely high viewpoint, with a slight time delay between the two photographs. Traces of a subjective mode of viewing are discernible in this diptych, in so far as the photographer adopts an unusual perspective on his subject. The *Neues Sehen* employed similar artistic techniques: individual details, extreme perspectives, oblique and out-of-focus views, pictorial elements tending towards abstraction, all belonged to the photo-optical aesthetic of the 'Bauhaus style'. This group also sought to liberate itself from reality and to stylize the medium as 'pure' photography. In most instances, the subject of the photograph was of no particular importance. As Louis Kaplan has observed in his witty essay about the 'Photo-Egg', a banal object was often deliberately chosen as the most suitable vehicle for the exploration of various positions in contemporary debates about painting, photography, perception and photo-optics.

In *Cairo*, however, Gursky undermines the theoretical framework of the Bauhaus group. The extreme perspective neither draws attention to the relative banality of photo-optics, nor does it offer great insight into the chaos of the Egyptian street. Rather it appears that the chaos has its own order, entirely independent of the modes of representation used in an attempt to master it. In this, the 'real' perspective is also evident; the subject itself belongs to a 'different order'. It is already at a distance and unmanageable on account of the barriers imposed by a cultural relativity. We see the image from our Eurocentric viewpoint and cannot judge it by disinterested aesthetic demands alone.

In conclusion, however, it should be noted that the decoding of the references in Gursky's photographs is only one part of interpreting his work. What makes Gursky's photographs unique is much more the manner in which

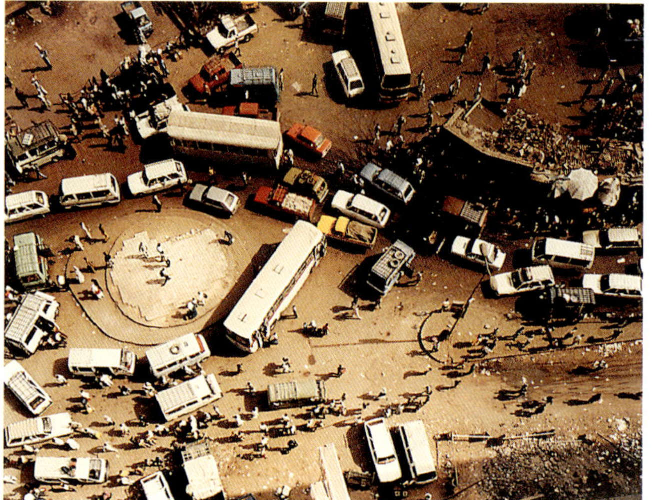
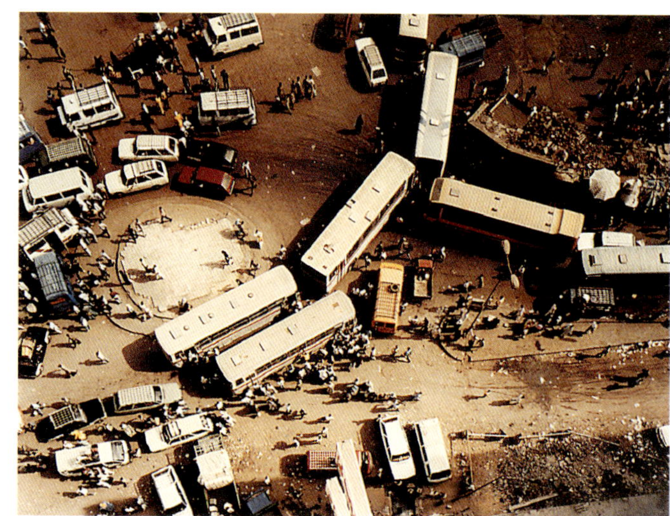

Andreas Gursky, Cairo, Diptych, 1992

Lucia Moholy, **Bauhaus Balcony, 1928**

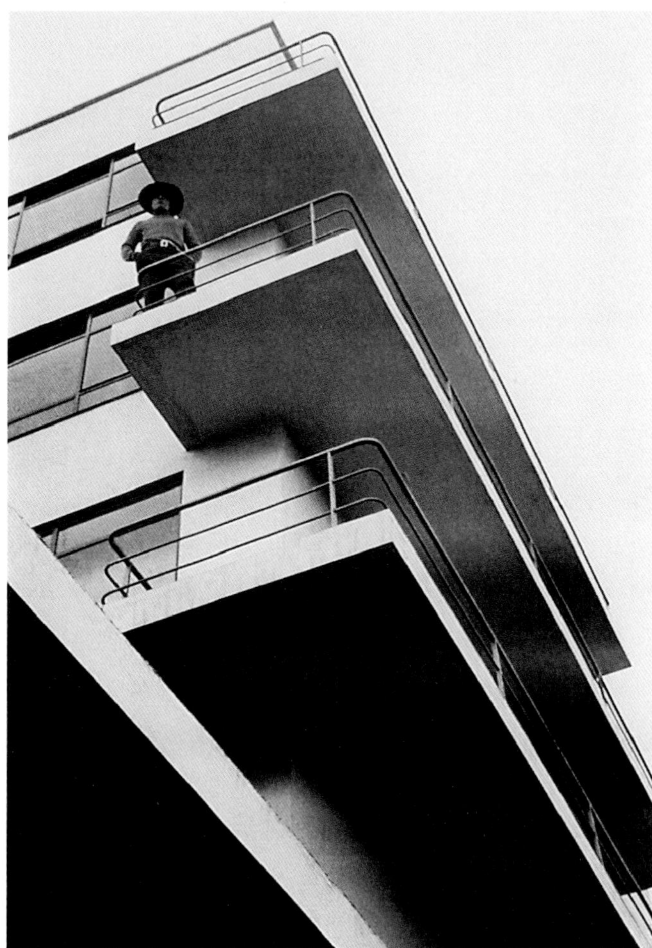

he playfully overcomes photography's desire to retain the autonomous status of art. He neither imitates art nor fences himself off from it, but locates himself right at the centre of contemporary discussions about both photography and art.

Translation Christian Braun

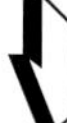

1 Most recently in: '... im Allgemeinen gehe ich die Dinge langsam an', Interview with Andreas Gursky, Supplement to the exhibition catalogue *Andreas Gursky 1994–1998* (Kunstmuseum Wolfsburg, 1998) p. iv.
2 Other paintings by Friedrich, such as his *Mountainous Landscape with Rainbow* (circa 1810), or his *Sea-shore with Fisherman* (1807), could be seen as an impetus for similar pictorial stratagems.
3 Friedrich Schlegel: 'Fragmente', quoted in Hans-Egon Hass, Gustav-Adolf Mohrlüder, eds., *Ironie als literarisches Phänomen* (Gütersloh, 1973) p. 293.
4 *Andreas Gursky 1994–1998*, op. cit.
5 It can be added that Gursky was inspired by a Prada display in a Düsseldorf shoe shop, but for the purposes of the photograph had a copy of the New York shop window built in an art gallery.
6 See Marie Luise Syring, 'Where is "Untitled"?', in exhibition catalogue, *Andreas Gursky: Photographs from 1984 to the Present*, (Kunsthalle Düsseldorf, 1998) p. 7.
7 Gursky, Interview, loc. cit., p. v.
8 ibid., footnote 1, p. vi.
9 ibid., p. v.
10 ibid., p. vi.
11 ibid., p. iv.
12 Otto Steinert, Gursky's teacher at this institution (where he studied from 1978 to 1981), should also be credited as having had a strong influence on his development.
13 A period that, in Germany, lasted from around 1860 until the first decades of the twentieth century.
14 Quoted in Lothar Romain, 'Systematische Inspektionen von Wirklichkeit', *Bernd und Hilla Becher*, in the series *Künstler. Kritisches Lexicon der Gegenwartskunst* (Munich, 1989) p. 6.
15 Interview with Bernd and Hilla Becher, in *Künstler. Kritisches Lexicon*, op. cit., p. 14.
16 On the subject of the connection between architecture and photography in the work of Becher's students compare Breuer, ed., *Außenhaut und Innenraum. Mutmaßungen zu einem gestörten Verhältnis zwischen Photographie und Architektur* (Gießen, 1997). See also Breuer, ed., *Axel Hütte. London. Photographien 1982–84*, studio catalogue of the Museum Künstlerkolonie Mathildenhöhe Darmstadt (Munich/Paris/London, 1993).
17 The term 'modernism' is used here to denote the American concept of 'modernism', which is much more firmly linked to the 1960s than the German concept.
18 Supplement, loc. cit., p. vii.
19 Rosalind Krauss, 'Allusion and Illusion in Donald Judd', *Artforum*, 9, May 1966, pp. 24–6, in Gregor Stemmrich, ed., *Minimal Art. Eine kritische Retrospektive* (Dresden/Basel, 1995).
20 Dan Flavin, 'Some remarks ... excerpts from a spleenish journal', *Artforum*, 4, December 1966, pp. 27–9, in Gregor Stemmrich, ed., *Minimal Art*, loc. cit.
21 Compare Arthur C. Danto, *The Transformation of the Commonplace: A Philosophy of Art* (Cambridge, MA, 1981).
22 Rosalind Krauss, op. cit., p. 26.
23 Quoted in Hans Irrek, *Andreas Gursky, Montparnasse*, exhibition catalogue Portikus (Frankfurt am Main, 1995) p. 5.
24 Gursky, Interview, loc. cit., p. v.
25 ibid., p. v.
26 Lynne Cooke, 'Andreas Gursky: Visionary (Per)Versions', in Marie Luise Syring, ed., *Andreas Gursky: Photographs from 1984 to the Present*, op. cit., pp. 13–17.
27 Compare Clement Greenberg, 'Jean Dubuffet und Jackson Pollock, 1947', and Jackson Pollock, 'Inspiration, Vision, intuitive Entscheidung, 1967', in Karlheinz Lüdeking, *Clement Greenberg. Die Essenz der Moderne. Ausgewählte Essays und Kritiken* (Amsterdam/Dresden, 1997) pp. 114–20 and 353–62.
28 Siegfried Kracauer, *The Mass Ornament: Weimar Essays* (London, 1995) pp. 75–9.
29 Gursky, Interview, loc. cit., p. v.

Behind: A Paralipomenon to Bernd & Hilla Becher

Hubertus von Amelunxen

'The back alone gives me hope, for it can never be seen.'
Sören Kierkegaard

It would be presumptuous to claim that the photographs of architecture taken by Bernd and Hilla Becher over the past four decades are *lacking in background*. It would likewise be hard to say that their views – mainly of industrial structures, compiled and ordered in series – are all *foreground*-orientated. Nor is their way of showing buildings anthropocentric; they do not seek to give us an image of man and his dwelling, so to speak. Through their circumspect approach, Bernd and Hilla Becher reject the very canon that defines the buildings within their work. The *typologies* may well be categories of architecture – the *water towers* and *lime kilns* listed relics of contained functionality – but what is behind the photographs? What, indeed, is meant by behind? Defined spatially (according to Grimm's dictionary), behind is 'a place lying at the back'. Is behind the back of a building, architecturally speaking, or is it understood as the invisible reverse of that which lies in front of our eyes? In the case of the Bechers' photographs of spherical gasometers, how can we determine the points of reference that orientate our perception? Is there a law that reverses the relative values of behind and in front? If we walk around a building we find ourselves behind the facade, but also behind the space to which our backs are turned. To perceive a building in its entirety, we must force ourselves into the intermediate spaces. But seeing through a building – through a transparent facade or an arcade – does not allow us to grasp the dimension of time. Nor, least of all, does photography. Despite this, photography has always insisted (disastrously) on its own perfection. The Bechers expose the insolence of this claim, which has more to do with Balzac's *Comédie Humaine* than with Renger-Patzsch's *Neue Sachlichkeit*. In the majority of their typologies of industrial buildings the back is imagined as a continuation of the functionality represented on the front. Pipes snake their way around blast furnaces. Cooling towers, water towers or gasometers are mostly cylindrical, and have circular bases that are also determined by the processes of industrial production. Coal mines are photographed from the diagonal, and pipes run through the images as if to catalyse our perception – channel our all too easily distracted view.

The back is like a secret which is destroyed once it is out in the open. Yet it remains inexhaustible; if it is lost an inversion arises: back becomes front, front becomes back. If we go *behind someone's back*, we keep them in the dark; if we attack *from behind*, we take them by surprise. The preposition *behind* has many applications and connotations, most of them related to invisibility, secrecy, and death. 'I am *already* (dead) means that I am *behind*. Absolutely behind, the Behind that has never been seen from the front, the Already that nothing has preceded, which therefore has conceived and created itself, but as a cadaver or glorious corpse' (Jacques Derrida). Transposed to the photography of architecture, this could be expressed in a single phrase: We never see what has been *left behind*.

In 1972, the year of *Documenta* 5, Bernd and Hilla Becher took eight photographs of the house at Sternbuschweg 362 in Duisburg (*1 House with 8 Views*). In the series the house turns *almost* once around a vertical axis, growing into its representation. It is photographed from eight precisely calculated positions: from the starting point, each view progresses forty-five degrees beyond the previous one. The 1870s house was certainly once part of a terrace on a busy street but war, clearance and speculation have left it standing on its own. In the first of the views, the house appears defiantly proud of its solitary status, fenced in and seemingly cut off by overhead cables. The narrow facade – and that is all we see – expresses dignity. The second view, taken after moving around forty-five degrees, shows the windowless right side of the building as it extends to the rear, to an overgrown, desolate backyard. The third view, taken at an angle of ninety degrees from the first position, reveals the stacking of the rear of the building and brings a tree into the foreground. The photographs communicate an impression of repetition, comparable to a pirouetting ballerina on a music box, only that here it is the photographers who carry out the movement, offering the viewer the present moment in saccades. The sixth view, with its stark contrast between shadow and light, makes the building seem almost like a cubed expressionist work – but the impression quickly fades when we are confronted with the seventh view of the facade, now massive, blind and refusing any external reference.

On the one hand *1 House with 8 Views* is typical of the Bechers' work, with its precisely calculated perspectives, repeated subject, suggestion of seriality, clear distancing from the object, careful contextualization, and absence of authorial presence. On the other hand (and now I come to my argument) this series may help us put into context the 'distance' that seems to accompany any evaluation of the work of the Bechers and their disciples or imitators. The talk of *distance*, or of a *distanced* attitude to the subject, evokes Gustave Flaubert's famous trinity – impartiality, impassivity, impersonality – as if the Bechers' photography was invoking the litany of modernism, as if the work was characterized by the (fictitious, of course) absence of the author. In a contribution to *art* magazine ten years ago, Hilla Becher said that the essence of the objects could only be grasped and translated into the typical from the correct standpoint. Is that correct standpoint aware of the rear? *1 House with 8 Views* sets each view within a time frame which is itself split into the linear irreversible time of the historical presence of the building, and the circular reversible time required to go around the object. Viewed as a whole, the eight photographs have a strongly analytical contour, evident in the linking back of the eighth view to the first (315 degrees to 360 degrees = 0 degrees), and in the suggestion of a circular progression of time. This is negated, however, by the photographic performance itself. The back of architecture is also the front, viewed at a different moment in time. Setting the object in a space–time continuum results in the loss of the *Present* as a site which, with each new view, makes a secret out of what has been seen. The *Present* cannot be the site of a series.

With *1 House with 8 Views* Bernd and Hilla Becher have created an allegory, and not just of architectural photography. 'Is it true', Jean Genet asks in *Pompes funèbres*, 'that philosophers doubt the existence of the things that are behind them? How, then, are we to discover the secret of the things that disappear? By turning around quite fast? No. Or even faster? Faster than anything? I dared to cast a look behind me. I eyed. I spied. I waited attentively. I turned my eye and my head, ready to … No, it was all in vain. The things are never caught out. You would have to turn at the speed of an aeroplane propeller. Then you would perceive that the things have disappeared, and you along with them.'

Translation Pauline Cumbers

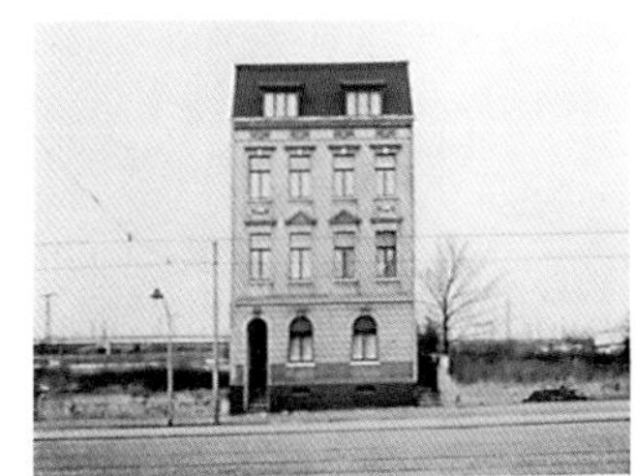
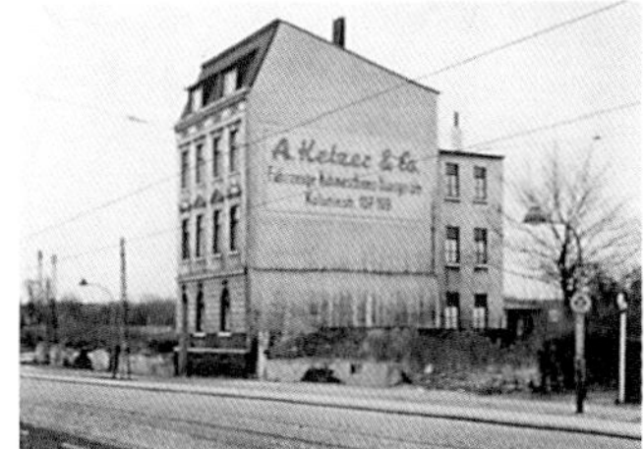
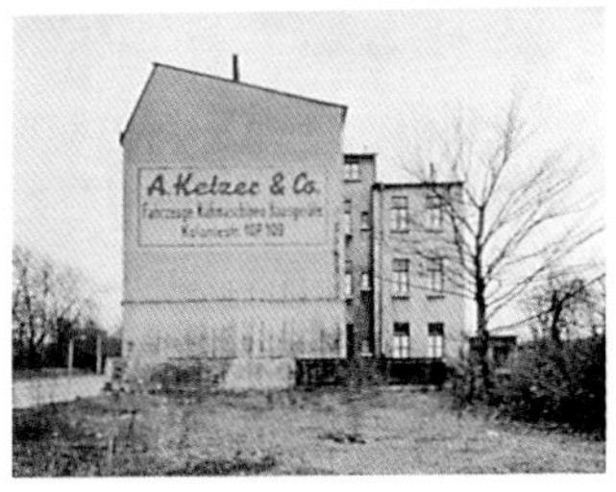
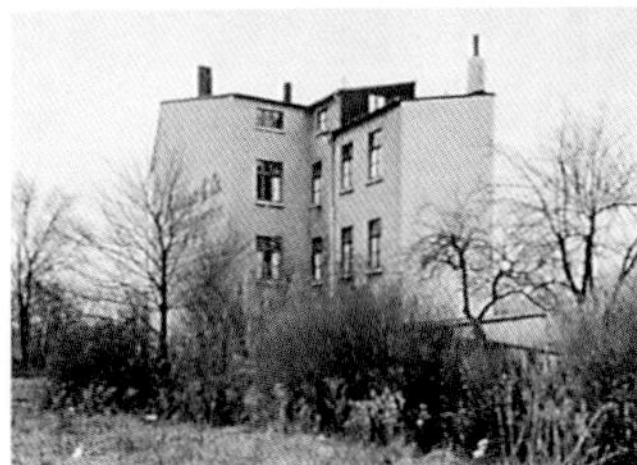
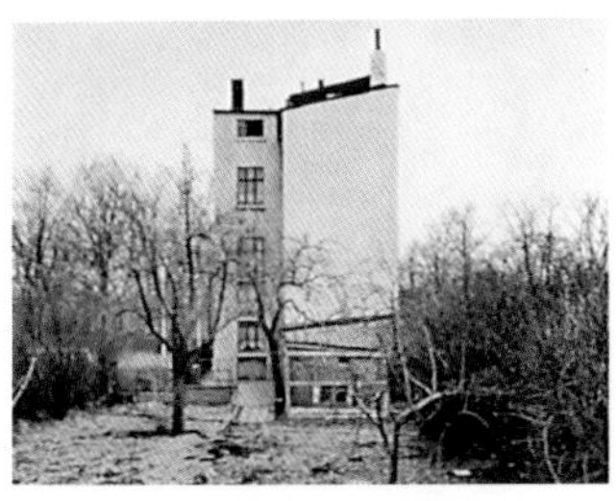
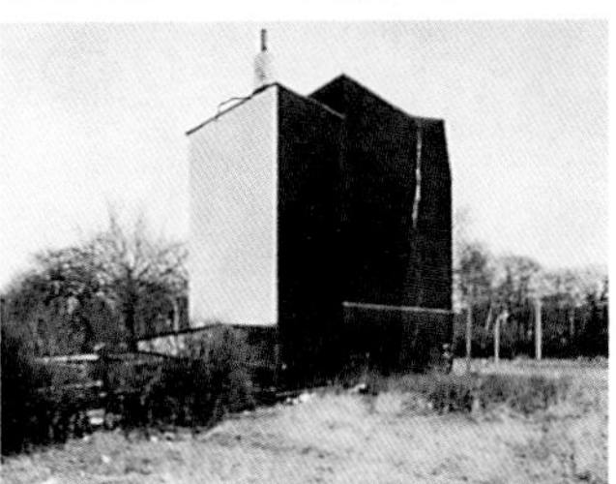
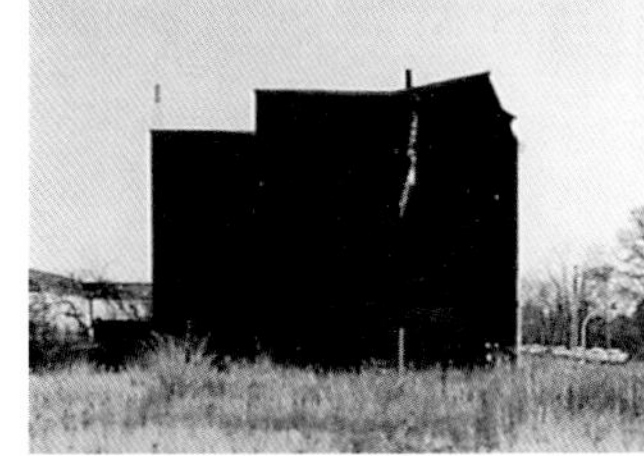
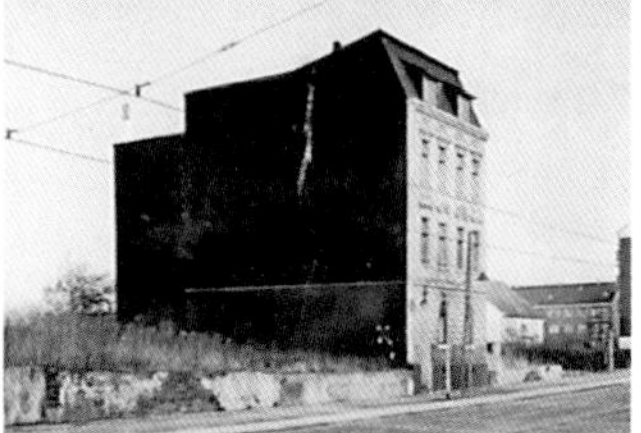

→ Bernd & Hilla Becher, 1 House with 8 Views, 8 Views of Sternbuschweg 362, Duisburg, 1972

Images on Buildings

Rolf Sachsse

Postmodernism and late modernism have passed on. Long live the second modernism, deconstructivism, the new simplicity and, above all, long live virtuality!

As information architecture, Robert Venturi's decorated shed[1] is enjoying an eschatological revival, albeit in modified form: the shed has become a factory hall, the fire station a library, the office building a cultural centre, and everything, in the end, has become a museum. The prophets and main proponents of this development are the Swiss architects Jacques Herzog and Pierre de Meuron, who design simple boxes for every purpose, and envelop, penetrate and light up old buildings with new cubes or slit windows.[2] Over the past few years Herzog & de Meuron have cultivated techniques for dressing up their work, beginning with the use of photography in three buildings: a sweet factory and storage facility for Ricola Europe, a sports centre in Pfaffenholz, and a library for Eberswalde University of Applied Sciences.[3] Today, in collaboration with the artist Rémy Zaugg, they are planning even more ambitious media facades. And these architects are not the only ones who are propagating such collaborations: from Rotterdam to Tokyo, image and information facades are in preparation, under construction, or already on view.

Covering a facade with ornament is nothing new; on the contrary, it is one of the oldest architectural practices. Moreover, ornament has been characterized by abstraction throughout the ages – from the friezes of Mesopotamian antiquity to Adolf Loos's montage of materials (which his contemporaries already saw as an absence of ornament).[4] The primary models for ornament are biological motifs, simplified to permit multiple reproduction and remove any overt symbolism. The function of ornament is doubly coded: on the one hand it serves as the bearer of meaning, an indicator of the building's uses, on the other it conceals elements of construction which are considered to be aesthetically unpleasing. But, above all, ornament serves to establish or maintain aesthetic conventions, especially when it is combined with new technology or means of construction. In the nineteenth century, floral decoration was deployed in railway stations and in buildings such as the Crystal Palace or the Eiffel Tower in order to disguise the unbearable lightness of the cast-iron filigree structure. Ornament is always camouflage, though this role is subject to periodic historical re-evaluation.

The use of photographs to furnish buildings is nothing new either. Monumental exhibition designs by El Lissitzky[5] and Herbert Bayer[6] inspired permanent installations of photographic murals in the inter-war years. Probably the most famous examples are Margaret Bourke-White's motifs from radiotechnology which filled the entrance lobby of the first Rockefeller Center in New York.[7] The pavilions at the World Fairs of the 1930s were also full of huge canvases; the entrance of the German propaganda exhibition, *Gebt mir vier Jahre Zeit*, even had canvases mounted on rollers, changing the picture every half hour.[8] After the war abstract representations from electronic engineering and chemistry became popular themes for murals in universities and large industrial corporations. Heinz Hajek-Halke made photograms and negative montages of this type from small-scale technical photographs.[9]

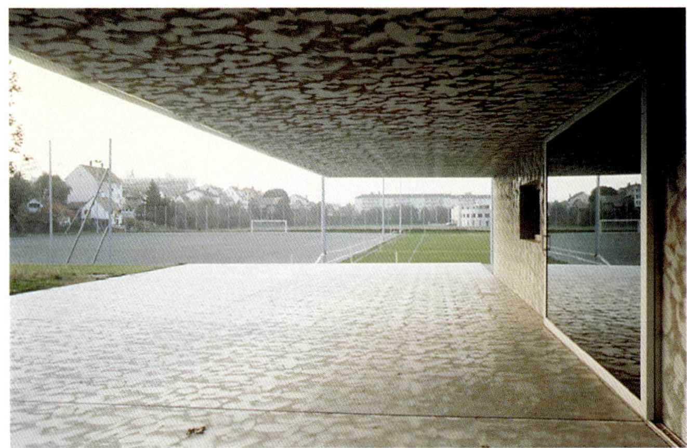

➩ Herzog & de Meuron, Pfaffenholz sports centre, 1993

Heinrich Heidersberger, in response to a commission from the University of Wolfenbüttel, built a 'rhythmogram' machine capable of systematically and precisely recording trajectories of light on large-format film.[10] Similarly, Peter Keetman developed Lissajous figures[11] out of a simple pendulum motion and decorated the walls of many a Munich office block and entrance lobby with the results.

A less well-known variant of the ornamental and decorative use of photography in architecture takes the form of etched glass. The *Cliché-Verre* technique, which evolved out of the transfer of drawn patterns in stained glass, began to incorporate photographic images from around 1900. A special form of this process can be seen in a cycle of stained glass windows in the church of Sts Chrysanthus and Daria in Bad Münstereifel, near Cologne, which contain tiny photographs of biological, mineral and chemical specimens. Executed as *grisailles*, the images correspond to a high-contrast black and white photography. (The miniature scale of the photographs may also correspond to what visitors expect to see in a small-windowed late Romanesque basilica.) From this development it was only a small step to the etched glass that Jean Nouvel incorporated into his Institut du Monde Arabe in Paris and, from there, an even smaller step to the newest kind of holographic window surfaces.[12] In this respect the works of Herzog & de Meuron – and, to be precise, the printed glass panels of the sports centre in Pfaffenholz – represent an intermediate step rather than an advanced position (in the same way that the architects describe their approach as being halfway between minimalism and deconstructivism).[13]

It is often forgotten that photography entered the fine arts via conceptualism and as performance documentation, accompanied by a series of experiments in bringing together architecture and photography: the endless pop montages that Archigram and the Vienna actionists used to define and describe their ideas; the grainy representations of architectural models that were directly inspired by the actionist photographs; the attempts by SITE, among others, to represent buildings in the same way as pictures – all helped to define an architectural style founded on a 'real' mimesis. These projects were reinforced by the direct action artworks conjoining photographs and facades (including countless projections of images on to urban buildings), the incorporation of photographic images into open-air concerts in the city, and the creation of photographic stage sets. In France and Italy, in particular, image and film projections became essential to nocturnal tourist attractions – many a Palladian villa was reduced to a projection screen for rock concerts or light shows – *son et lumière* was everywhere. Around this time, too, began the vogue for projecting advertising messages on to urban pavements, building facades and other receptive surfaces.

Jacques Herzog and Pierre de Meuron are acquainted with all this – they saw and experienced enough of it during their student years. Half a generation younger than the actionists, they have taken their repertoire – as well as the Hannes Meyer brand of strict Basel modernism – and not so much deconstructed as remoulded it into a stylistic programme adaptable to any individual project.[14] In this context they have undertaken an interdisciplinary collaboration with artists which has gone beyond the conventional scope of 'art in building' projects. It is significant that the artists they have chosen work between several disciplines and media: Rémy Zaugg occupies himself with sculpture, literature and drawing; Balthasar Burkhard is known for his sculptural photographic works; and Thomas Ruff's name is synonymous with a peripheral area of the so-called Becher School. The first two artists have worked and exhibited together,[15] and are also known for various collaborations with other artists, curators and architects. Their proposals for Herzog & de Meuron include complex media facades, such as those on the Museum of the Twentieth Century on the former site of the Turkish barracks in Munich.[16]

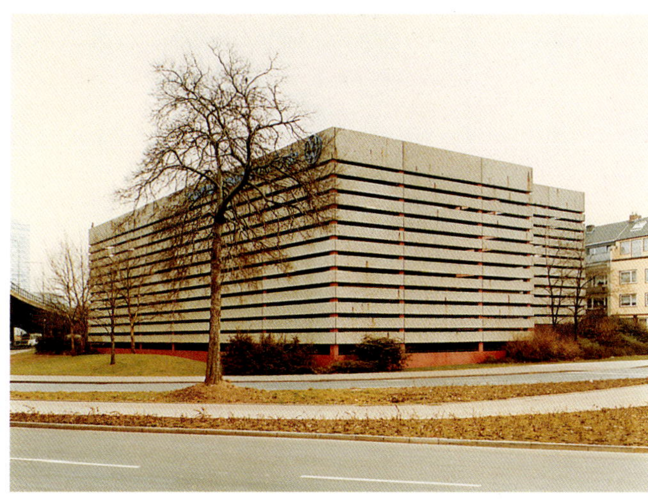

➾ Thomas Ruff, House No. 8 I, 1988

Since finishing his studies in Bernd Becher's class at Düsseldorf Art Academy[17] the third artist, Thomas Ruff, has developed two distinctive methods for distancing the worlds pictured in his photographs from possible physical realities. These methods are seamlessly juxtaposed in his work: one is defined by the reproduction of found material, which might include old astronomy charts or photographs, newspaper cuttings or other media paraphernalia; the other is characterized by the digital manipulation of documentary photographs – for example, he may lengthen a simple apartment block by one section, or join together two orthogonal facade views to make a panorama. In both cases he is attempting to question the unconditional reference of all photographic representation to a given reality and to negate its claim to documentary status – the very claim consolidated by Bernd and Hilla Becher and their School.[18] In the process, Ruff remains laconic and unliterary. His representations reinforce or complete real things. They allude to nothing but the possibility of minimally altering, through processes of reproduction and completion, that which (in the words of William J. Mitchell) the Reconfigured Eye can see.[19] In conceptual terms this places Ruff some way behind positions taken by Polish avantgardists in the 1970s,[20] but he compensates with the enormous size and extraordinary finish of his photographs.

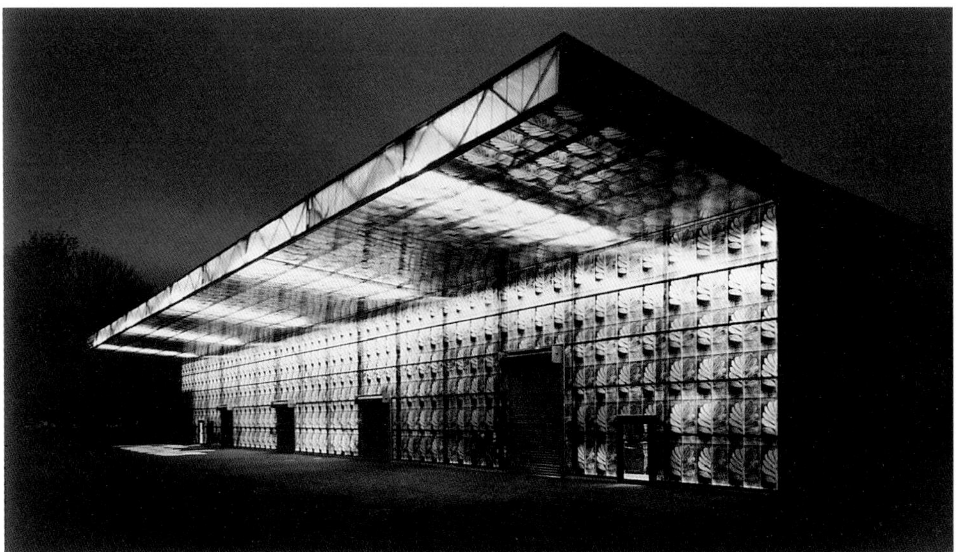

Thomas Ruff, Ricola Mulhouse, 1994

The collaboration between Ruff and Herzog & de Meuron has, to my knowledge, also been extended to two overlapping levels of reproduction. On one level Ruff has published photographs of a series of earlier buildings by the practice, thereby taking his place, as a documentary-maker, in the compartmentalized world of the architectural profession.[21] In this work he occasionally uses the form of digital montage described above; with a long facade, for example, he may splice together two or three frontal shots to make a single long picture, and then use retouching to blur the foreground in the resulting double- or triple-centred perspective. These photographs have always been published in black and white – a further abstraction from reality[22] – and since Ruff photographs and prints in colour as well as grey tones this must be seen as a conscious, and therefore significant, decision. It appears to me to be a reference to sculptural minimalism, the style brandished by the architects like an aesthetic banner – and the only reference to Ruff's formation in the Becher School that he acknowledges in interviews.[23] At the same time, this approach establishes the basis for the conceptual and practical collaboration between the architects and the photographer.

The collaboration begins with two steps: the choice of vehicle for the photographic ornament, followed by the choice of motif. In the case of the Ricola building in Mulhouse a series of translucent panels were screenprinted with a motif based on a Karl Blossfeldt photograph. The motif was sufficiently familiar to be conventionalized for design use; it was also out of copyright.[24]

At the library for Eberswalde University the images were applied in horizontal bands; an alternation between reflecting and transparent photographs was intended to distract from the rather banal composition of the facade. For this project Ruff used newspaper images from a personal archive collected over a number of years. The photographs refer to pictorial models such as river meanders, 'running dogs' and rows of acanthus leaves. As motifs these appear somewhat unspectacular, but they were selected more for formal characteristics – such as curvatures, or an intense progression from dark to light – which accentuate their decorative quality. For a third collaboration, on the sports centre in Pfaffenholz, Ruff chose an abstract image resembling old-fashioned sheets of Formica,[25] which was imprinted on to the continuous concrete surfaces of the facade, while the translucent roof panels were screenprinted in imitation of the surface patterns of Heraklith mineral wool insulation board.

Precisely this work contains a clue to the technical-aesthetic basis of the collaboration. The Formica motif corresponds to those little pictures (with no message, no meaning) which are used as a backdrop to all kinds of web pages, minimizing the *horror vacui* of potential transmission failures. Often these backdrops allude to a materiality which is intended to evoke a source product or thought process connected with the offering on the web. In this respect they are clearly in the lineage of the surrogate problematics of late-nineteenth-century architectural historicism. In true postmodern fashion the collaboration between Ruff and Herzog & de Meuron extends this surrogate materiality through multiple codings of the media employed. Rough grids, unfinished corners, blurring, monochromy, traces of scratching – all of these devices point to the derivation of the decorative images from technical media, a process presented as entirely natural. In this sense they are no more than a (wholly unironic) recourse to the automatic self-reproduction of all technical media, as described by Friedrich Kittler.[26]

It would be pointless to look for meaning in the pictorial motifs. Whilst Blossfeldt's leaf may be considered appropriate for a herbal sweet factory, the use of newspaper cuttings on the walls of a university library is harder to fathom, and the sports hall's evocation of 1950s interiors, complete with Formica and Heraklith fittings, ultimately descends into the realm of the arcane. Thomas Ruff may, of course, be expressing the artistic freedom to select autonomous pictorial motifs modelled on earlier subjects – indeed this is a tradition of the painting school at Düsseldorf where he studied. However we may question the applicability of such a concept to the everyday practice of architecture, in the same way that we may question the applicability of that tradition to sacred art a hundred years ago. Both achieve a transformation of medium at the expense of the aura of the work: the price of technical progress is a standardized aesthetic. There is something almost tragic about the fact that the artist's approach – which above all illuminates the infinite reproducability of all arts and genres – has been yoked to the decorative convention of a recognizable motif, with the ultimate aim of securing a superficial acceptance of the building in itself.

The technical achievement of the collaboration between Ruff and Herzog & de Meuron has been to advance the decision-making process regarding the role of art within the building. The artist is no longer excluded until the design has been finalized, but is involved at a very early stage in the planning process. For artists this represents the fulfilment of a long-nurtured dream, yet it could also turn out to be a false dawn. This is because such an advance is the result of an innovation in media design, namely the use of CAD technology to assemble animations and perspective views out of a variety of architectural elements. When two-dimensional images are inserted into virtual constructs, when the materiality of a future object is represented by artificially generated colours and surface effects achieved by computer morphing techniques, the surrogate clearly becomes dependent on the media. Today the role of the artist (including the photographer) is to click the mouse to insert a few small pictures, distribute these over defined surfaces, erase the crops, and then select materials online, from suppliers' web pages (which at least guarantees a temporary connection with the real building process). The earlier the intervention is set in motion, the more minimal it need be. In principle this is all fair and good but, paradoxically, it makes the artist's work seem more meaningless.

In the meantime Herzog & de Meuron have gone one step further. They are presenting their virtual house on the Internet and in workshops, and presenting it with a wide selection of visual candy from the brave new world of modern media.[28] For the most part these images are drawn from film history, from private, anonymous archives, from advertising or from daily life. Derived from the video-clip, this aesthetic arranges all the images next to one another as minimalized particles of equal value, edits them only in terms of time sequence, and avoids any repetition in favour of an ungraspable fullness of iconic quotations and references. As the pages become a riot of colour, the house is volatized in a chaotic mass of pretty pictures. Goethe's pre-photography rallying cry, 'petrify the waves of time', is now washed away unheard. It is for this reason that architects such as Herzog & de Meuron no longer require a photographer for projects of this type, not even one with such a distanced view as Thomas Ruff.

Translation Pamela Johnston

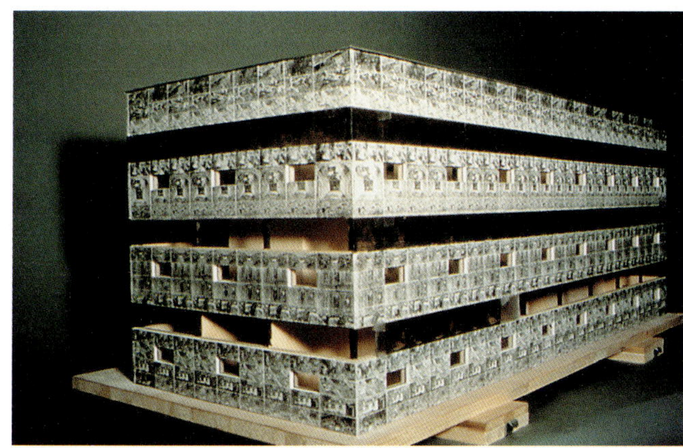

Herzog & de Meuron, Eberswalde University library, 1996

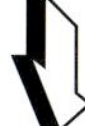

1 Robert Venturi, *Learning from Las Vegas* (Cambridge MA, 1978) pp. 101-20.
2 As in the Duisburg Copper Mills, for example, which are being transformed into the Grothe Museum of Modern Art.
3 For Ricola Europe, Pfaffenholz sports centre and Eberswalde University library see *arch +*, 129/130, December 1995, pp. 26-45 and 129-30. This special issue of the magazine contains comprehensive descriptions and illustrations of the building facades and details.
4 Burkhard Rukschcio, Roland Schachel, *Adolf Loos Leben und Werk*, (Salzburg, 1982) pp. 148-54.
5 Exhibition catalogue, *El Lissitzky* (Halle/Saale, 1988).
6 Sachsse, 'Out of Austria: Herbert Bayer', in *Camera Austria*, 25, 1994, pp. 3-11.
7 Jonathan Silverman, *For the World To See: The Life of Margaret Bourke-White* (London, 1983) pp. 70-72.
8 Ulrich Pohlmann, 'Nicht beziehungslose Kunst, sondern politische Waffe', an essay on the National Socialists' use of photography exhibitions as a means of aetheticizing their economics and politics, in *Fotogeschichte*, 8, 1988, pp. 17-32.
9 Heinz Hajek-Halke, *Experimentelle Fotografie, Lichtgrafik* (Bonn, 1955).
10 Exhibition catalogue, *Heinrich Heidersberger* (Wolfsburg, 1986).
11 Peter Keetman, *fotoform* (Berlin, 1987). These figures are named after Jules Antoine Lissajous (1822–1880), who, when developing a method for studying vibrations, obtained curves by successively reflecting light from mirrors on two tuning forks vibrating at right angles. The figures are only seen because of persistence of vision in the human eye.
12 'Baumarkt: Glas', in *arch +*, 134/135, December 1996, pp. 110-38; Martin Winter, 'Farbiges Glas', loc. cit., pp. 110-12.
13 'Minimalism and Ornament, Herzog & de Meuron in conversation with Nikolaus Kuhnert and Angelika Schnell', in *arch +*, 129/130, December 1995, pp. 115-18.
14 J. J. Herzog, P. de Meuron, 'Rationale Architektur und historische Bezugnahme', in *The Village Cry* (Basel), March 1977, pp. 17-39. See also Sachsse, 'From 0 - 1 to 0 + 1: The Artist Placement Group', in John Latham, *Art After Physics* (Museum of Modern Art Oxford, 1991) pp. 45-50.
15 A collaborative exhibition of the work of Rémy Zaugg and Balthasar Burkhard was held at the Kunsthalle Basel in 1983.
16 <http://www.archINFORM.de/projekte/4091.htm>
17 Exhibition catalogue, *Distanz und Nähe, Die Becher-Klasse* (Stuttgart, 1992).
18 Rupert Pfab, *Stille, Form und Farbe. Bernd und Hilla Bechers Industriebauten und das Stilleben bei Claus Goedicke und Thomas Ruff*, in the proceedings of the colloquium *Bernd und Hilla Becher / Distanz und Nähe* (Kawasaki, 1996) pp.131-148.
19 William J. Mitchell, *The Reconfigured Eye. Visual Truth in the Post-Photographic Era* (Cambridge, MA, 1992)
20 Exhibition catalogue, *Andrzej Jurczak, Particle of Dust* (Warsaw, 1978).
21 *Architektur von Herzog & de Meuron*, photographed by Margherita Krischanitz, Balthasar Burkhard, Hannah Villiger and Thomas Ruff, with a text by Theodora Fischer (Basel, 1991).
22 Thomas Ruff, 'Freie Sicht auf das Objekt', conversation with Michael Corsar in *RISZ, Zeitschrift für Architektur* (Dortmund), February 1994, pp. 14-16.
23 See, for example, the contributions made by Thomas Ruff to a round-table discussion at a symposium accompanying the exhibition *Deutsche Fotografie*, Bonn, 8 July 1997.
24 The copyright-free status of the Blossfeldt photographs was made widely known by a mass-market publication, *Karl Blossfeldt Photographien* (Cologne, 1993).
25 Susan Grant Lewin, ed., *Formica & Design, From the Counter Top to High Art* (New York, 1991).
26 Friedrich Kittler, 'Gleichschaltungen. Über Normen und Standards der elektronischen Kommunikation', in Manfred Faßler, Wulf Halbach, eds., *Geschichte der Medien* (Munich, 1998) pp. 255-68.
27 Jacques Herzog, 'The Virtual House', in *Das virtuelle Haus. Dokumentation eines Workshops in Berlin, Brakel, Cologne 1998*, pp. 118-29. URL: <http://virtualhouse.ch>

Bernd & Hilla Becher

Grube Anna Alsdorf/Aachen Germany, 1992	Zeche Friedrich der Große Herne Ruhrgebiet Germany, 1978	Zeche Werne Werne Ruhrgebiet Germany, 1976	Zeche Pluto Wanne-Eickel Ruhrgebiet Germany, 1981	Dortmund-Hörde Germany, 1989	Rombas Lorraine France, 1992	Mines de Roton Charleroi Belgium, 1976
Grube Anna Alsdorf/Aachen Germany, 1992	Schafstadt/ Merseburg Germany, 1994	Zeche Lothringen Bochum Ruhrgebiet Germany, 1980	Zeche Concordia Oberhausen Ruhrgebiet Germany, 1976	Zeche Zollern II Dortmund Germany, 1971	Siège Simon Forbach Lorraine France, 1989	Werdohl Sauerland Germany, 1985
Zeche Werne Werne Ruhrgebiet Germany, 1976	Calais Normandy France, 1995	Harlingen Netherlands, 1963	Charleroi-Montigny Belgium, 1984	Rodange Luxembourg, 1979	Calais Normandy France, 1995	Werdohl Sauerland Germany, 1985

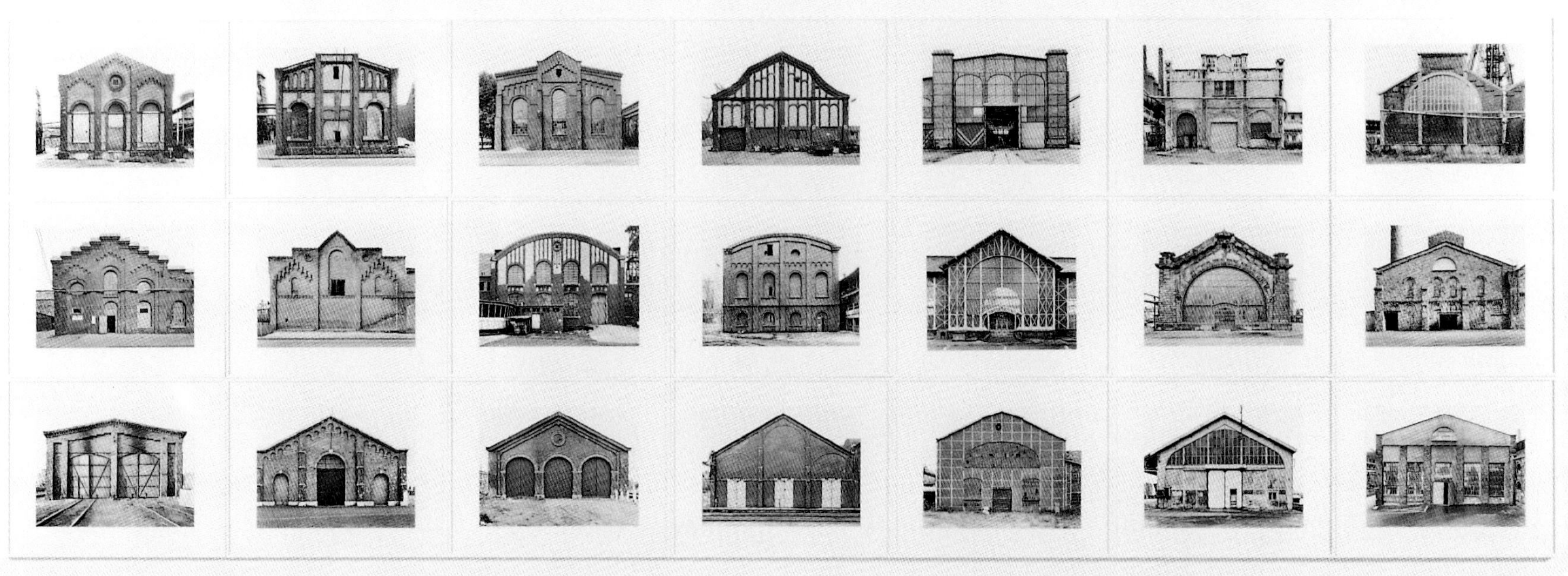

33 Industrial facades, 1996, twenty-one black and white photographs each 18" x 22" framed

34 Zeche Westfalen, Ahlen, Germany, 1968 35 Zeche Hugo, Gelsenkirchen, Germany, 1968

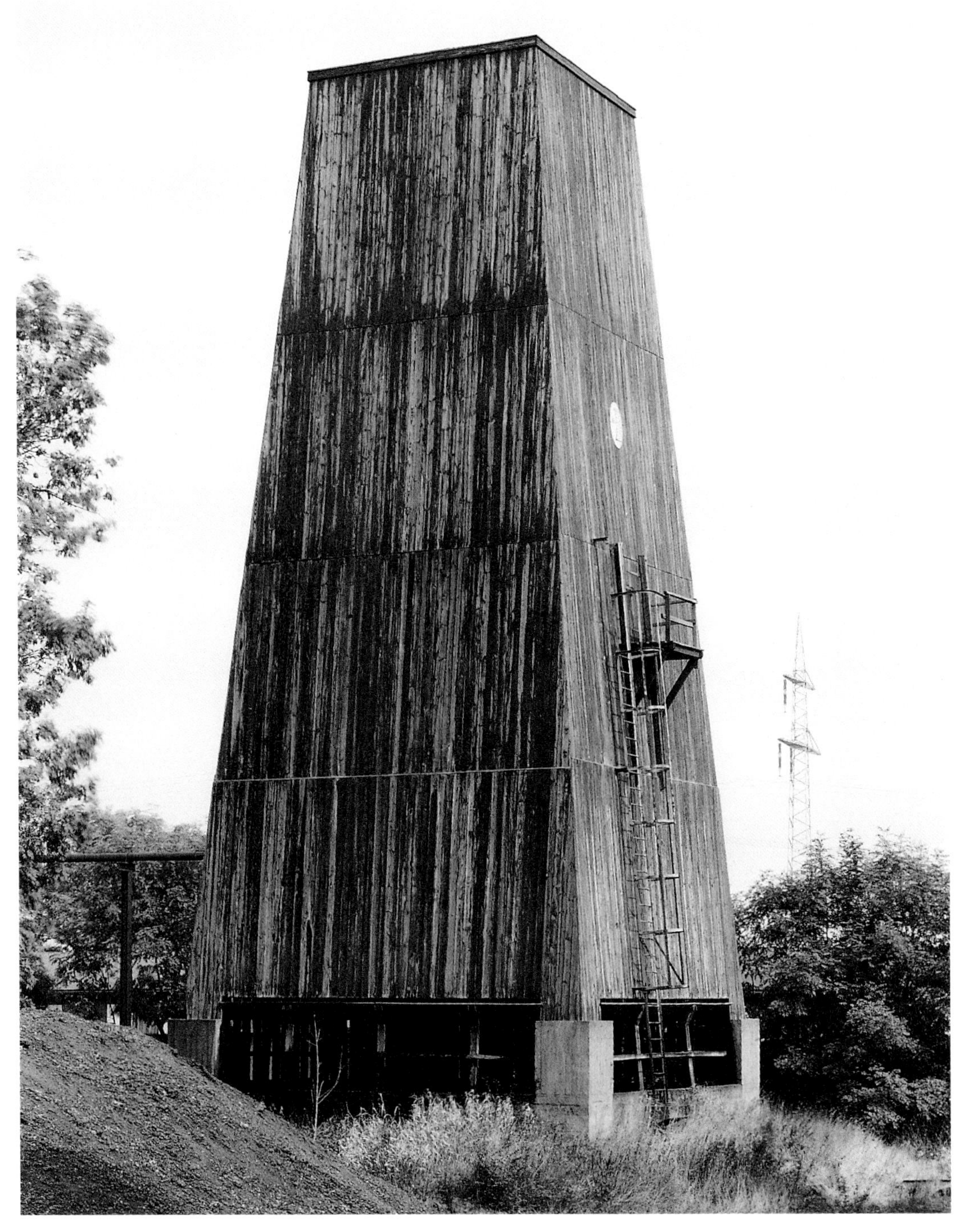

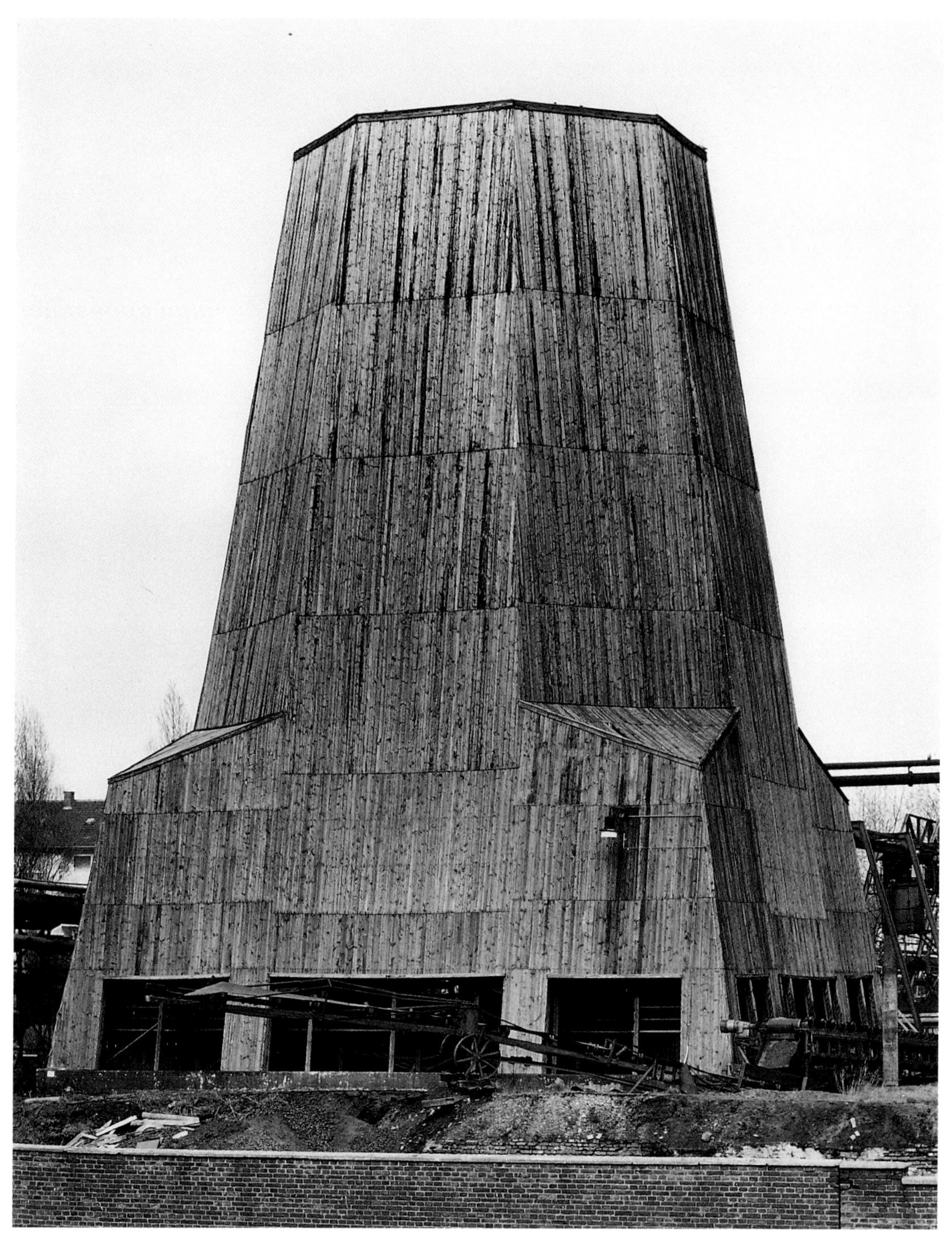

36 Liège, Belgium, 1971 37 Lübeck-Herrenwyk, Germany, 1983

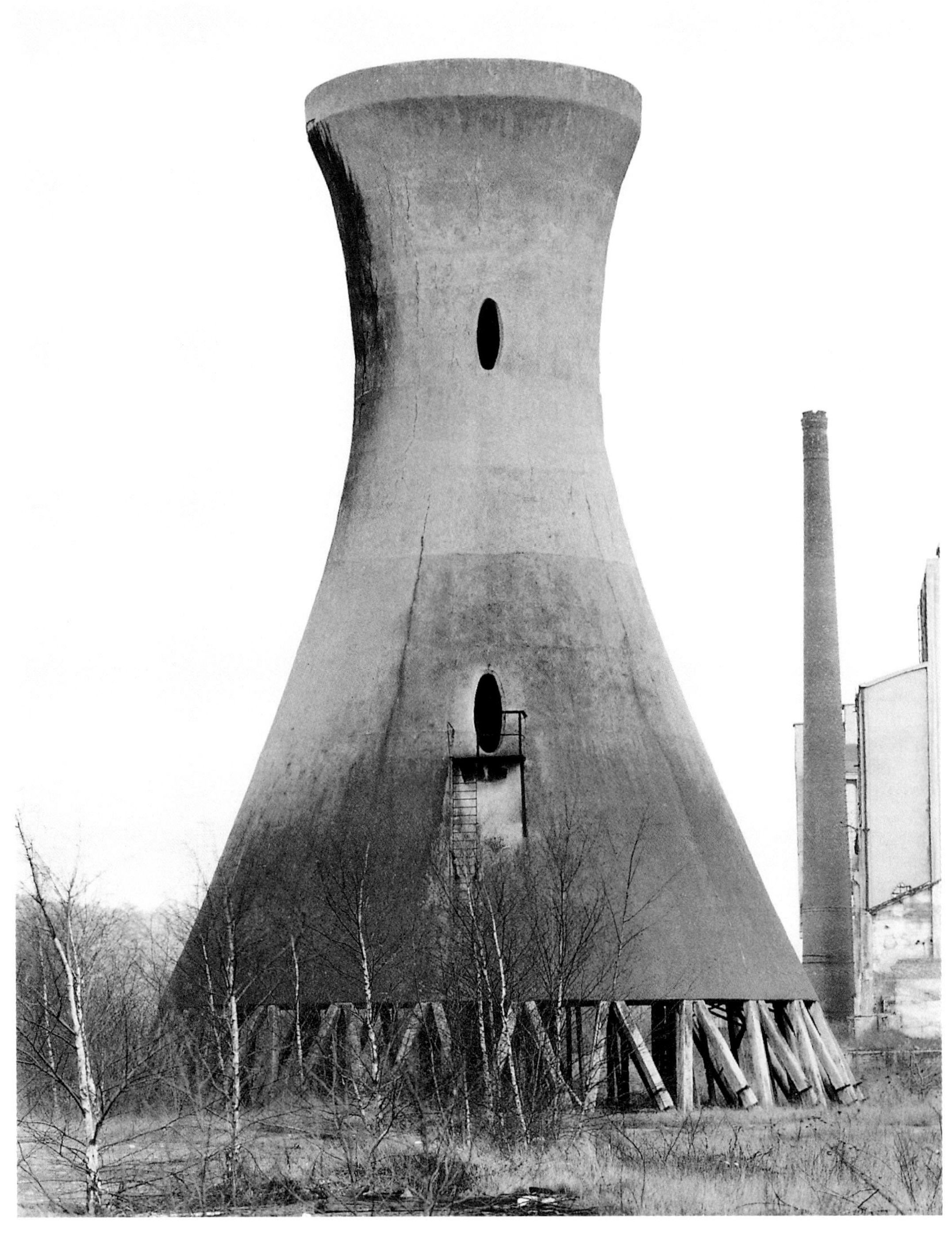

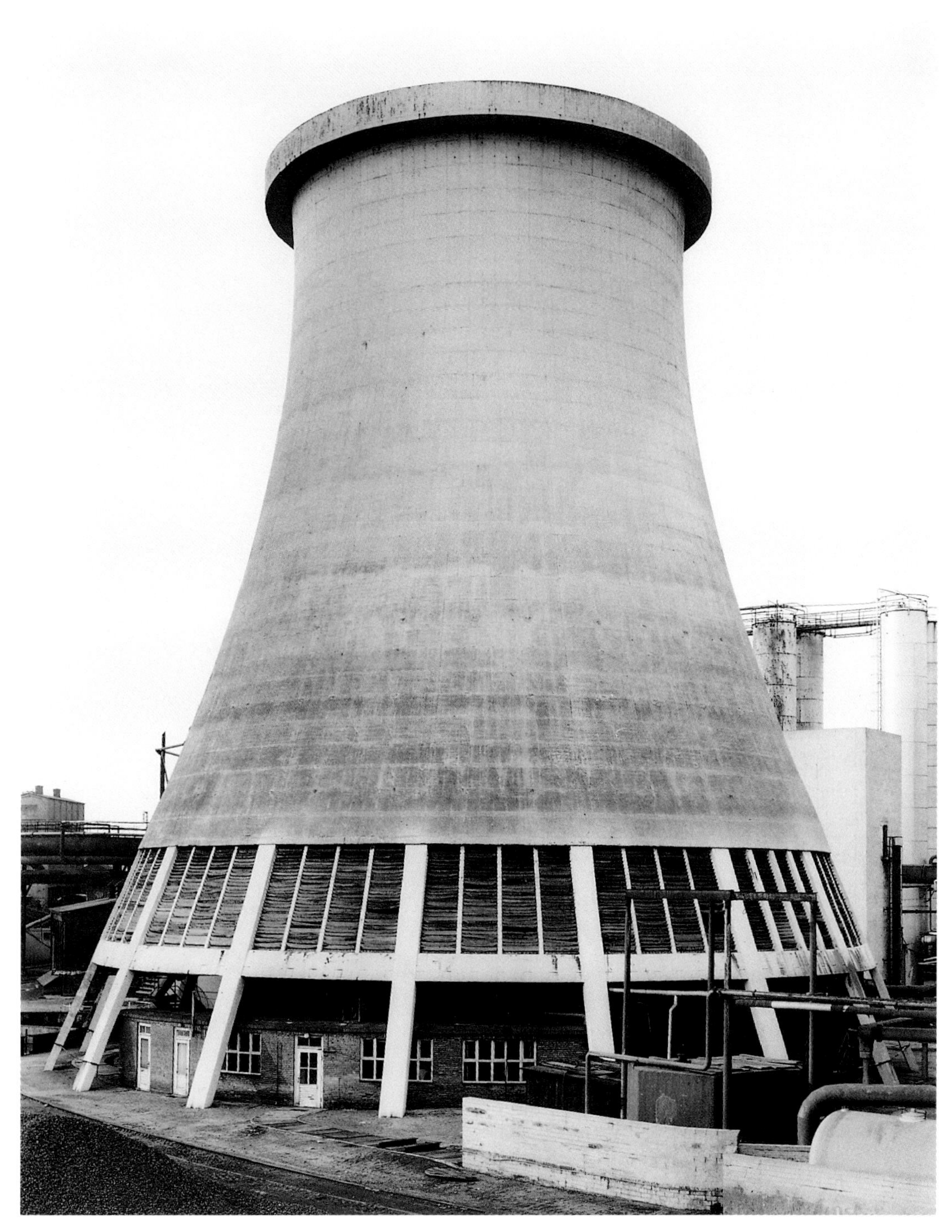

38 Oregon, Ohio, USA, 1977 39 Weirton, West Virginia, USA, 1977

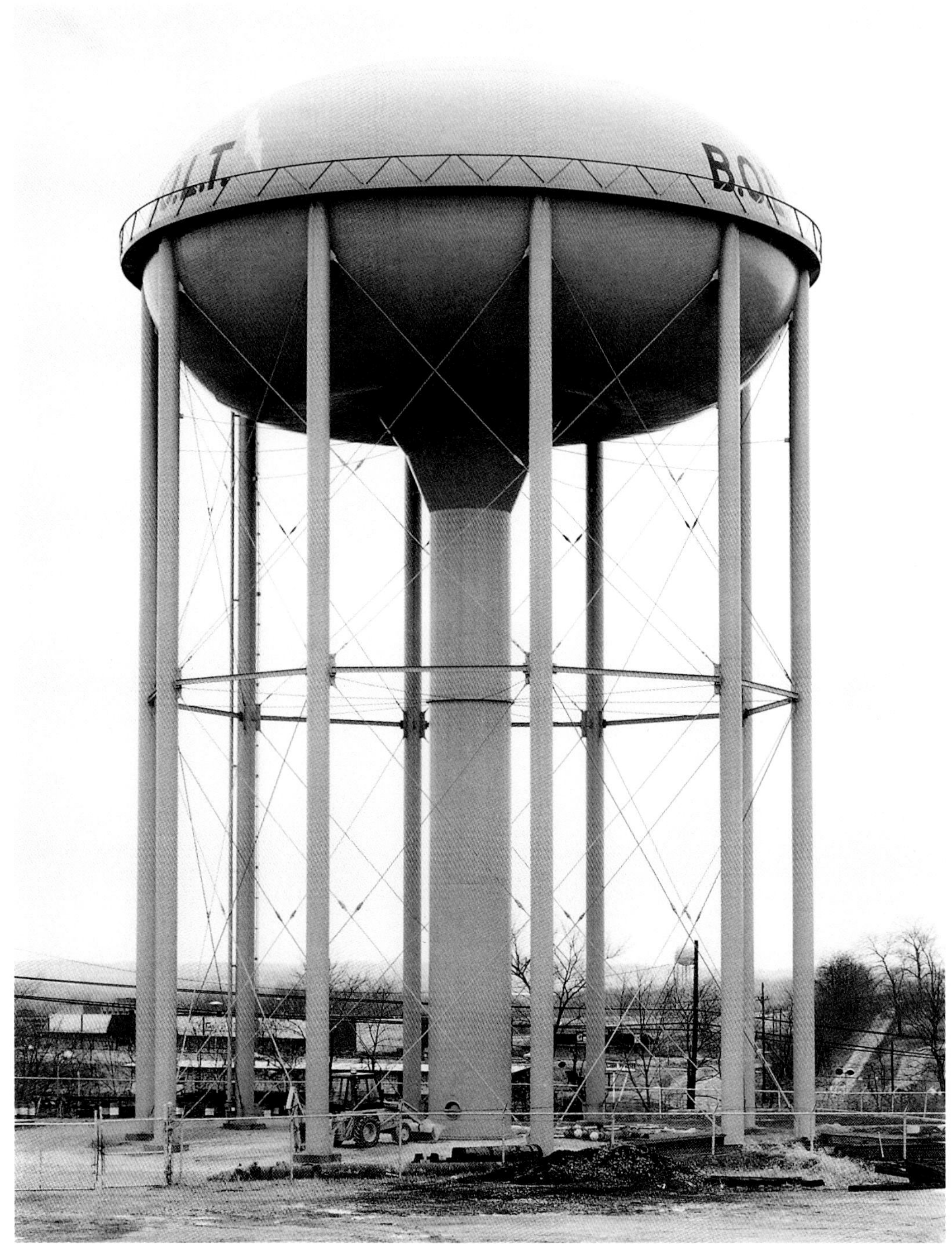

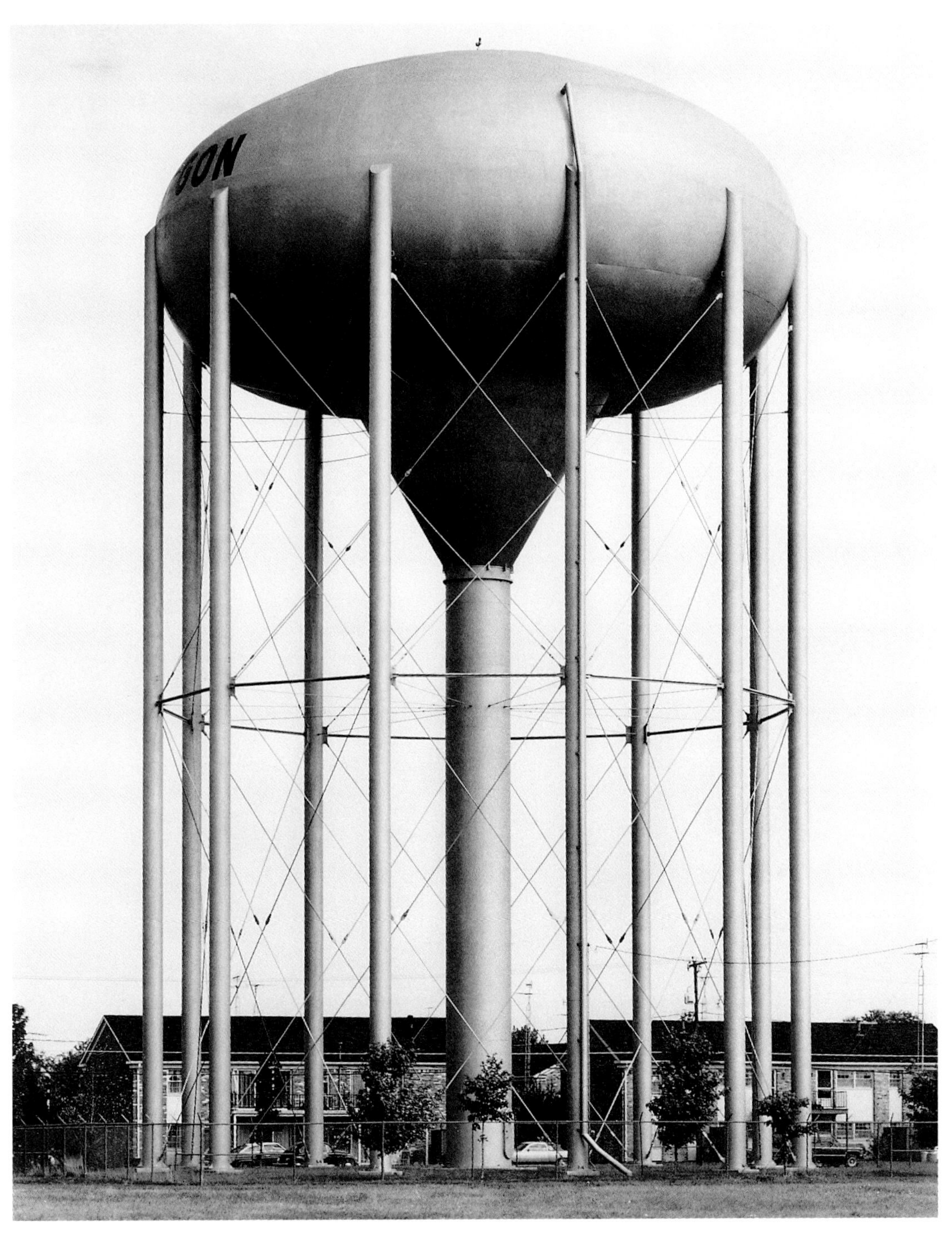

40 Neville Island, Pennsylvania, USA, 1980 41 Cleveland, Ohio, USA, 1980

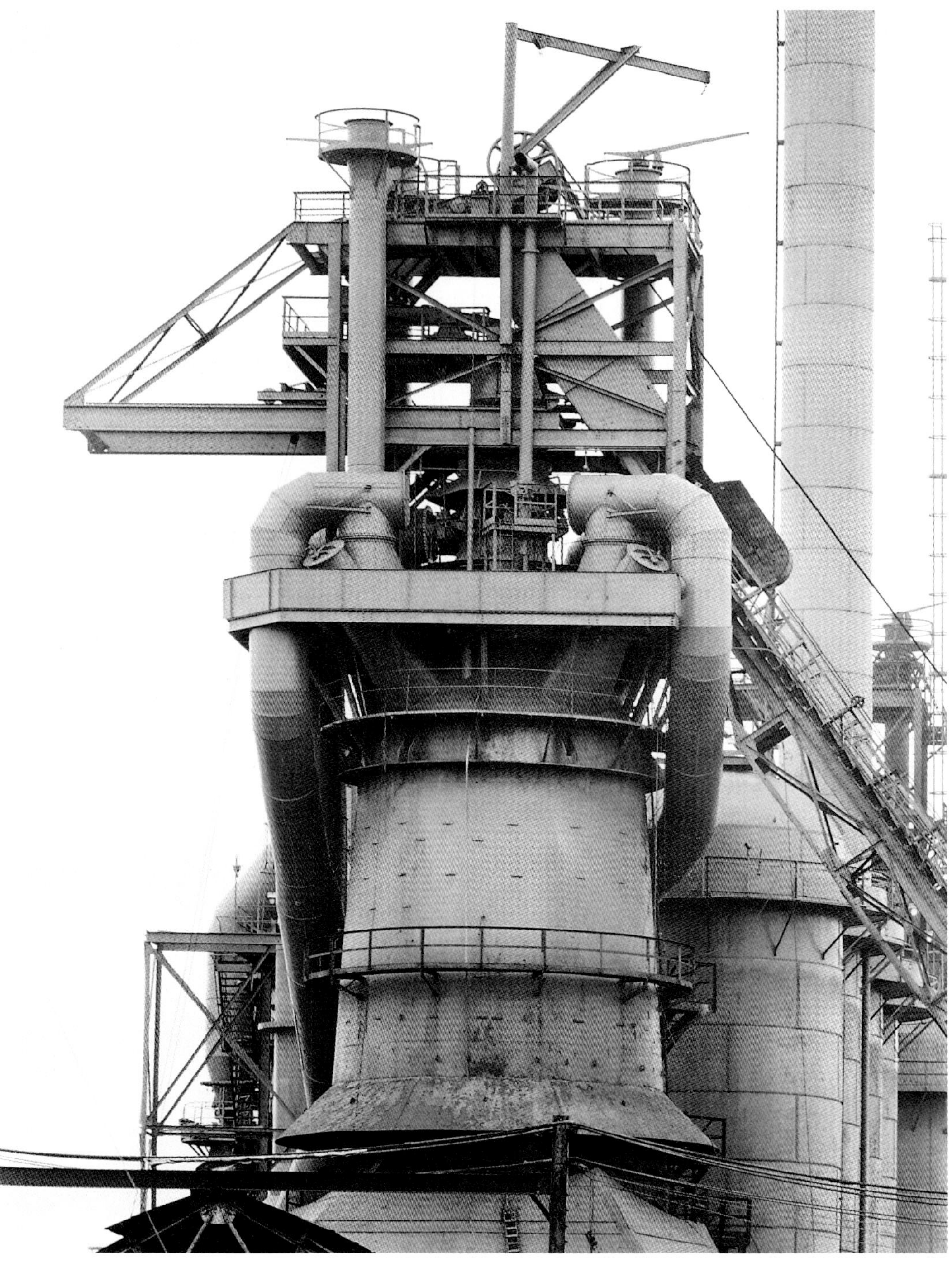

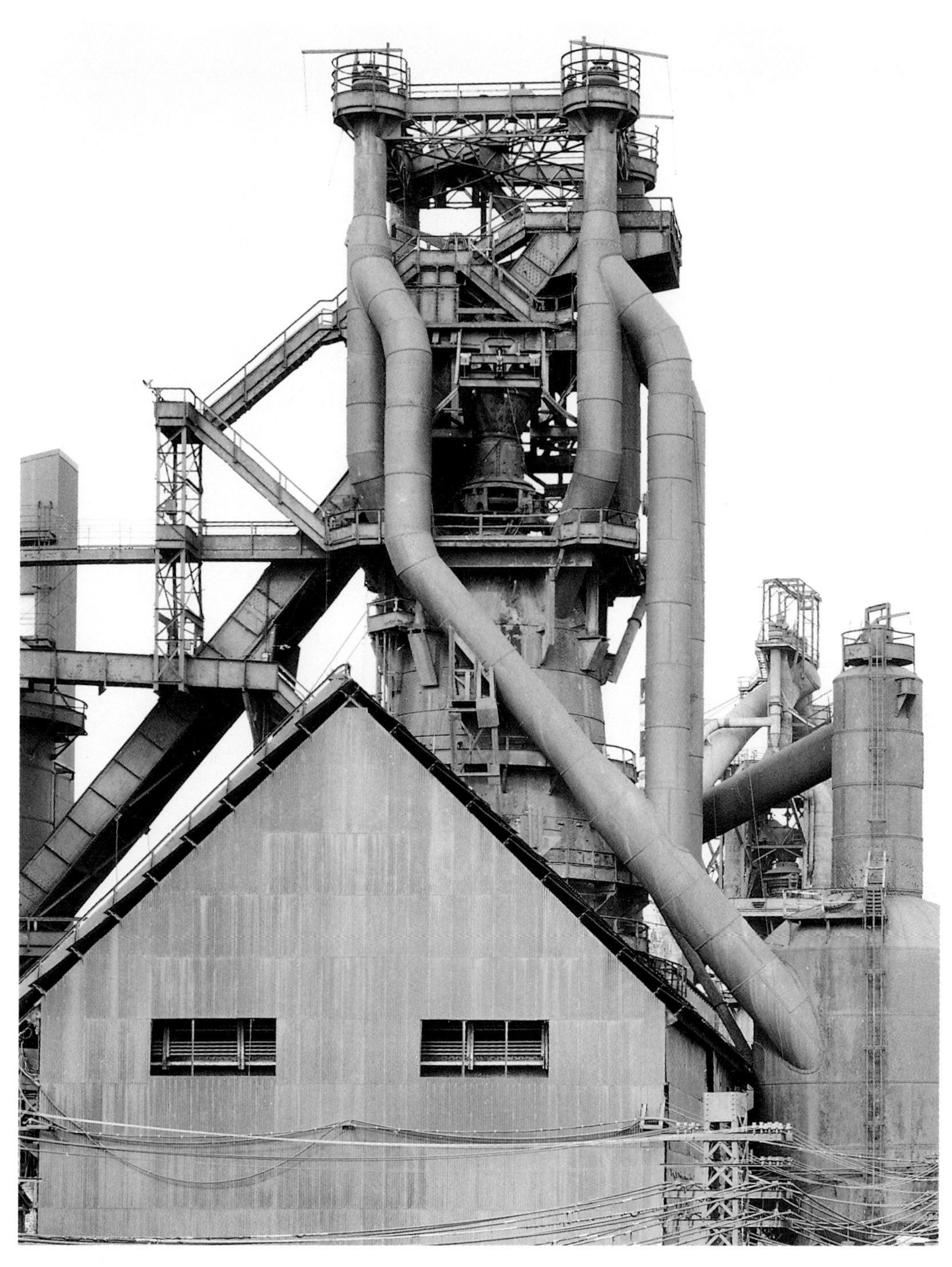

Johannes Bruns

The Treaty of Versailles prohibited Germany from establishing an air force. Despite this restriction, operational flight training was carried out under the cloak of diverse companies and institutions. Airfields were also constructed from 1928 applying the rational functionalism of the Weimar period, and the building programme intensified after the accession of the Nazis in 1933. Public access to the airfields was granted only after sixty years of continuous military use. Johannes Bruns has photographed the hangars just as their disrepair threatens to destroy them.

43 Döberitz, 1998

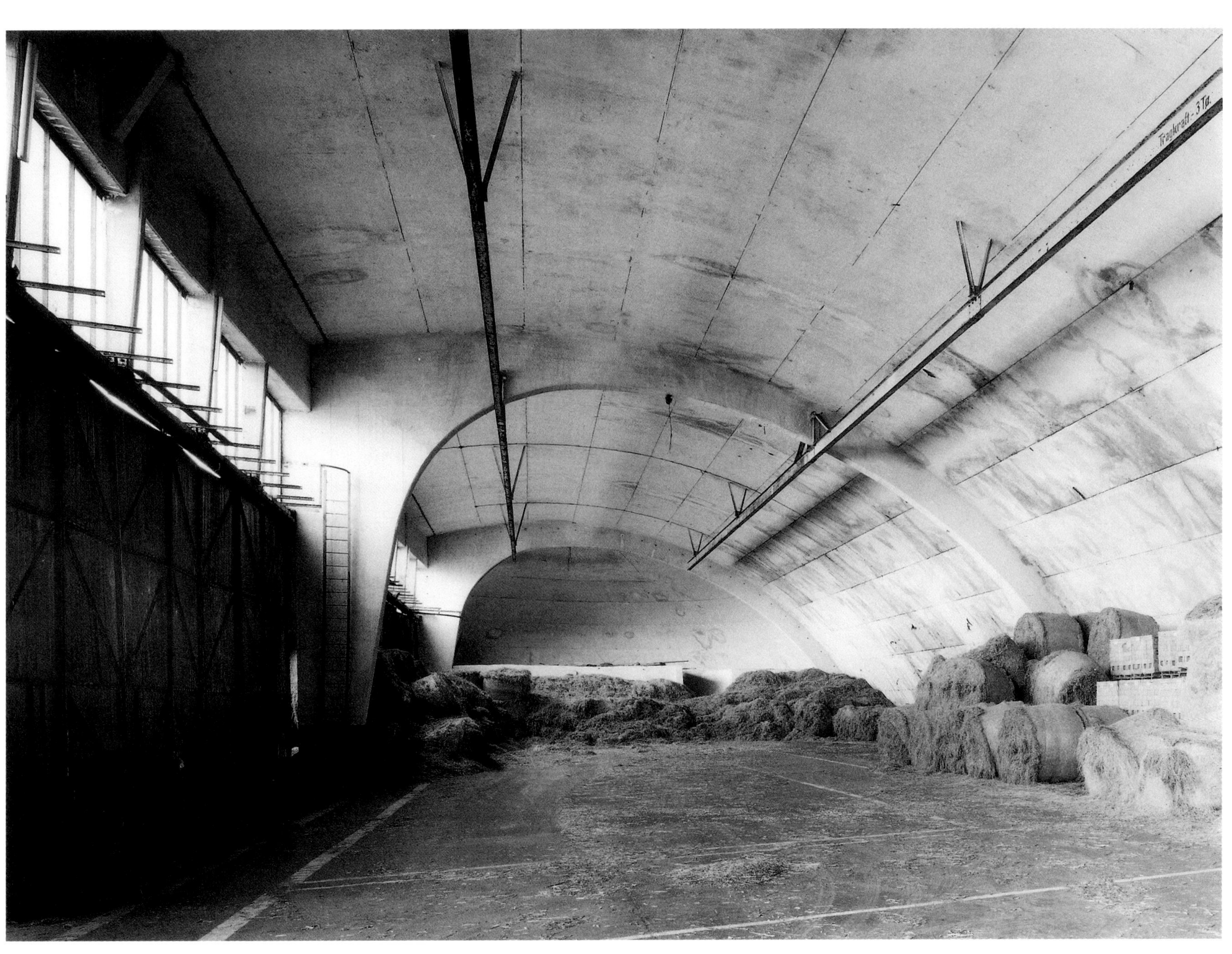
Tragkraft - 3 Tø.

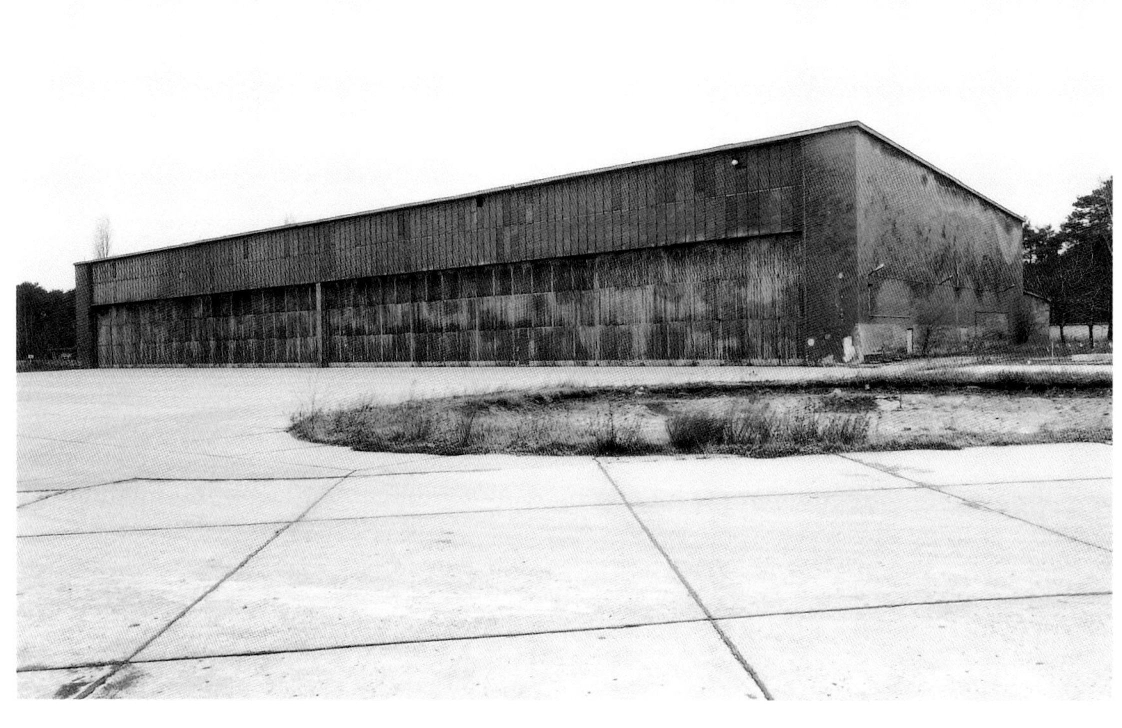

44 Jüterbog – Old Camp, 1997 45 Wittstock, 1998

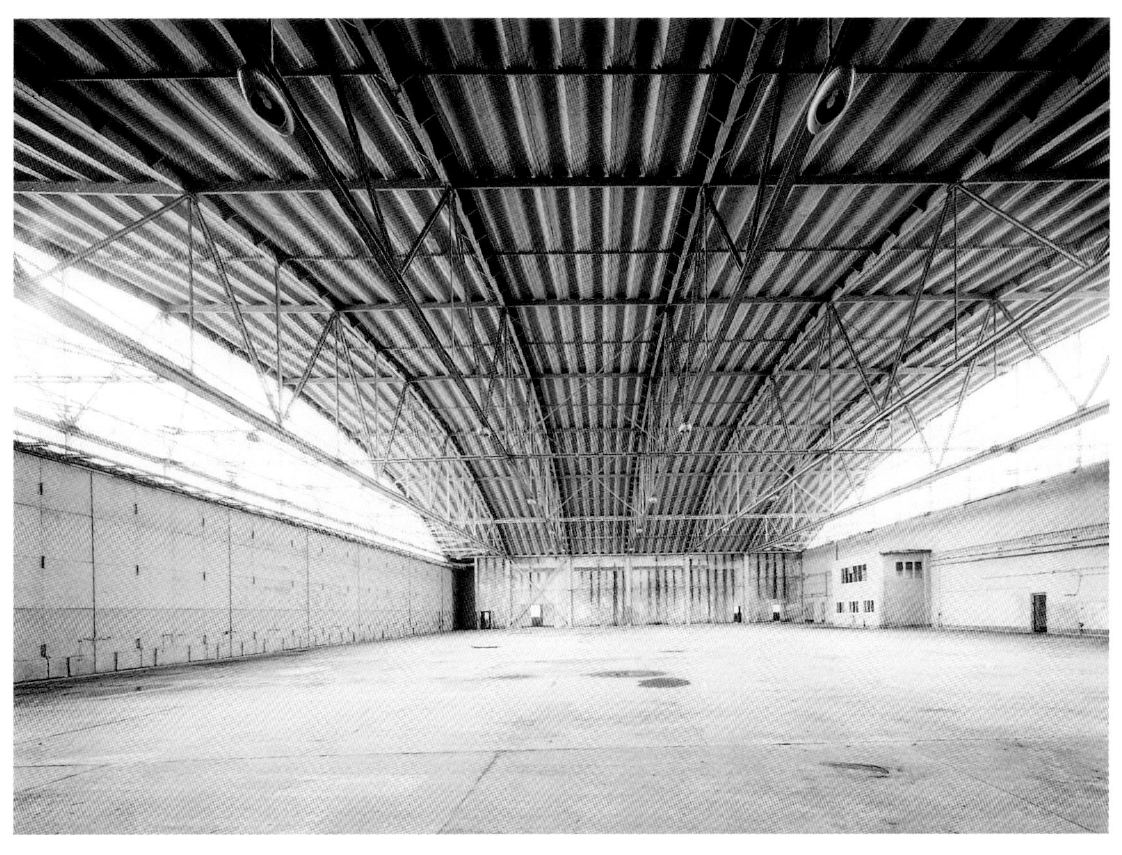

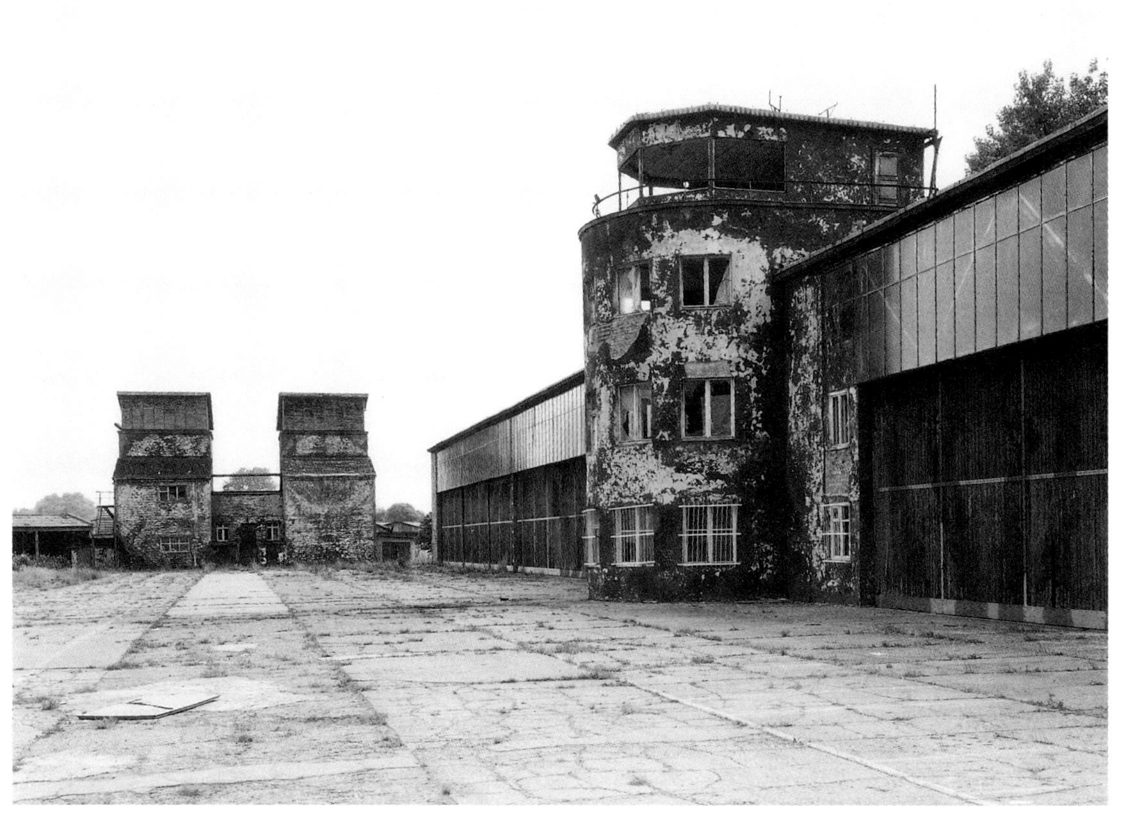

46 Rangsdorf, 1998 47 Jüterbog – Damm, 1998

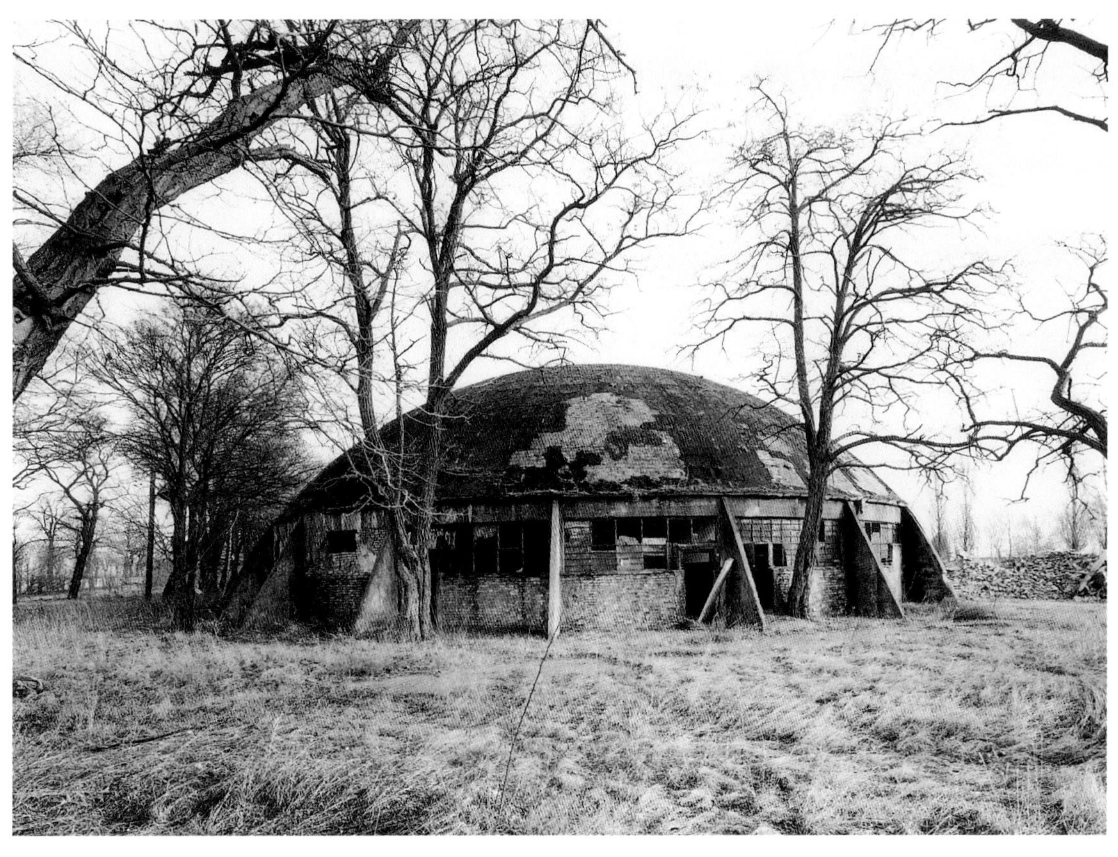

49 Dachau, watchtower at the eastern boundary of the camp

Dirk Reinartz

Dirk Reinartz's project, Deathly Still, portrays the banal and functional architecture which contained the barbarism of the Nazi concentration camps. Many of the camps were destroyed by the Allies, but have since been rebuilt as sites of remembrance.

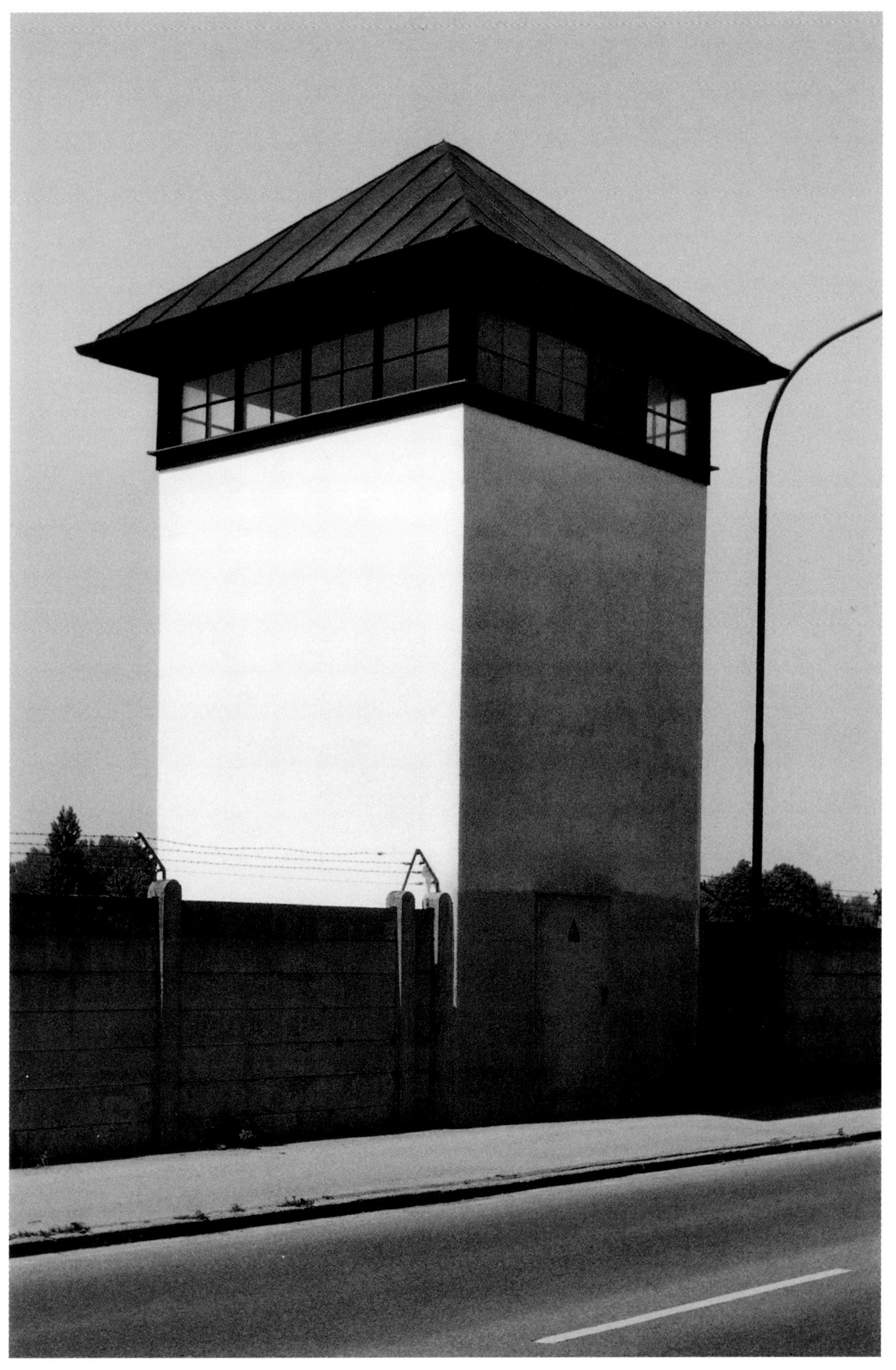

50 Dachau, symbolically retraced barracks foundations and reconstruction of an accommodation hut, with service building in the background
51 Dachau, inside an accommodation hut – a reconstruction of the early phase of the camp

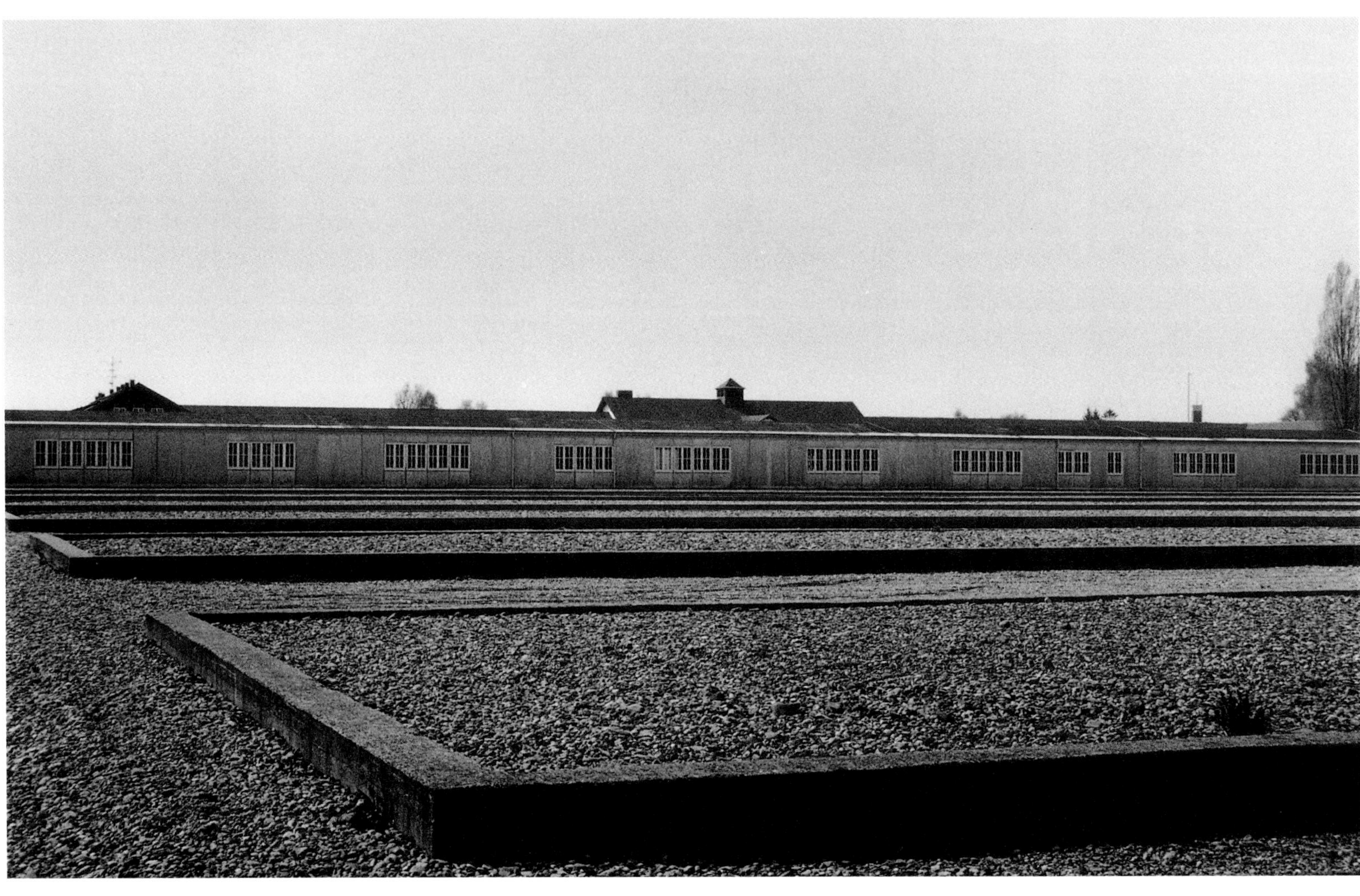

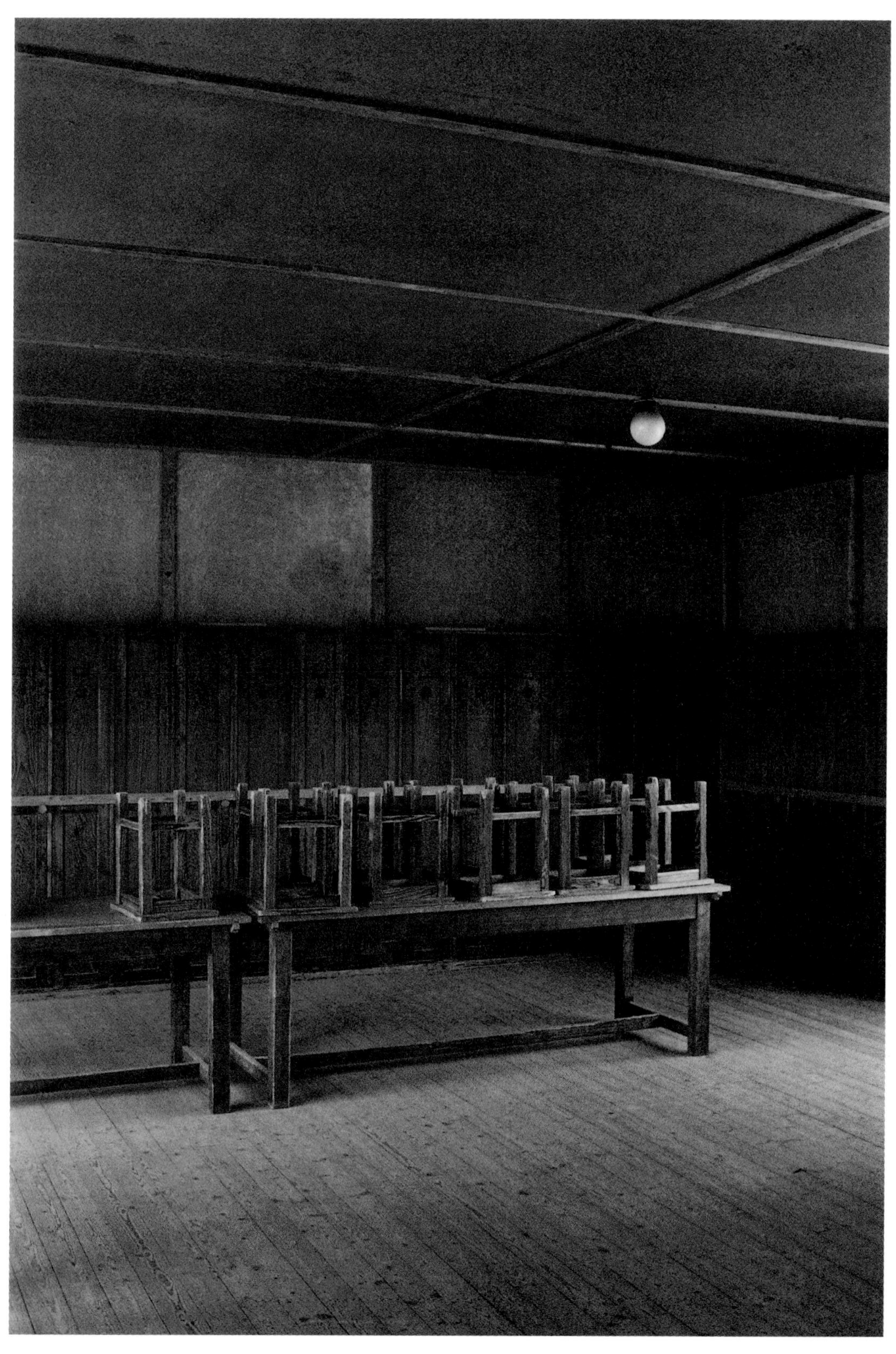

52 Neuengamme, ramp leading to the brickworks 53 Theresienstadt, prisoners' files in small fort office

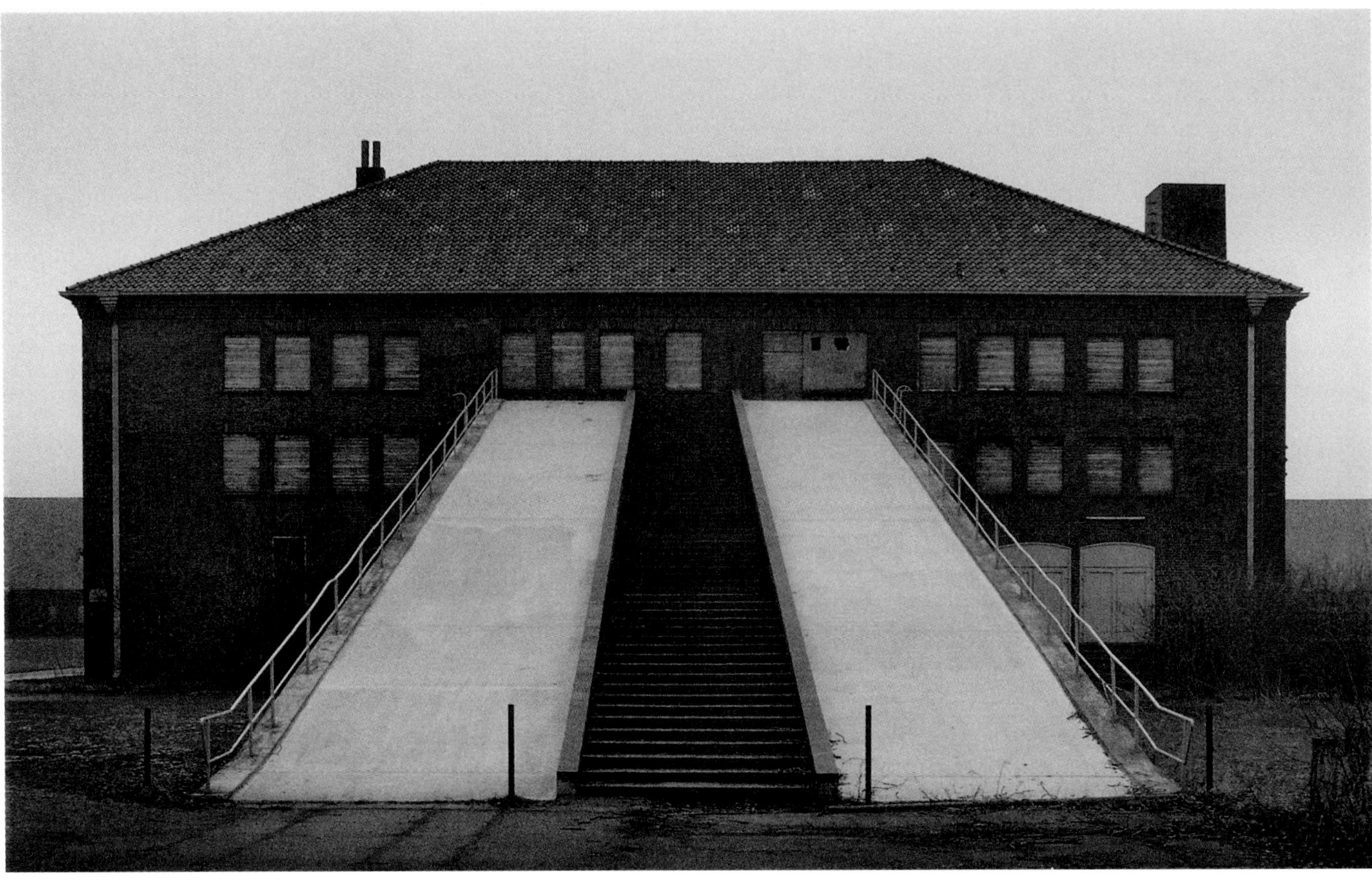

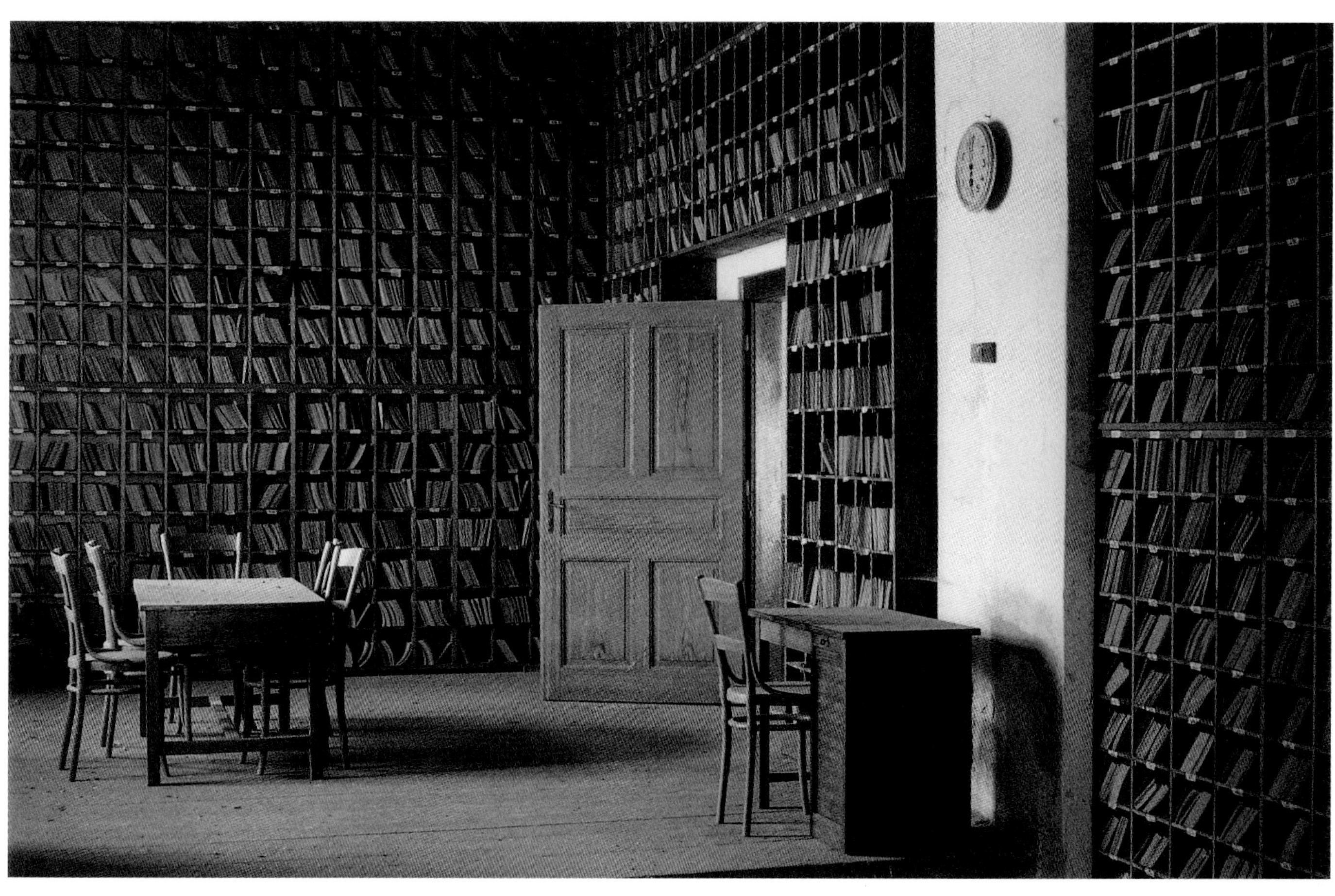

54 Lublin Majdanek, view of the grounds 55 Gross-Rosen, view of the grounds from the gate house, with street and admissions block

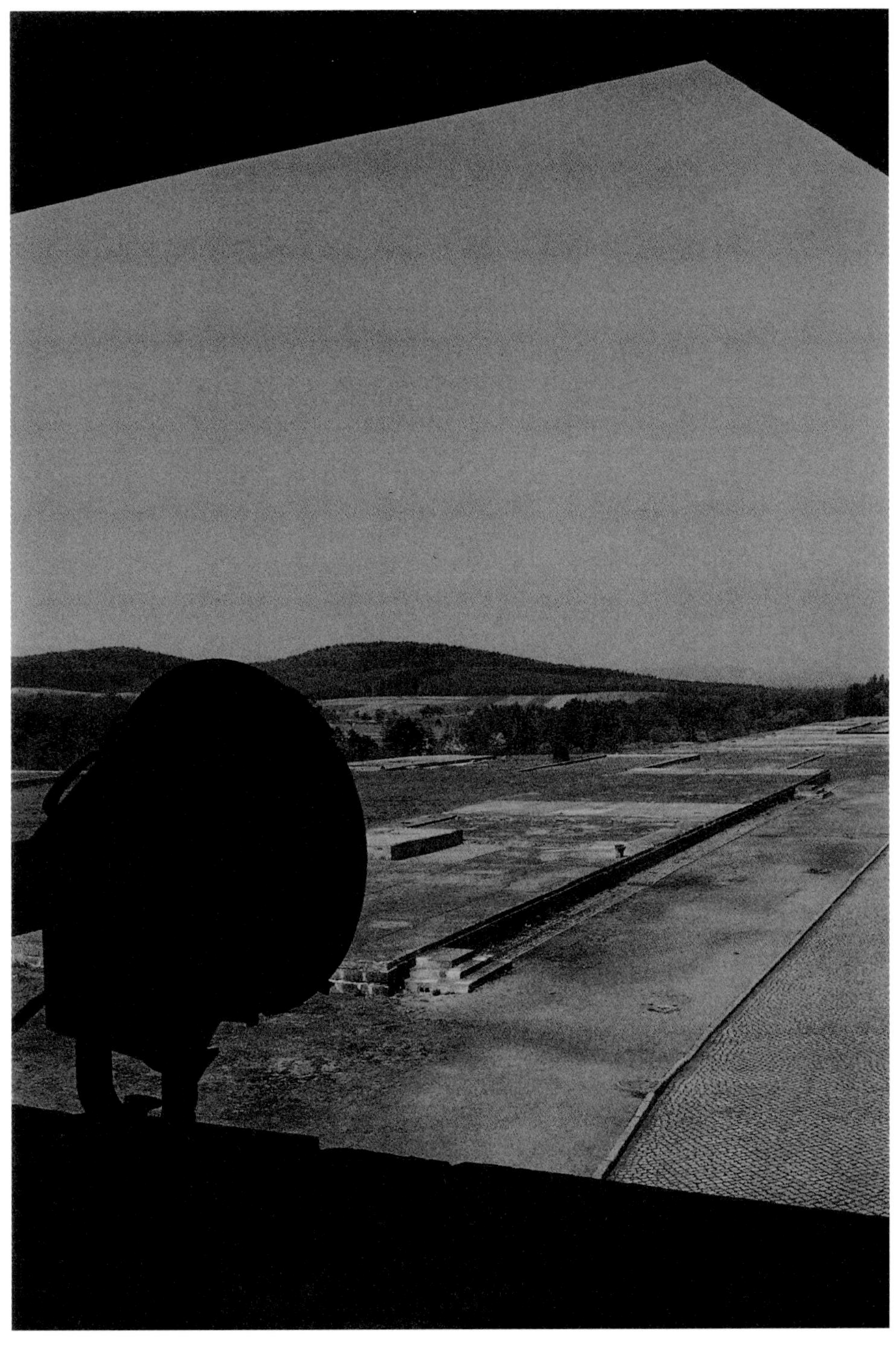

56 Auschwitz Birkenau, wooden stall-type barracks 57 Auschwitz Birkenau, barracks' chimneys

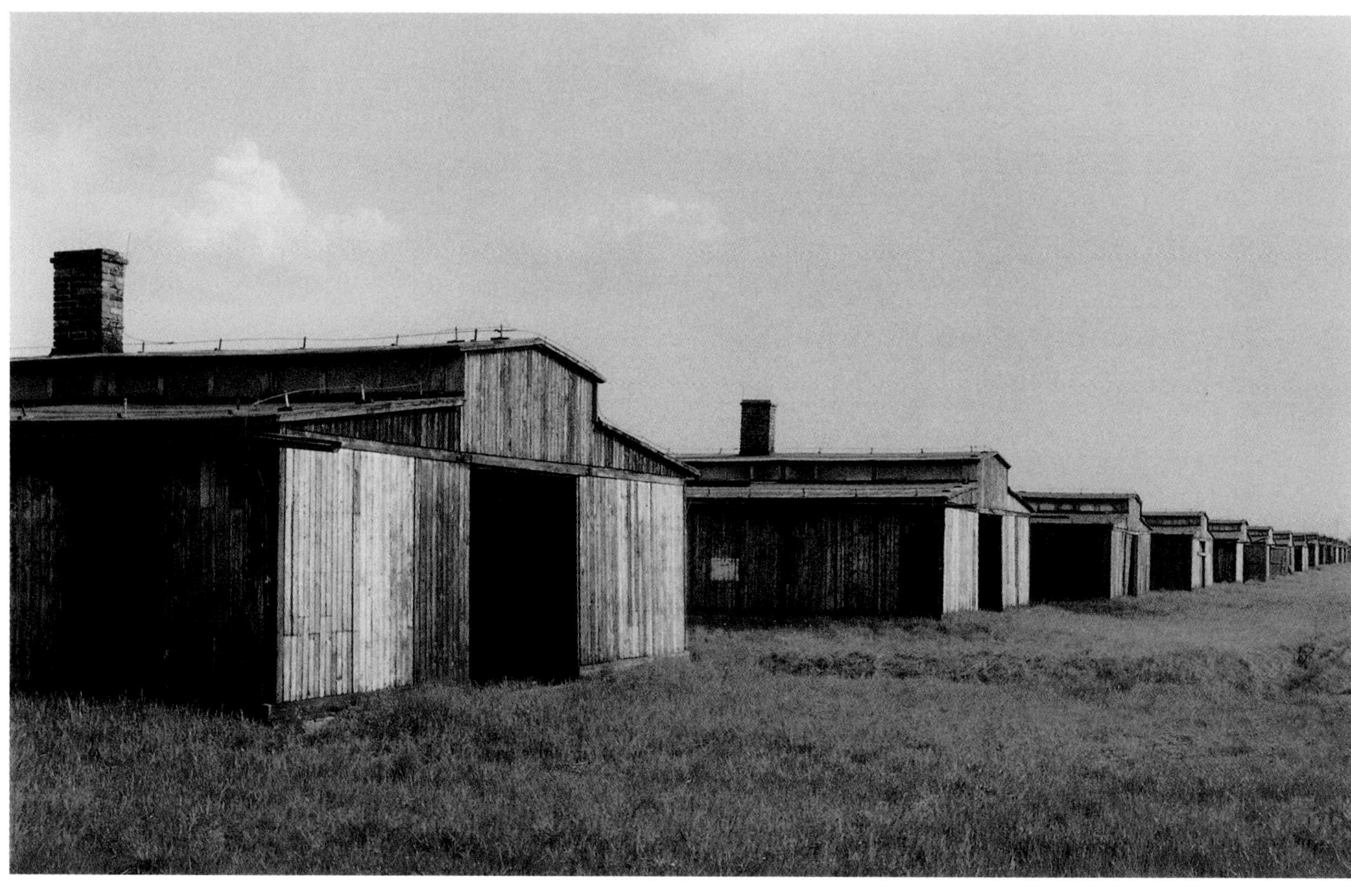

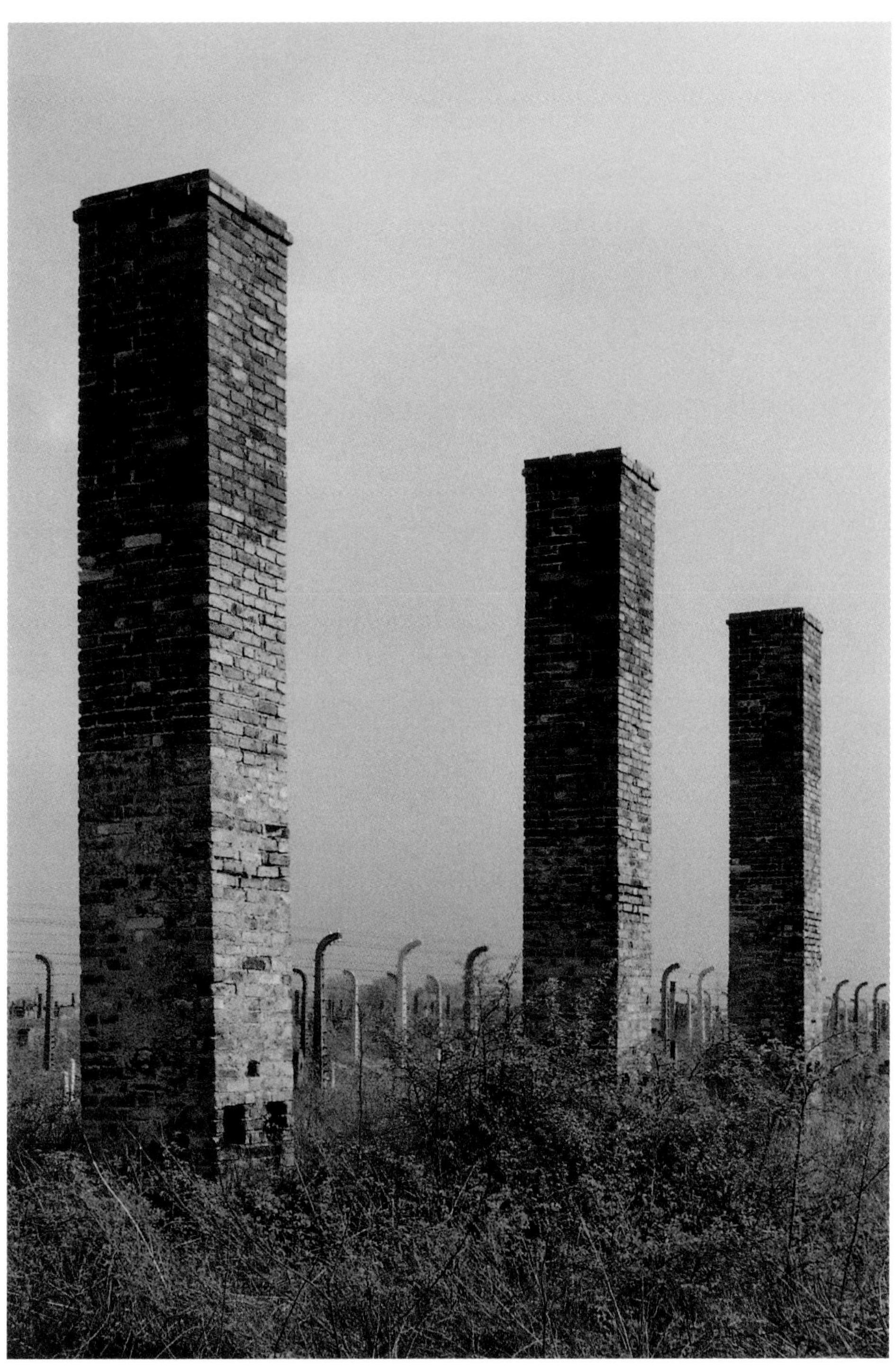

Since 1965 Michael Schmidt has been photographing the city of Berlin and its immediate vicinity. His work has traced the city's tumultuous history via its architecture and its people. This has usually involved a combination of urban views and portraits, but in his 1980 body of work, Berlin after 45, this practice was replaced by a series of thirty-two images documenting the urban framework of the city. The series is a topography of Berlin's empty sites, of bombed or undeveloped gaps in street frontages.

Michael Schmidt

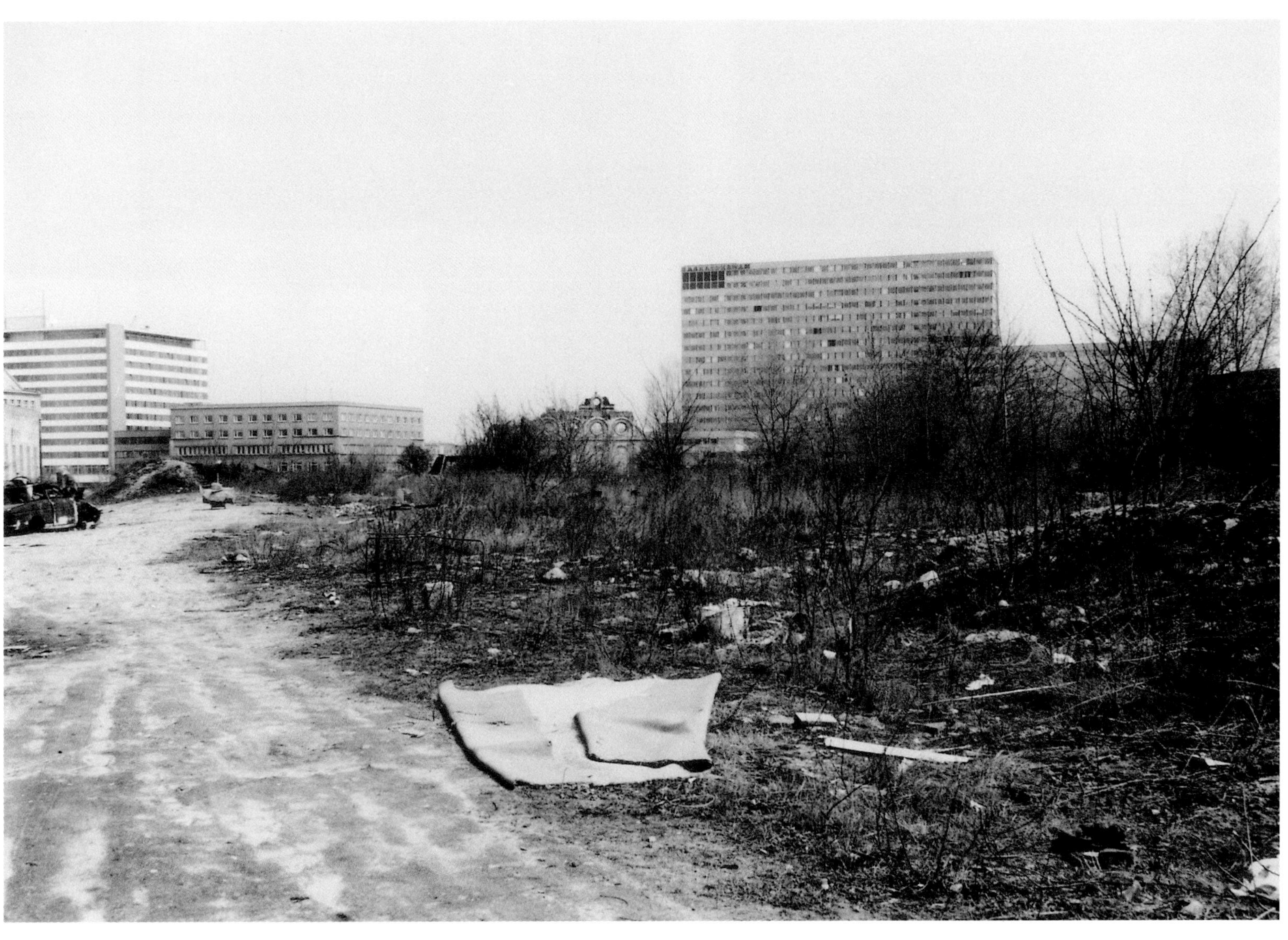

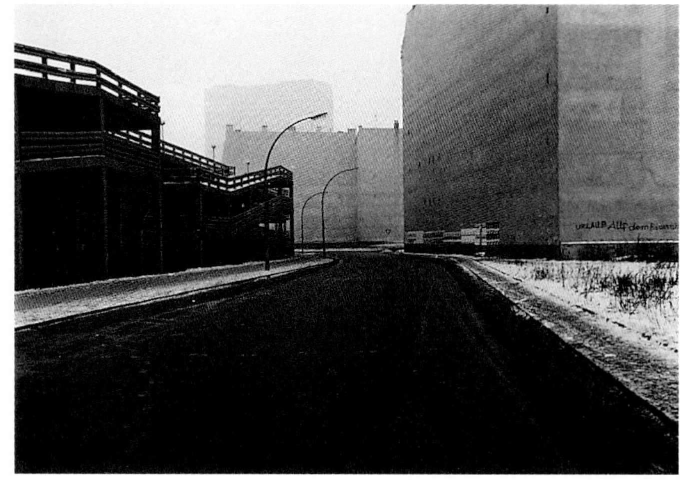

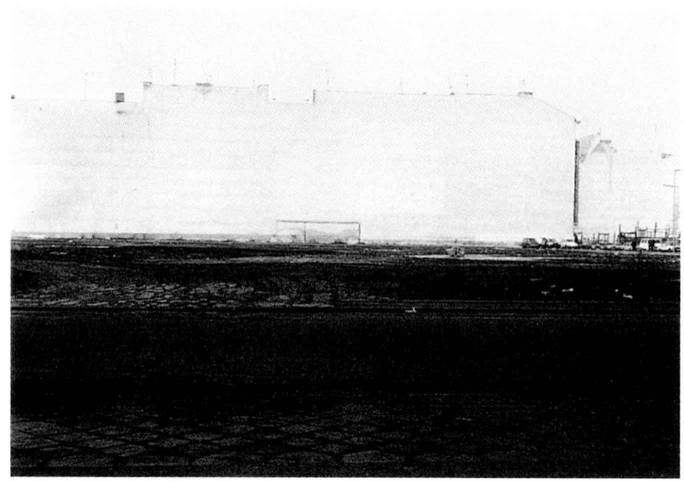

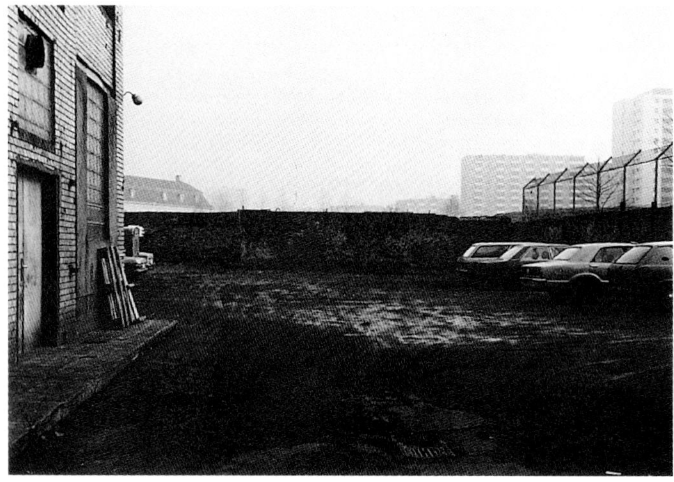

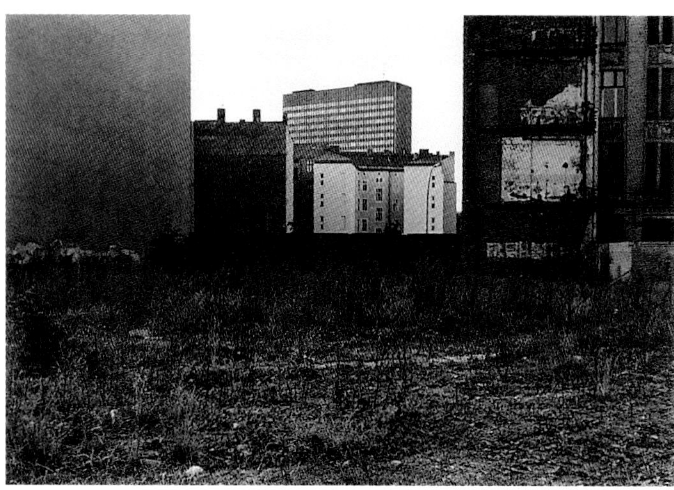

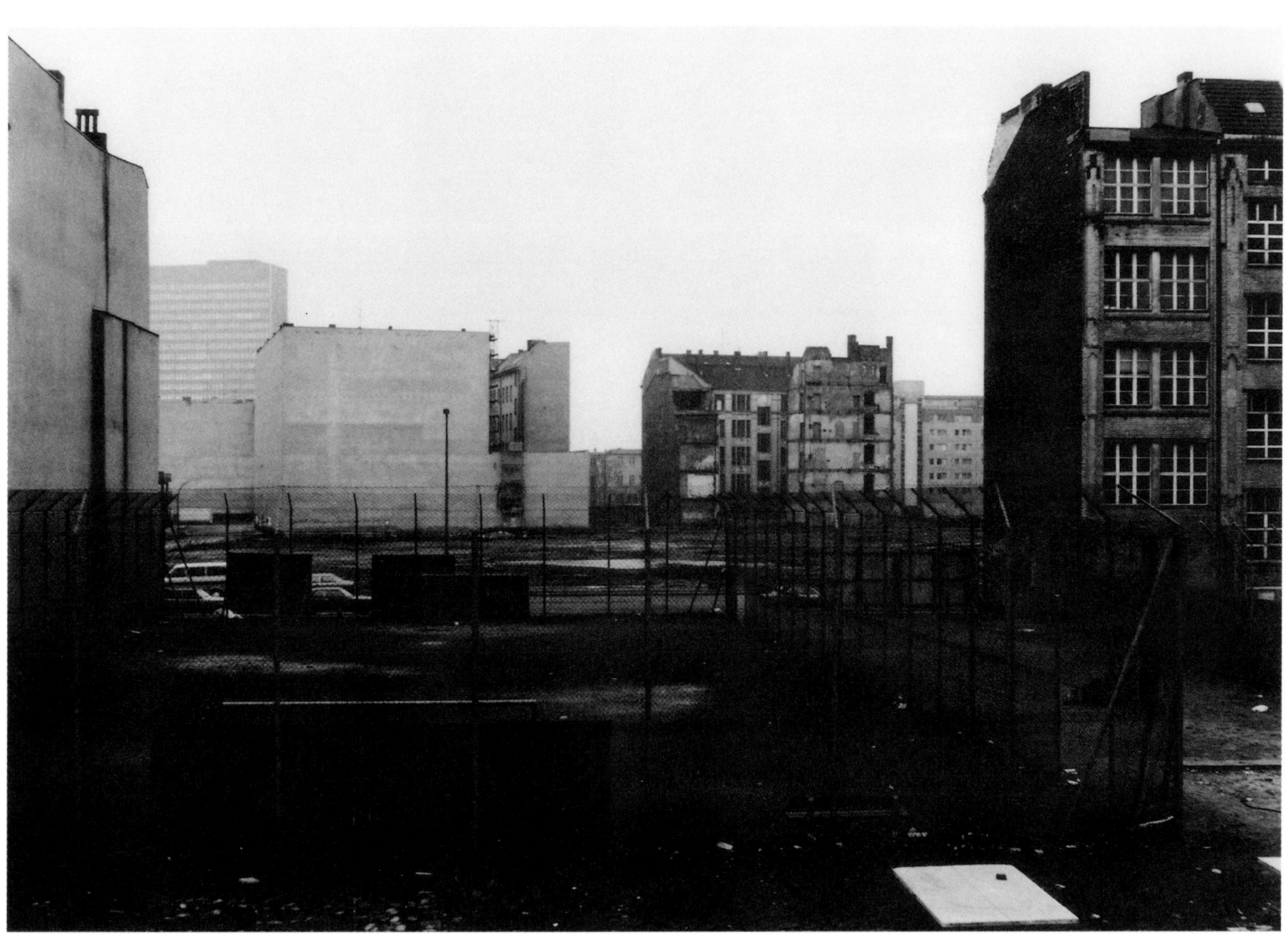

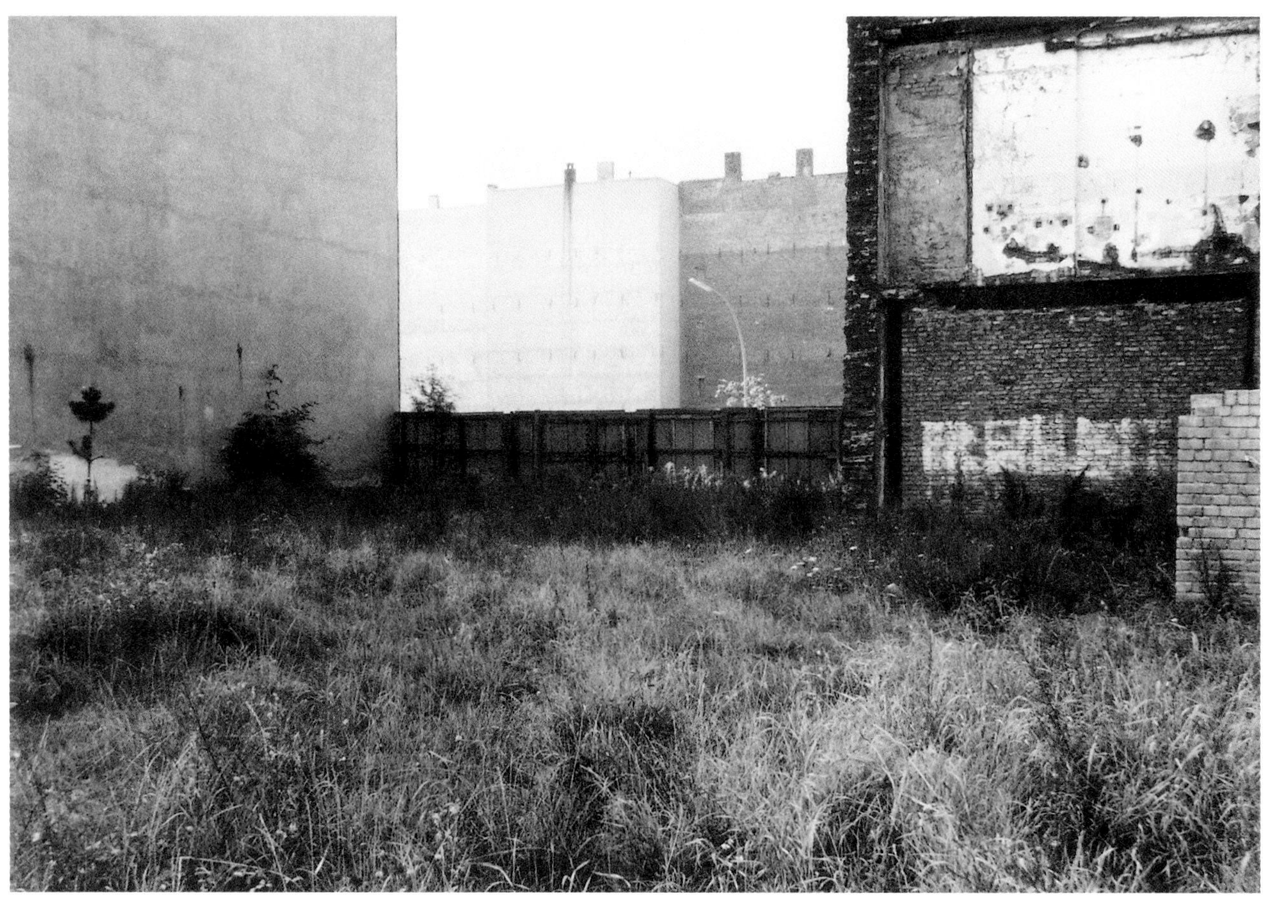

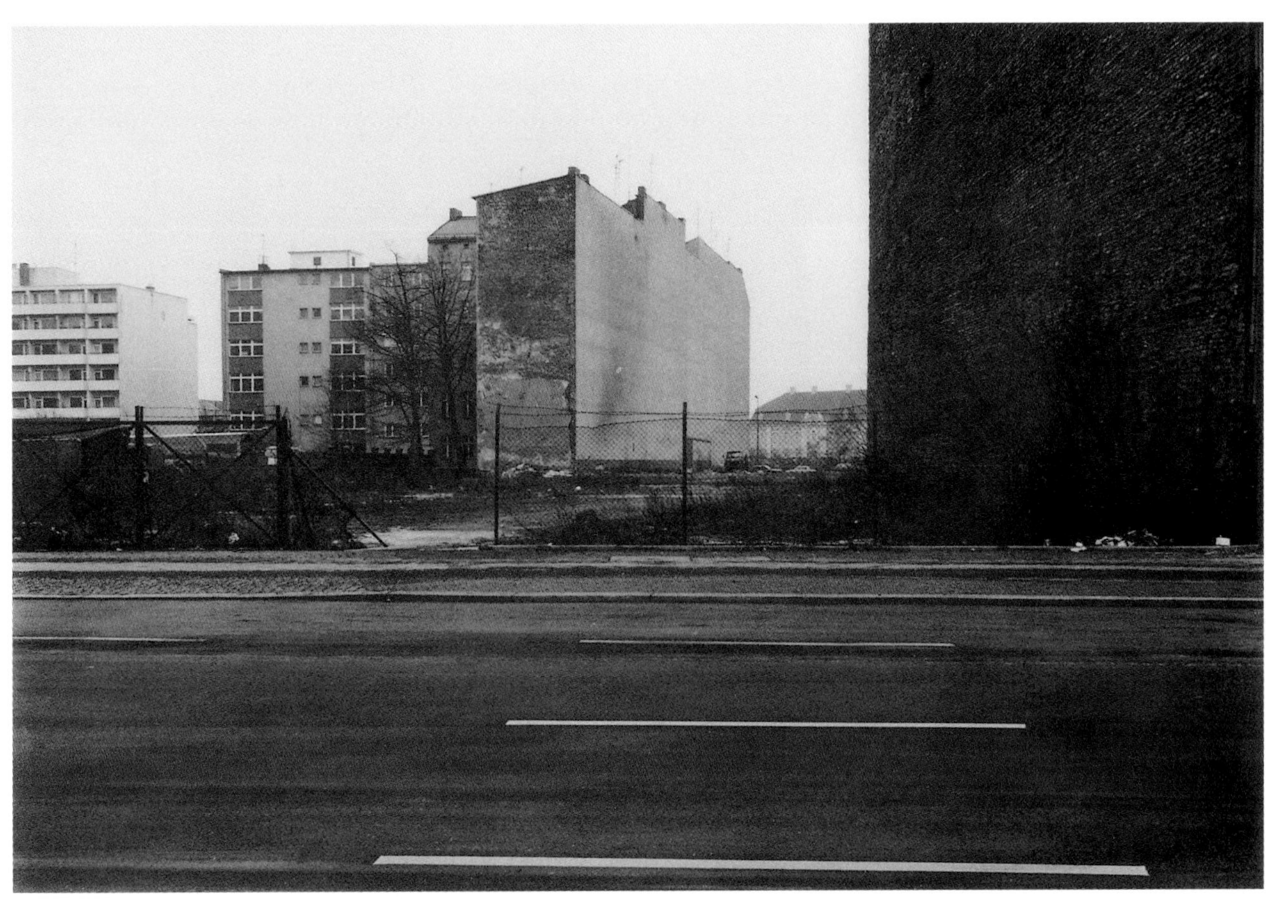

Ulrich Wüst

Ulrich Wüst has used photography to write his own history of Germany, portraying the nature of power through architecture and sculpture, the antecedents of Nazi fanaticism through found fragments of folk culture, and the decimation of the German Jews though a catalogue of gravestones. A constant subject has been the urban fabric of Berlin, and his recent work has concentrated on the massive upheavals in the city and the attempts to rekindle its role at the heart of Europe.

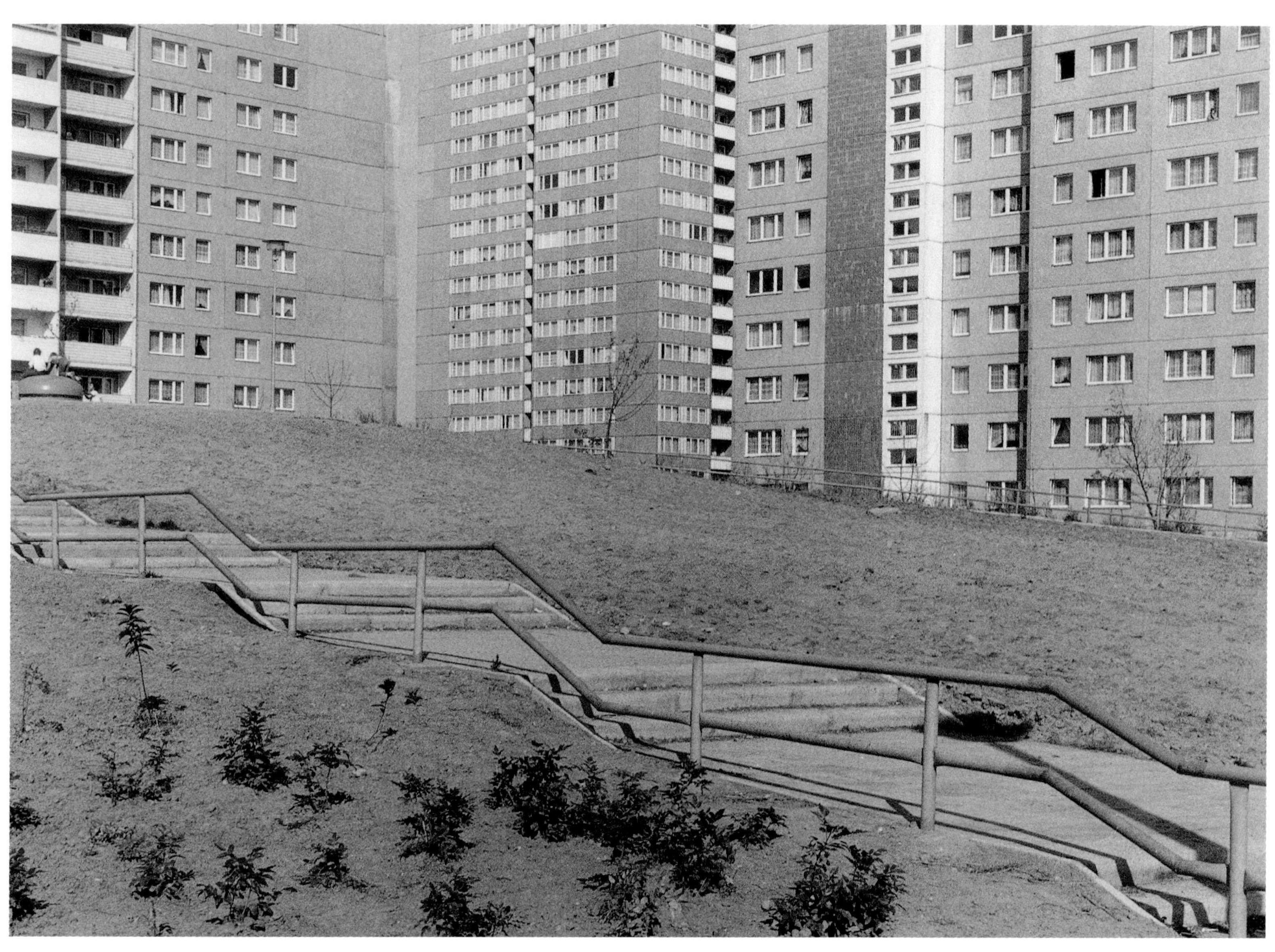

65 Berlin (East), 1982

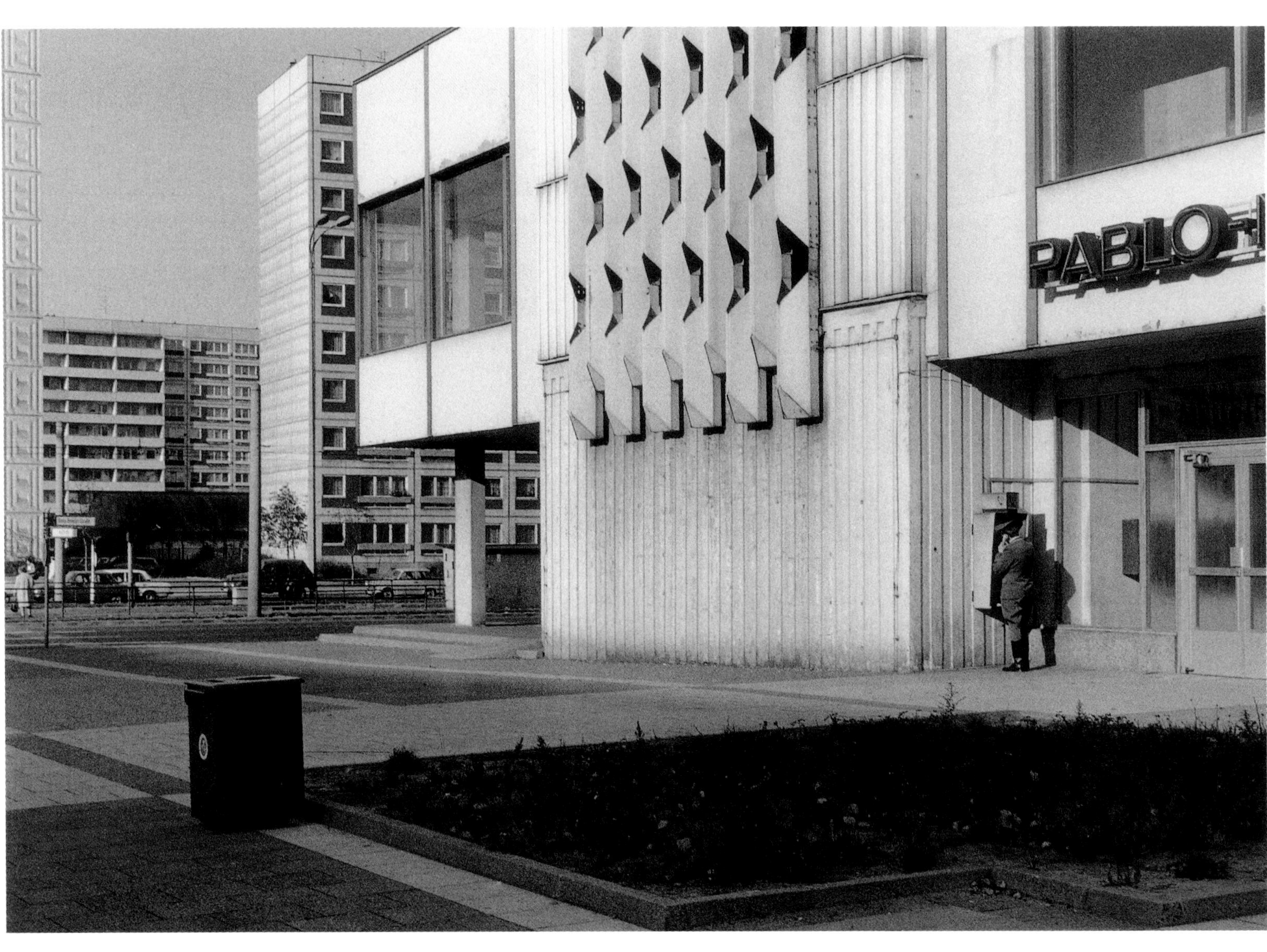
PABLO-

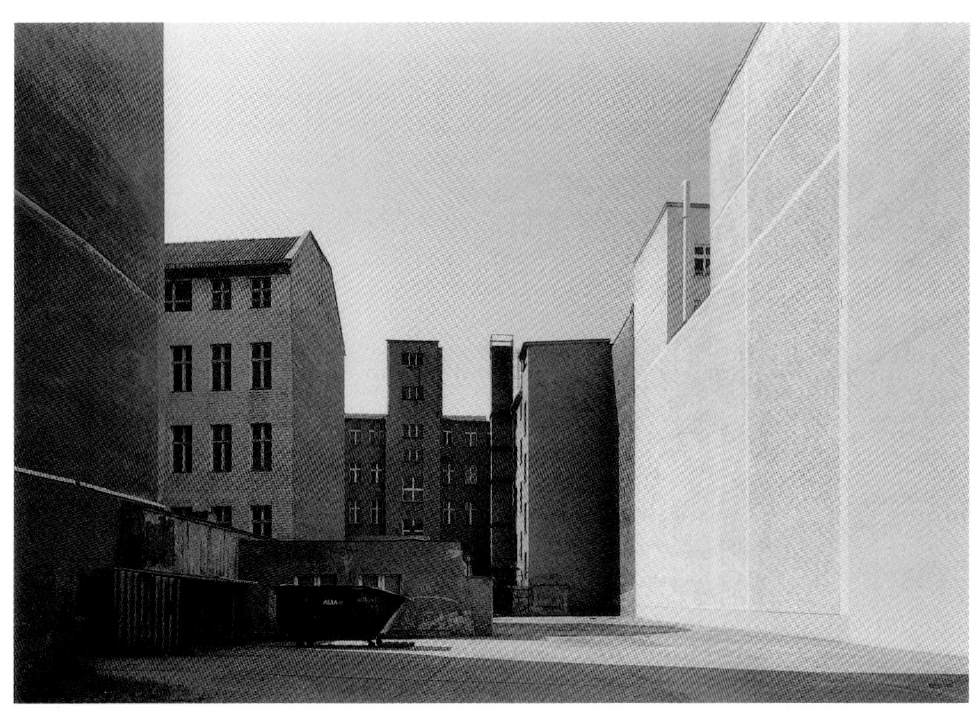

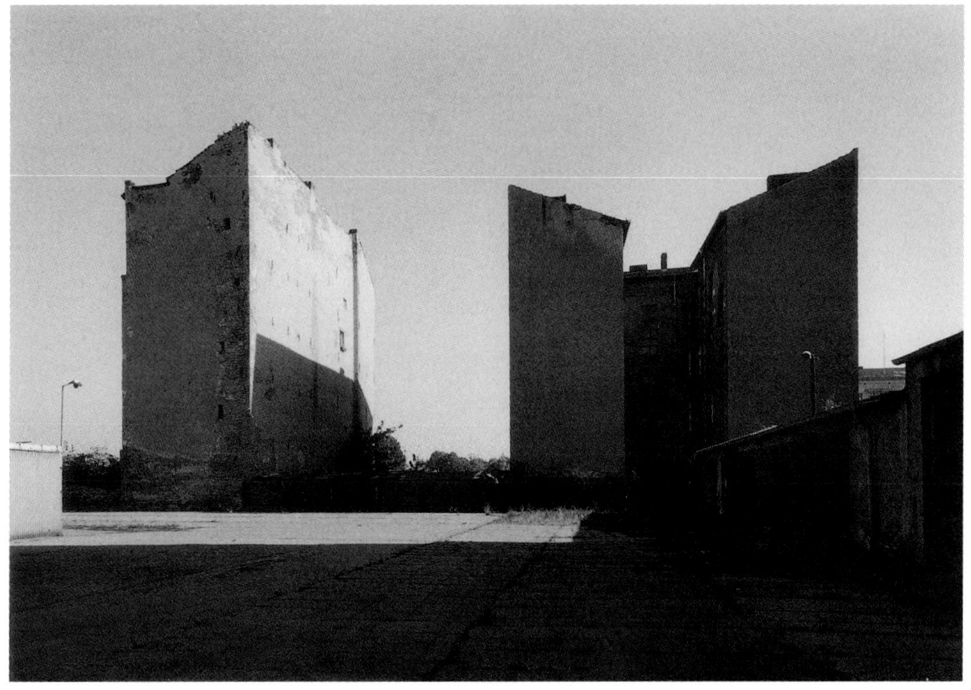

66 Berlin (East), Mollstrasse, 1983 67 Berlin, Oranienburger Strasse, 1996; Köpenicker Straße/Engeldamm, 1995

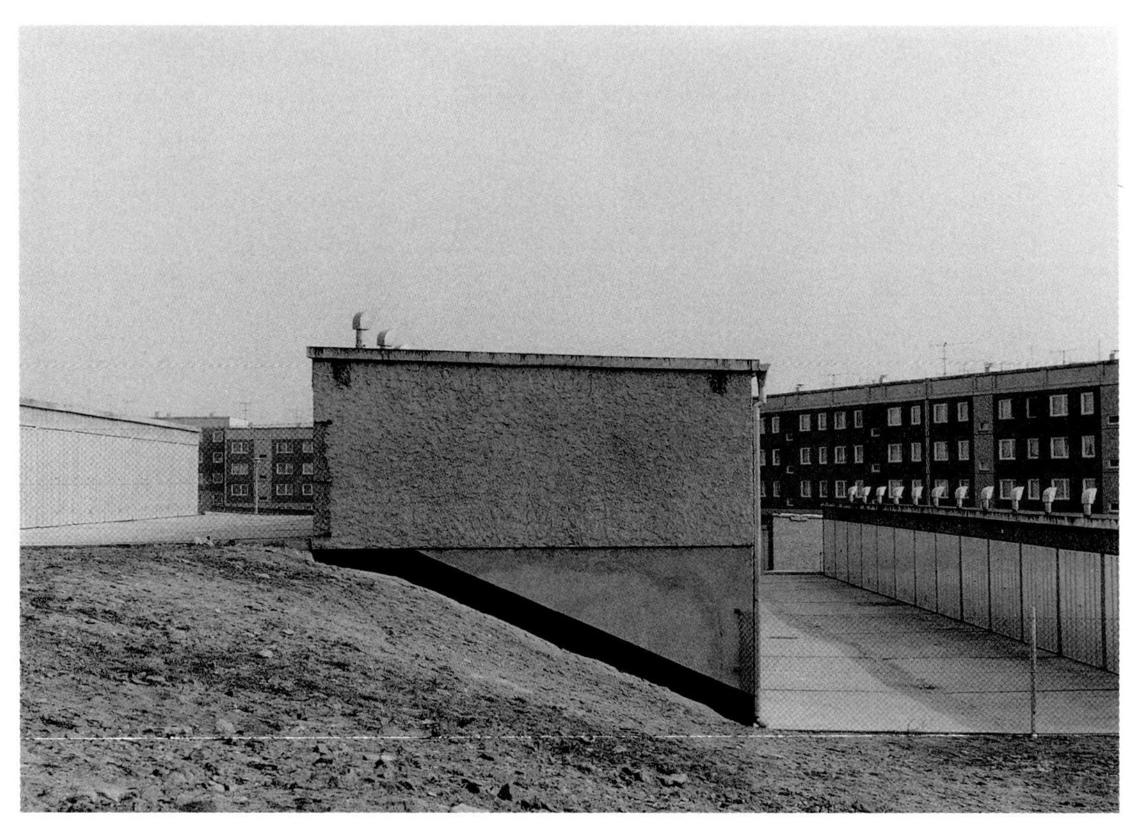

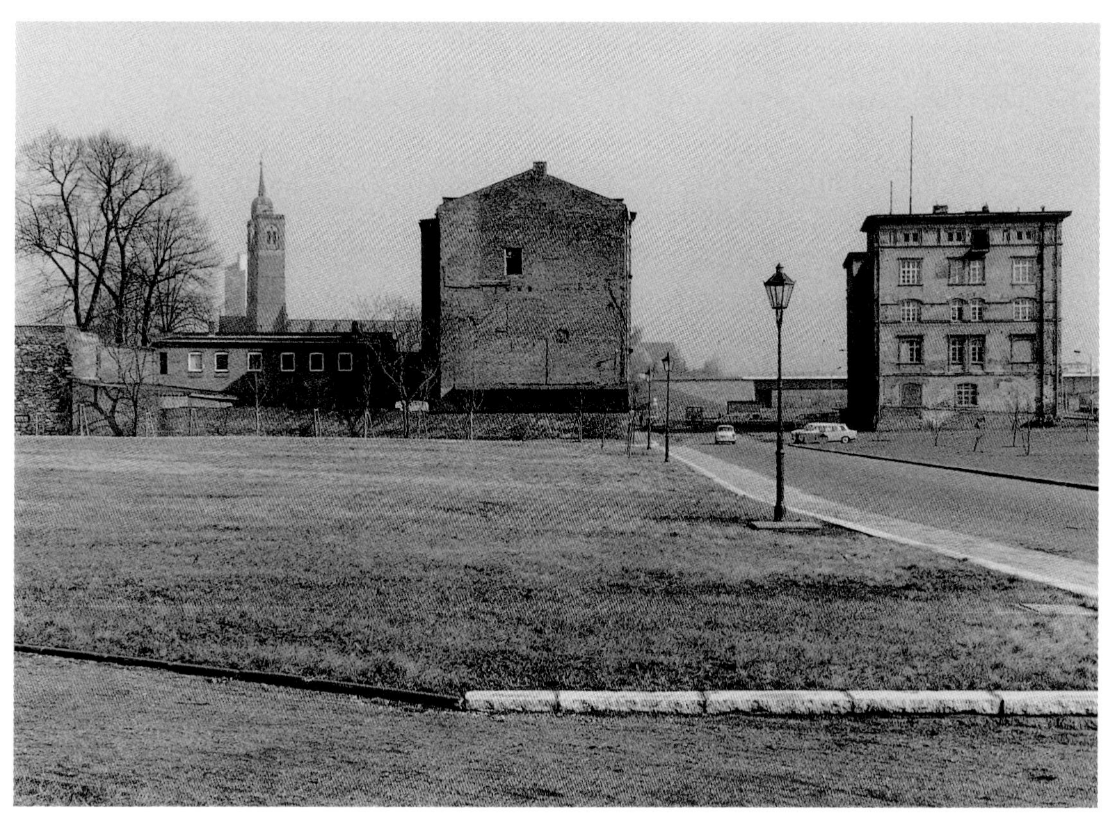

68 Gera, 1982 69 Magdeburg, 1982

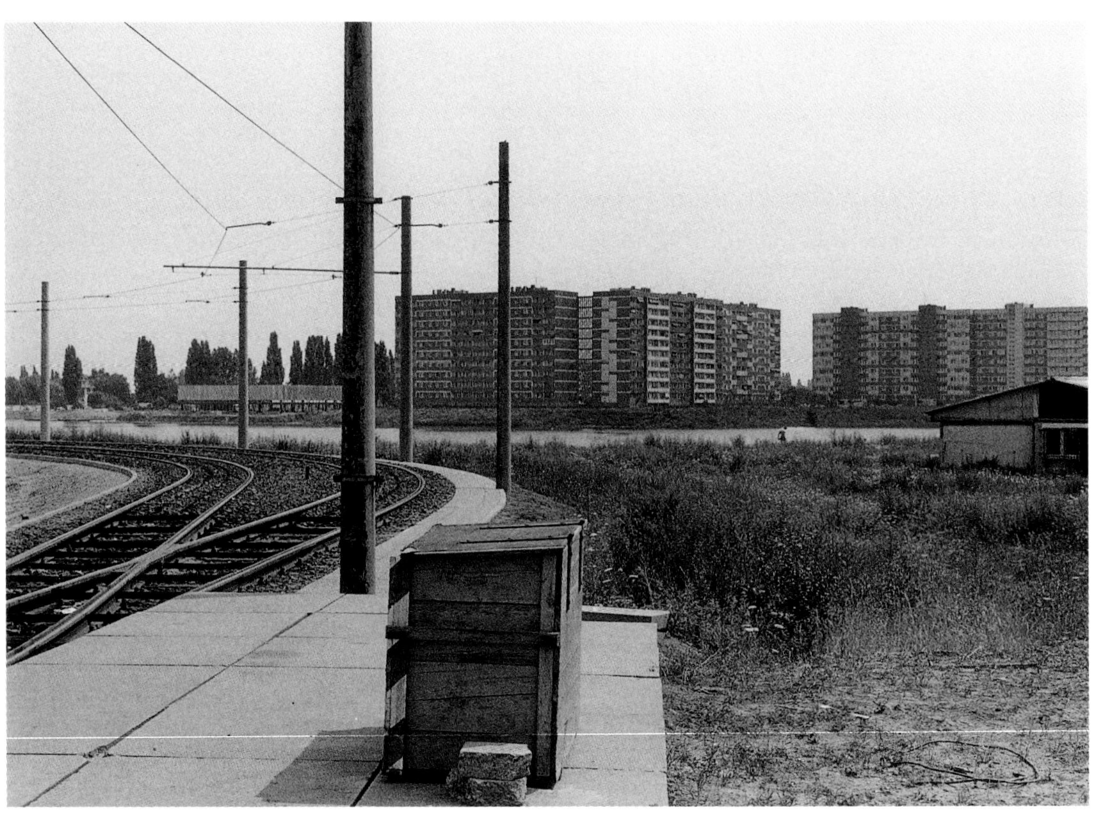

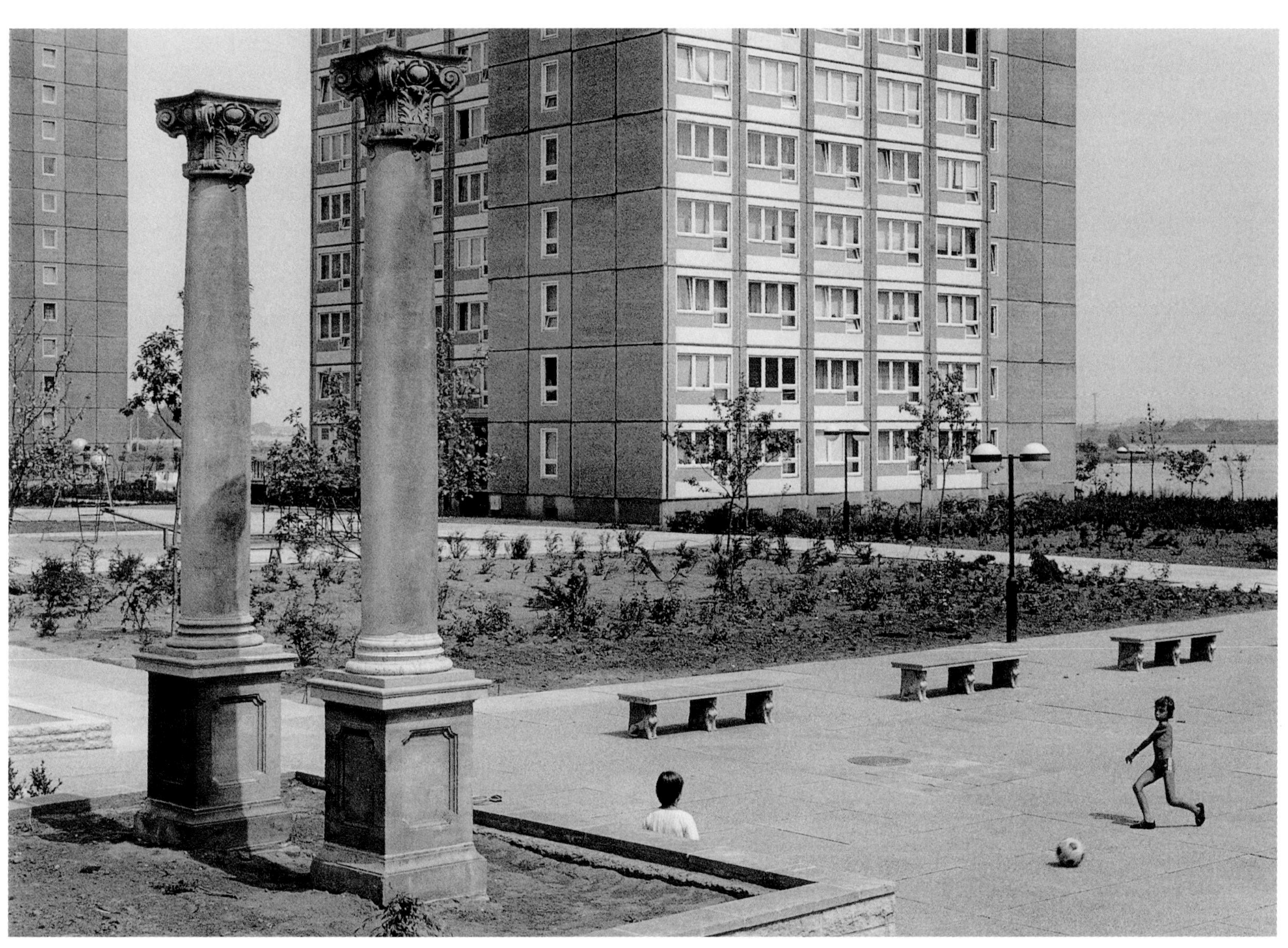

70 Magdeburg, 1982 71 Magdeburg, 1982

73 Potsdam, 1994

Laurenz Berges

The photographs of Laurenz Berges document the interiors of former East German state buildings – military sites built in the 1920s and 1930s, occupied by Soviet troops, and now dilapidated and empty. The work excavates accumulated histories from beneath the layers of dust.

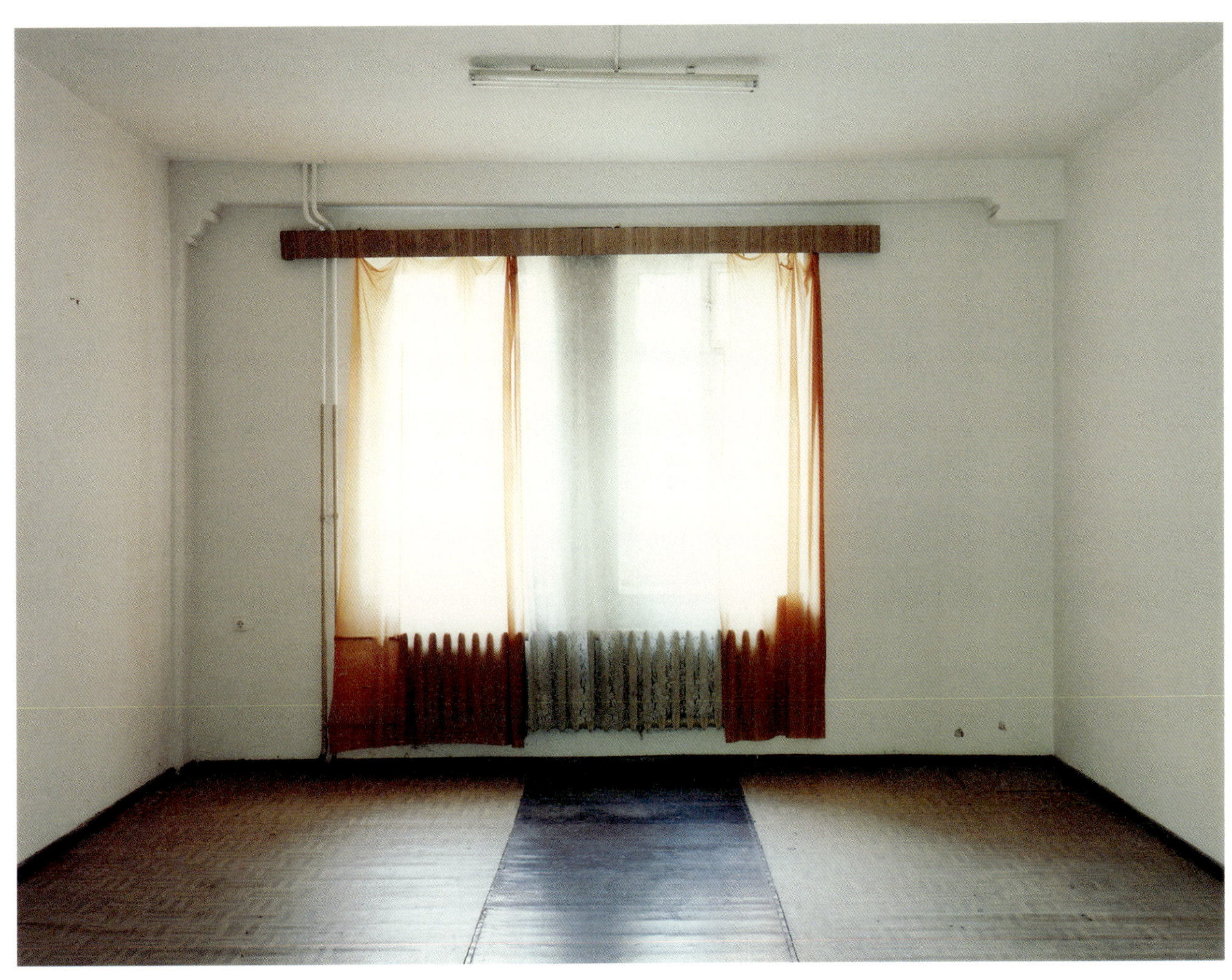

74 Stahnsdorf III, 1994 75 Potsdam, 1993

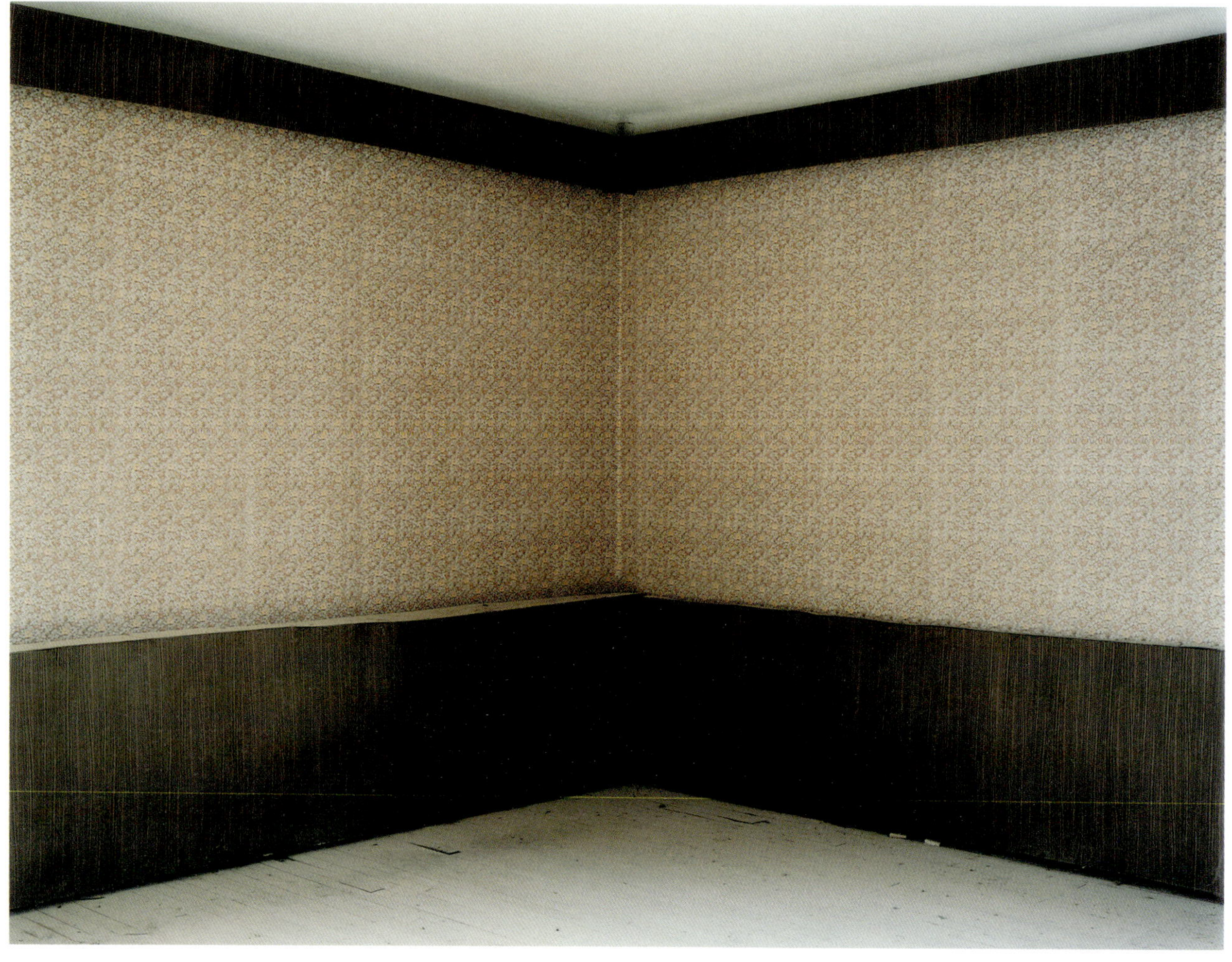

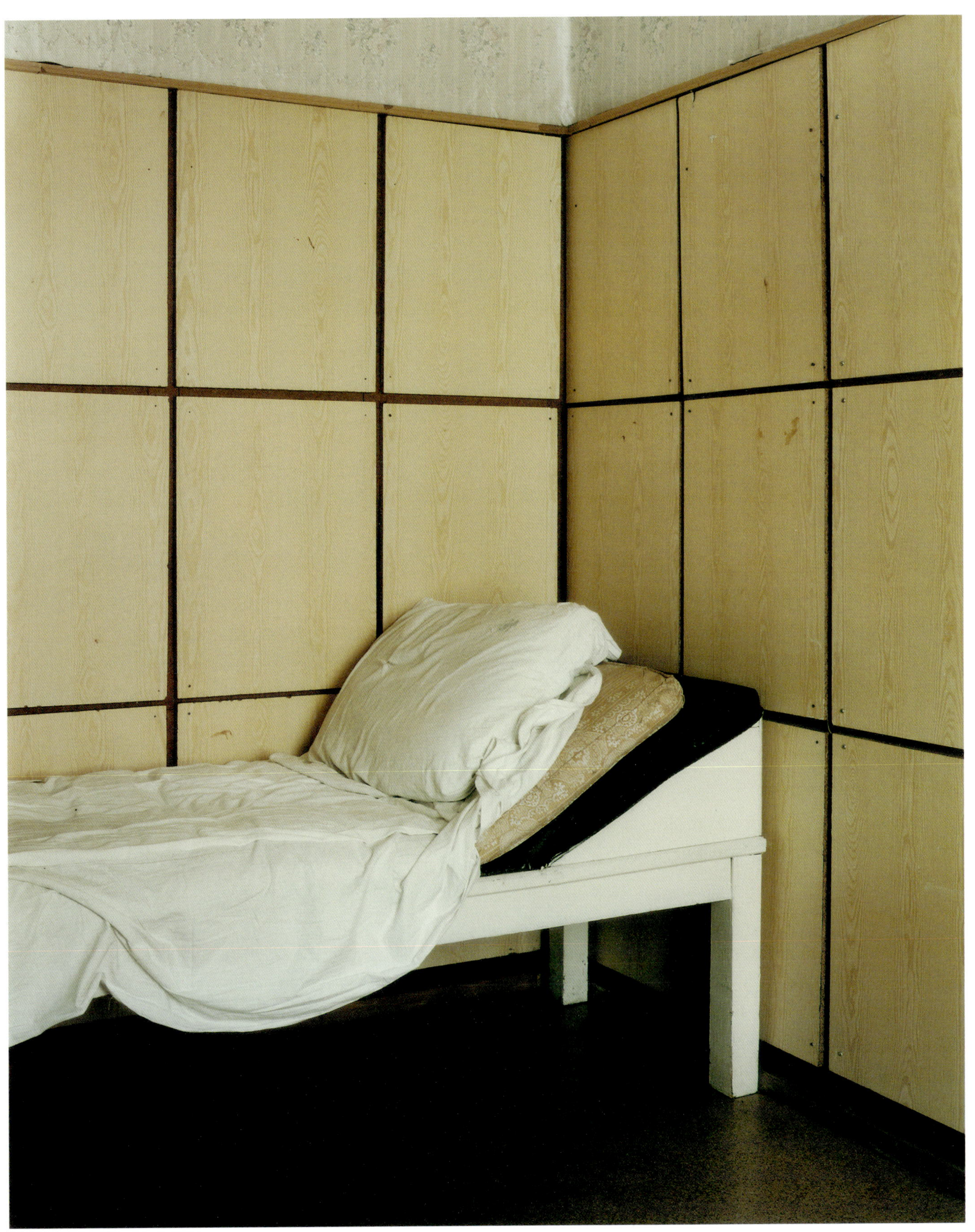

76 Wünsdorf, 1994 77 Leipzig, 1992

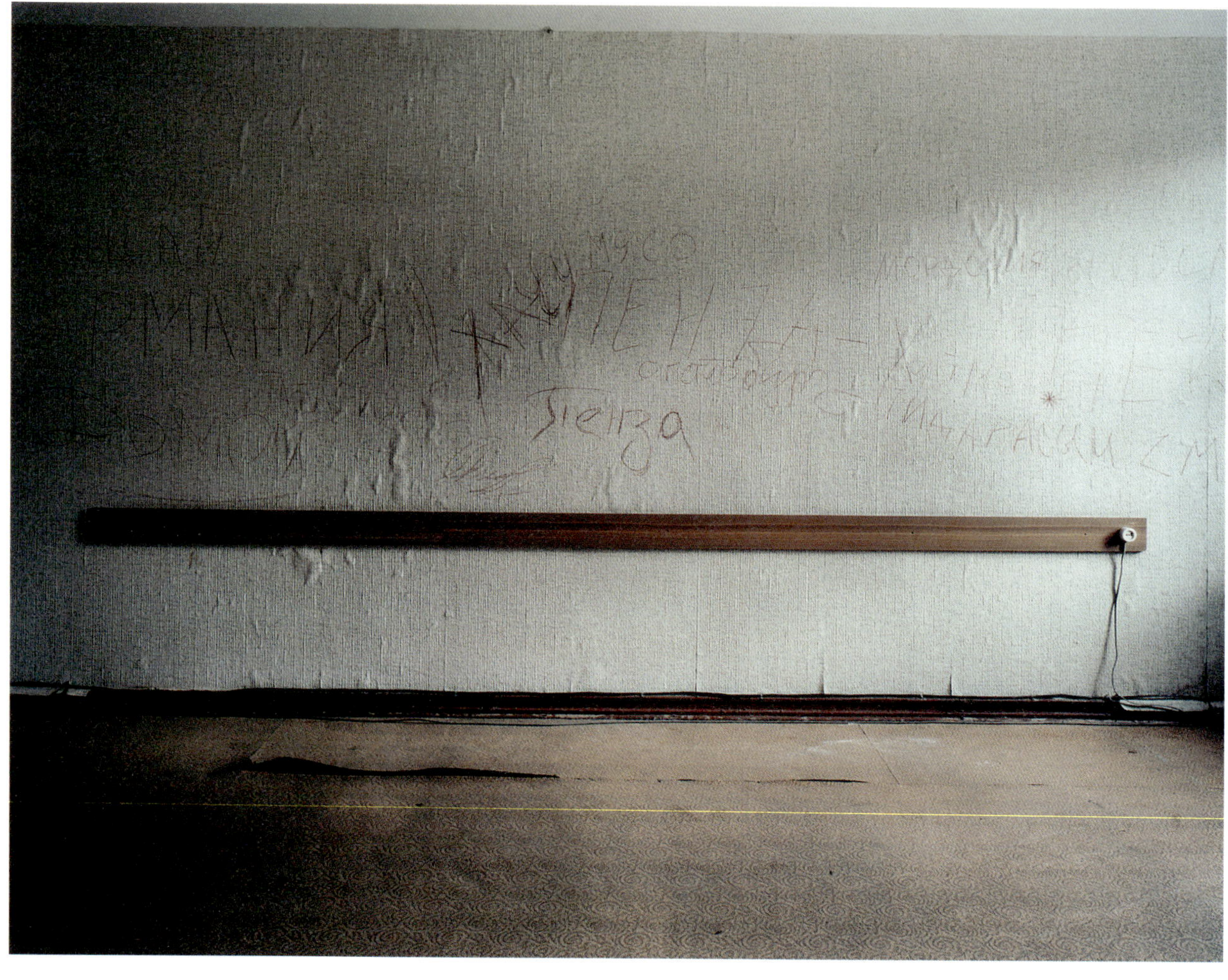

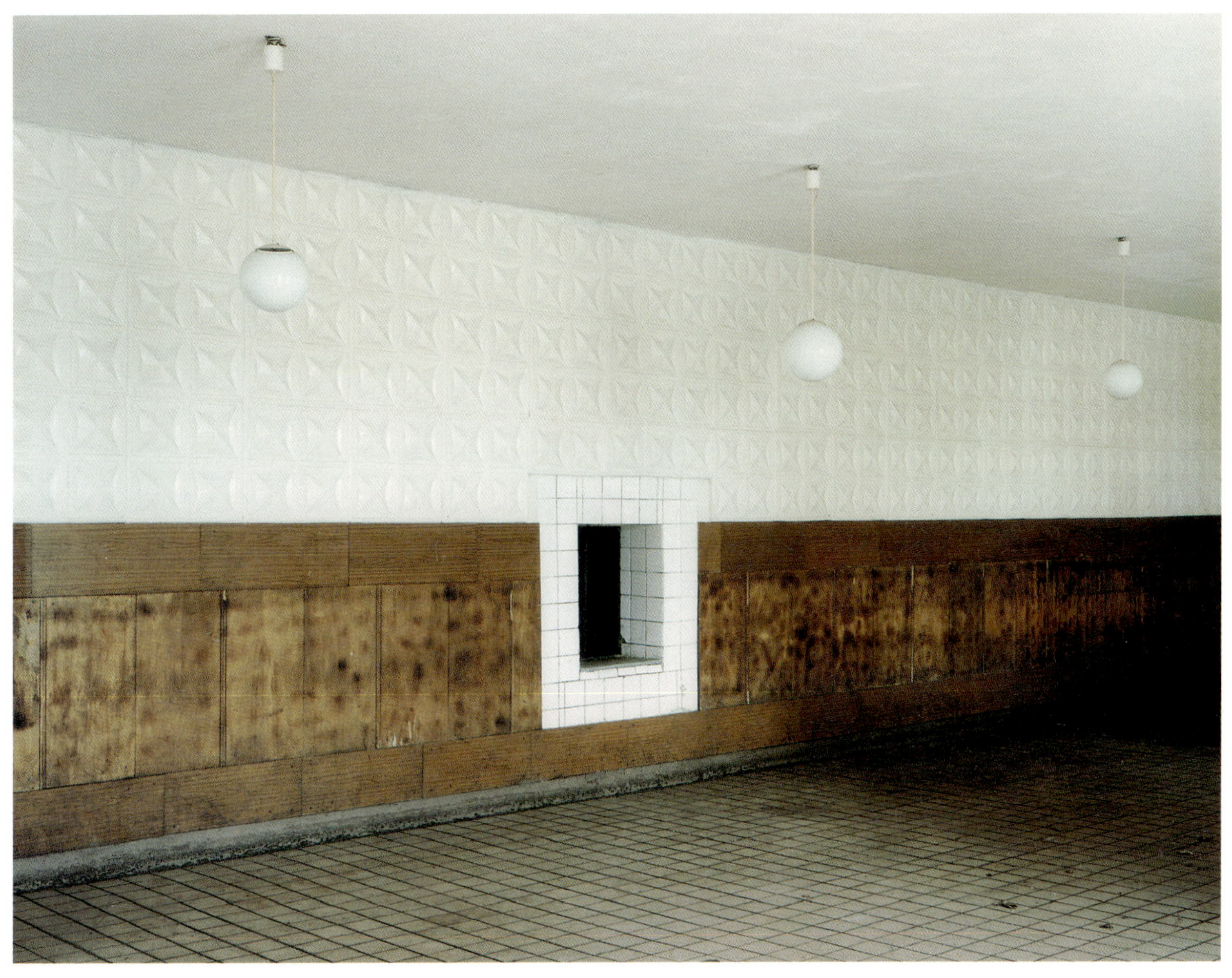

78 – 79 Rooms in the Russian barracks in Potsdam, 1994

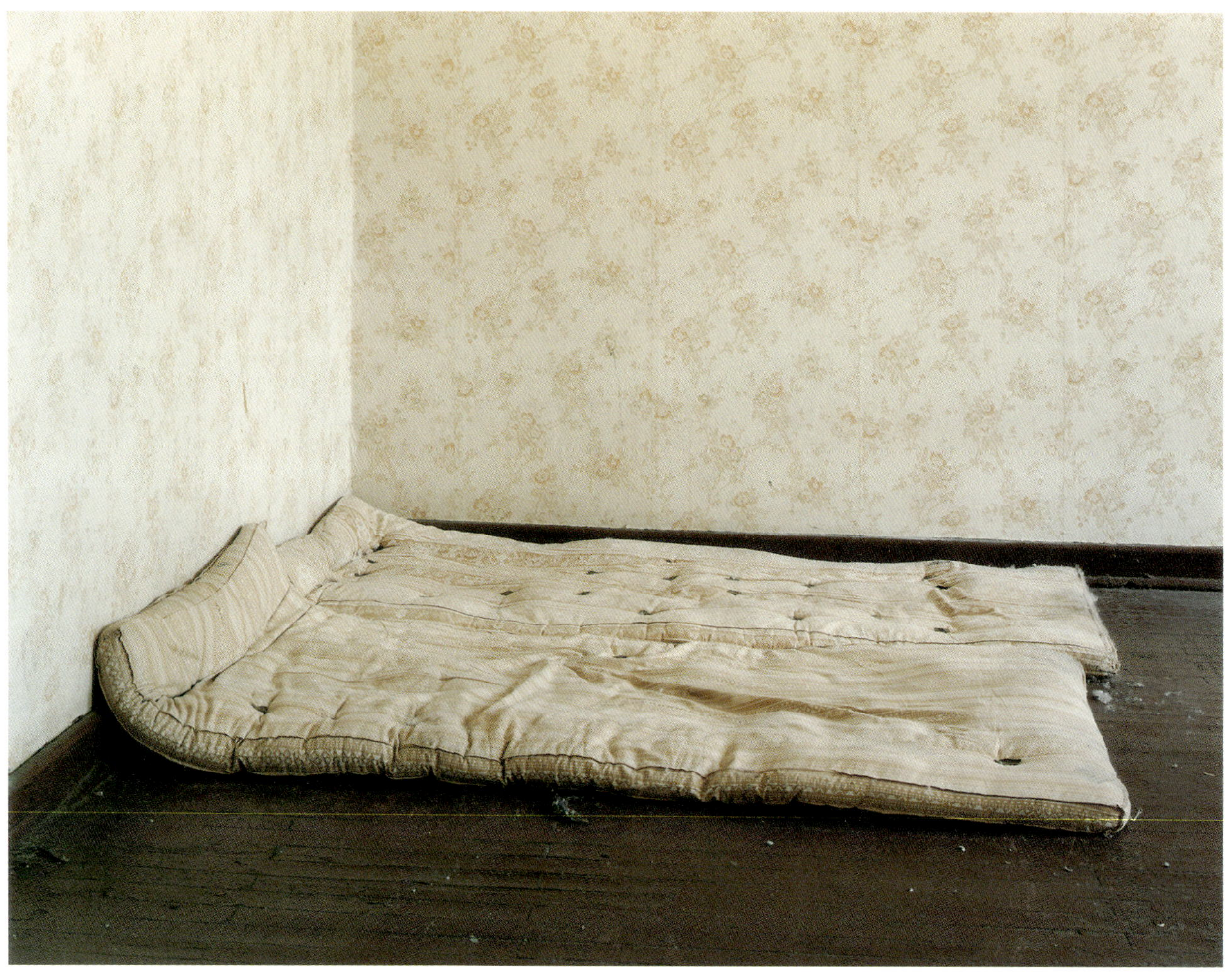

The work of Matthias Hoch – an artist from the former GDR – evidences a consistent preoccupation with the implications of reunification. In 1993 Hoch photographed the Reichstag as the embodiment of a 'new' Germany. Two years later, with his work on a clinic in Aachen, he began a documentation of the spaces developed under the new regime. The Speicher series considers automated sites of industry which are indicative of the rapid modernization of the infrastructure of former East German cities.

Matthias Hoch

81 Oschatz #17, 1997

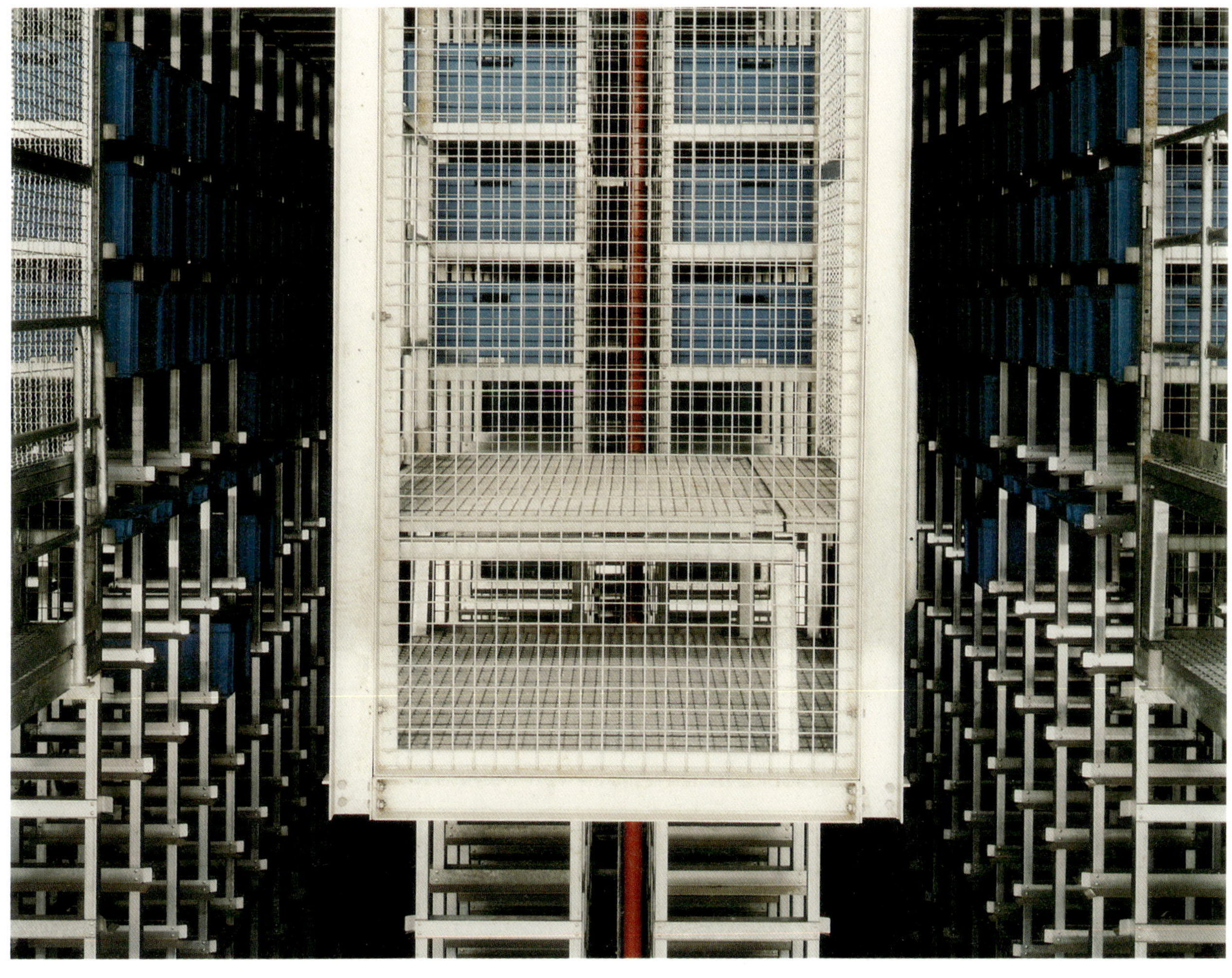

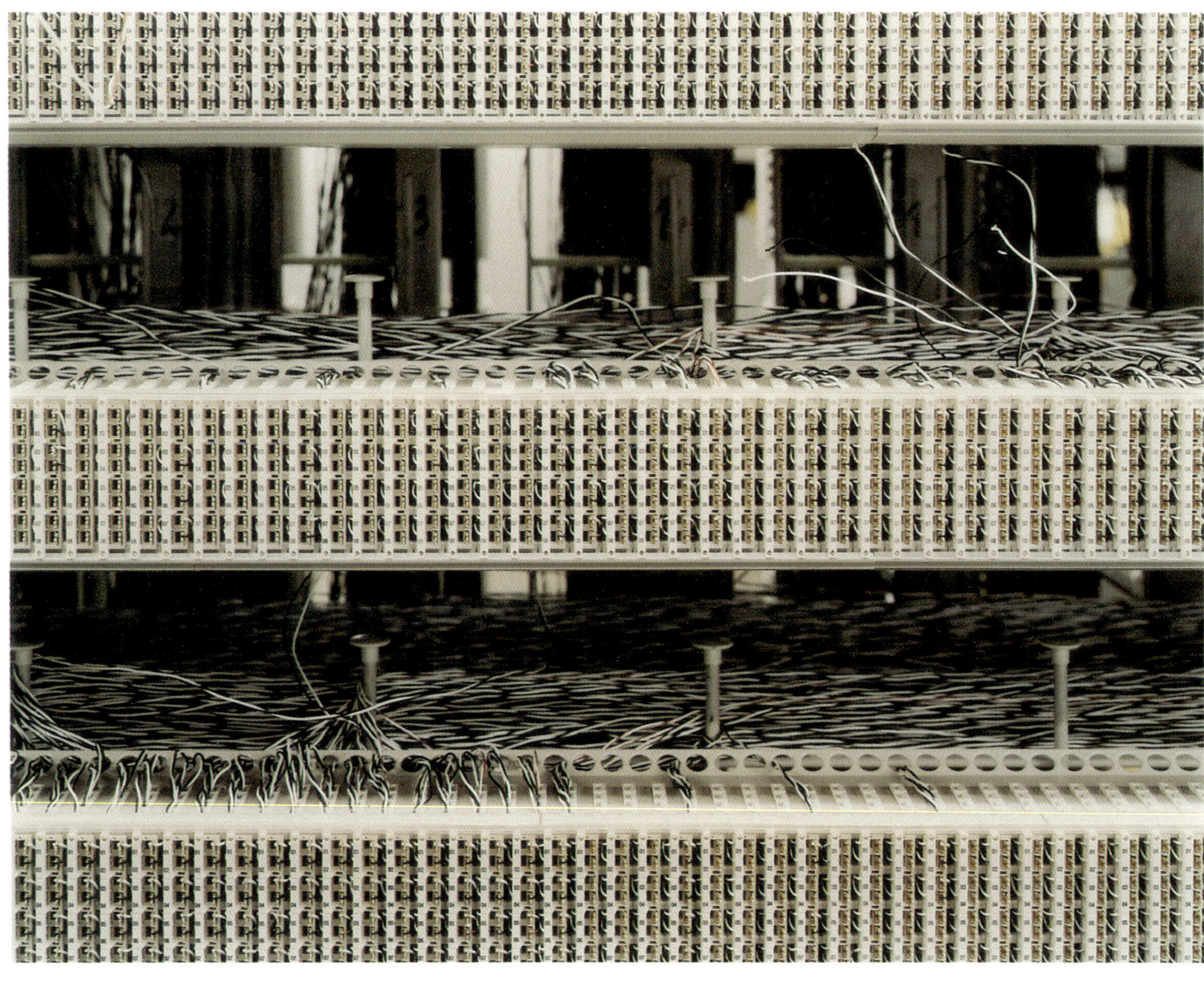

82 Leipzig #23, 1997 83 Leipzig #18, 1997

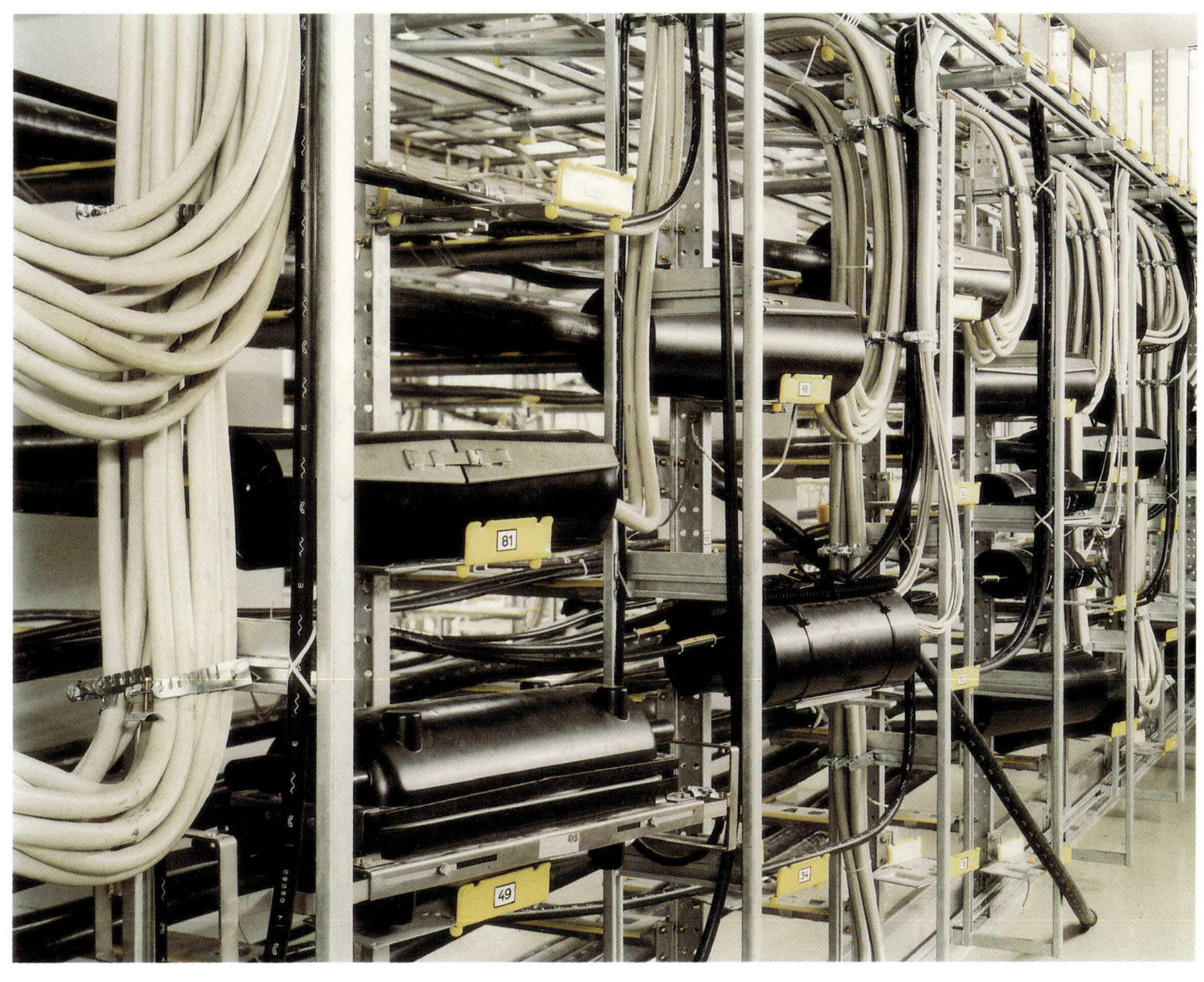

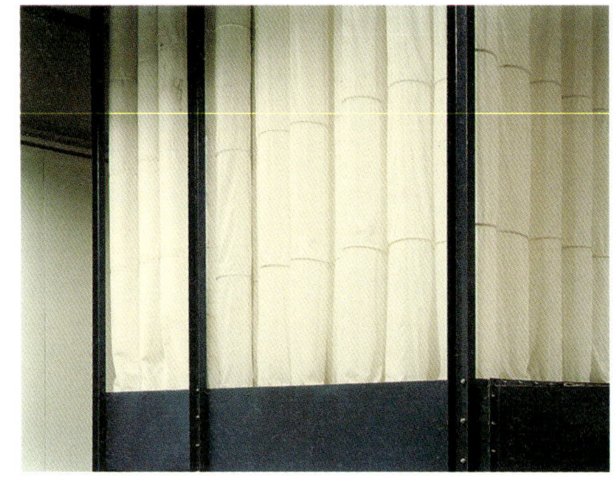

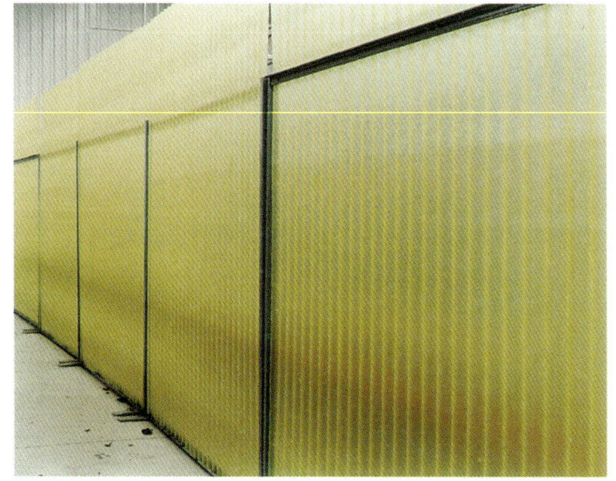

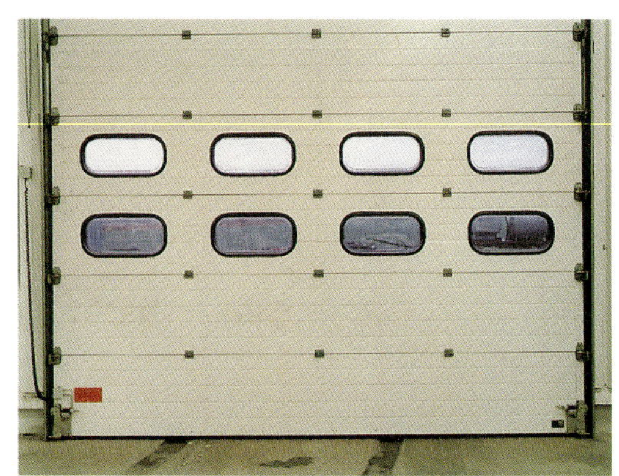

84 Zittau #39, 1998; Zittau #45, 1998; Zittau #36, 1998 85 Leipzig #29, 1997

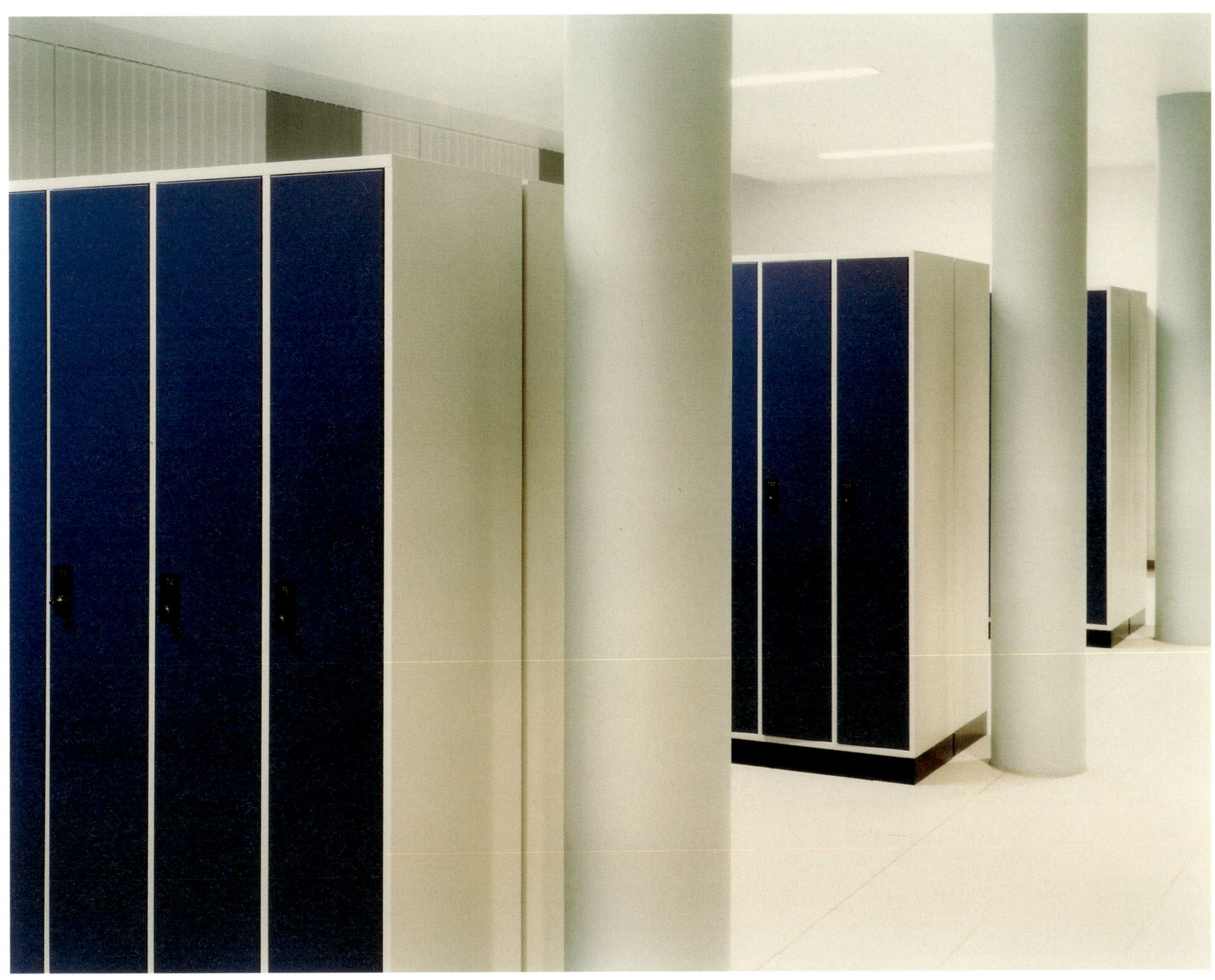

Andreas Gursky has traversed the extremes of German photography. He began his studies at Otto Steinert's school of 'subjective photography' in Essen, but then moved to the class of Bernd Becher at Düsseldorf Art Academy. He started out as a 'straight' photographer and appeared, with his interest in post-industrial culture, to carry on the Becher tradition, but he does not work in series and has now fervently embraced the possibilities of digitalization. Some of his recent images involve the construction of sets which are photographed and then digitally manipulated, in an attempt to construct imagery which faultlessly encompasses myriad references and conceptual complexities.

Andreas Gursky

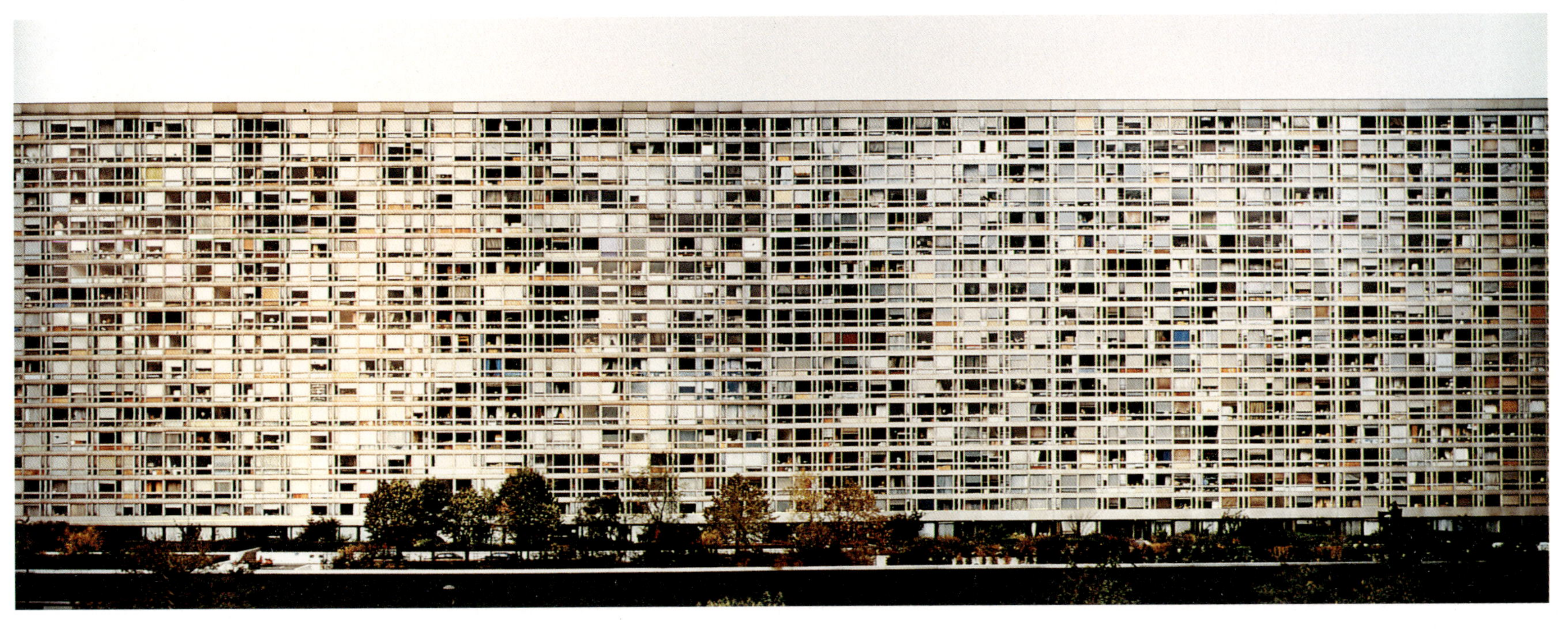

87 Paris, Montparnasse, 1993

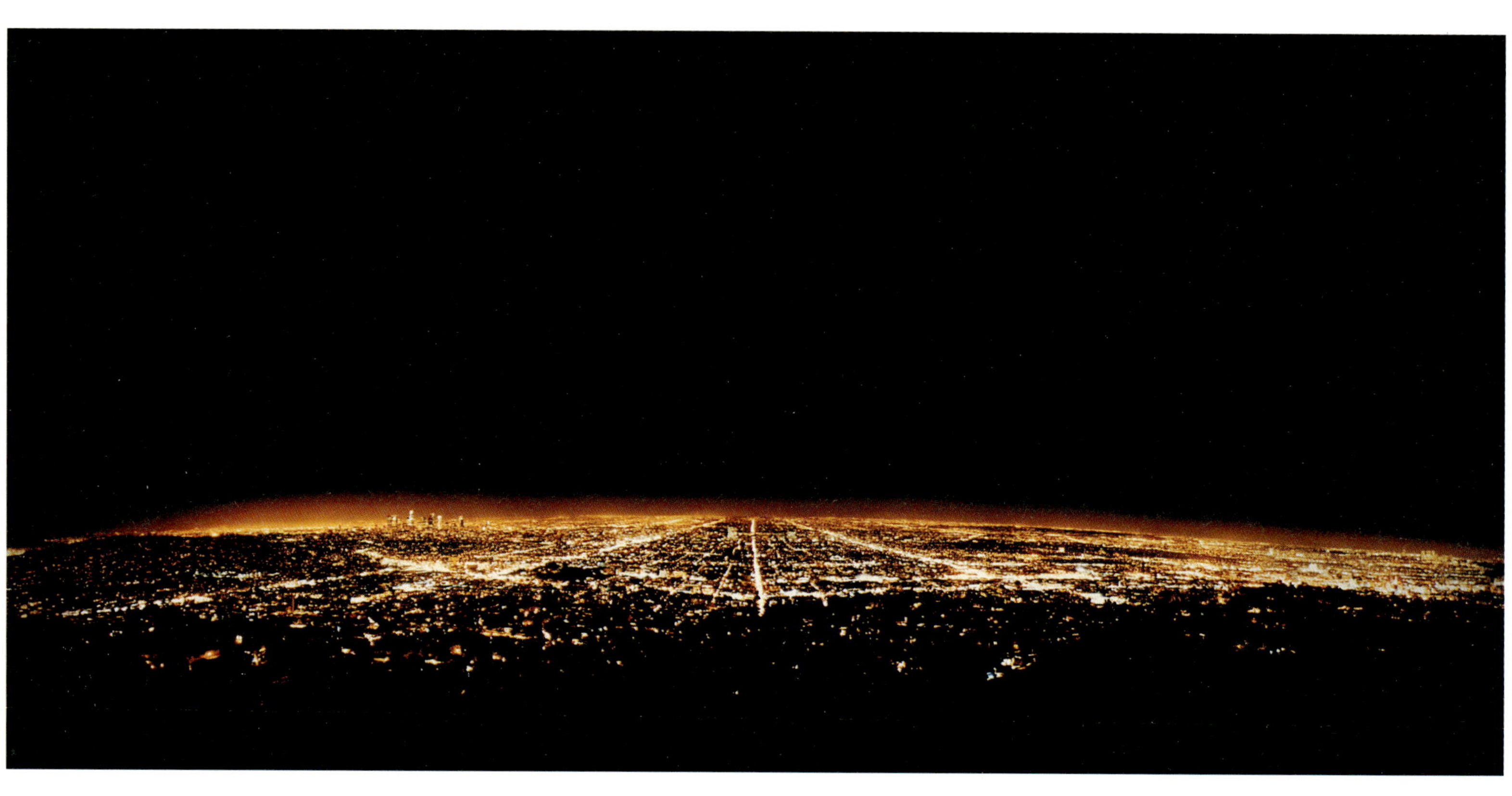

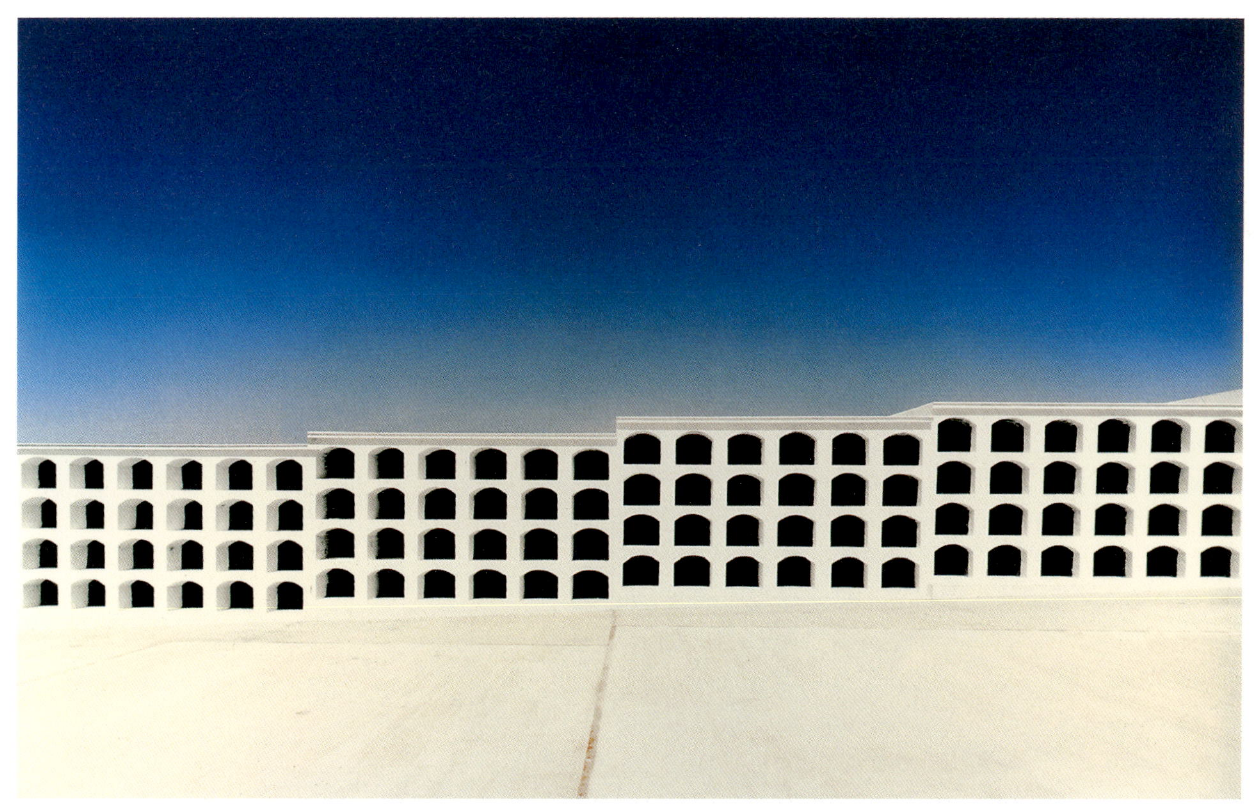

88 Los Angeles, 1997 89 Ayamonte, 1997

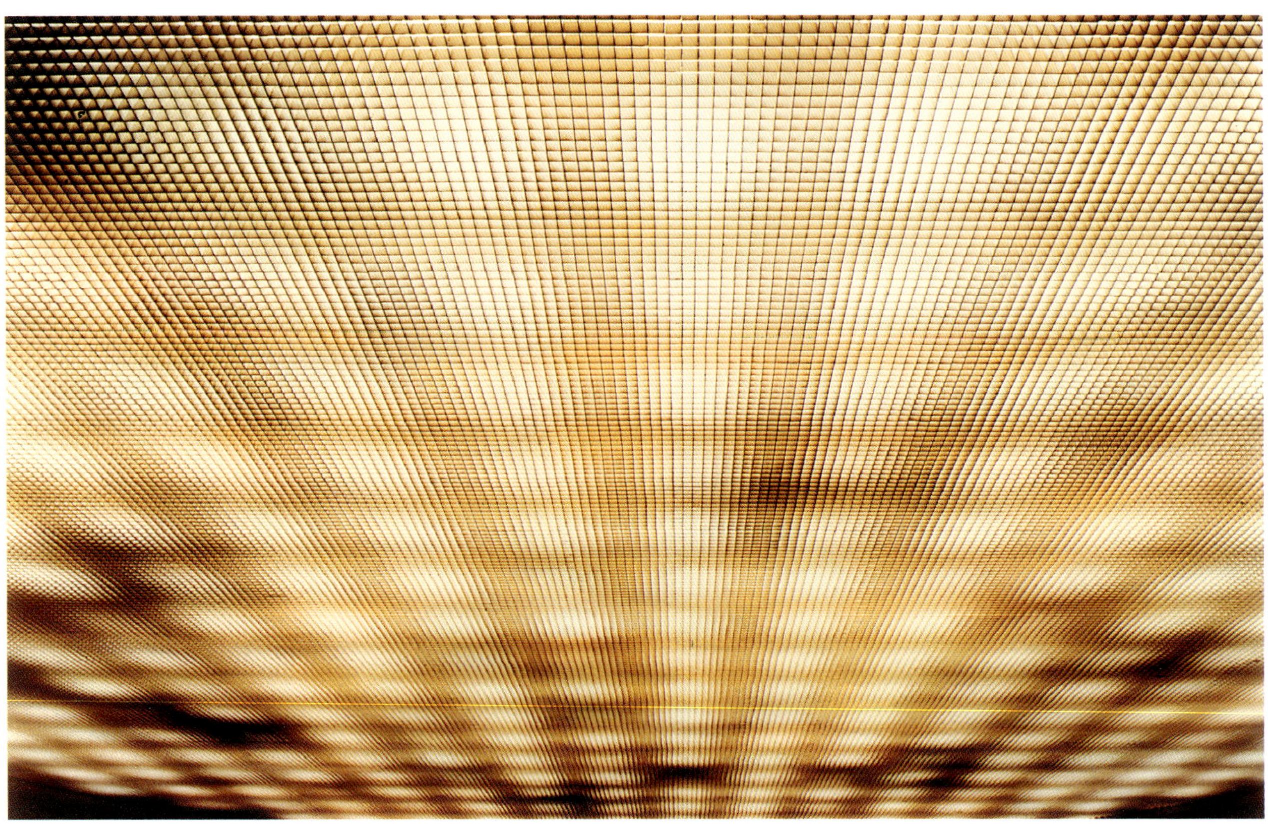

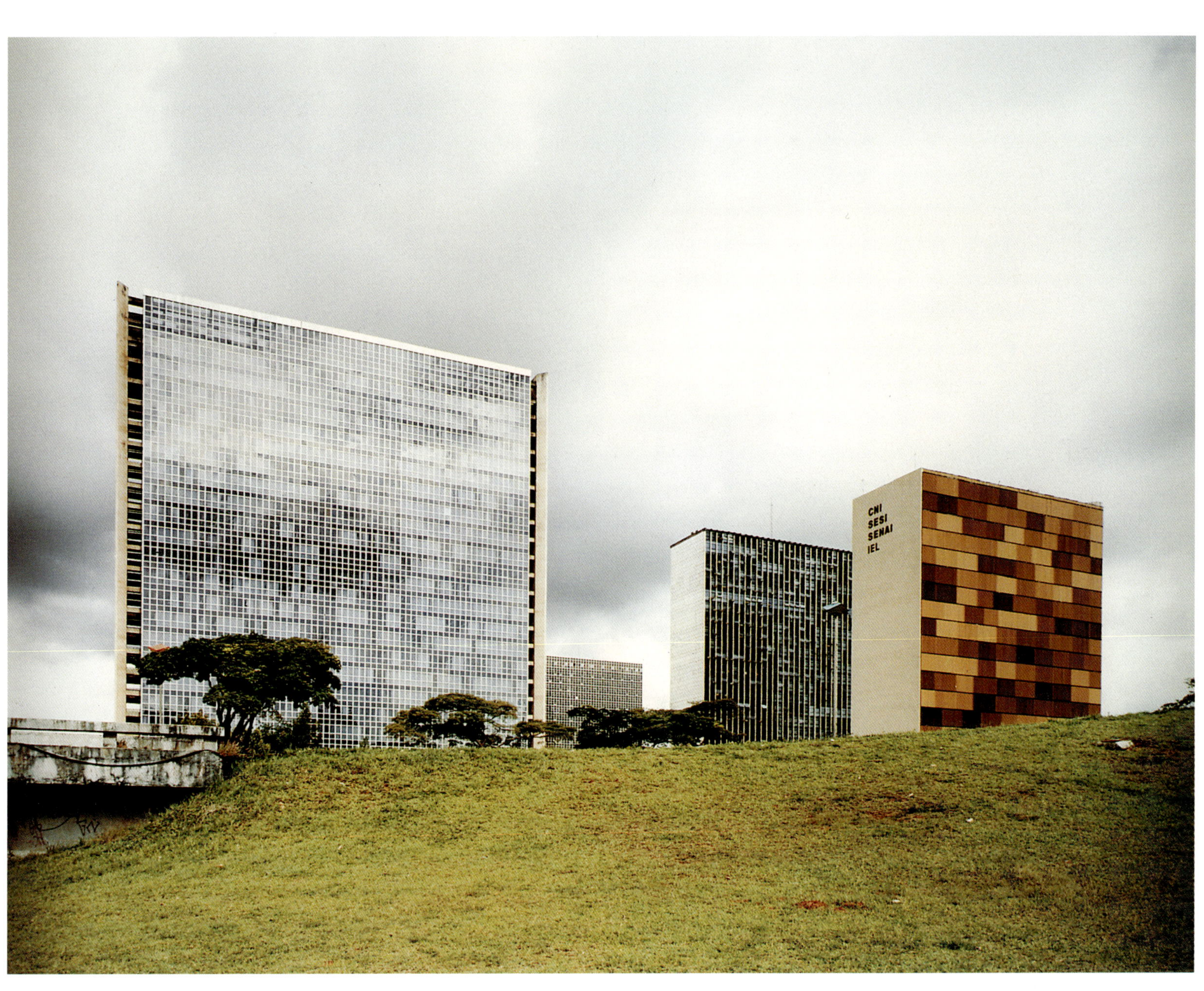

90 Brasília, General Assembly I, 1994 91 Brasília, North Banking Sector, 1994

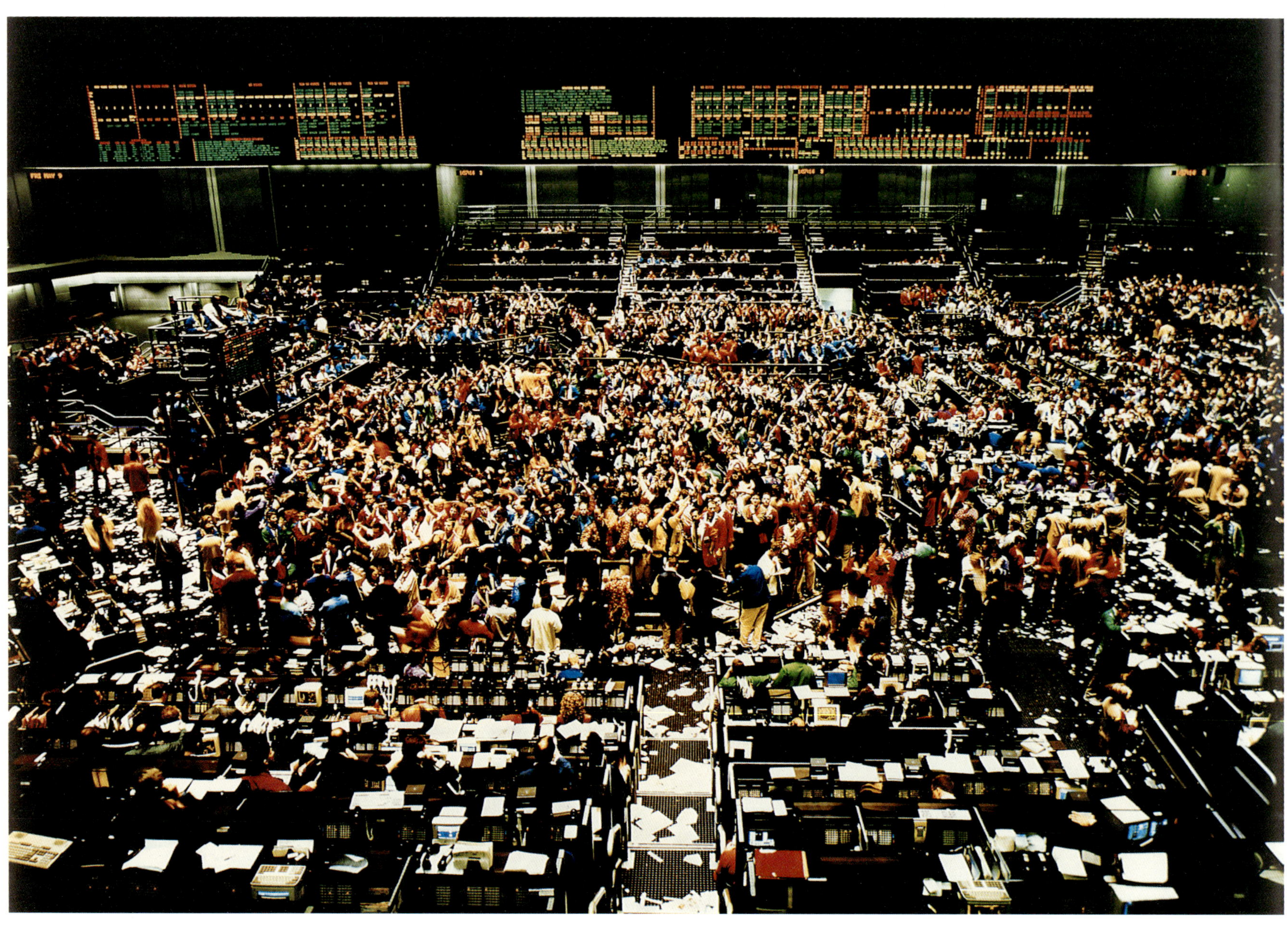

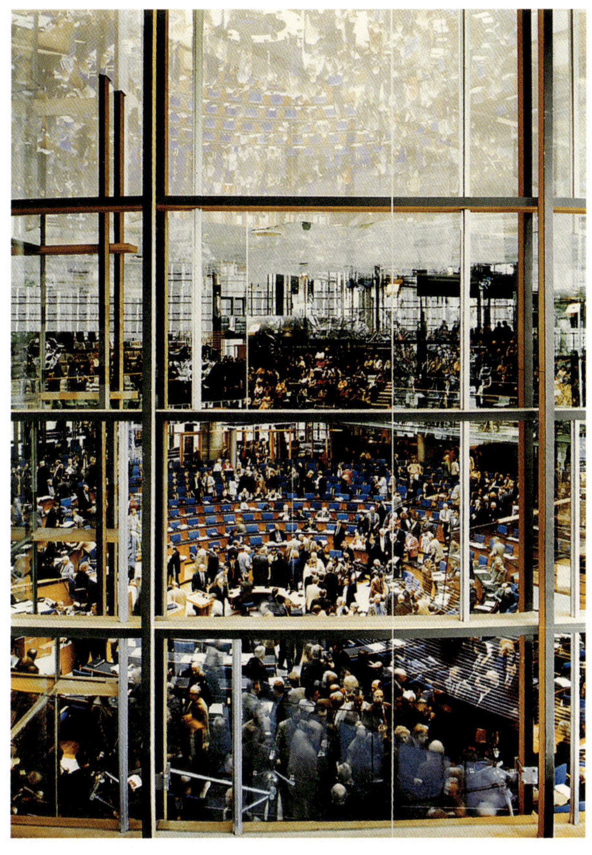

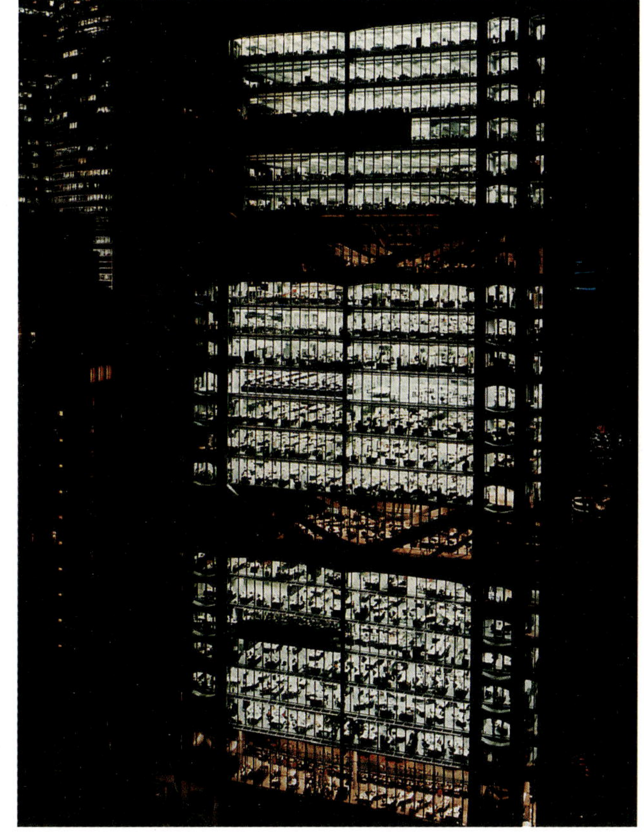

92 Chicago, Board of Trade, 1997 93 Bundestag, 1998; Hong Kong, Shanghai Bank, 1994

Thomas Demand

Thomas Demand builds fragments of the world in front of his camera: models of Utopian architecture, constructions based on photographs of historically significant sites and imagined structures. His 'cardboard architecture' interrogates the interwoven relations of architecture and photography, and the final images repeat history in such a way that it becomes fiction.

'*Cardboard architecture* is a term which questions the nature of the reality of the physical environment; *cardboard* is a term which attempts to shift the focus from the existing conceptions of form to a consideration of form as a signal or a notation which can provide a range of formal information; *cardboard* is a means for an exploration into the nature of architectural form itself, in both its actual and conceptual states.'

Peter Eisenman, 'Cardboard Architecture', *Casabella* 374 (1973) p. 24

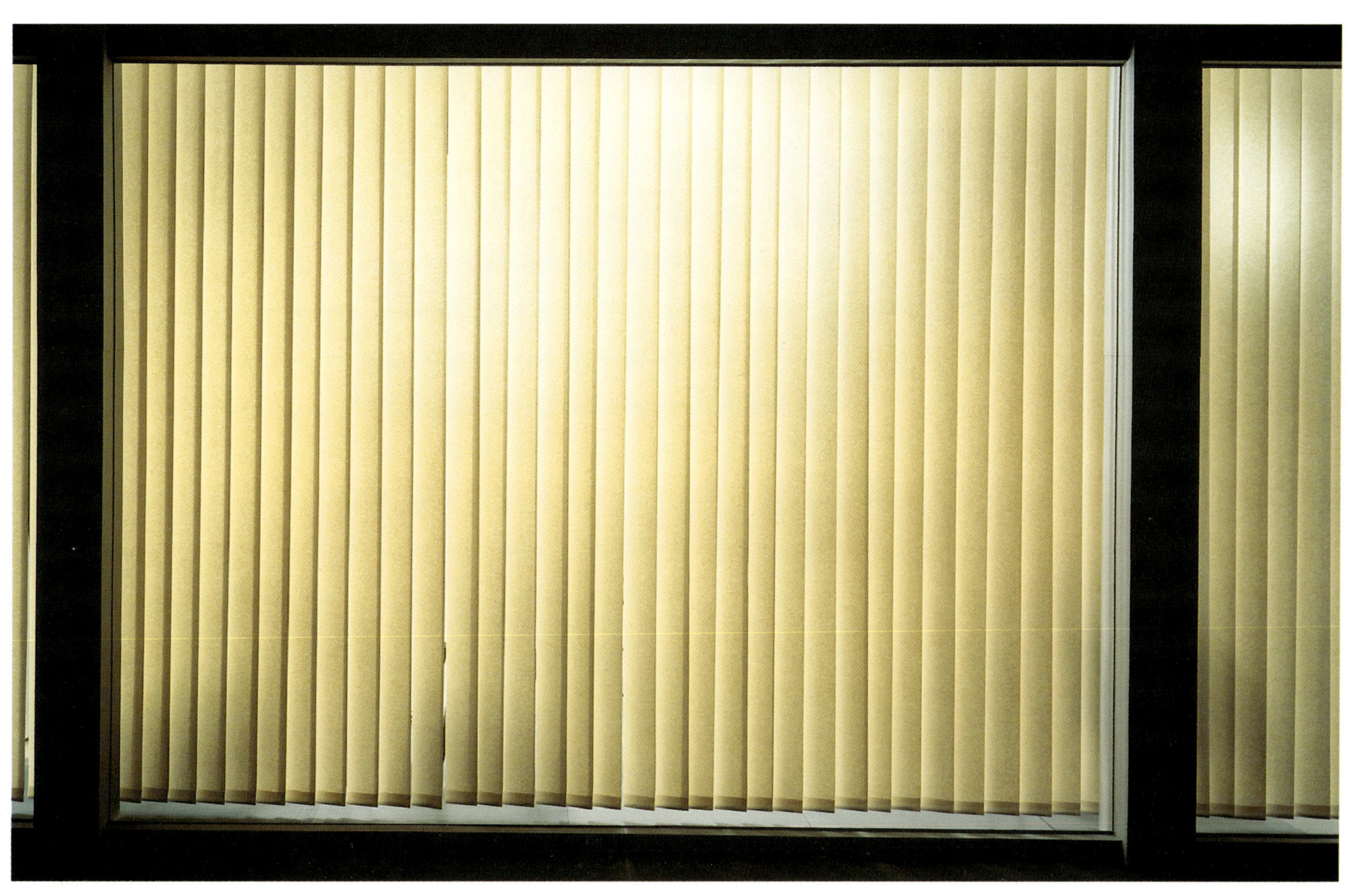

95 Fenster (Window), 1998

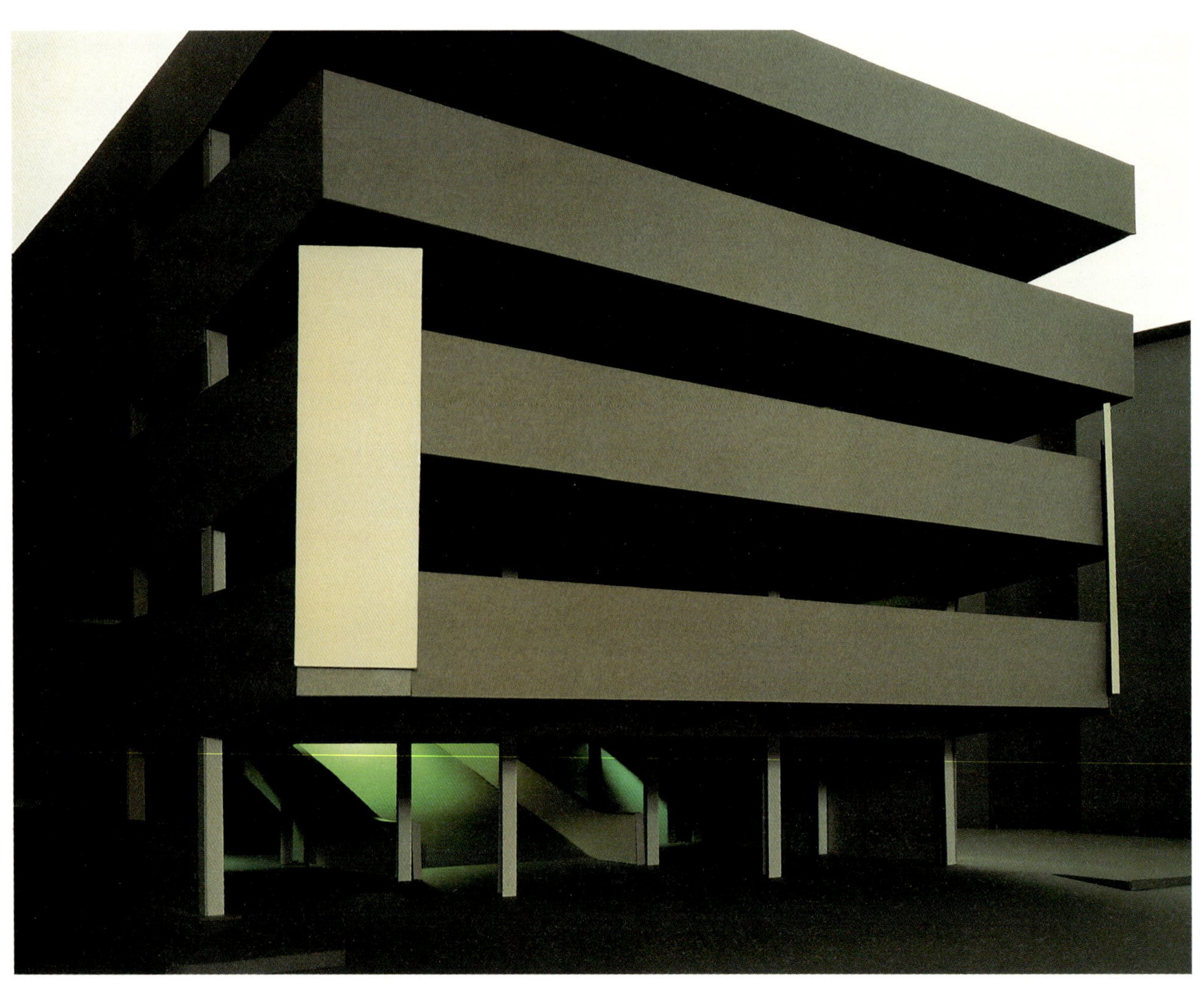

96 Carpark, 1996 97 Balkone (Balcony), 1997

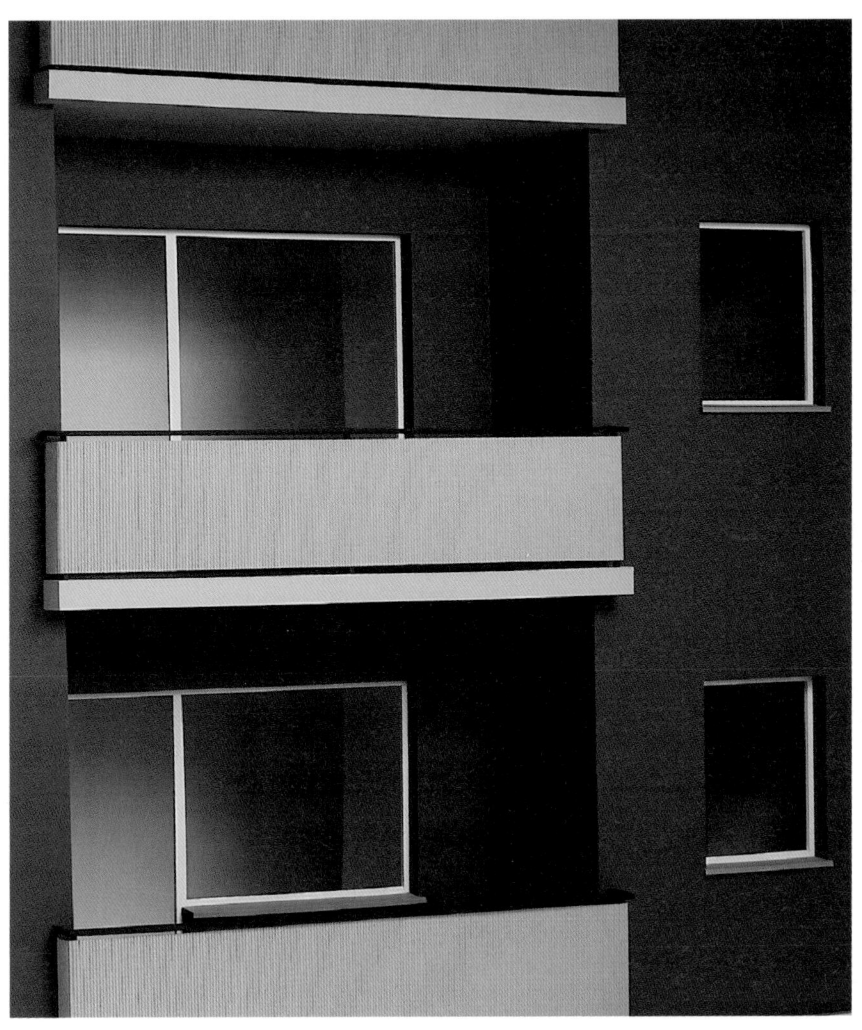

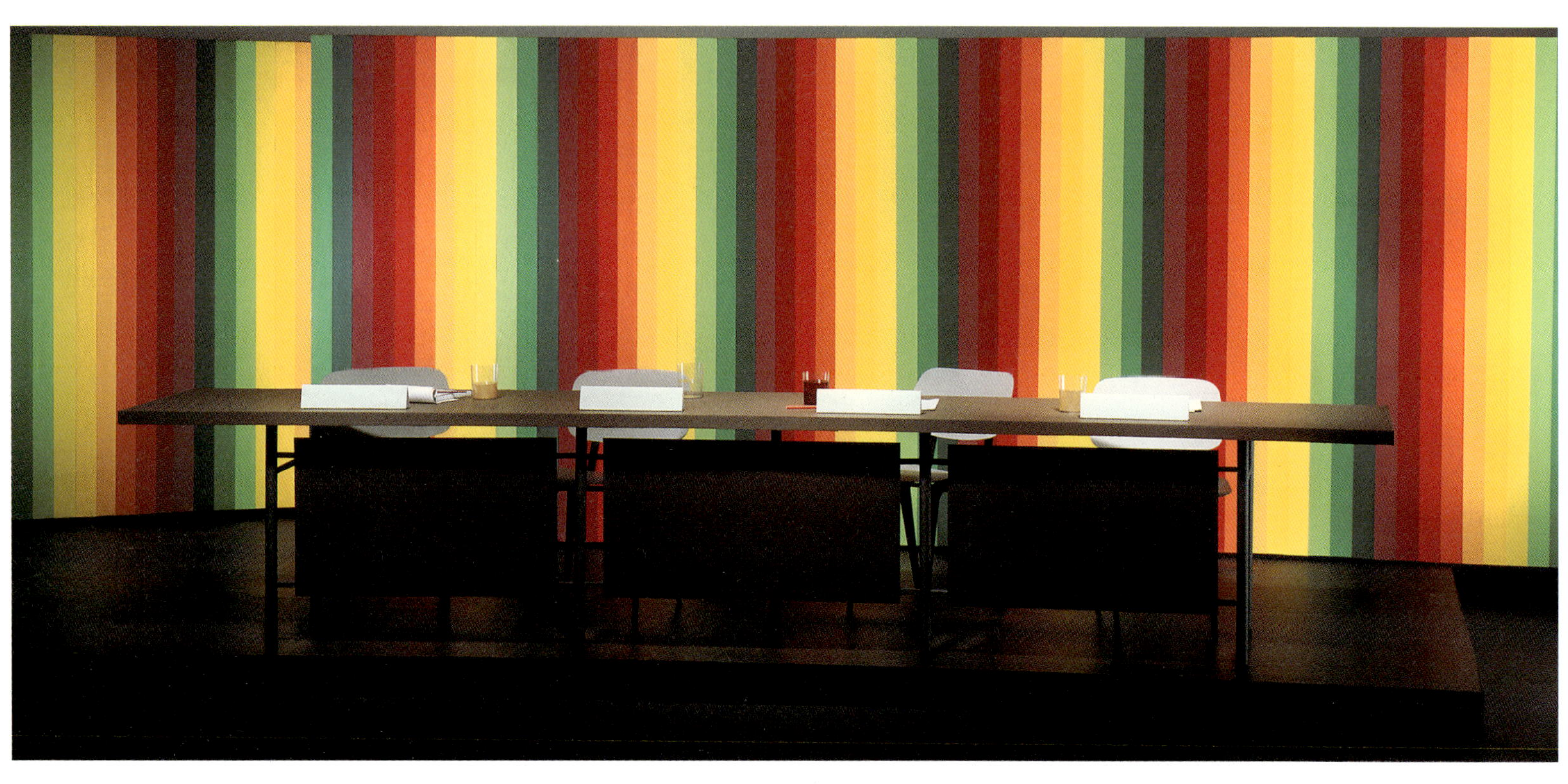

98 Studio, 1997 99 Treppenhaus (Staircase), 1995

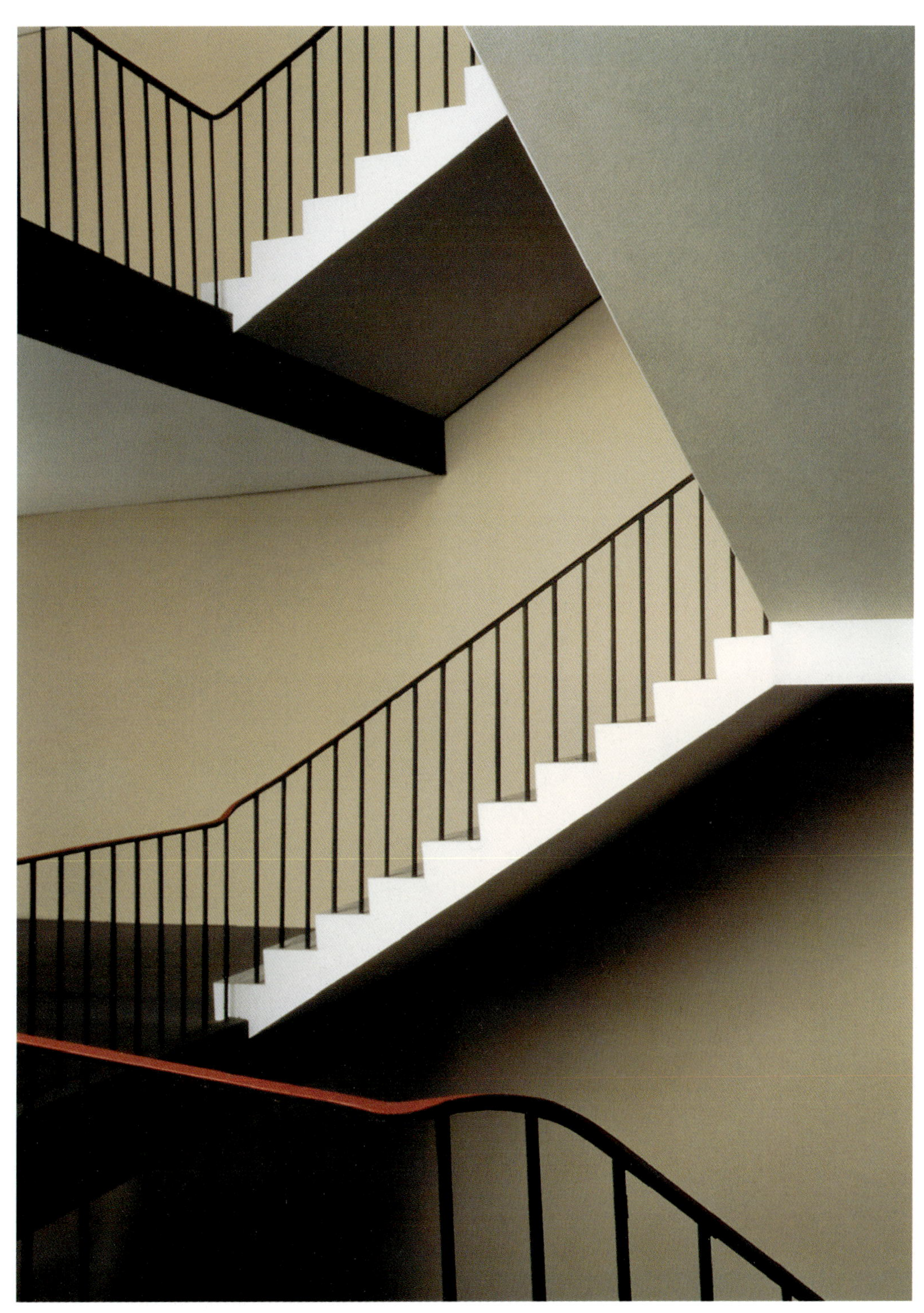

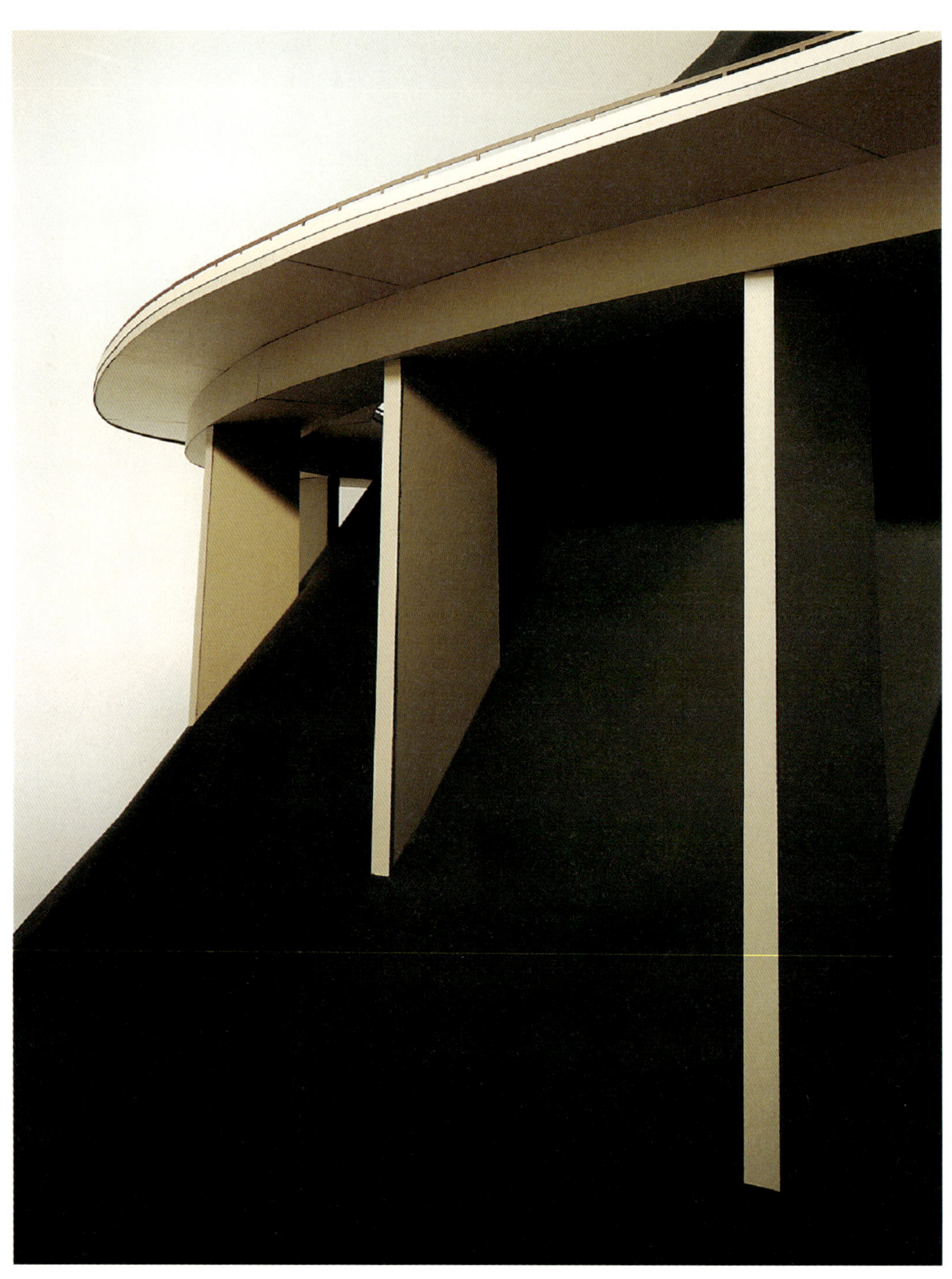

100 Brenner Autobahn, 1994 101 Drei Garagen (Three Garages), 1995

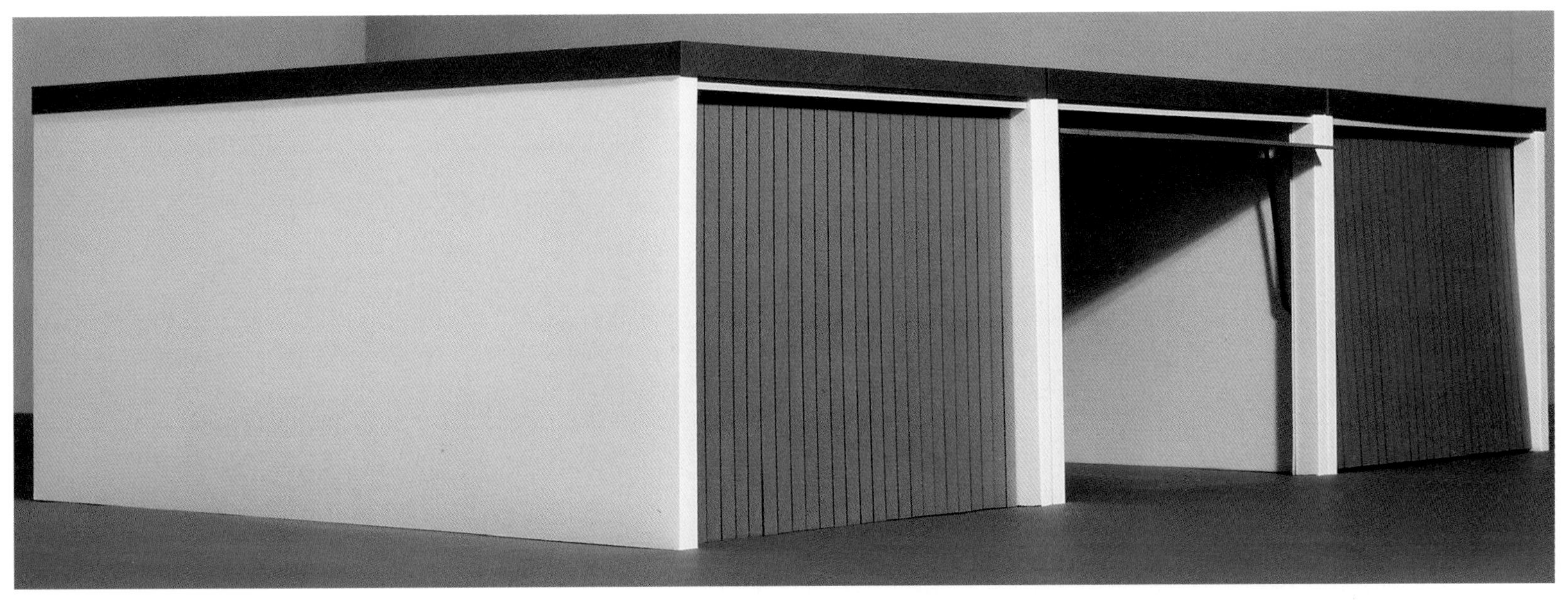

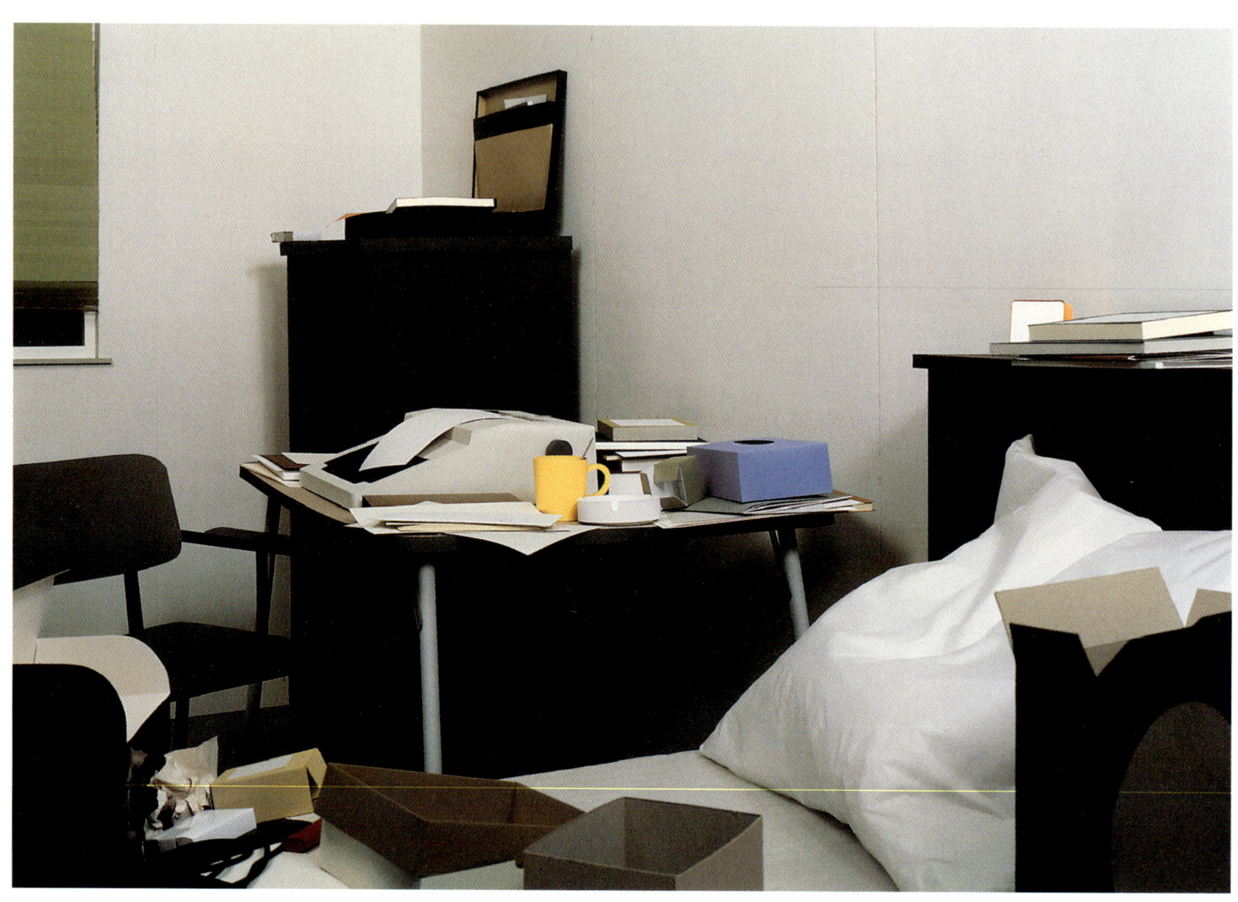

102 Zimmer (Room), 1996 103 Zeichensaal (Drafting Room), 1996

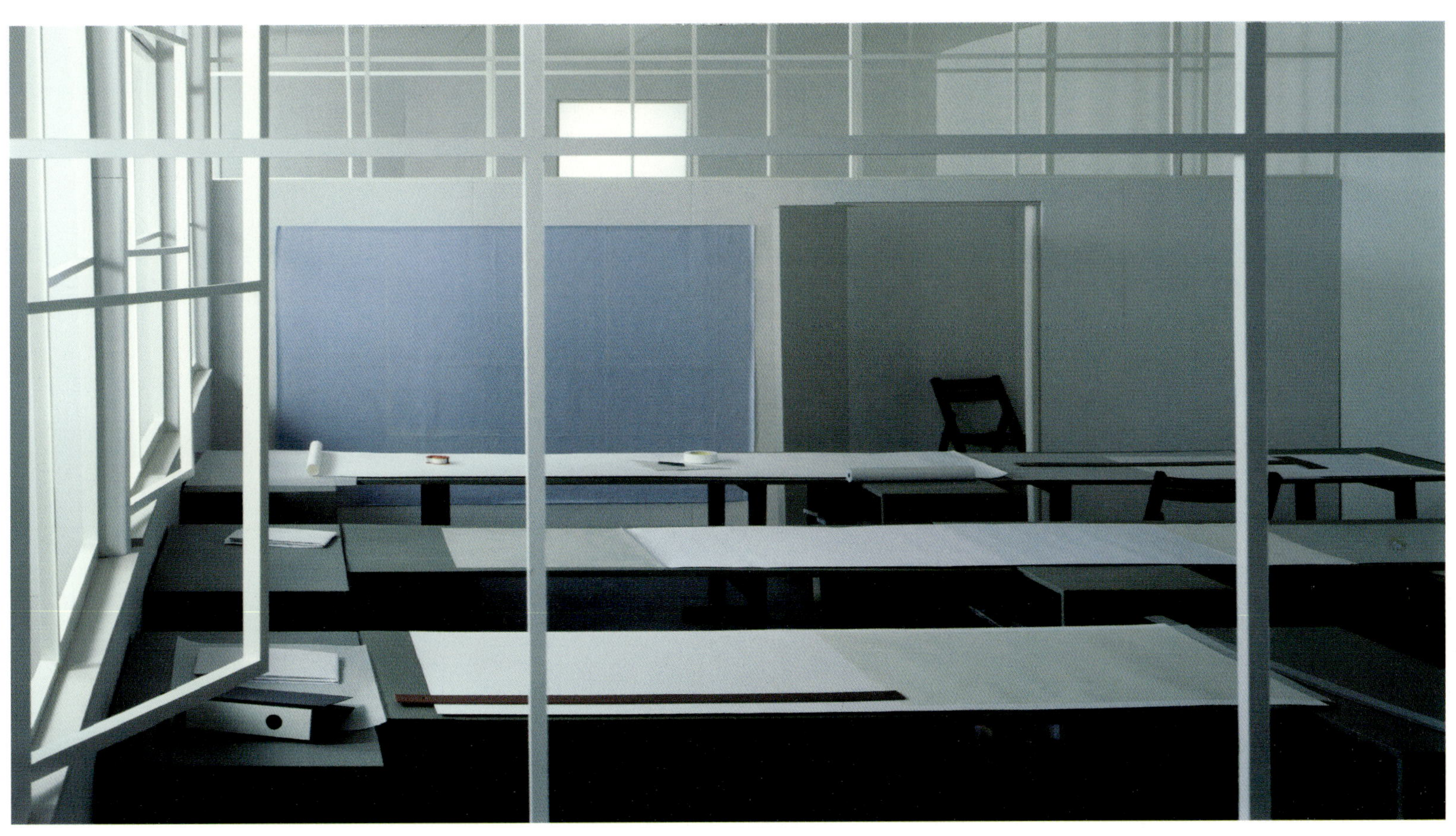

Christine Erhard

Christine Erhard's photographs show artificial model spaces constructed by bringing together single image elements collected from various sources, including photographs of architectural details, images from the mass media, and snapshots from private albums. The constructed photograph combines these layers into a common image plane, confusing the spatial relationships and fragmenting the interior space until it no longer appears to be clearly delineated in three dimensions.

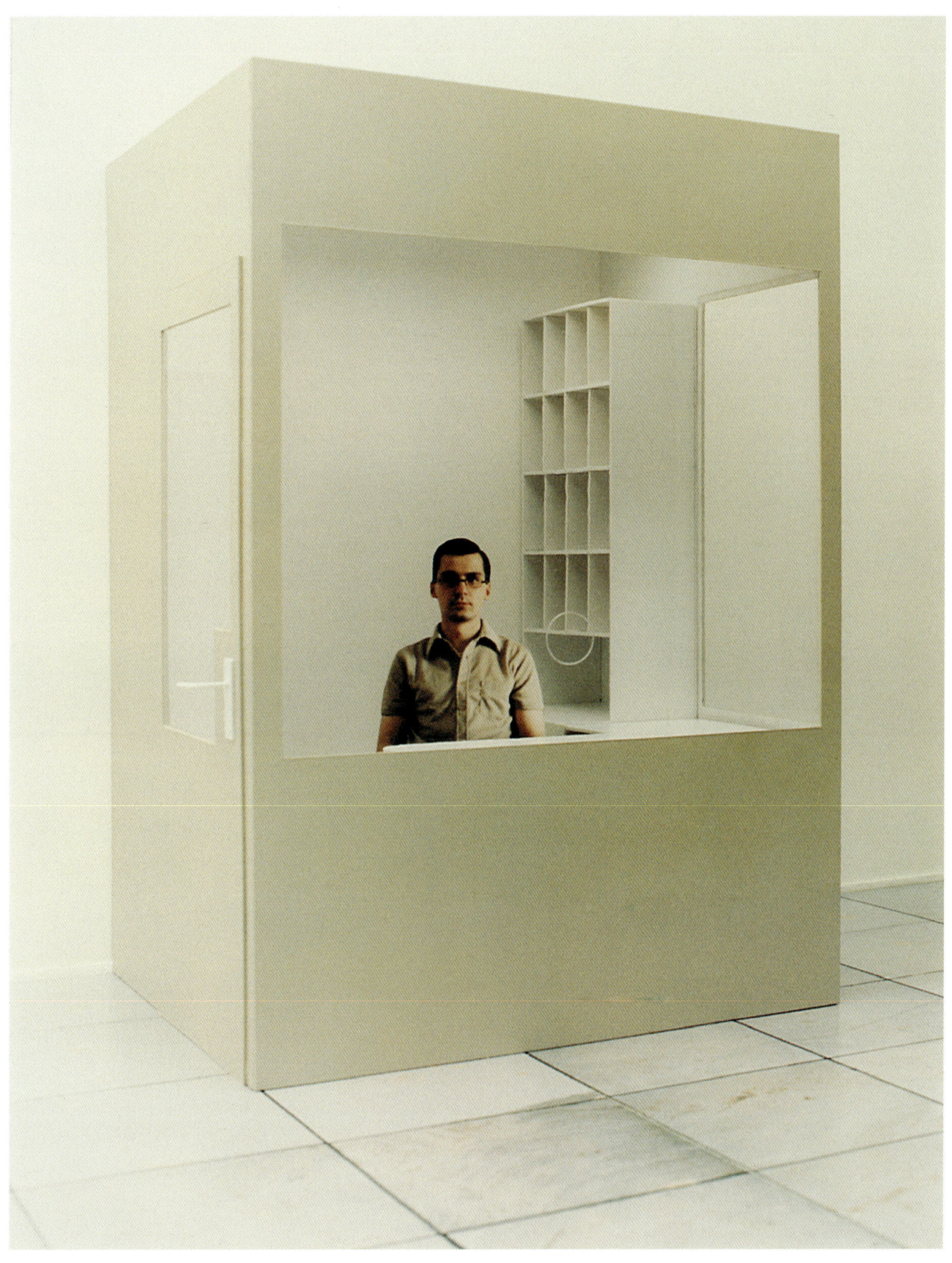

105 Christine Erhard/Ralf Werner, The Porter, 1998

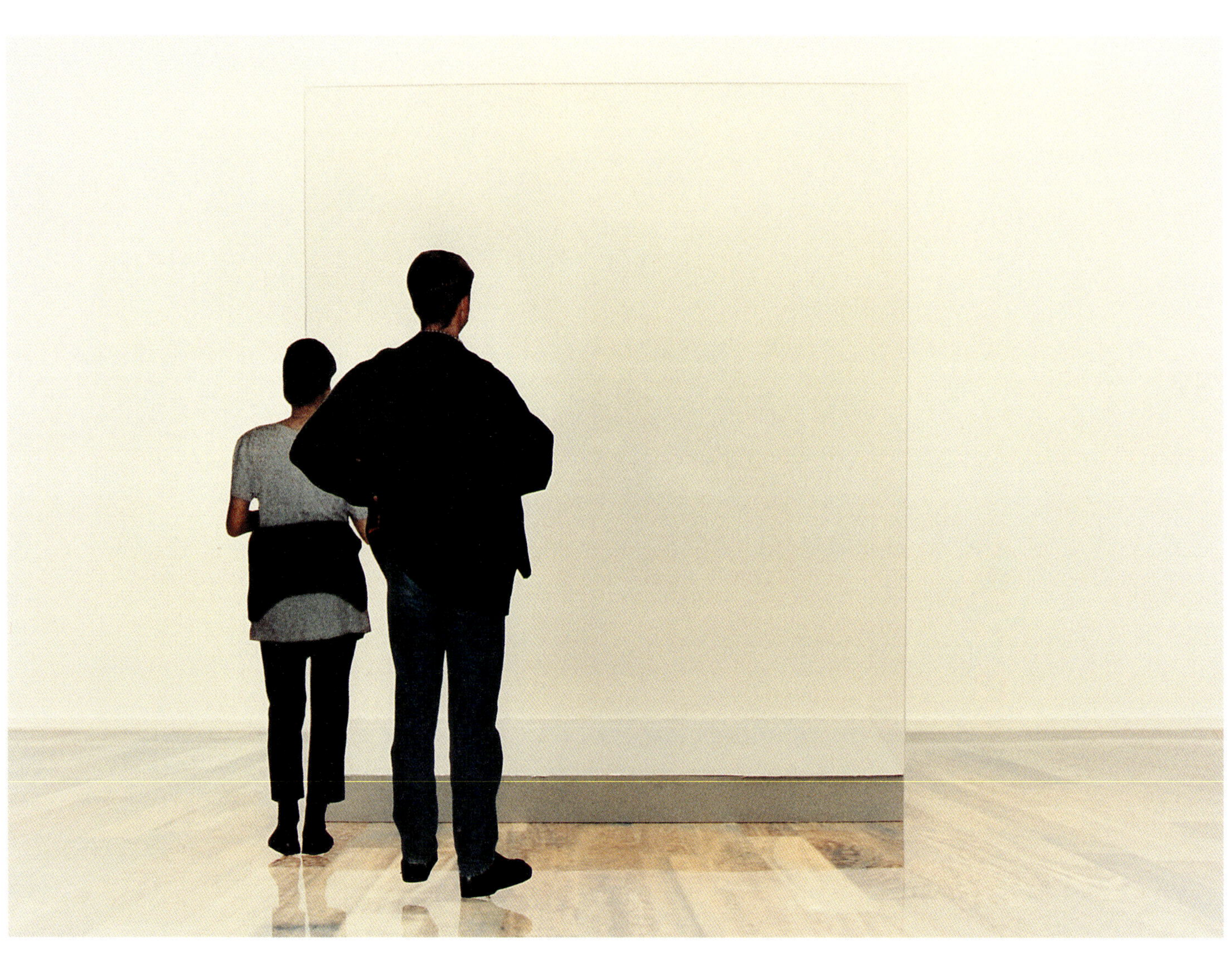

106 Visitors in front of a Display Case, 1997 107 Visitors in front of Curtain Blinds, 1998

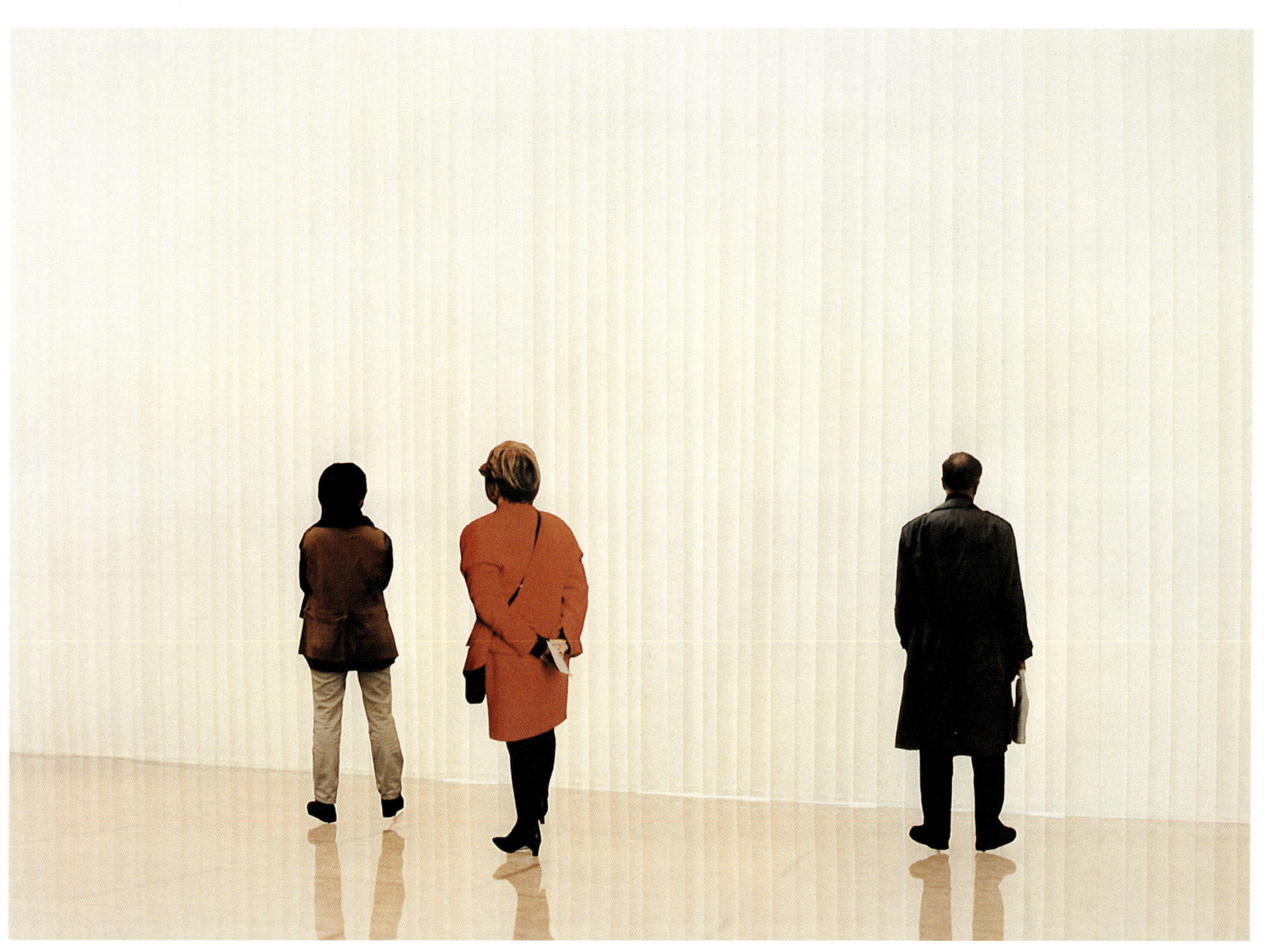

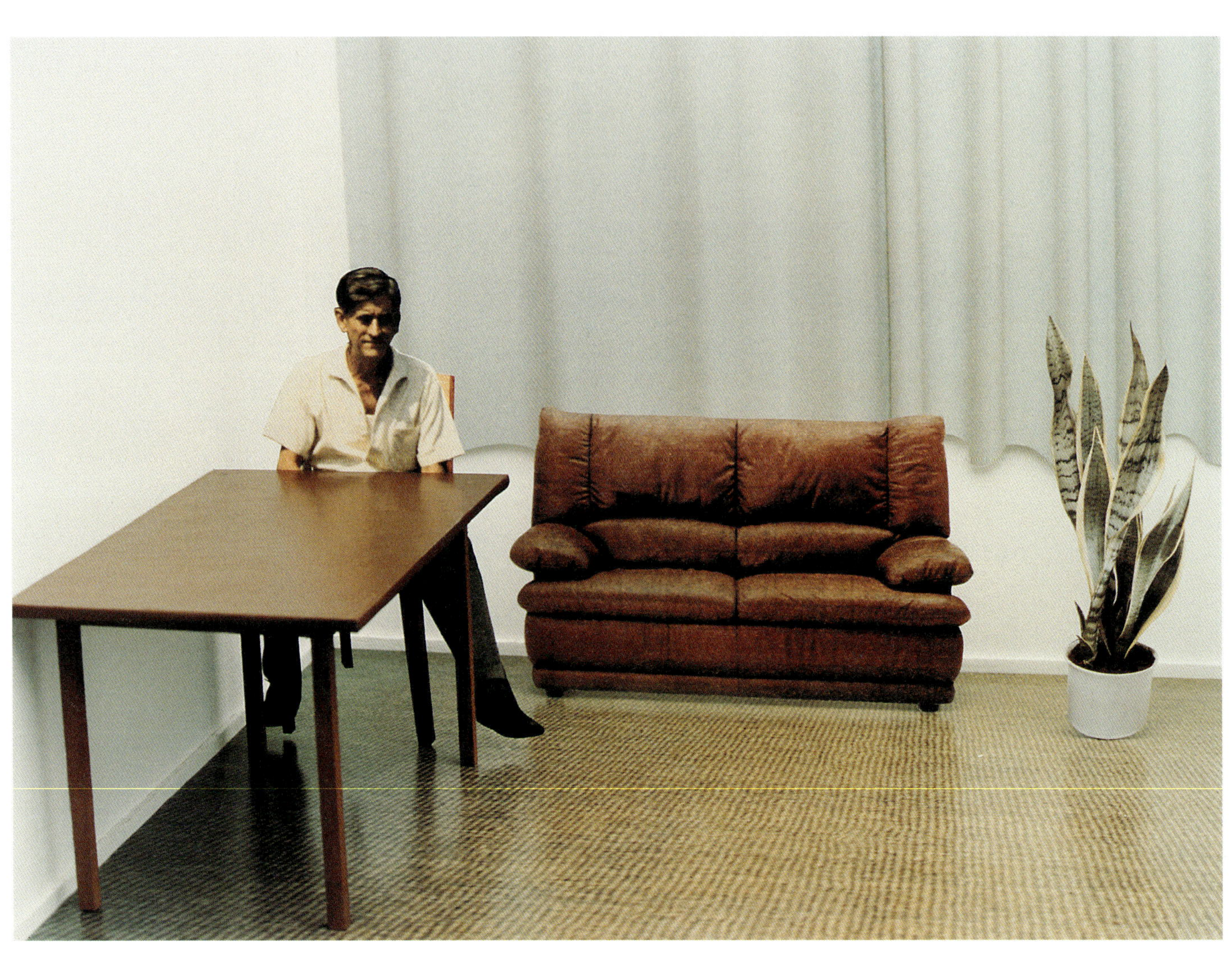

108 Summer '69, 1998 109 Hotel Room, 1998

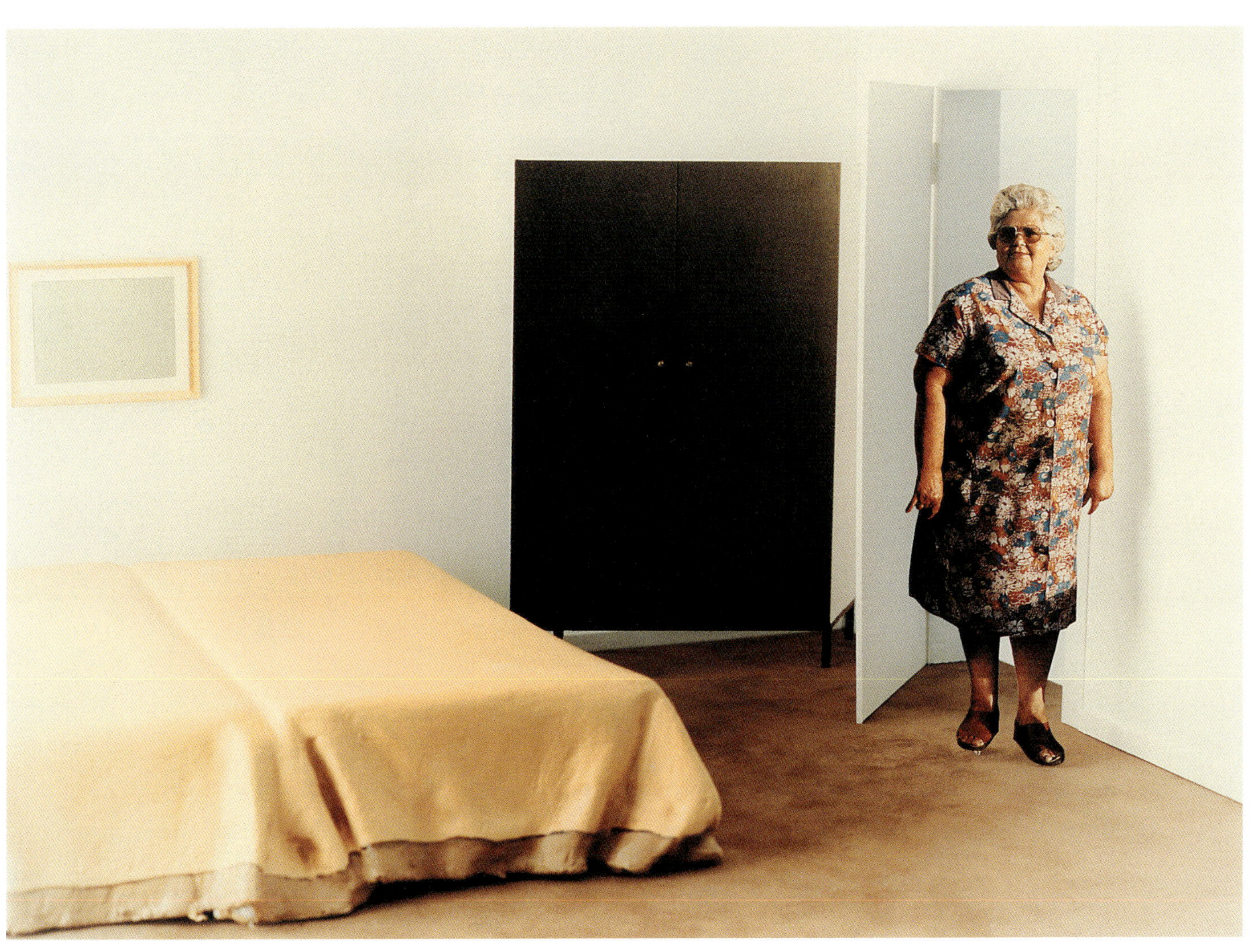

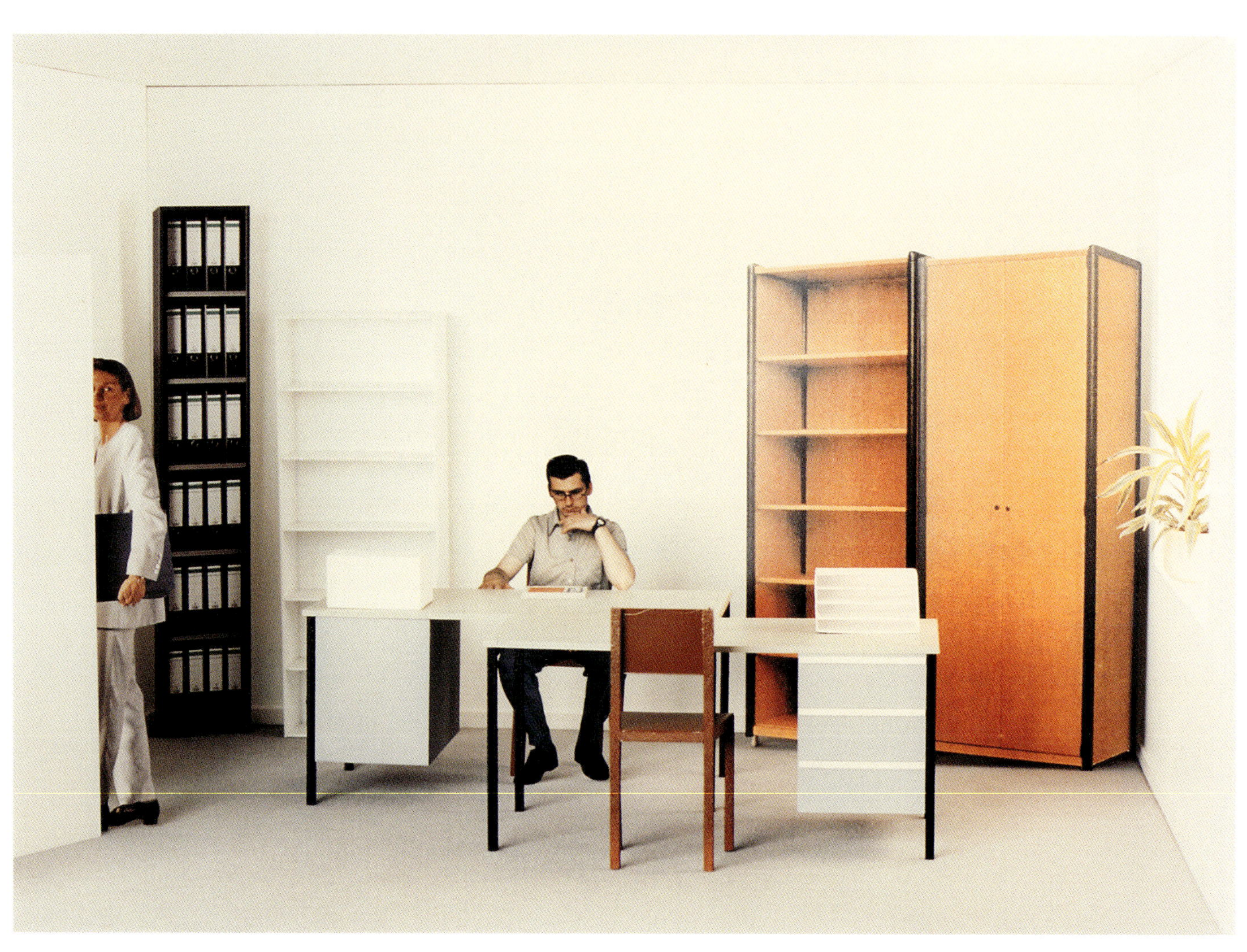

110 Office, 1998 111 Entrance Hall, 1998

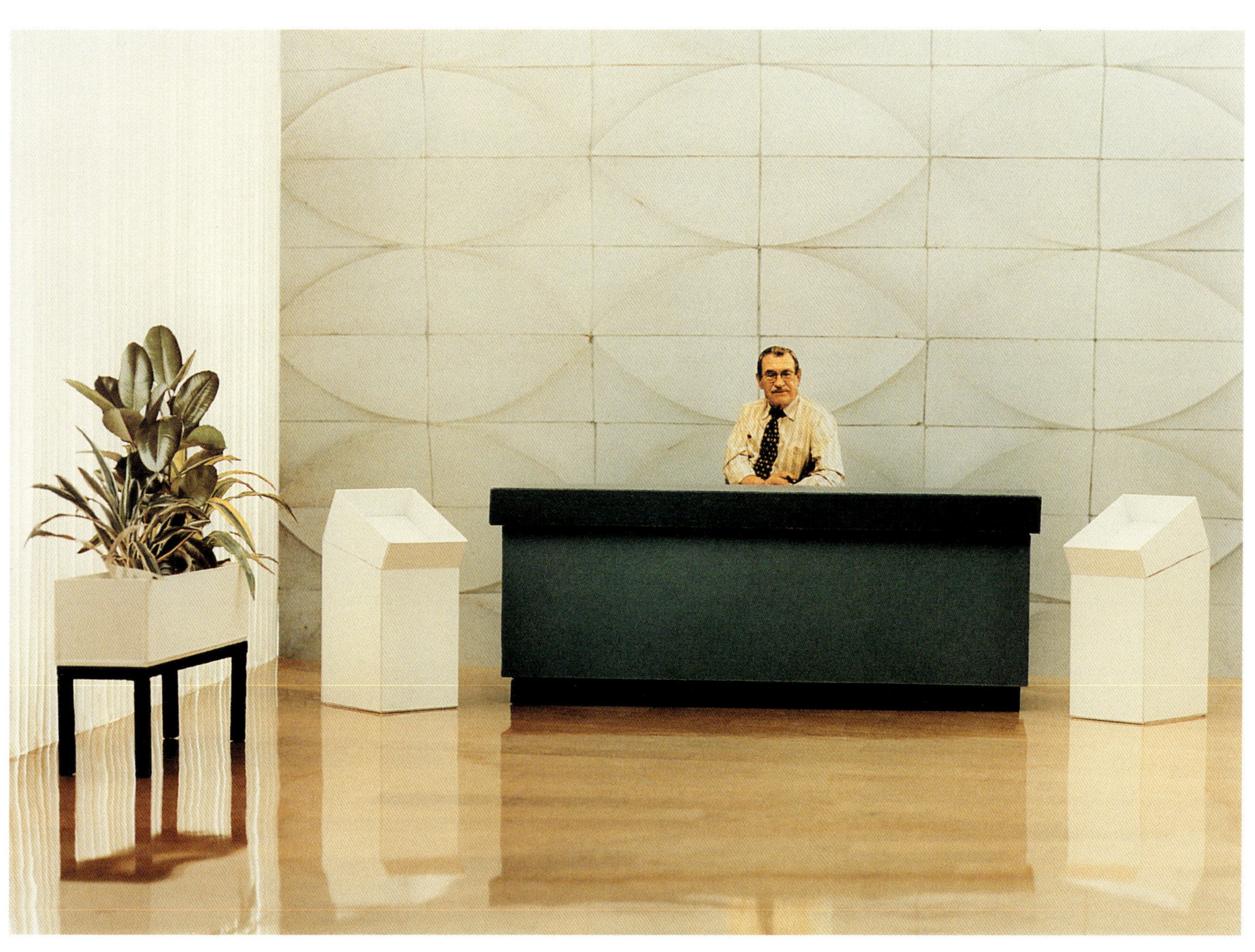

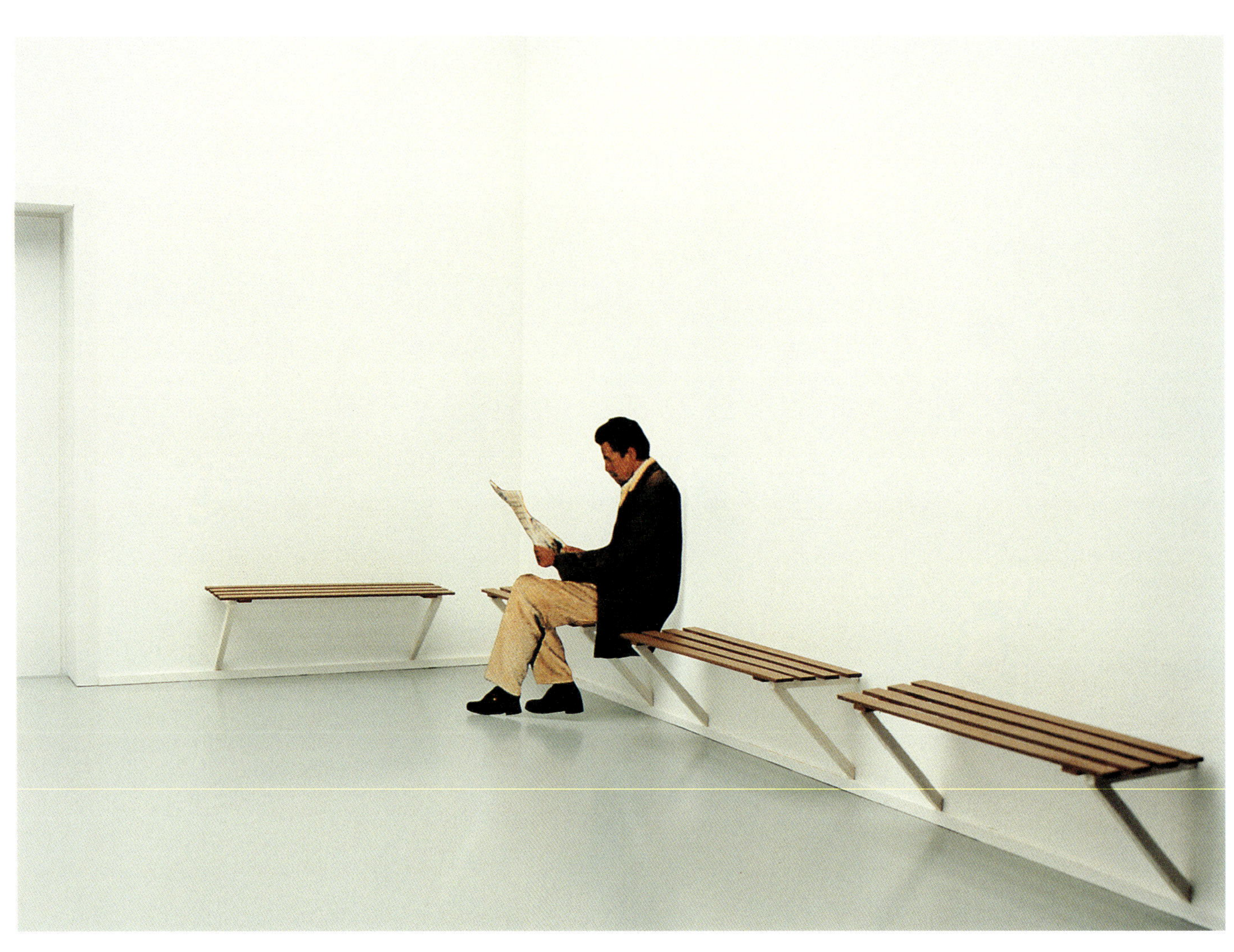

112 Man Reading Newspaper, 1998 113 Woodpanelling, 1998

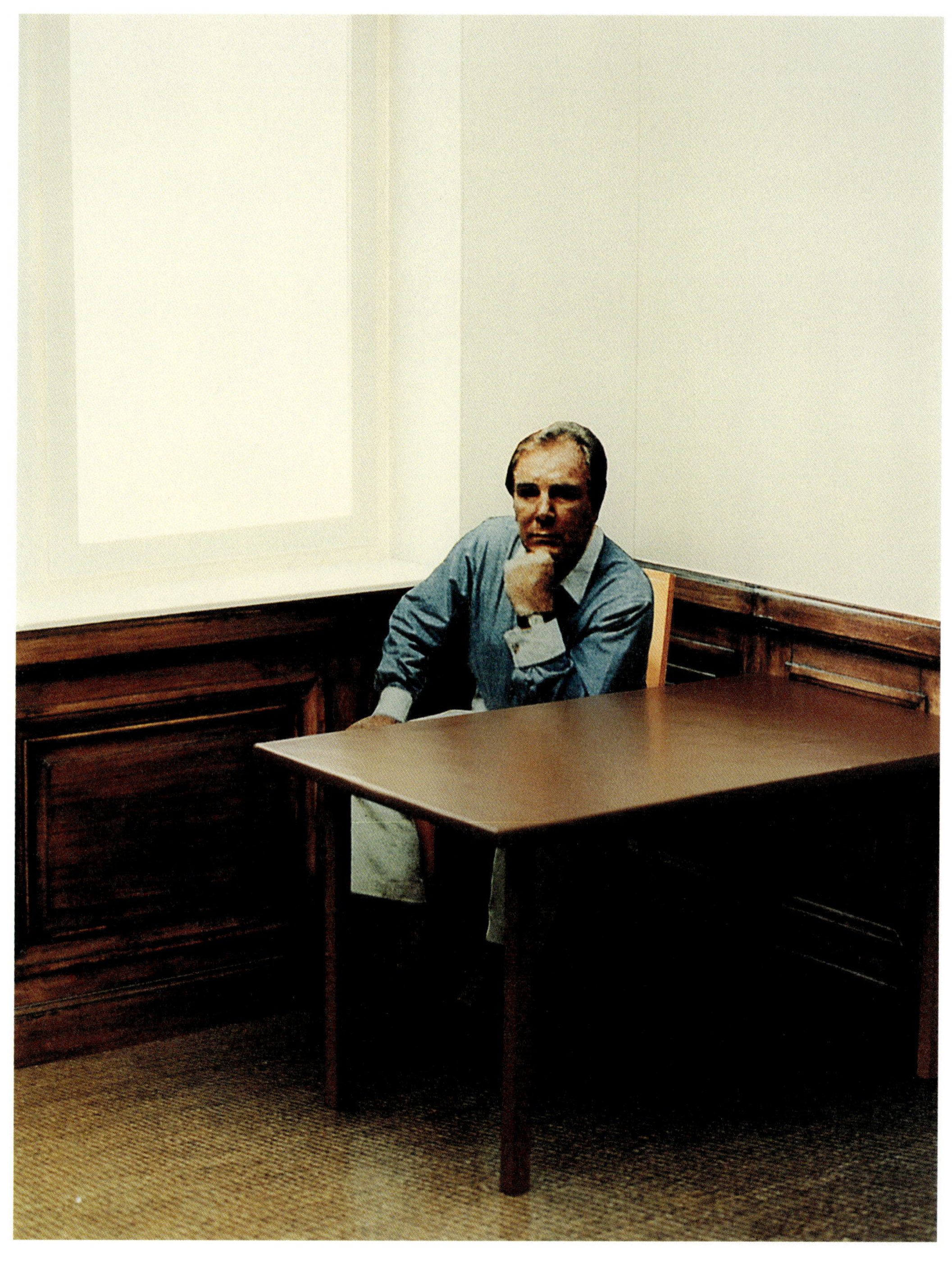

Heidi Specker

Heidi Specker photographs International Style architecture and superimposes a digital layer of pixelation on the images prior to making large format ink-jet prints. The resultant softening of the images highlights the structure as the dominant feature and deconstructs these icons of modernist design into patterned facades.

115 Speckergruppen, Berlin 1995/96

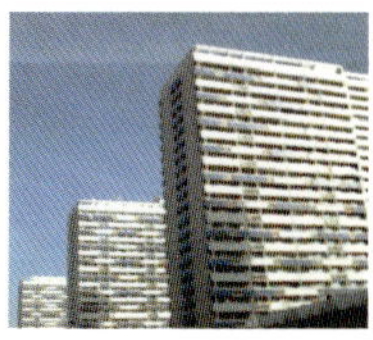
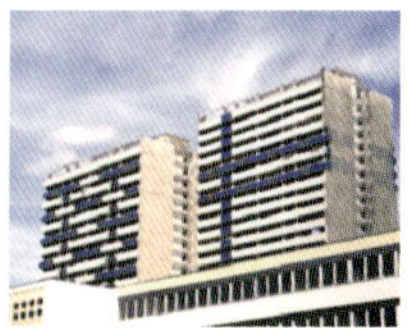
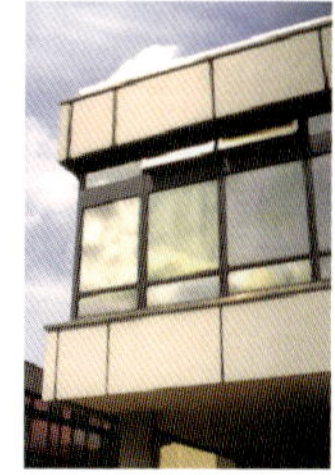
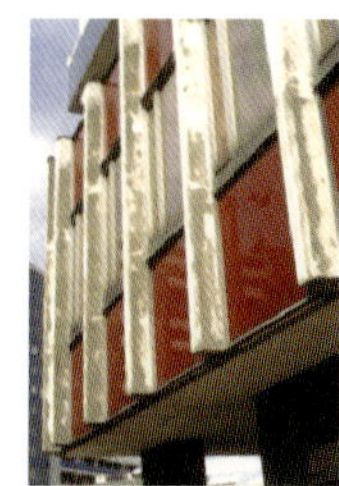
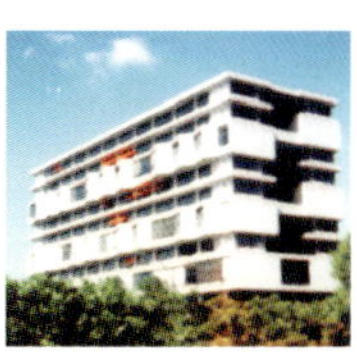
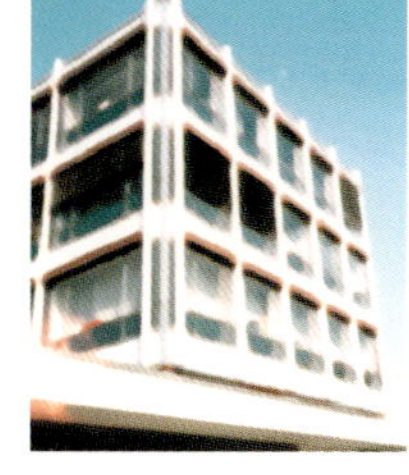
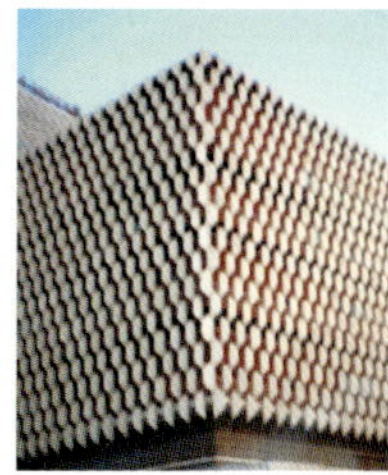
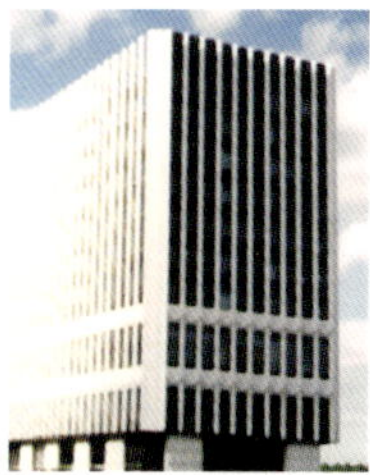
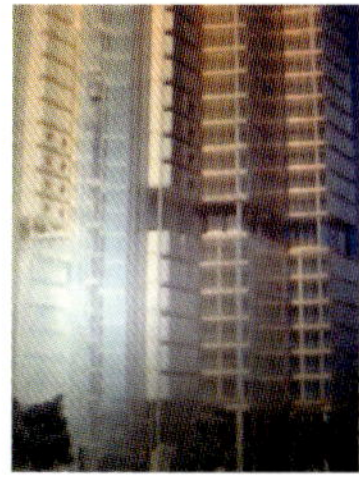
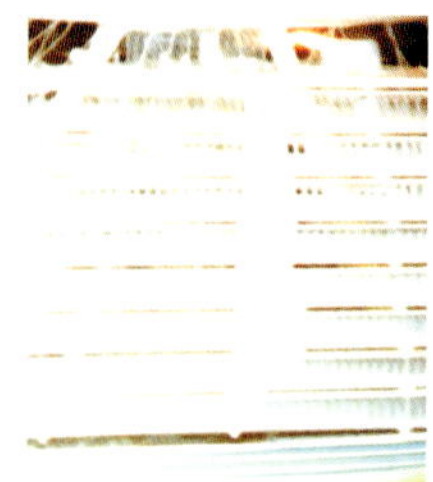
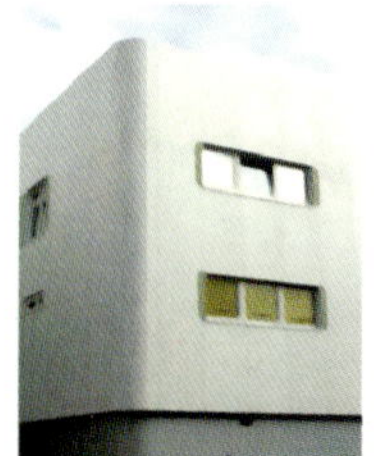
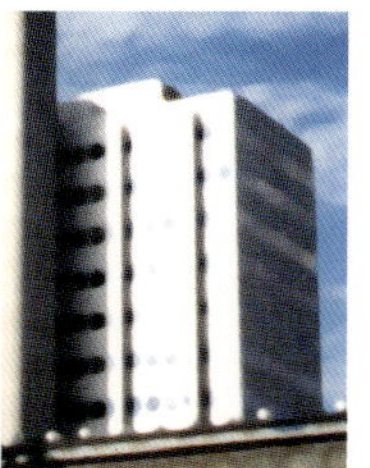
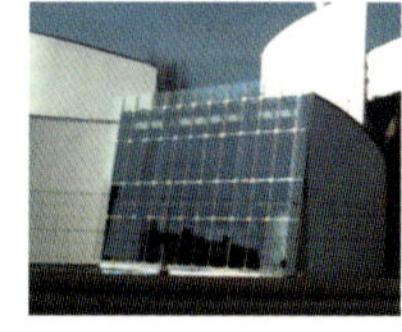
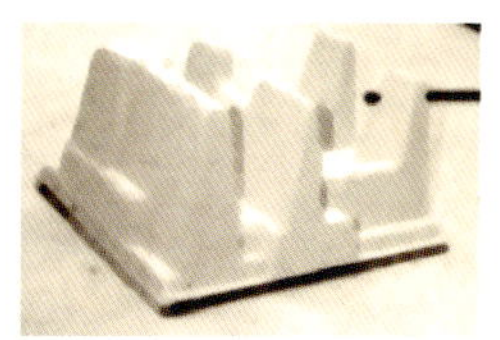
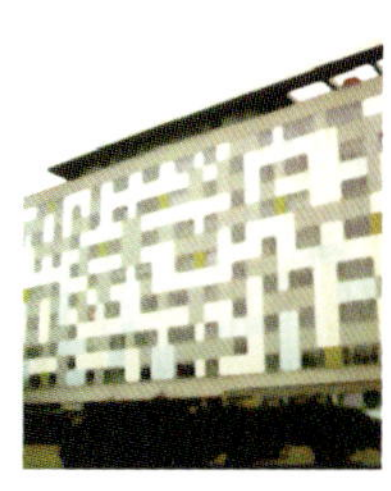
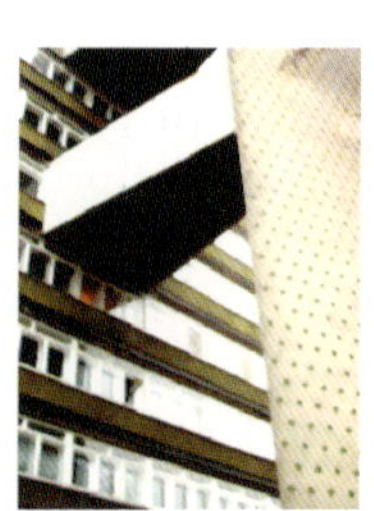
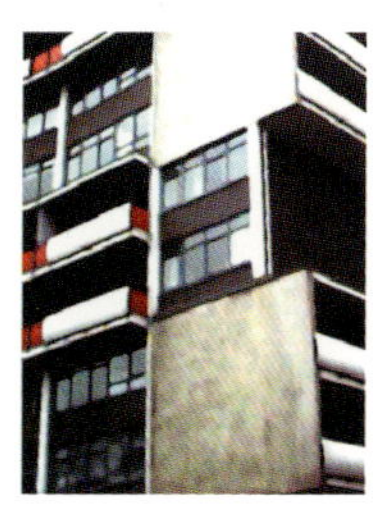
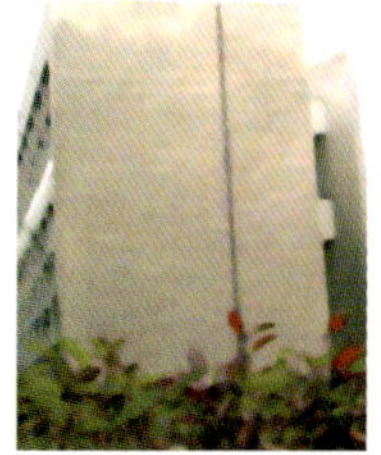

116 Teilchentheorie (Particle Theory), 1998

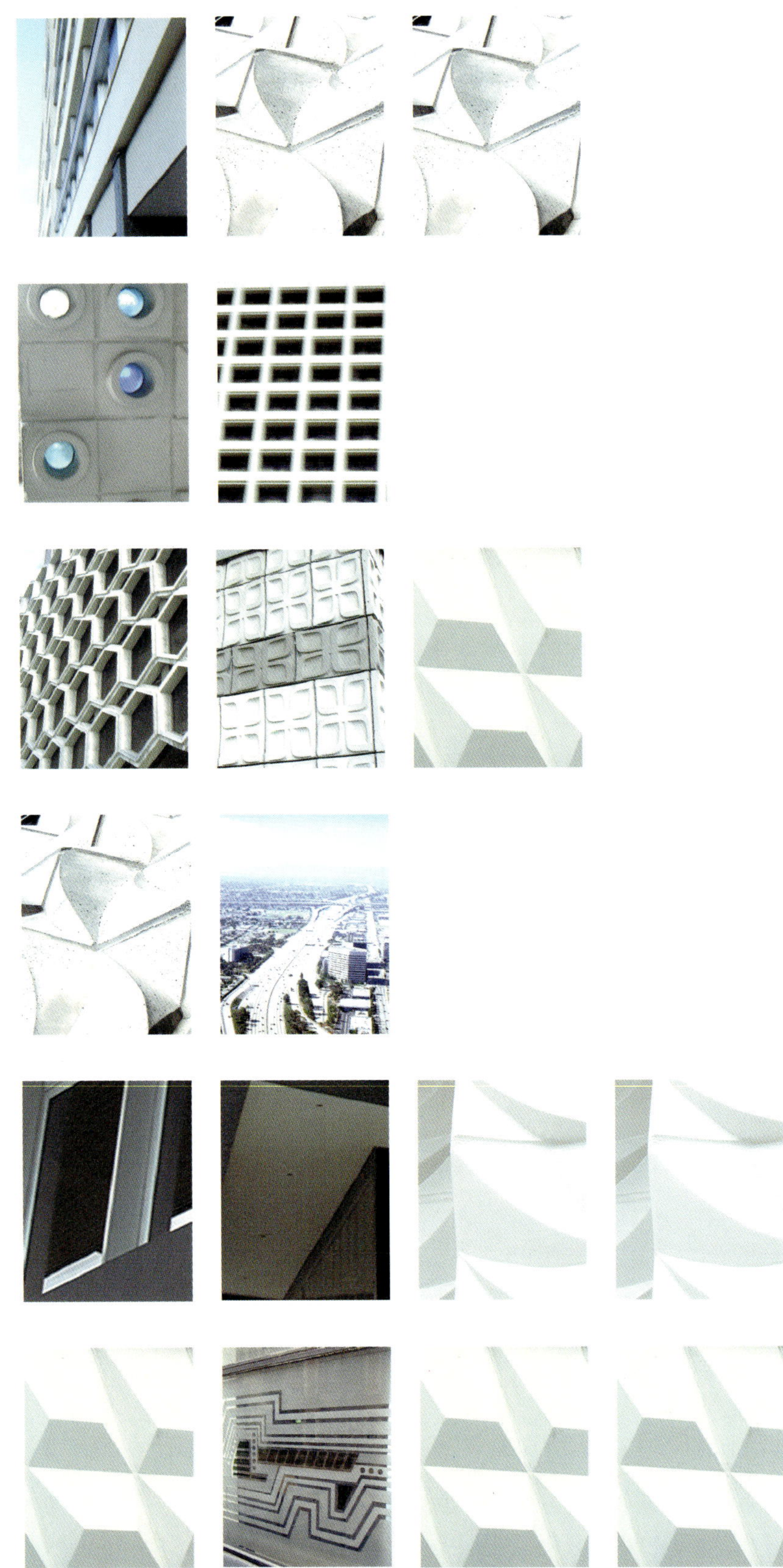

117 RGB Routine, 1997

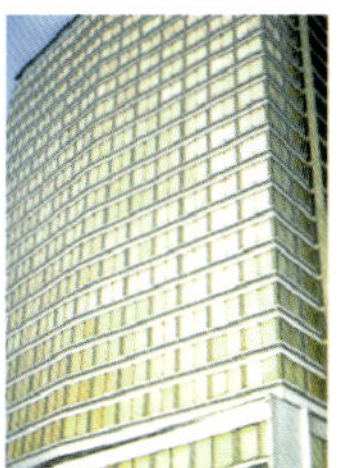
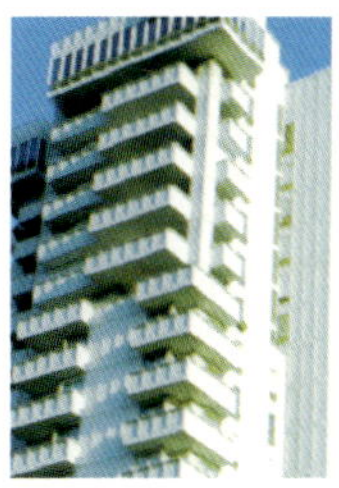
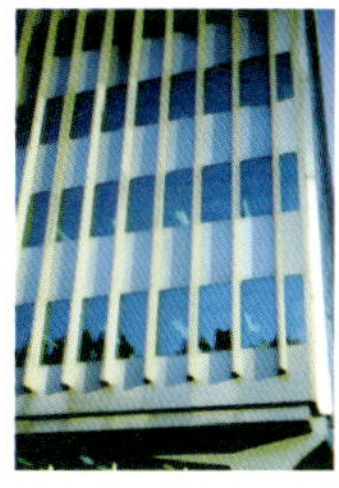
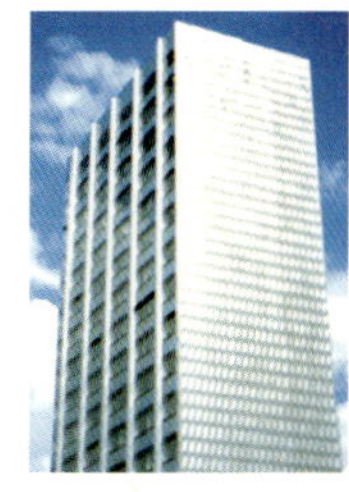
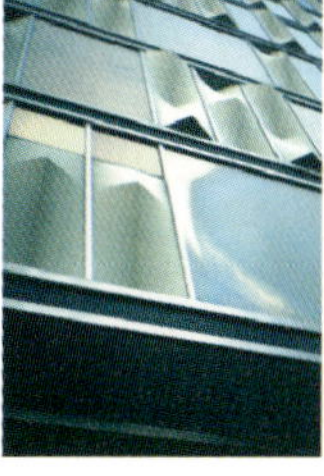
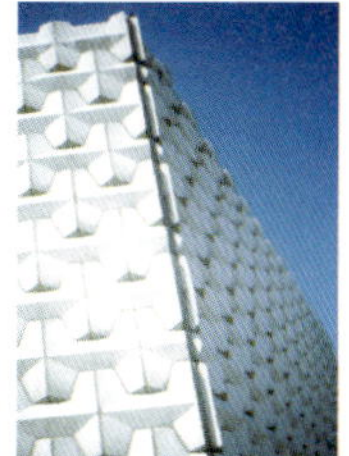

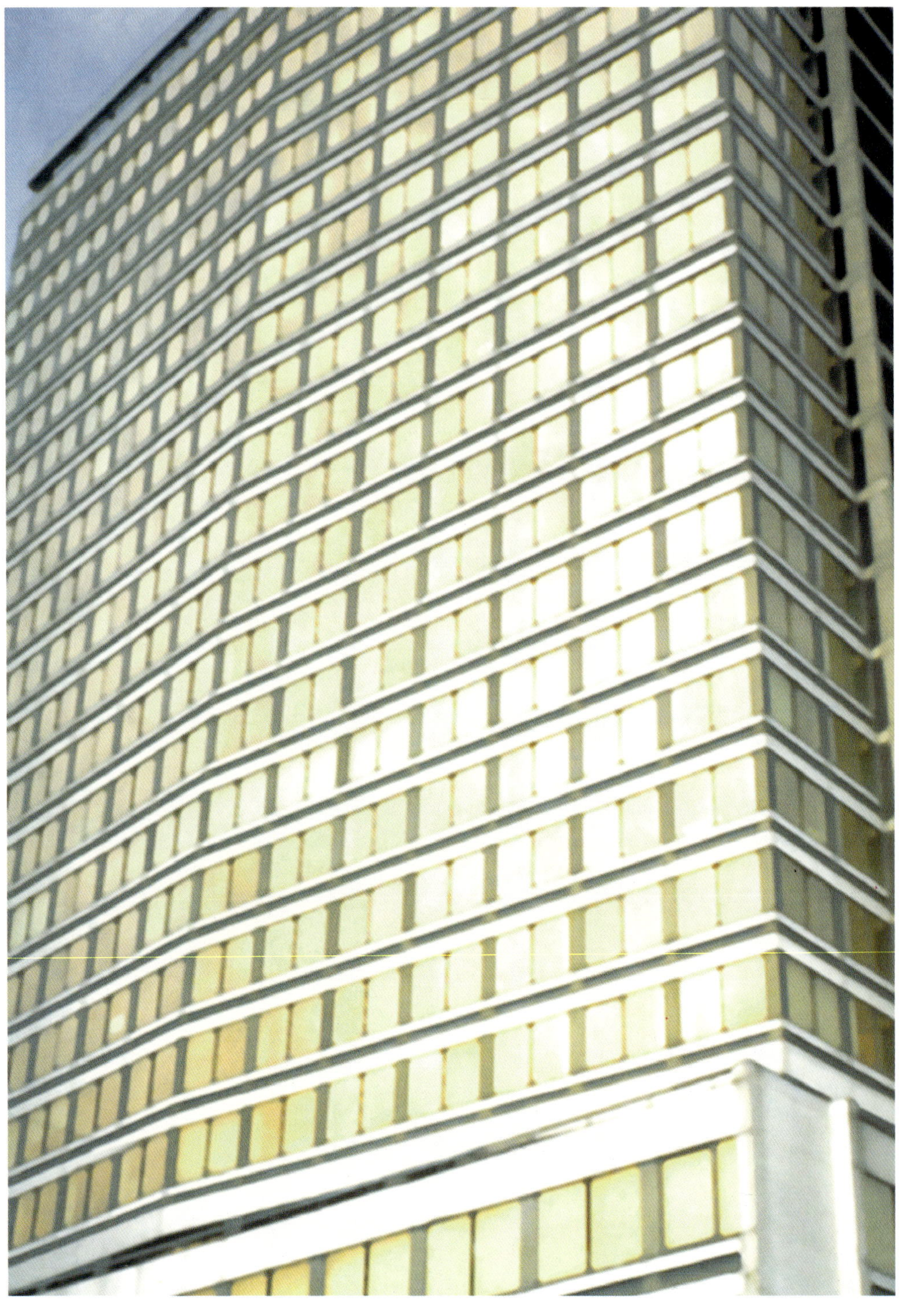

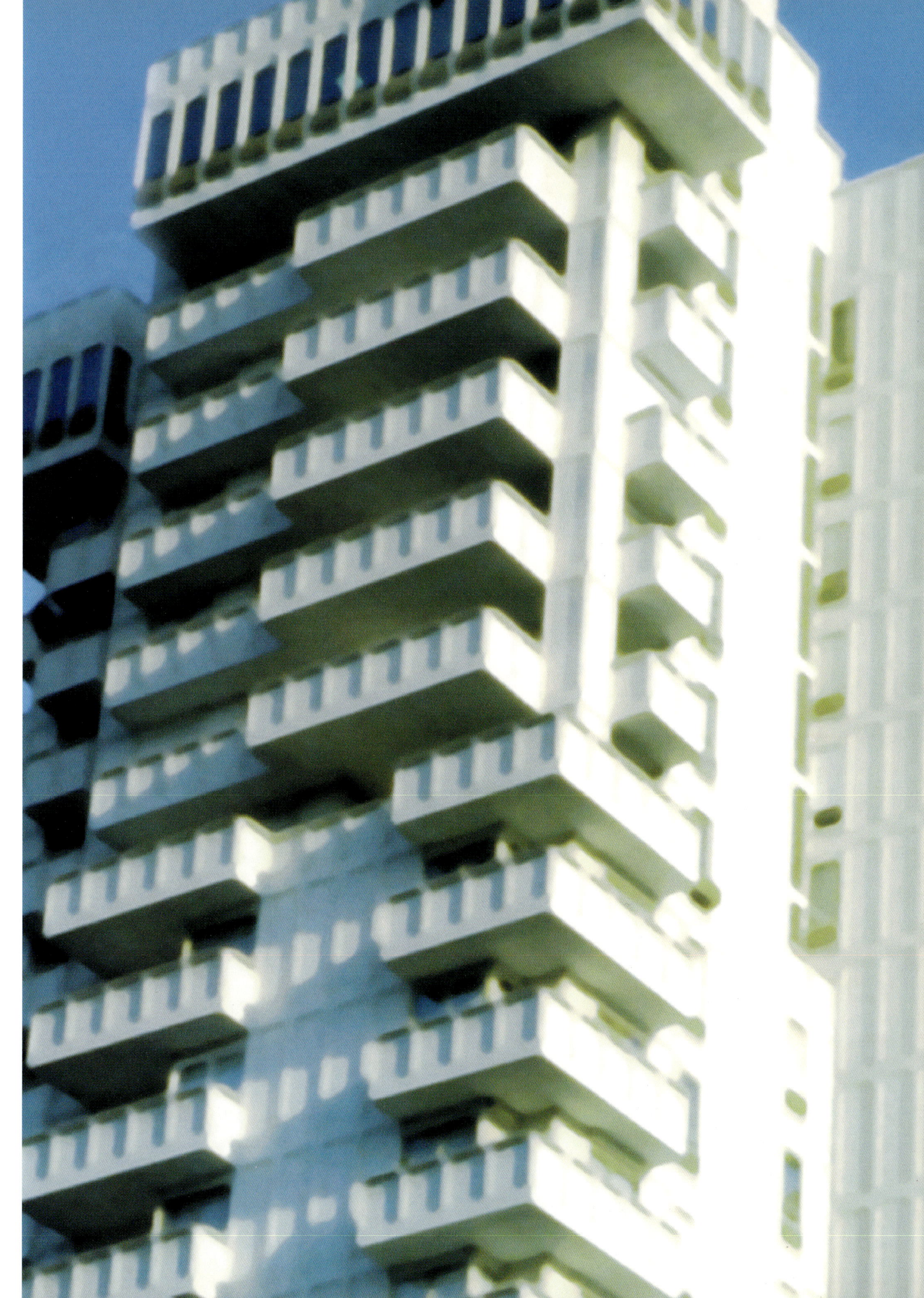

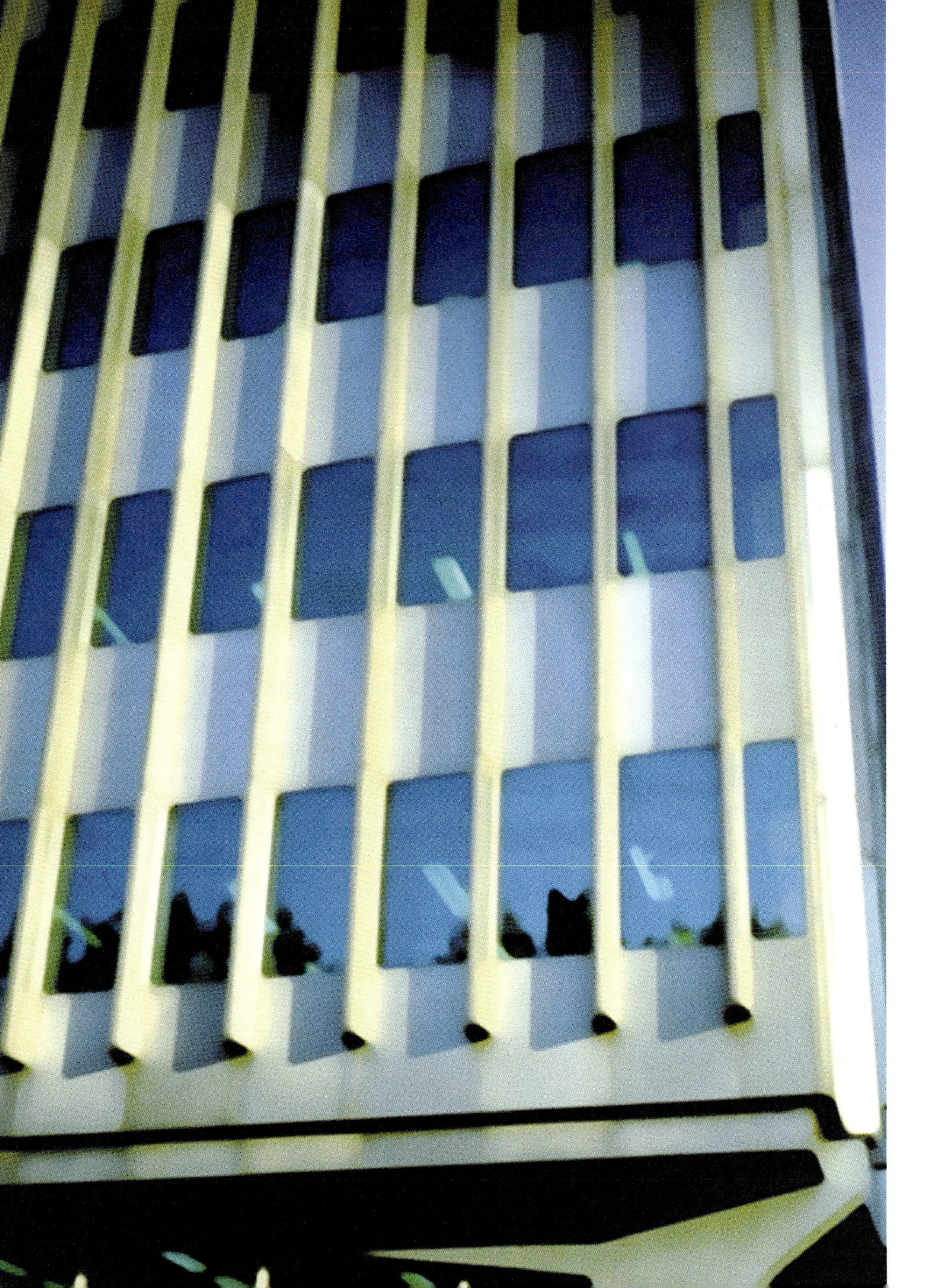

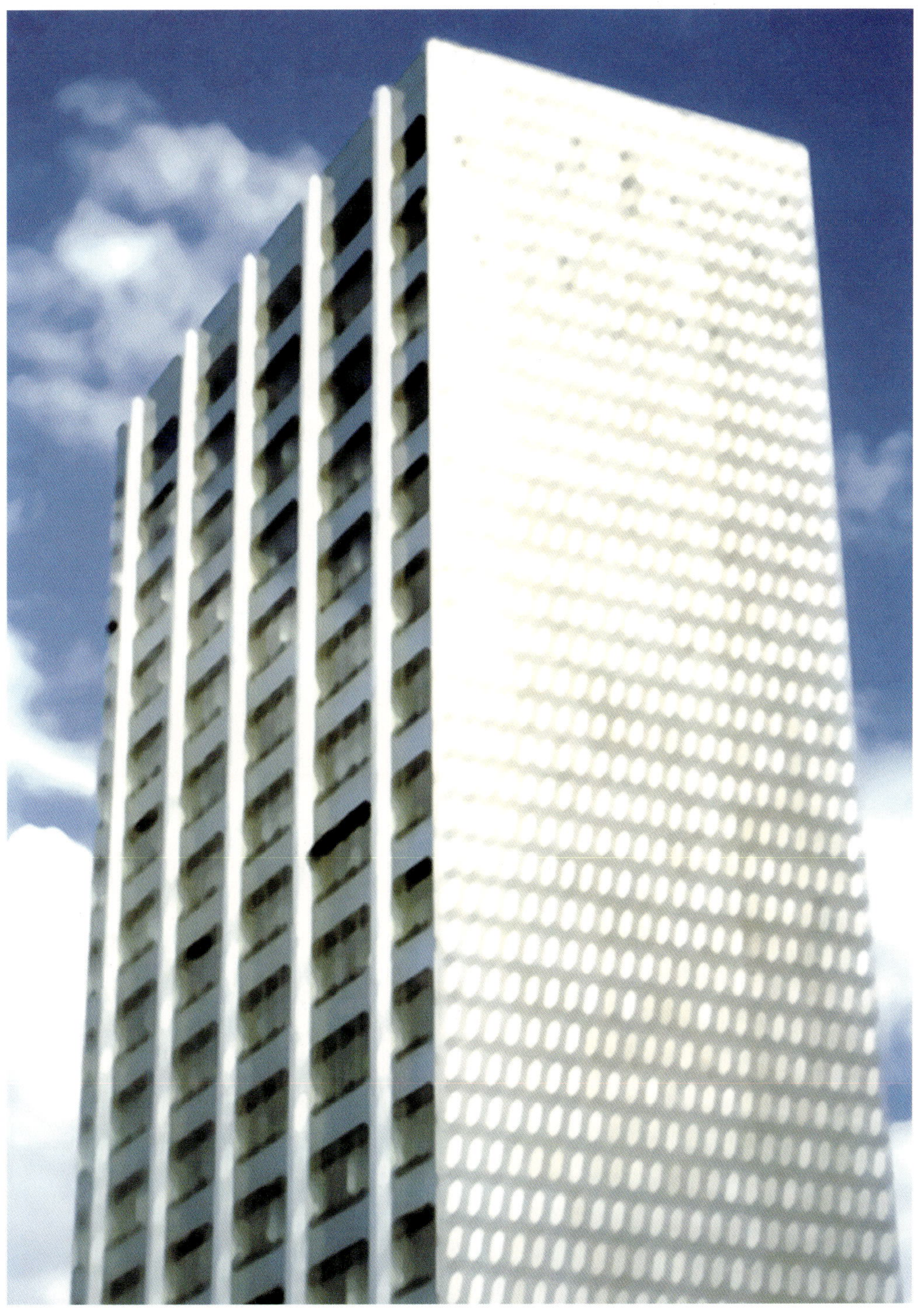

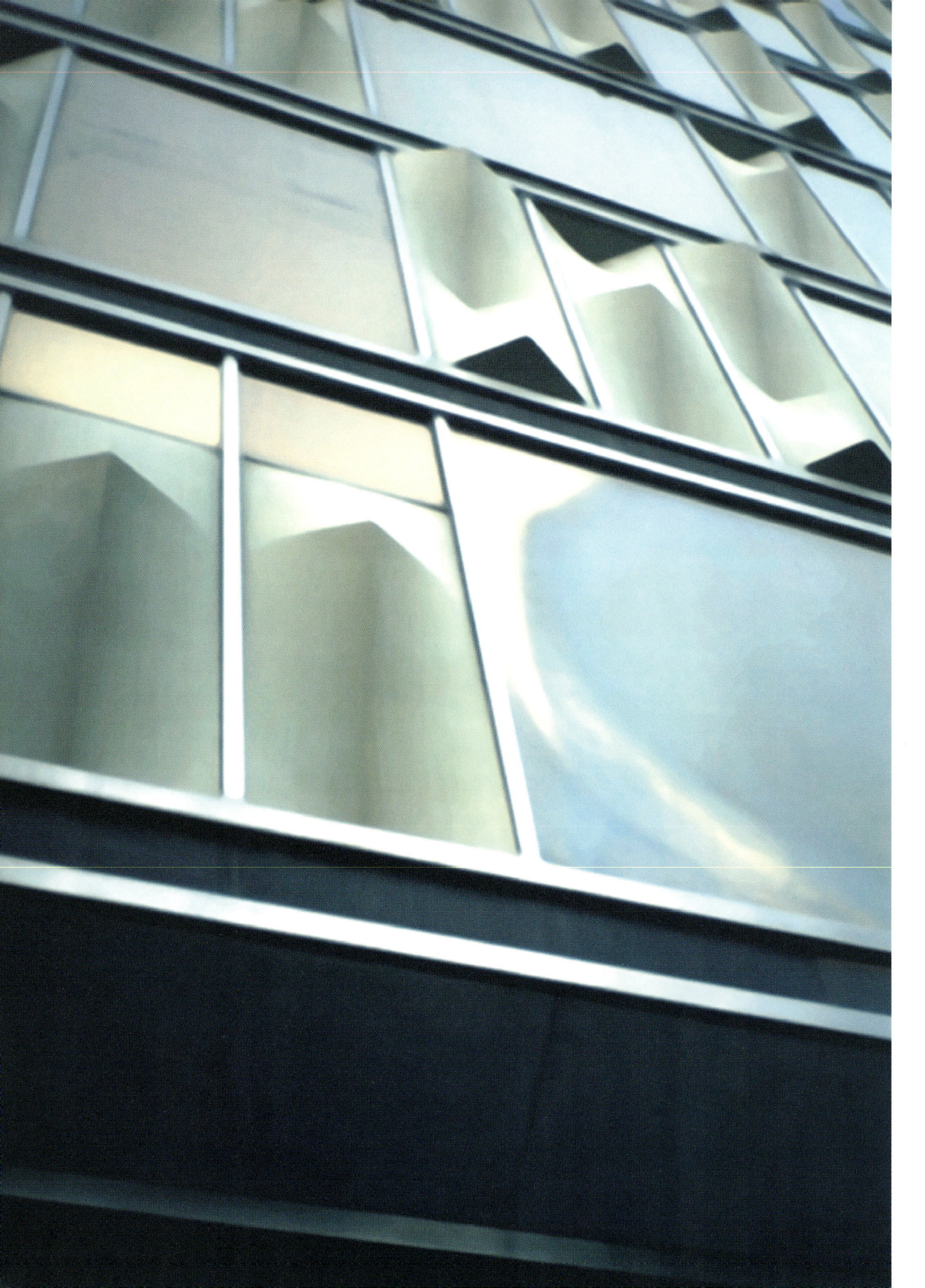

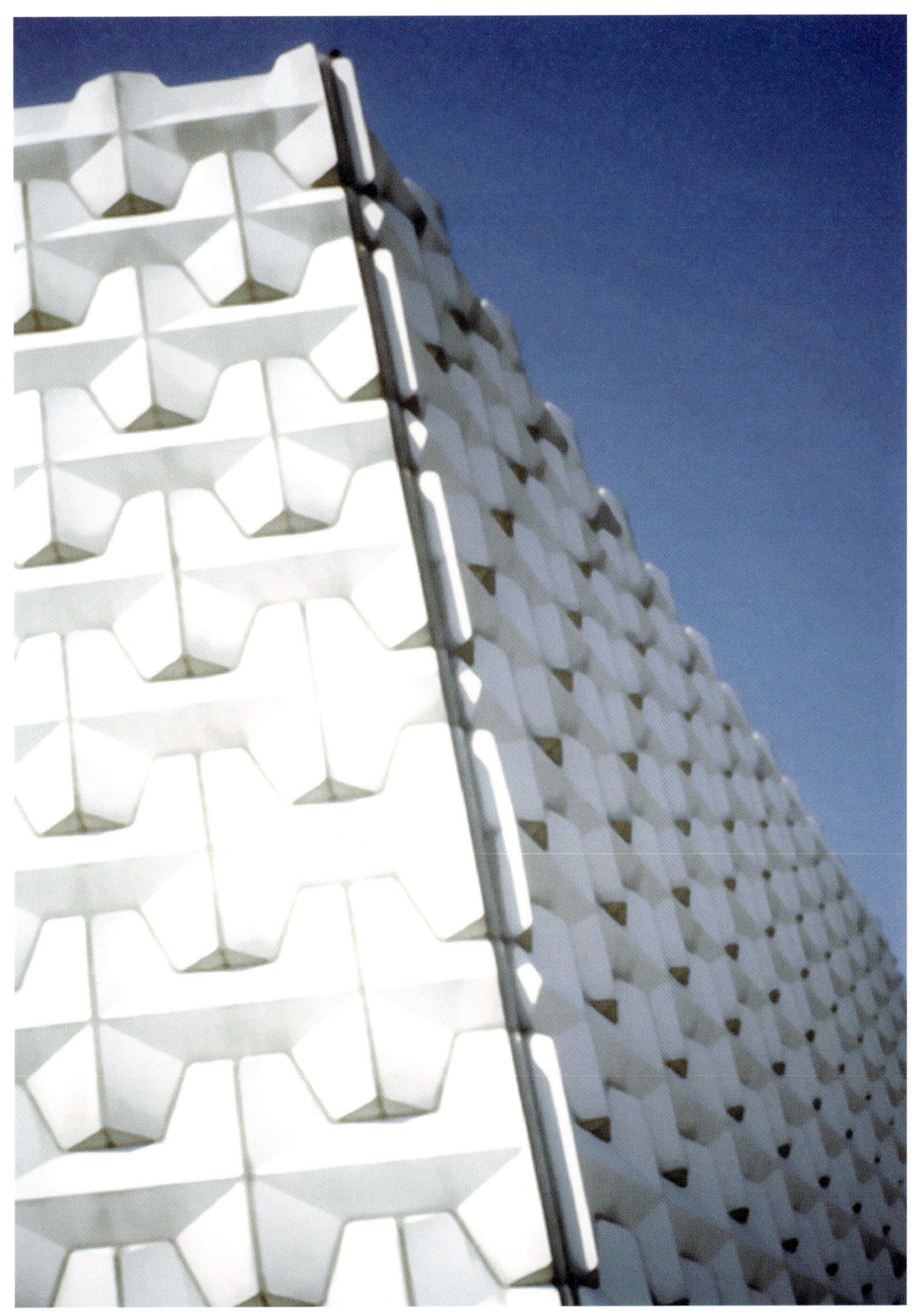

Susanne Brügger

Susanne Brügger's series Kartenwerk (Map Work) applies the scientific methods of cartography and documentary photography to an exploration of the relationship between objective representation and subjective sight. These rigid and often unsuitable methods for describing the environment influence and manipulate perception and ultimately represent templates for bureaucratic control.

Kartenwerk XIV, the Gustav series, dissects photographs of a circular survey of Paris from the Eiffel Tower using the cartographic methods of measurement applied by city planners to the urban landscape.

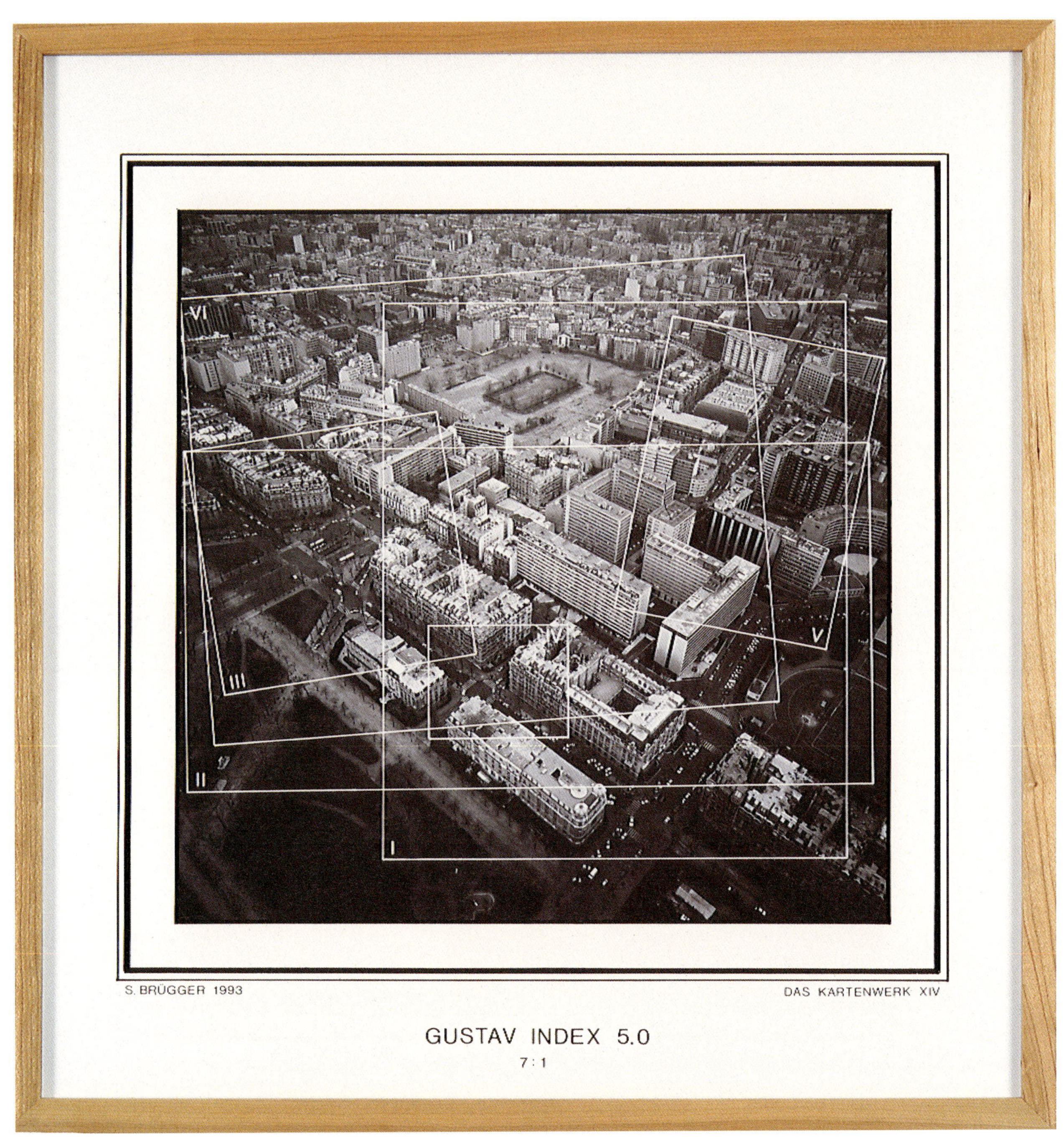

125 Gustav Index 5.0, 1993

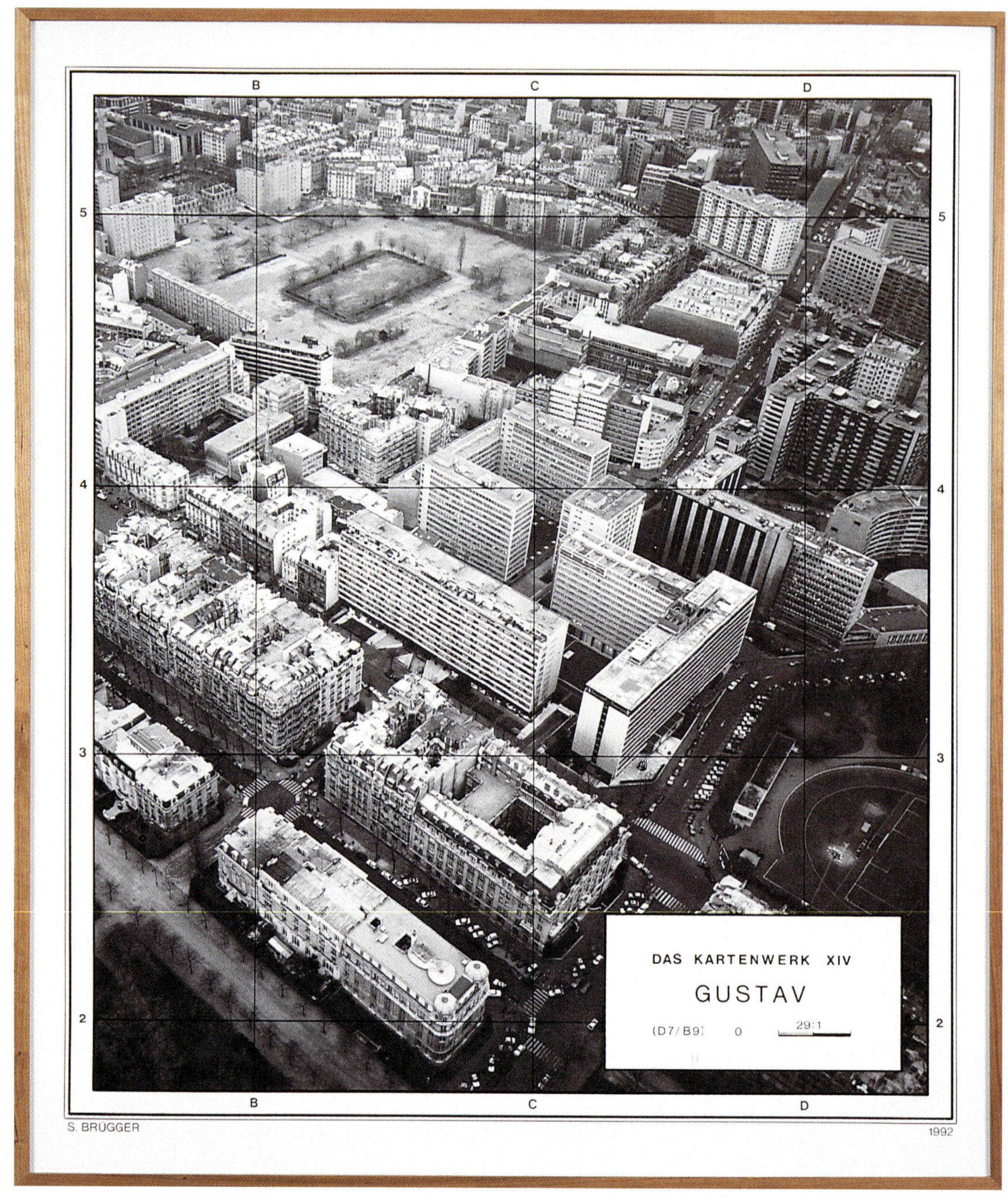
B
C
D
5
4
3
2
DAS KARTENWERK XIV
GUSTAV
(D7/B9)
0
29:1
S. BRUGGER
1992

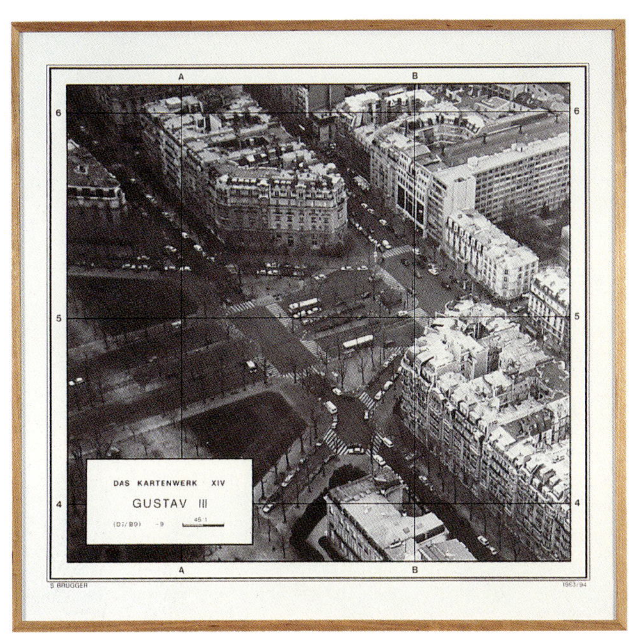

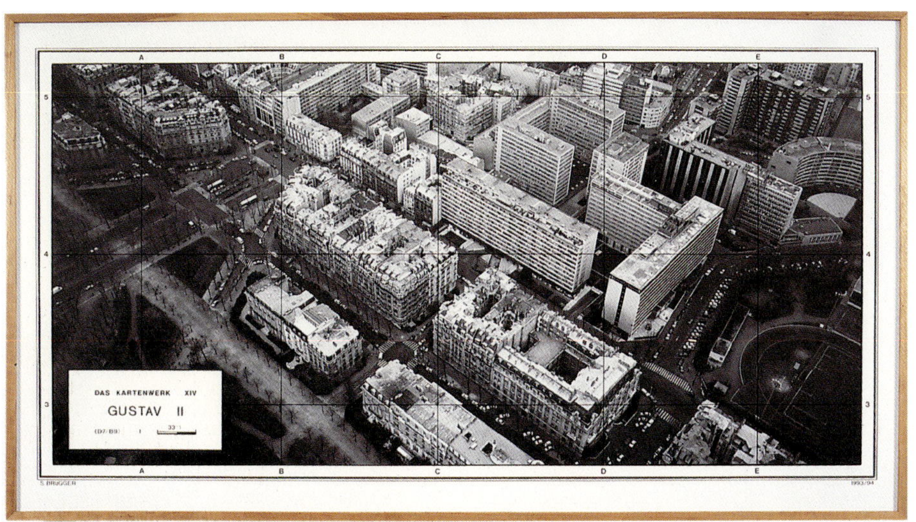

126 Gustav, 1992 127 Gustav II, 1994; Gustav III, 1994

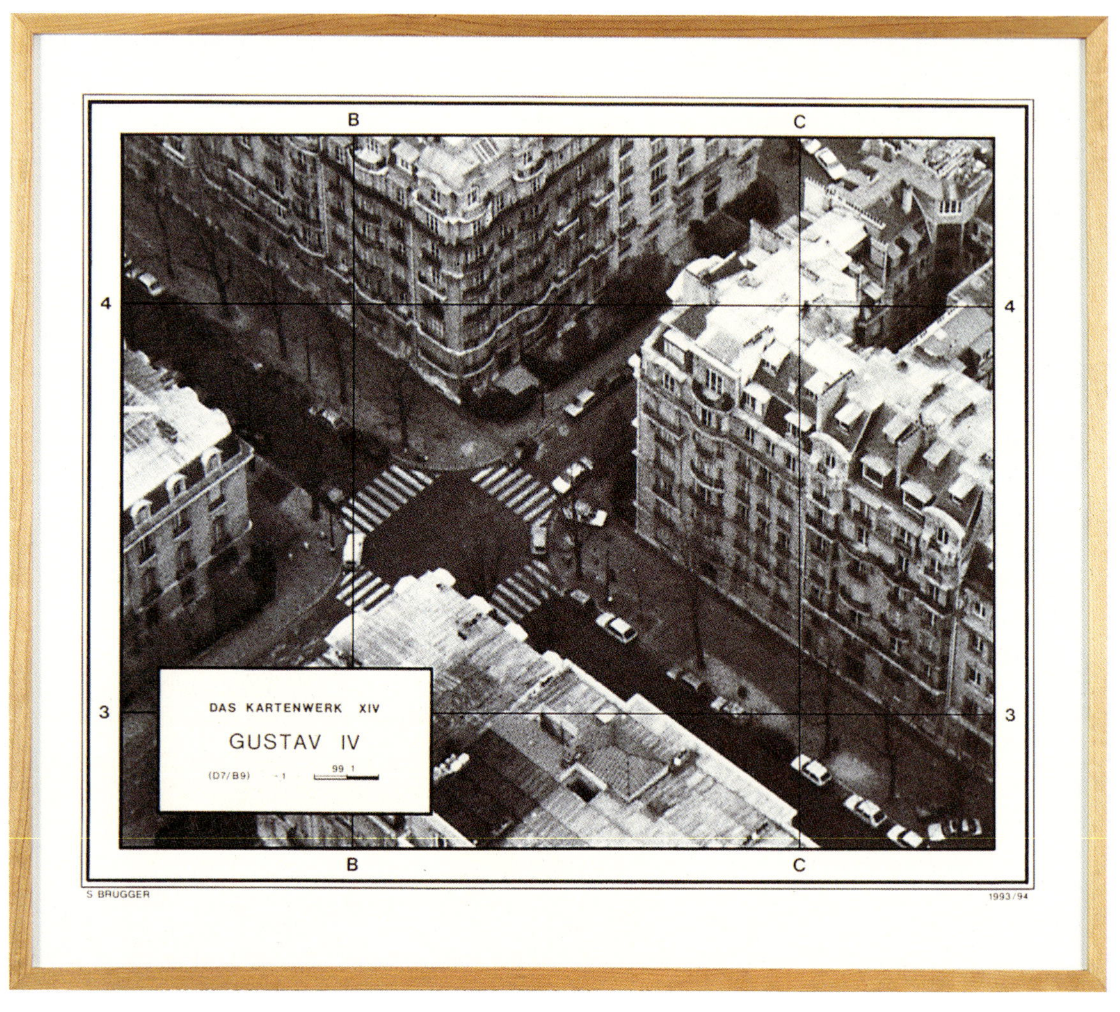
B
C
4
4
DAS KARTENWERK XIV
GUSTAV IV
(D7/B9) -1 99 1
3
3
B
C
S BRUGGER
1993/94

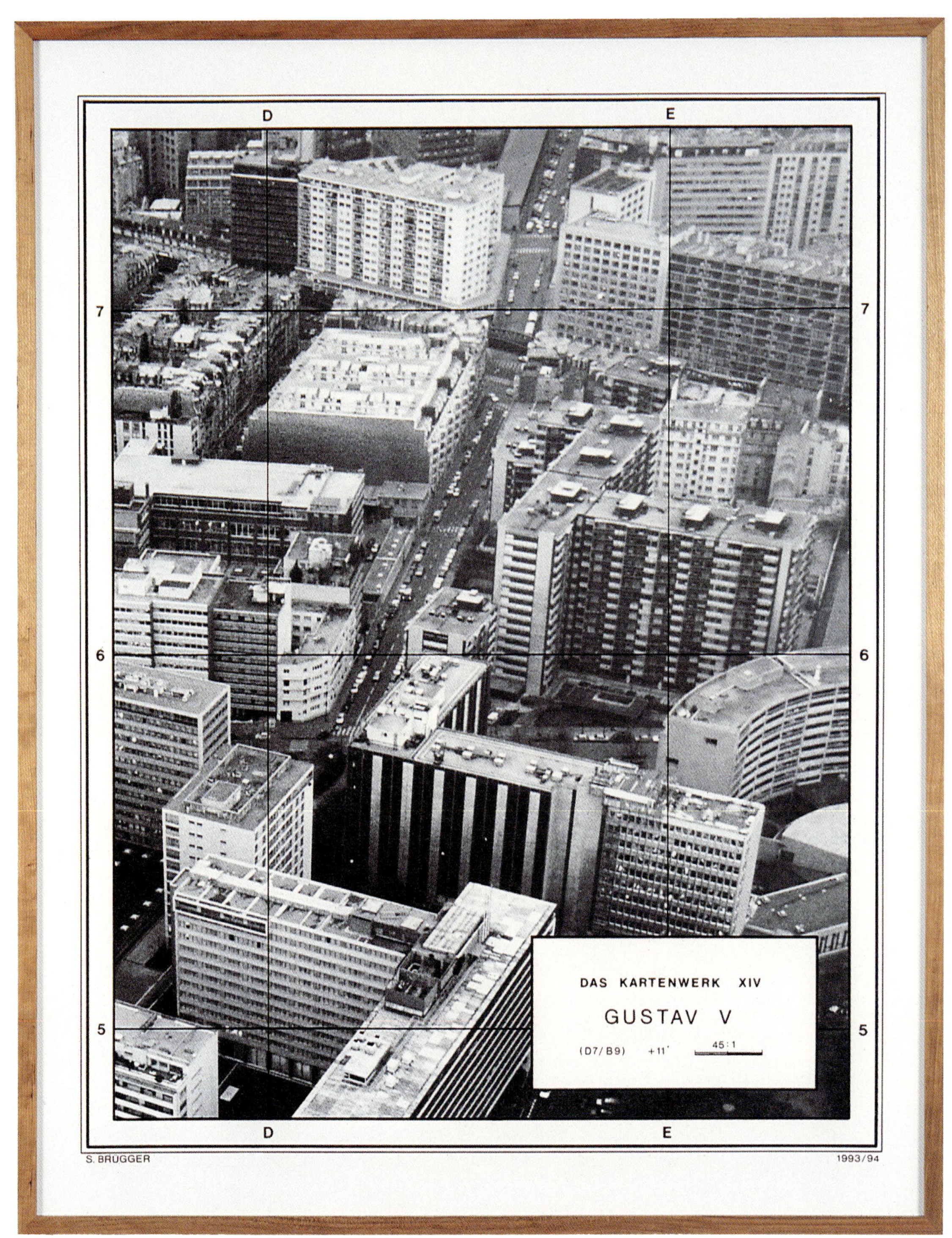

128 Gustav IV, 1992 129 Gustav V, 1994

130 – 131 Atlas, 1962 – 1998: Städte/Cities, 1968, Plate Nos. 113 (above) and 107 (below)

Gerhard Richter

In 1962 Gerhard Richter began collecting personal and mass media photographs and illustrations. Ten years later he collated some of these for the first exhibition of Atlas. Combined by reference to content and form, the 'found' photographs were the source of many of his photo paintings.

'I was attracted by those dead cities and Alps, which in both cases were stony wastes, arid stuff. It was an attempt to convey content of a more universal kind.' Gerhard Richter.

Interview with Benjamin H. D. Buchloh, 1986, in Gerhard Richter, *The Daily Practice of Painting Writings 1962–1993* (London, 1995) p. 146

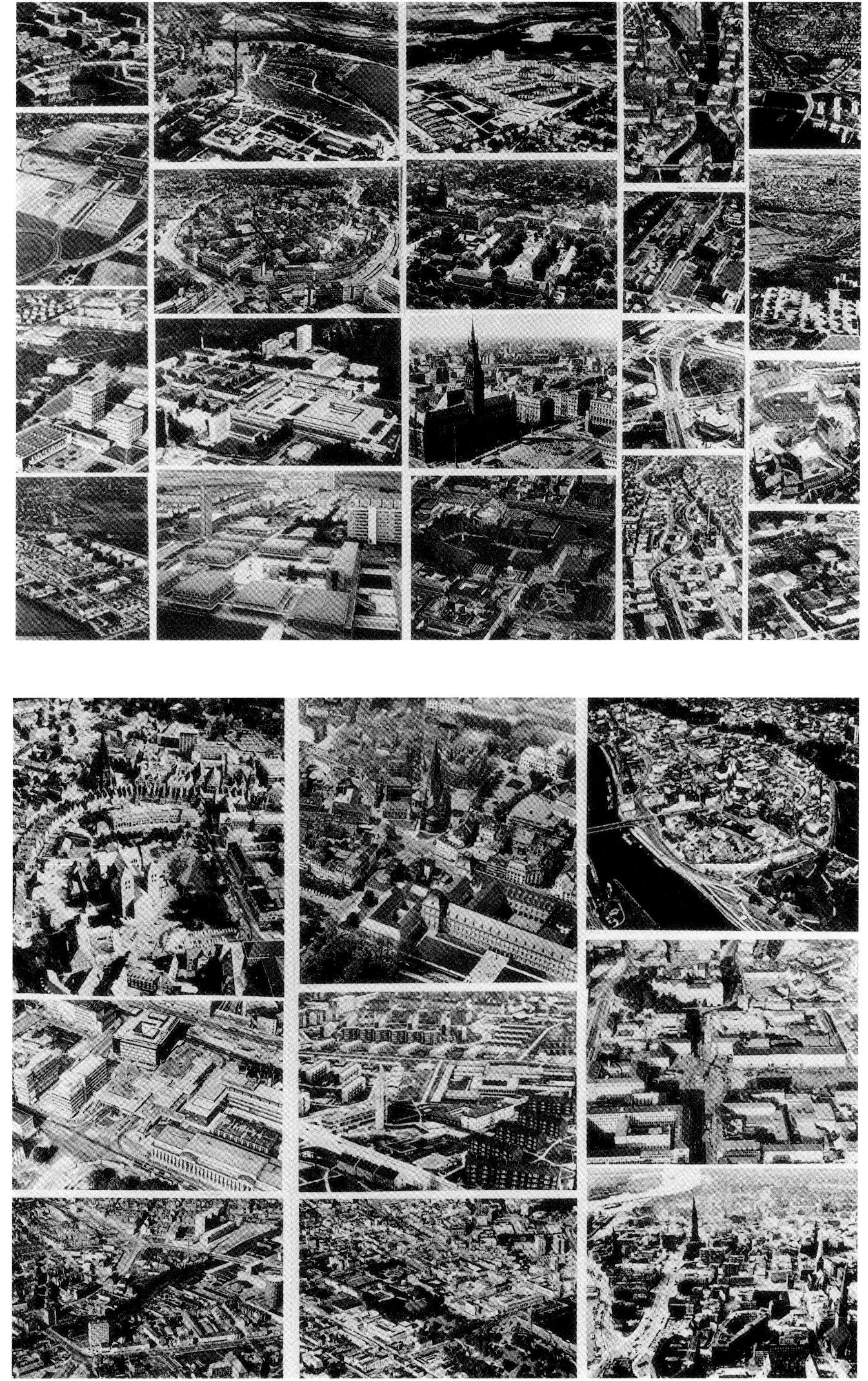

Thomas Struth has been photographing streets and apartment buildings since he began his practice in the mid 1970s. His first series of images of 1950s German architecture addressed issues of reconstruction and preservation. Later work has ranged from deserted street scenes in global cities to peopled public sites in the Far East. Struth considers architecture to be a signifier of a culture's values, and his photographs of public spaces present a reading of sites of social interaction.

Thomas Struth

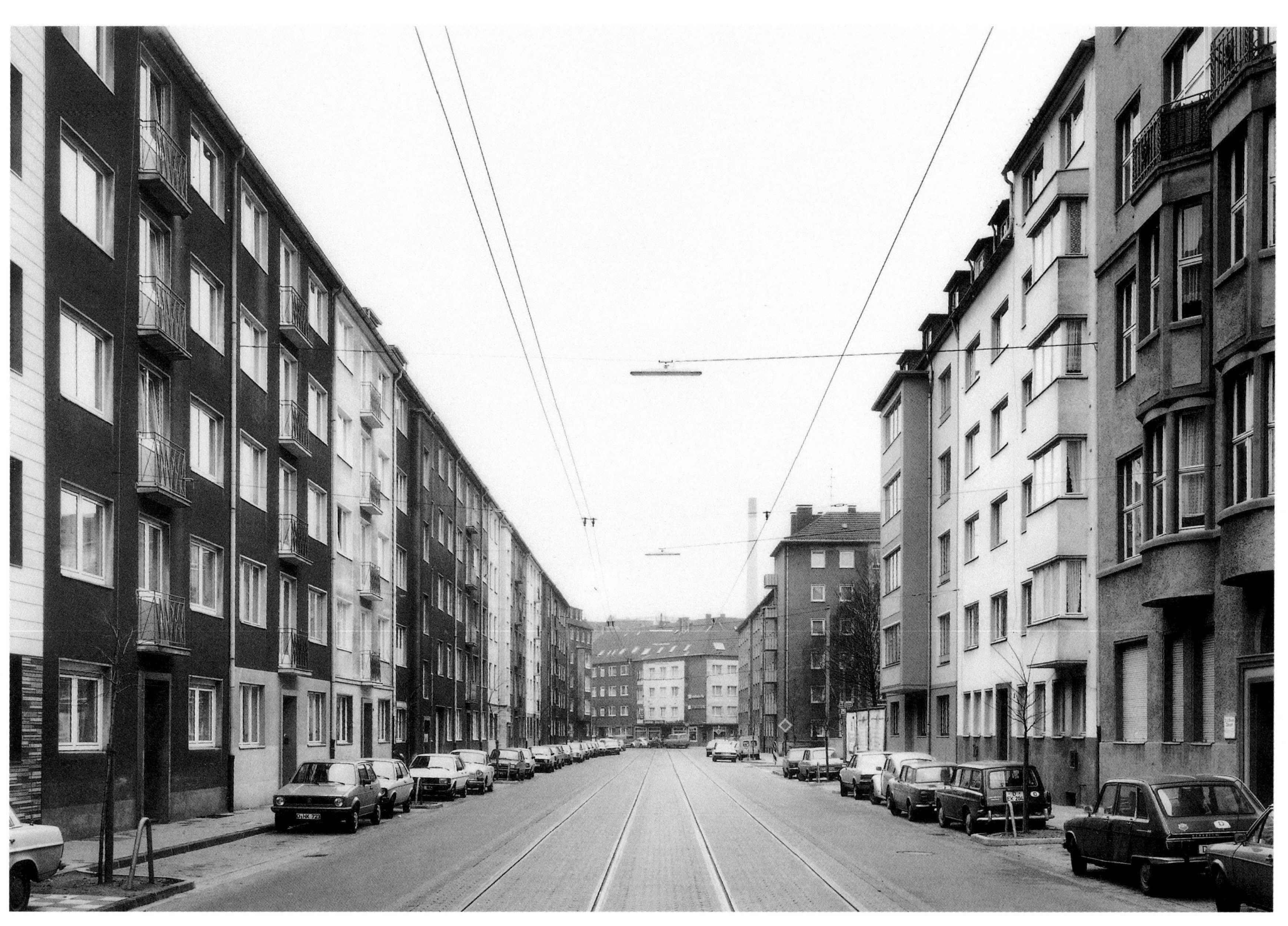

133 Sommerstraße, Düsseldorf, 1980

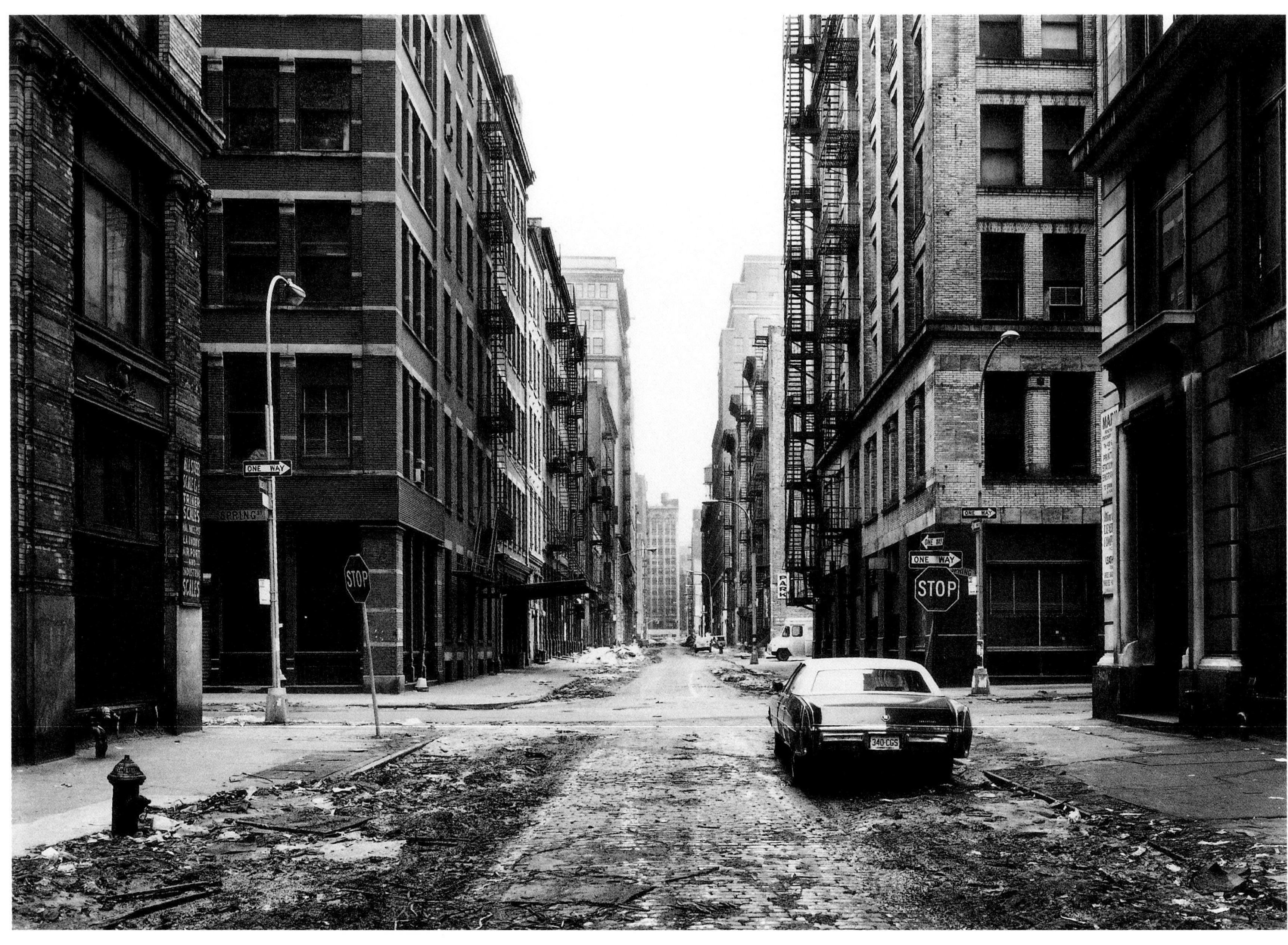
ONE WAY
STOP
ONE WAY
STOP

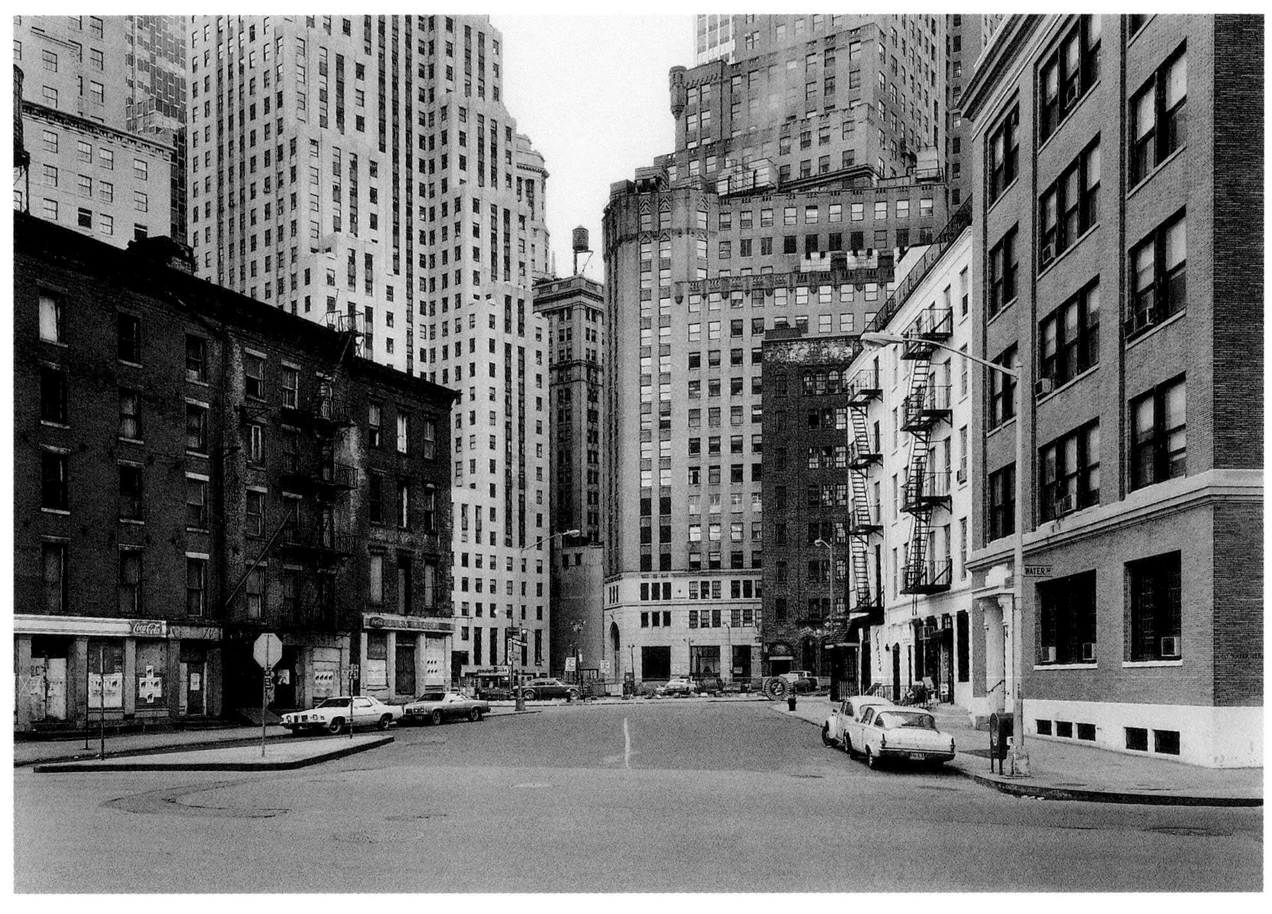

134 Crosby Street, New York/Soho, 1978 135 Coenties Slip, New York/Wall Street, 1978

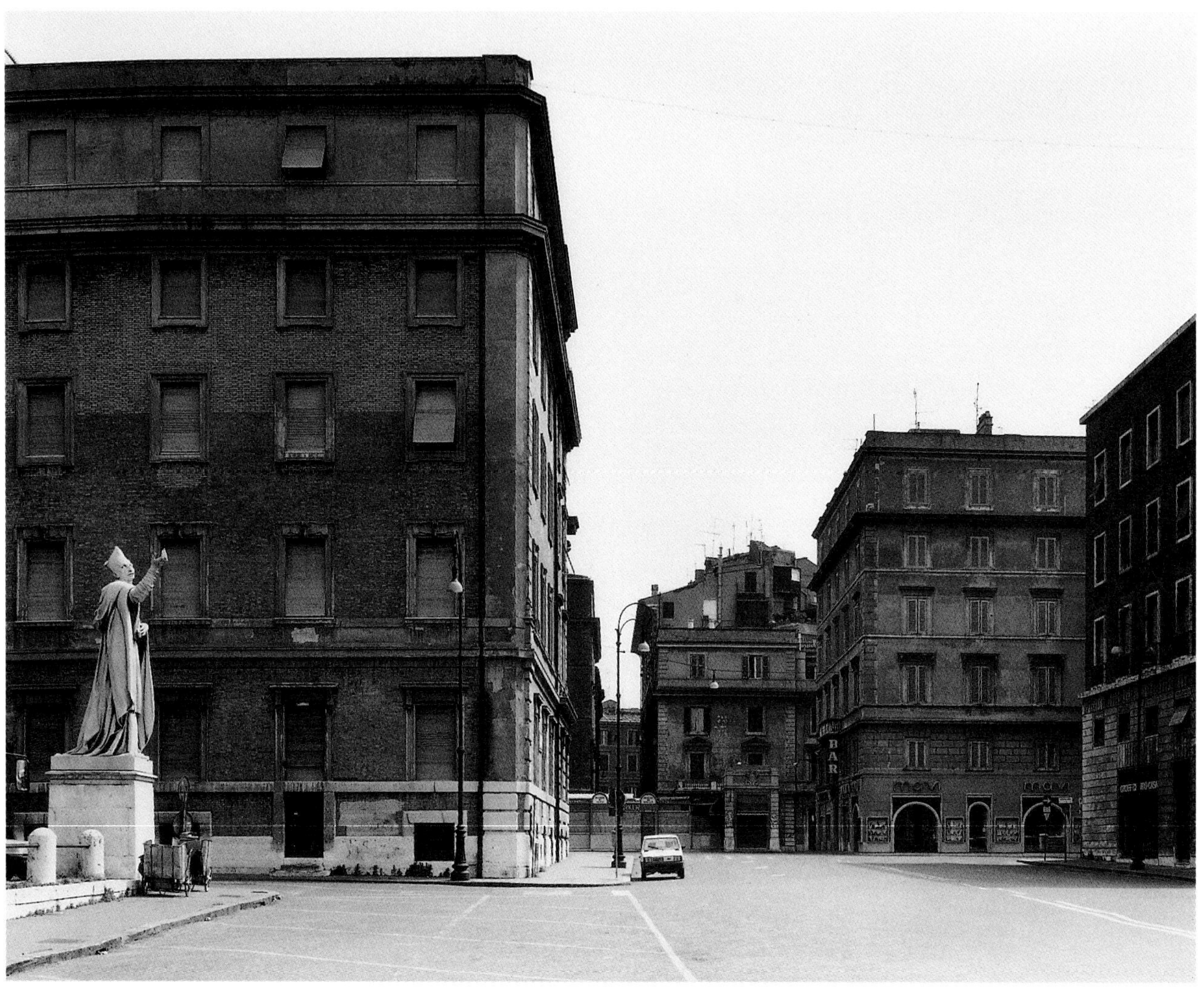
BAR

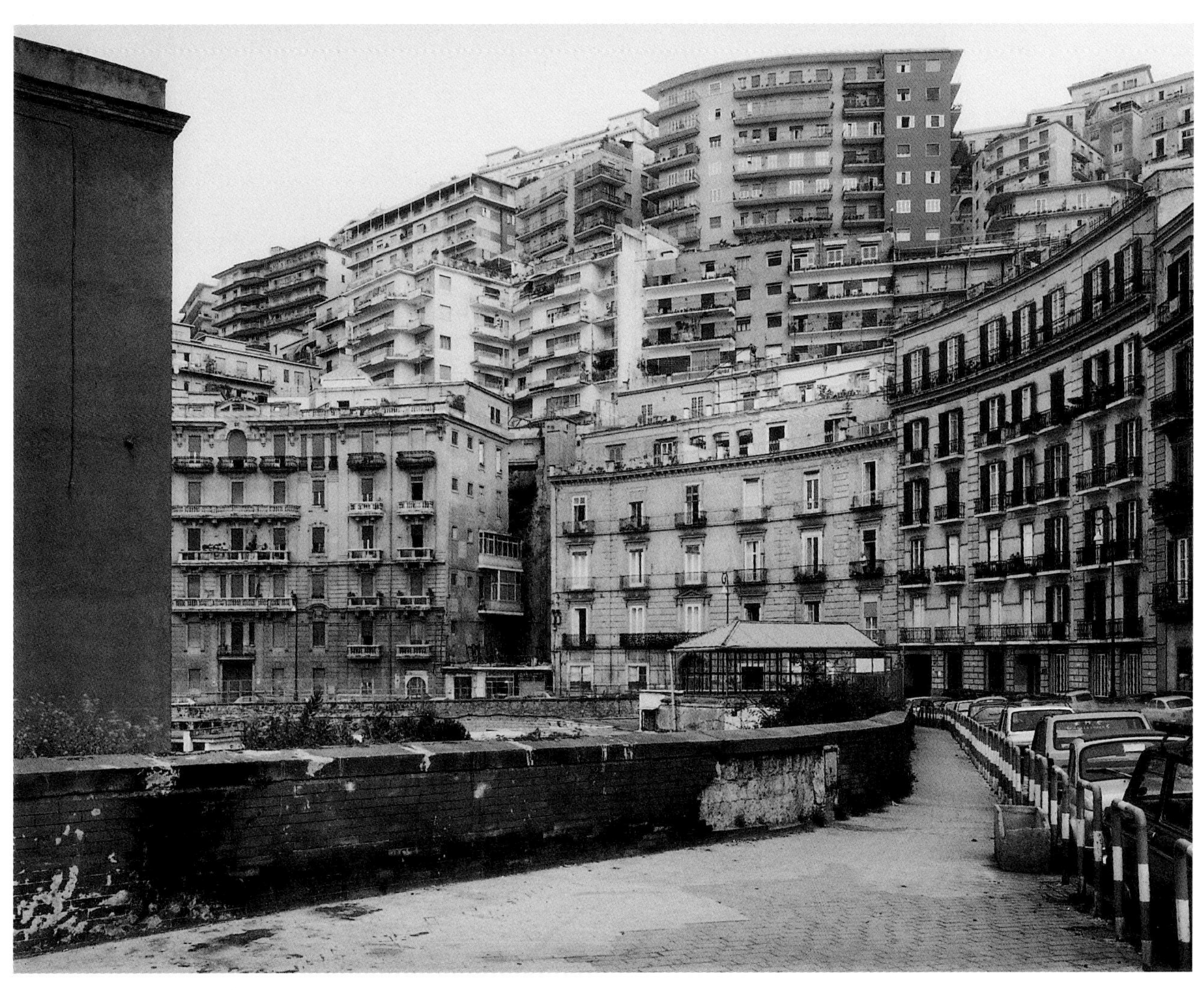

136 Piazza del Augusto Imperatore, Rome, 1984 137 Corso Vittorio Emanuele, Naples, 1989

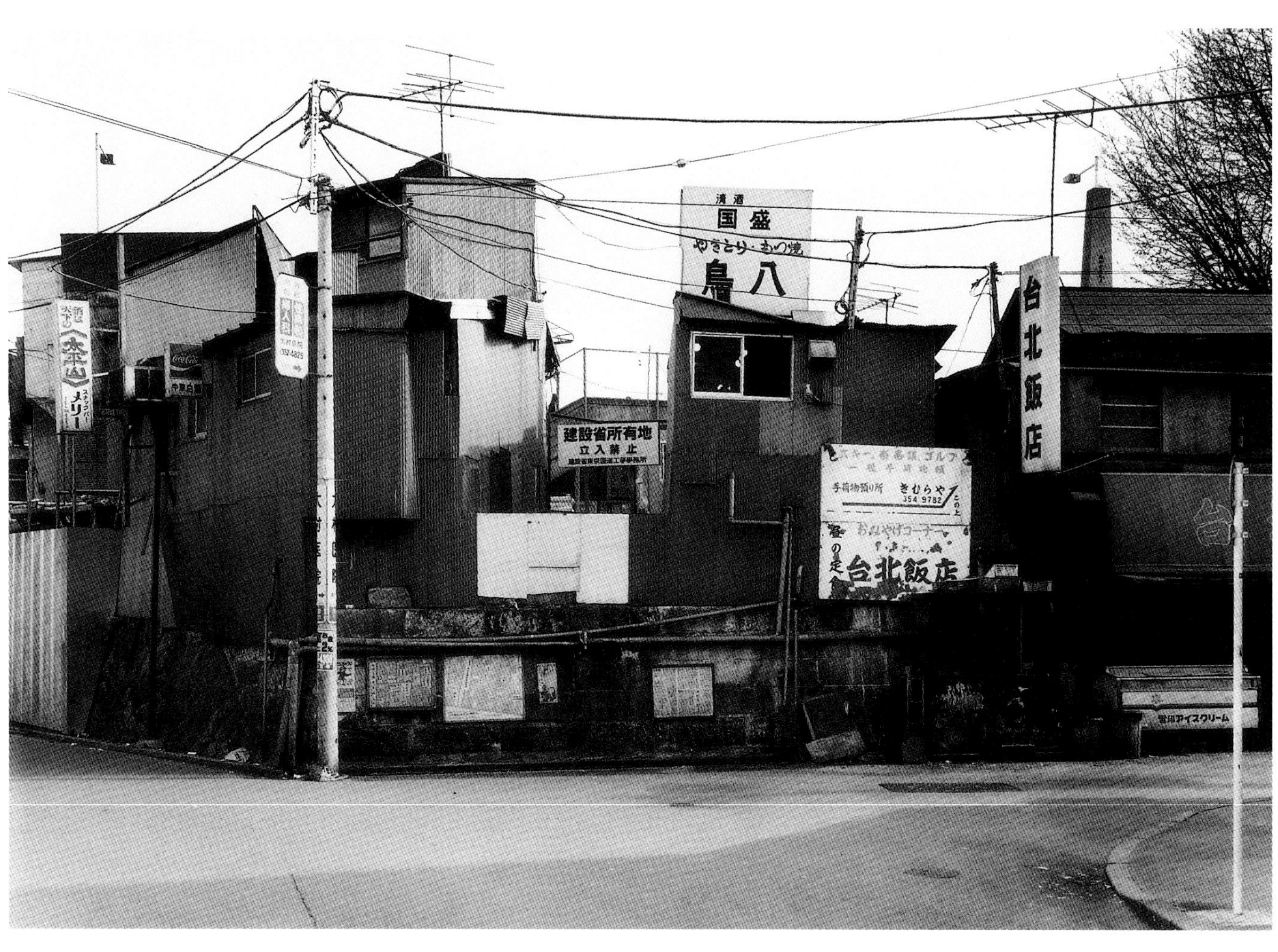
清酒
国盛
やきとり・もつ焼
鳥八
台北飯店
建設省所有地
立入禁止
メリー
一般手荷物類
手荷物預り所
きむらや
354 9782
この上
おみやげコーナー
昼の定食
台北飯店
雪印アイスクリーム

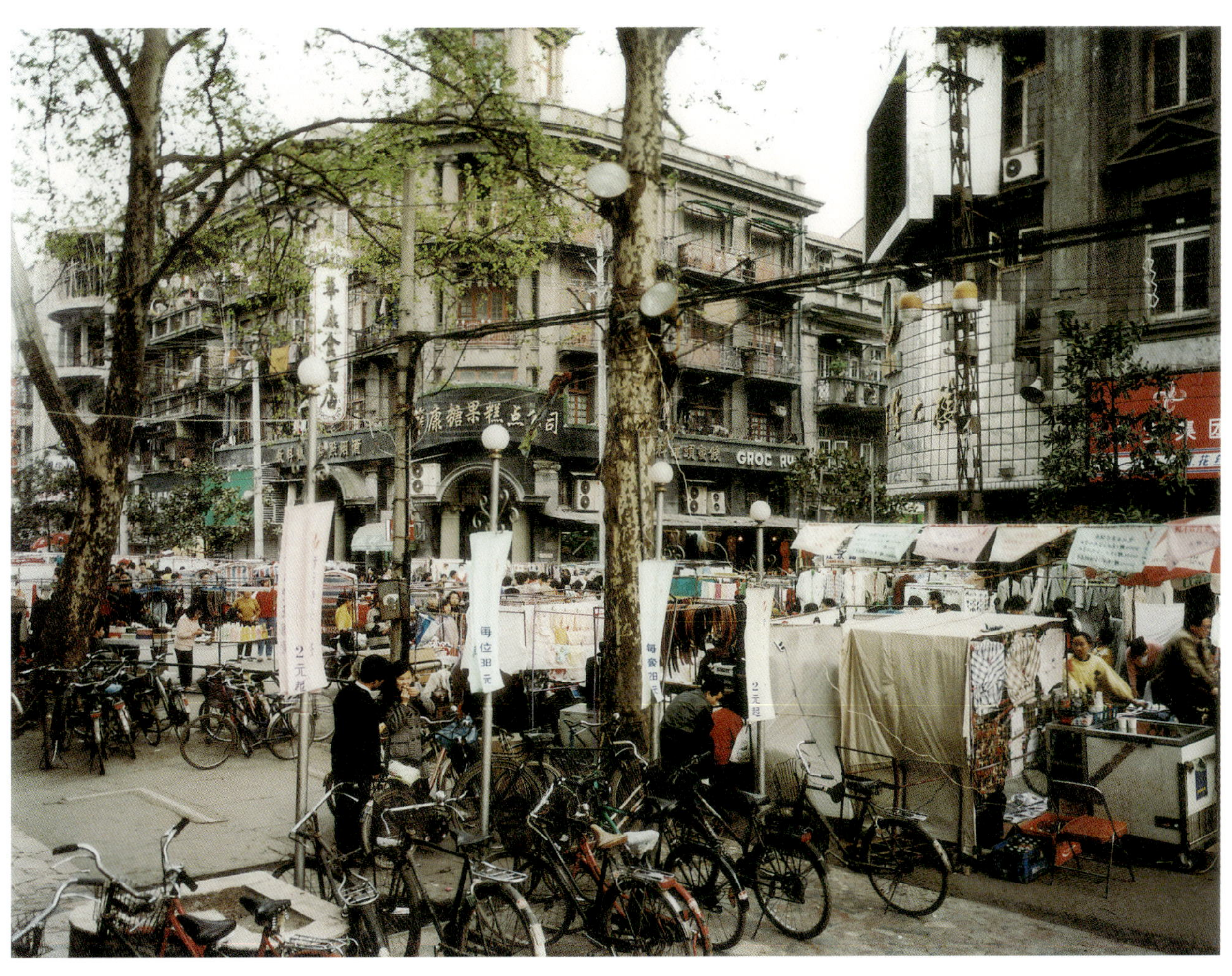

138 Metal shelters, Shinju-ku,Tokyo, 1986 139 Jianghan Lu, Wuhan, 1995

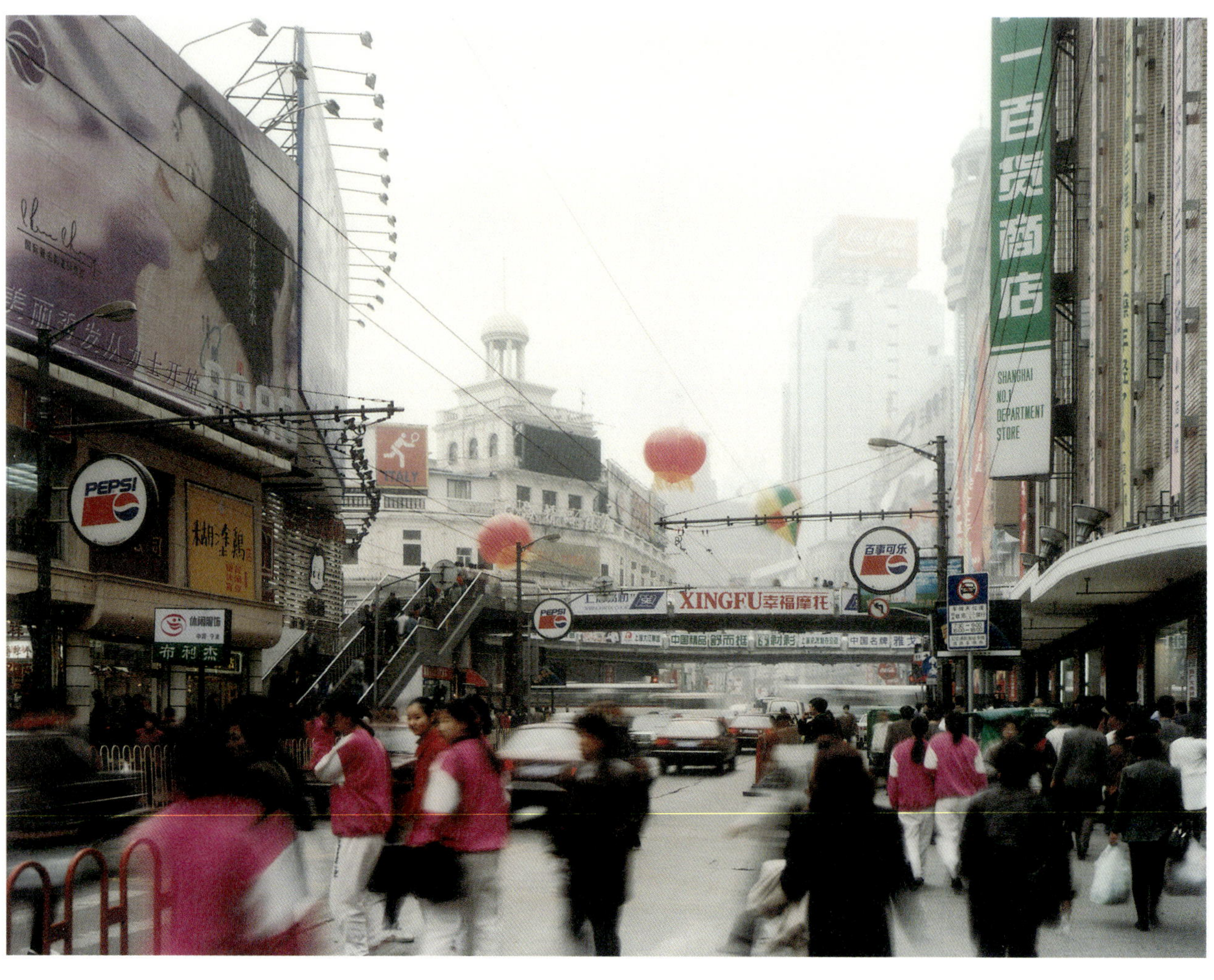
PEPSI
PEPSI
XINGFU幸福摩托
百事可乐
一百货商店
SHANGHAI
NO.1
DEPARTMENT
STORE

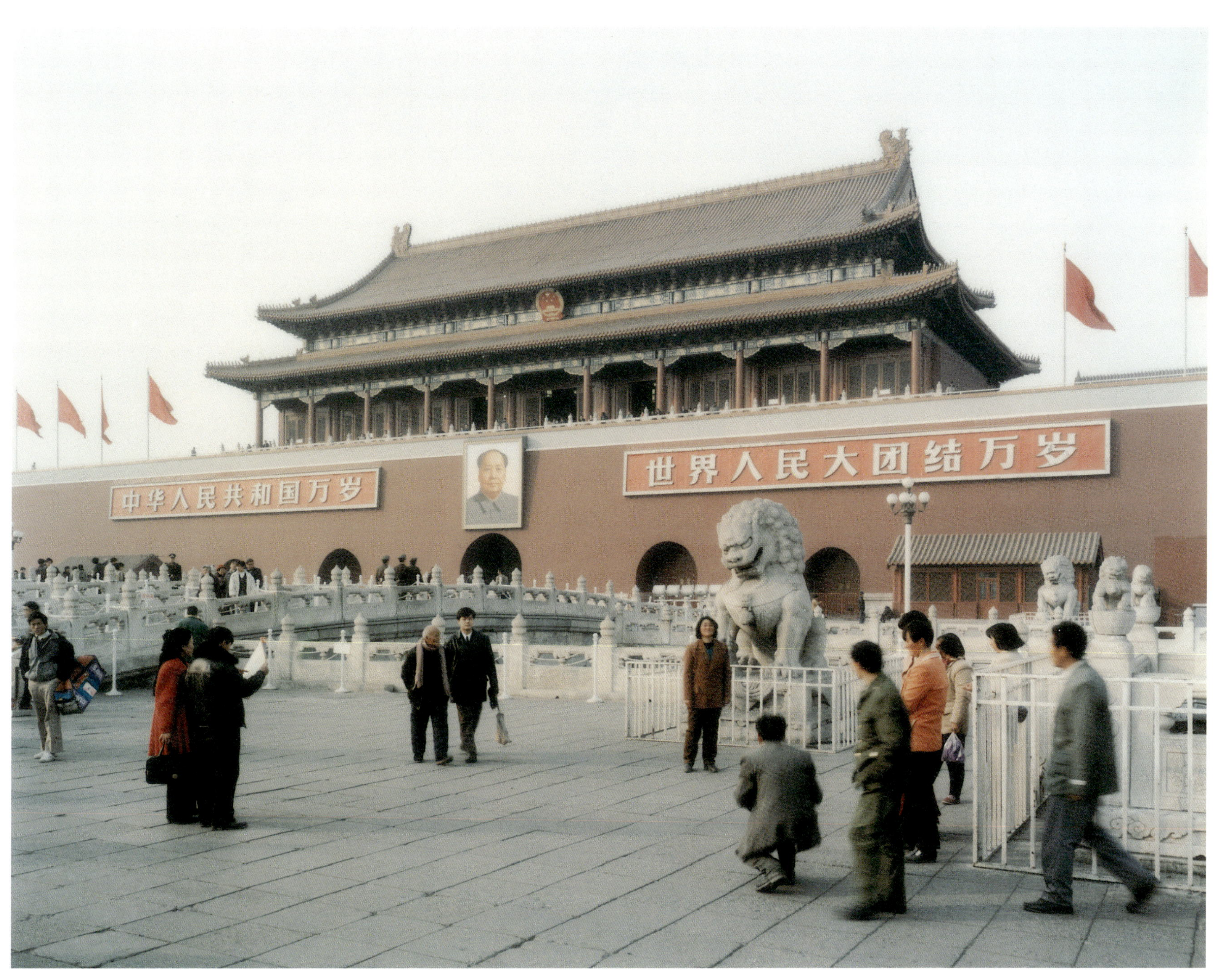

140 Nanjing Xi Lu, Shanghai, 1997 141 Tien an Men, Beijing, 1997

Mona Breede's photographs consider the 'choreography' of human figures in public space. Each work consists of a series of three or four images made at the same site and juxtaposed to develop a narrative that elaborates the relation of constellations of people to their environment.

Mona Breede

 Parc Citroen I – III, Paris, 1998

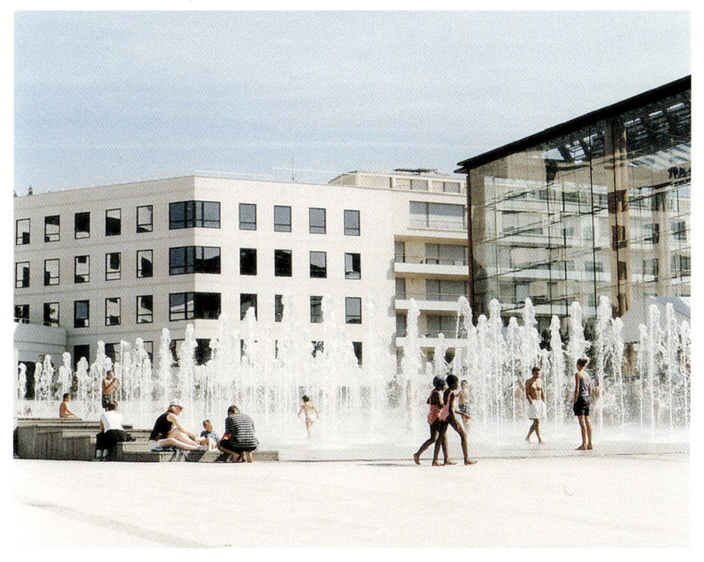

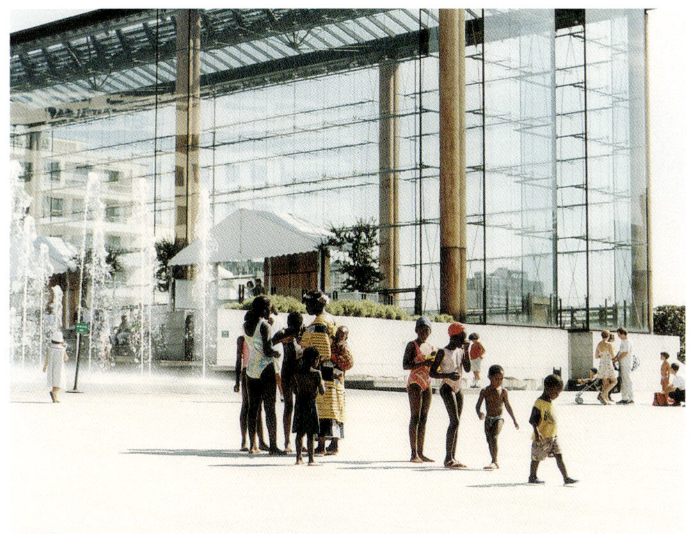

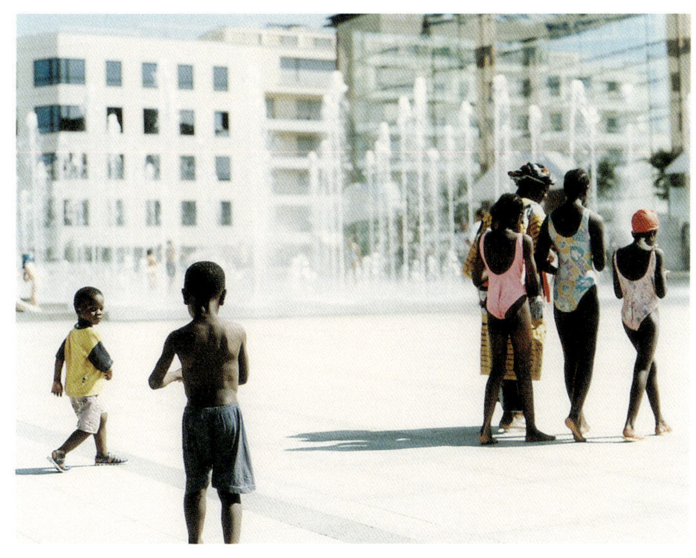

144 – 145 Durchgang (Passageway) I – IV, Paris, 1998

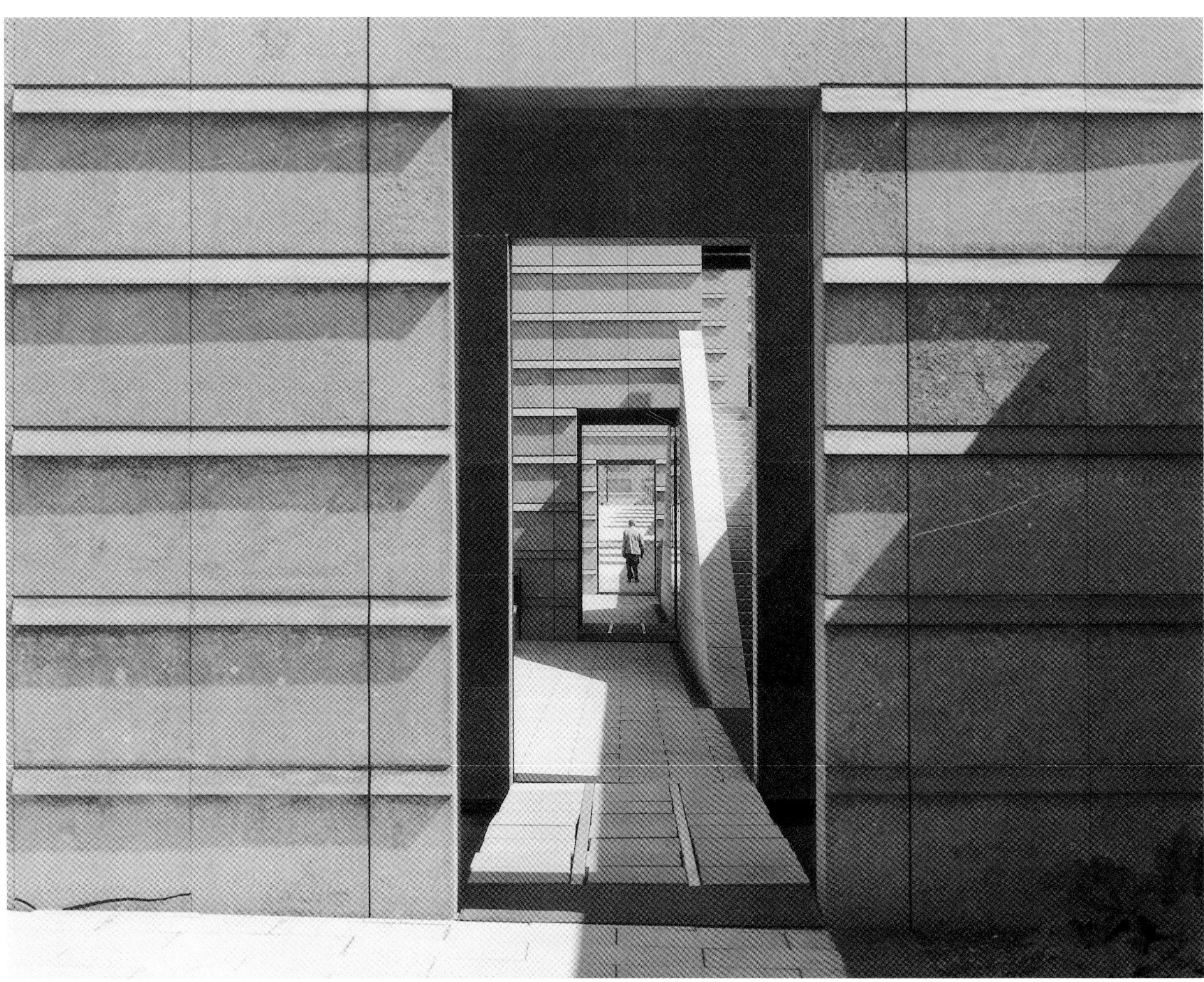

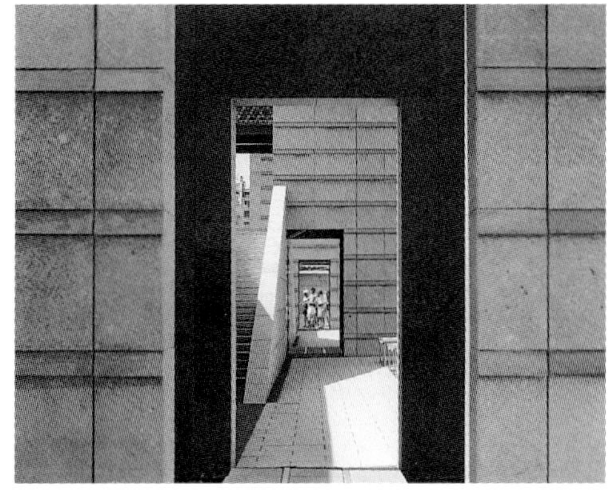

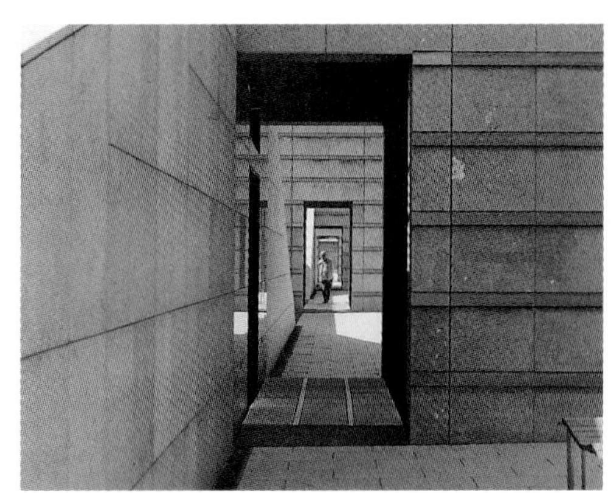

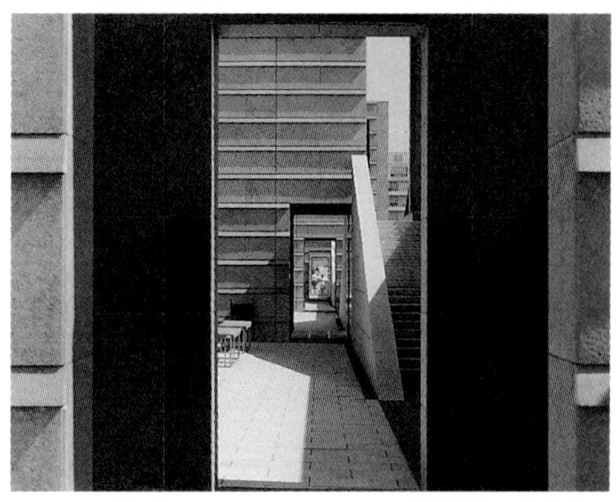

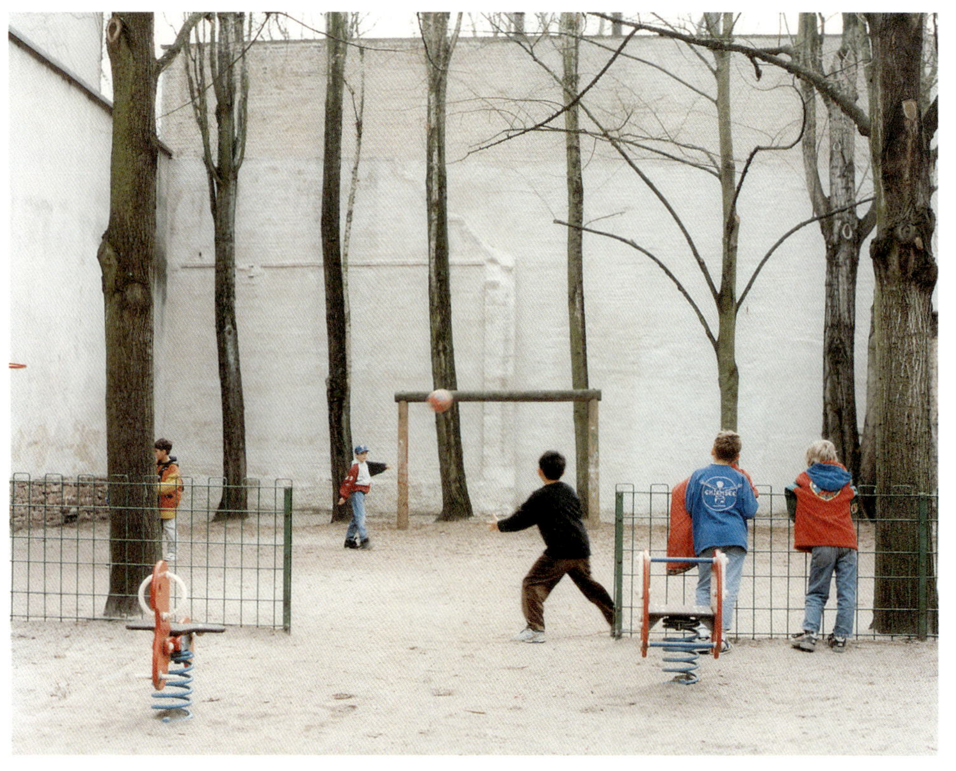

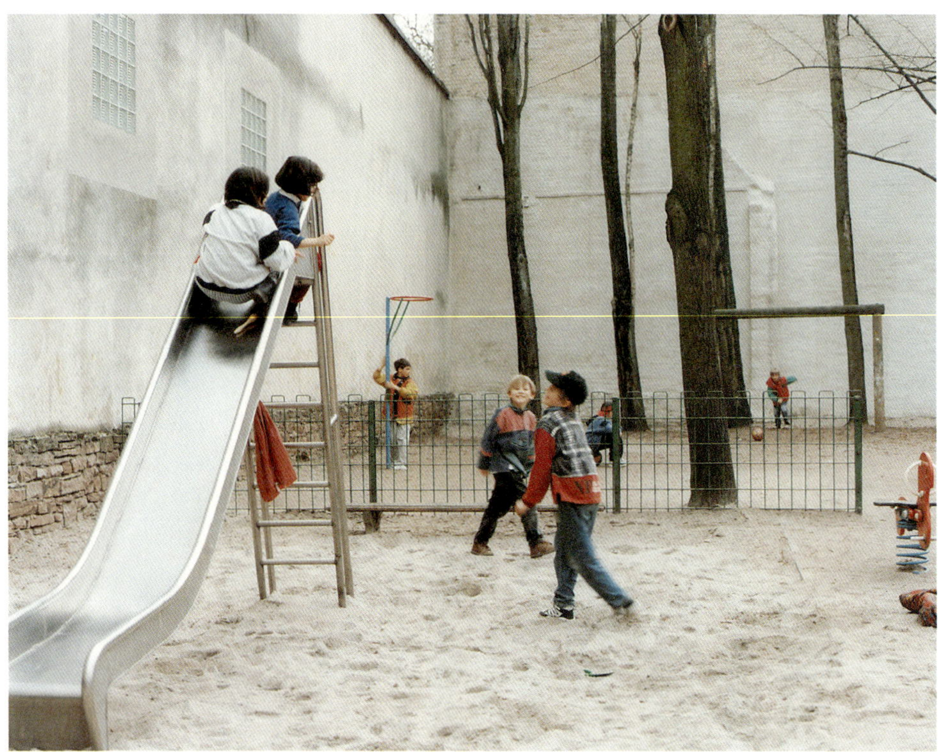

146 – 147 Spielplatz (Playground) I – IV, Karlsruhe, 1997

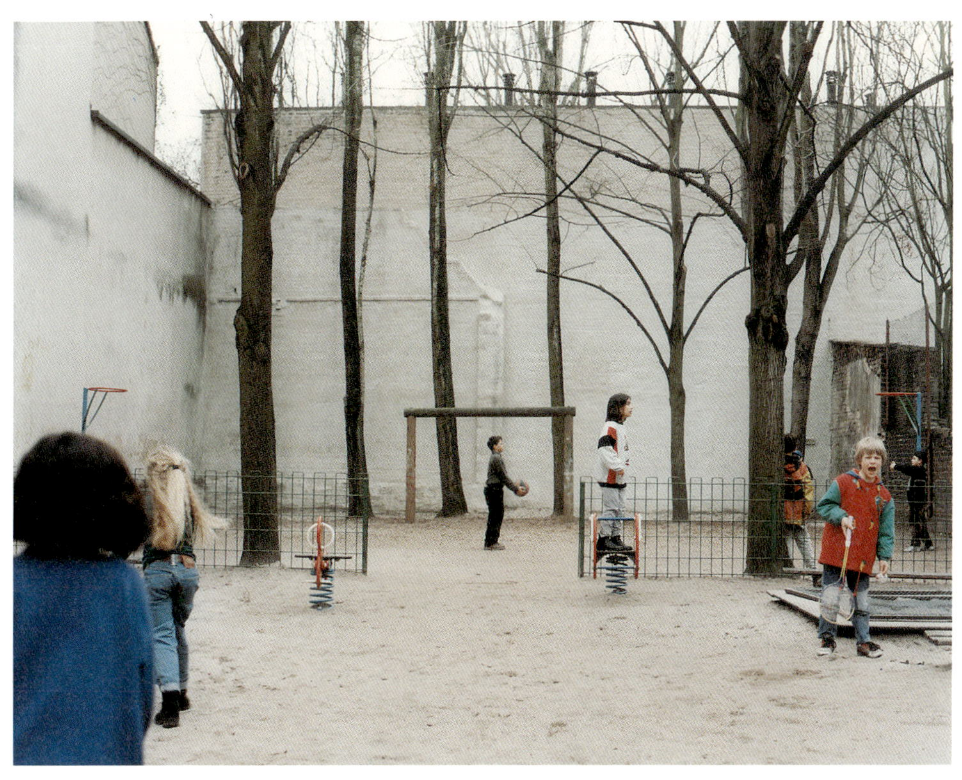

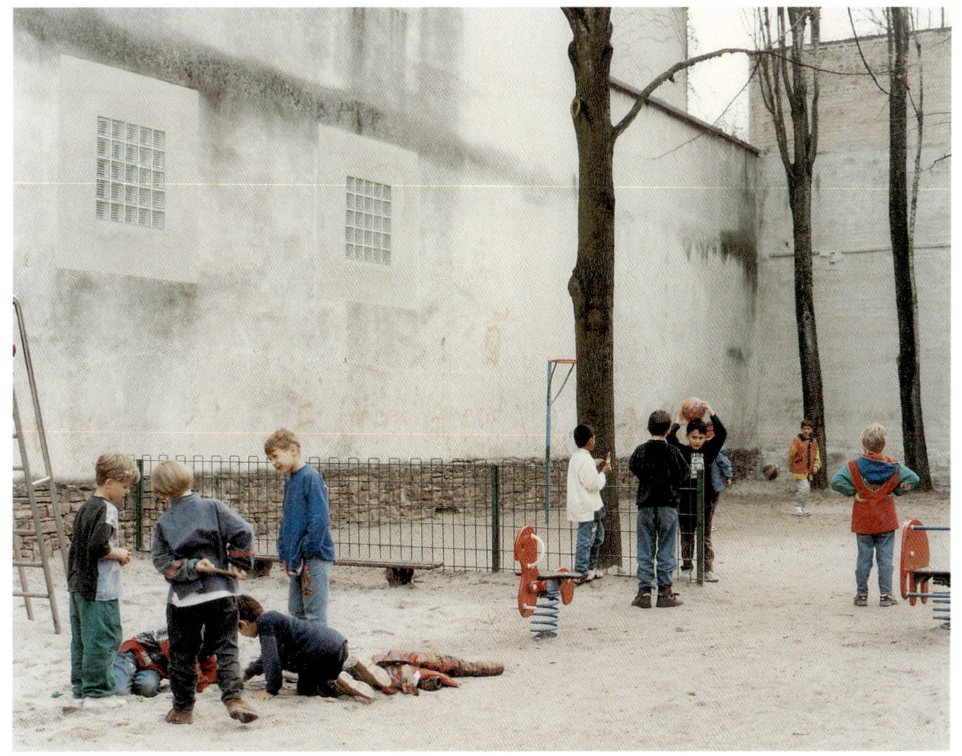

Matthias Schmidt

REALA 3000 is Matthias Schmidt's study of the aesthetics of modern cities, in which architecture is uniform and congruent. In streets and plazas human figures appear to define the use of the communal spaces, but as pedestrians their presence is transient. The pedestrians fulfil the function of the landscape in between the buildings, but the architecture fails to create socially meaningful sites.

149 – 153 REALA 3000

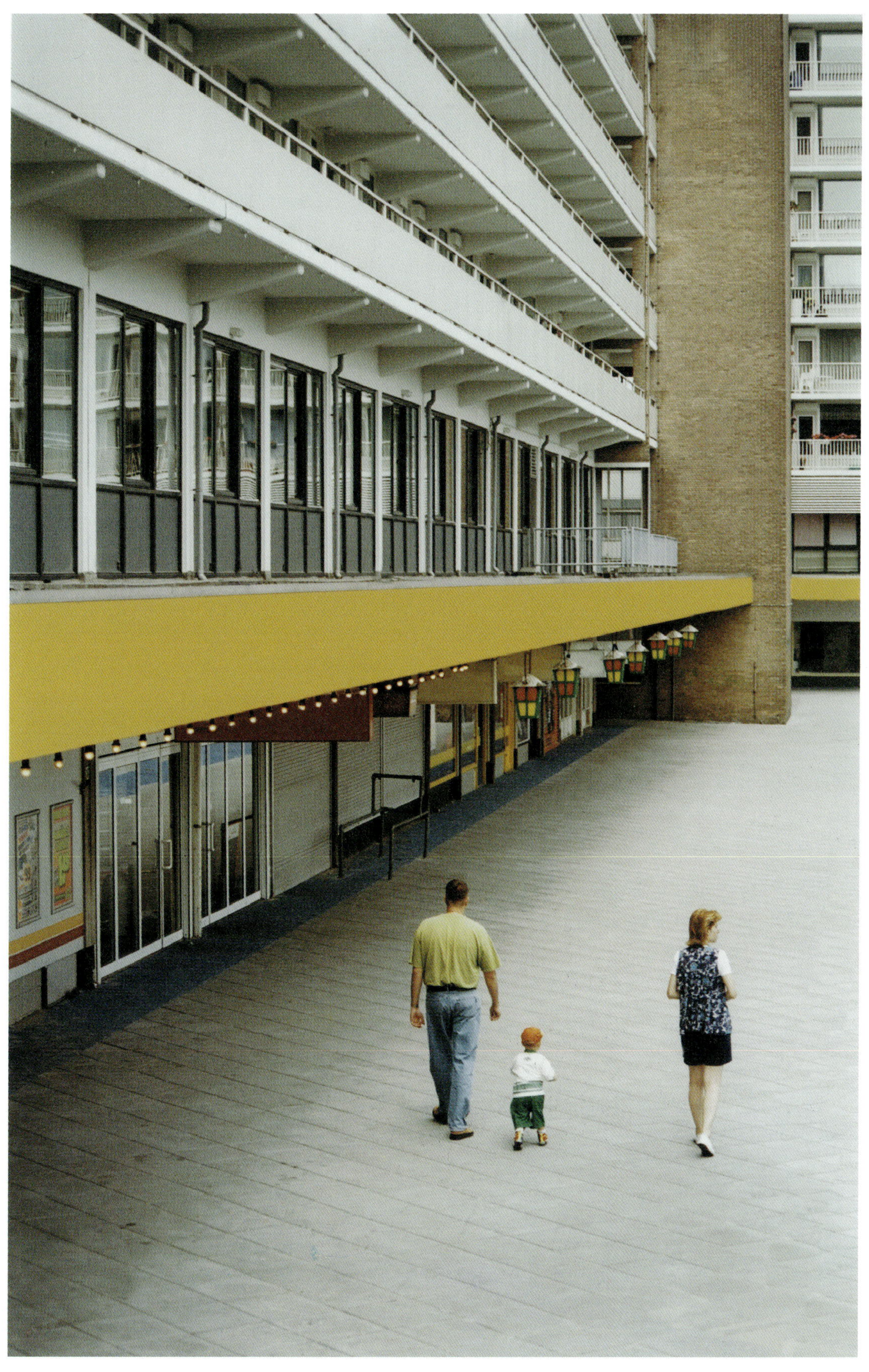

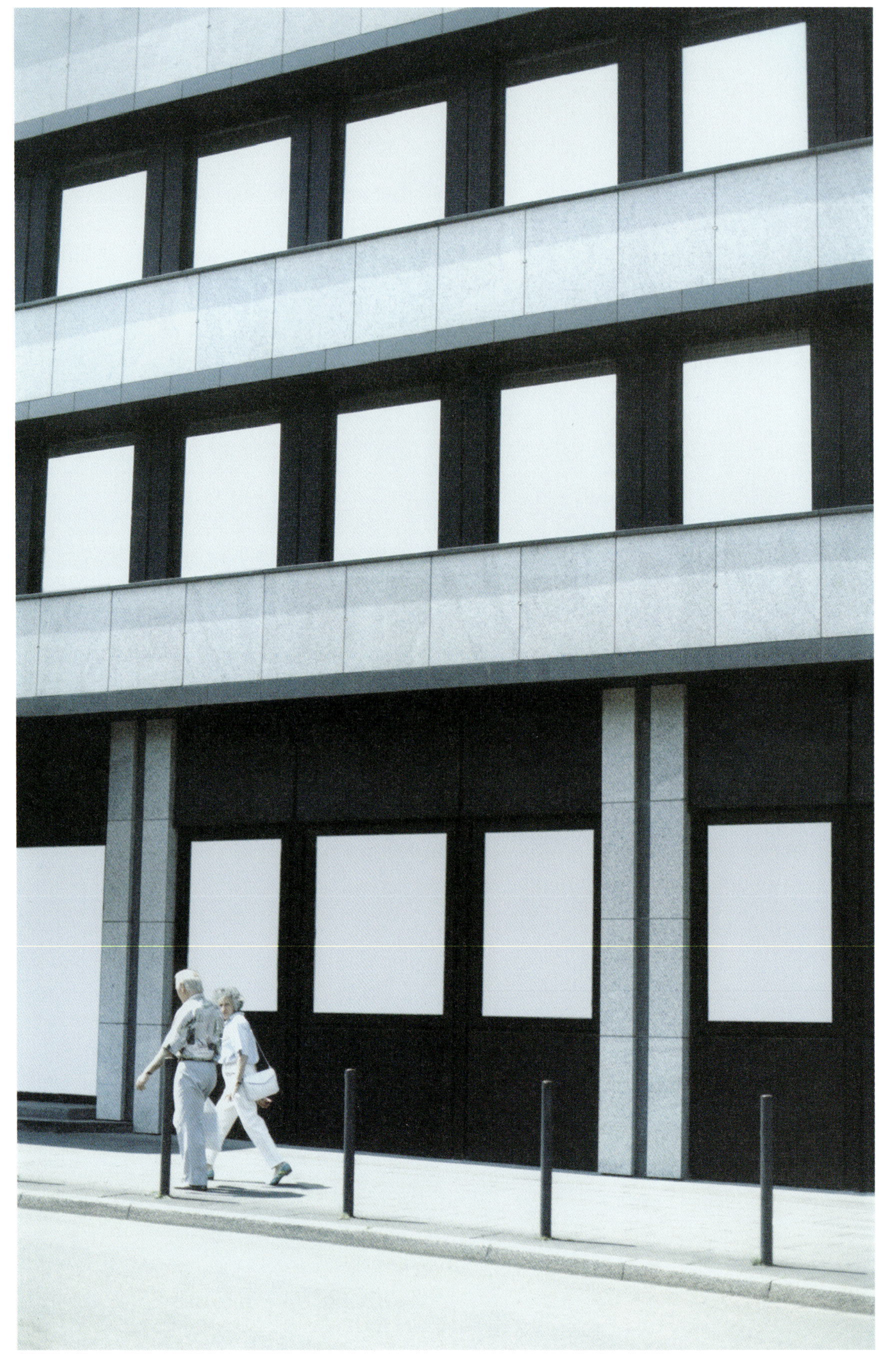

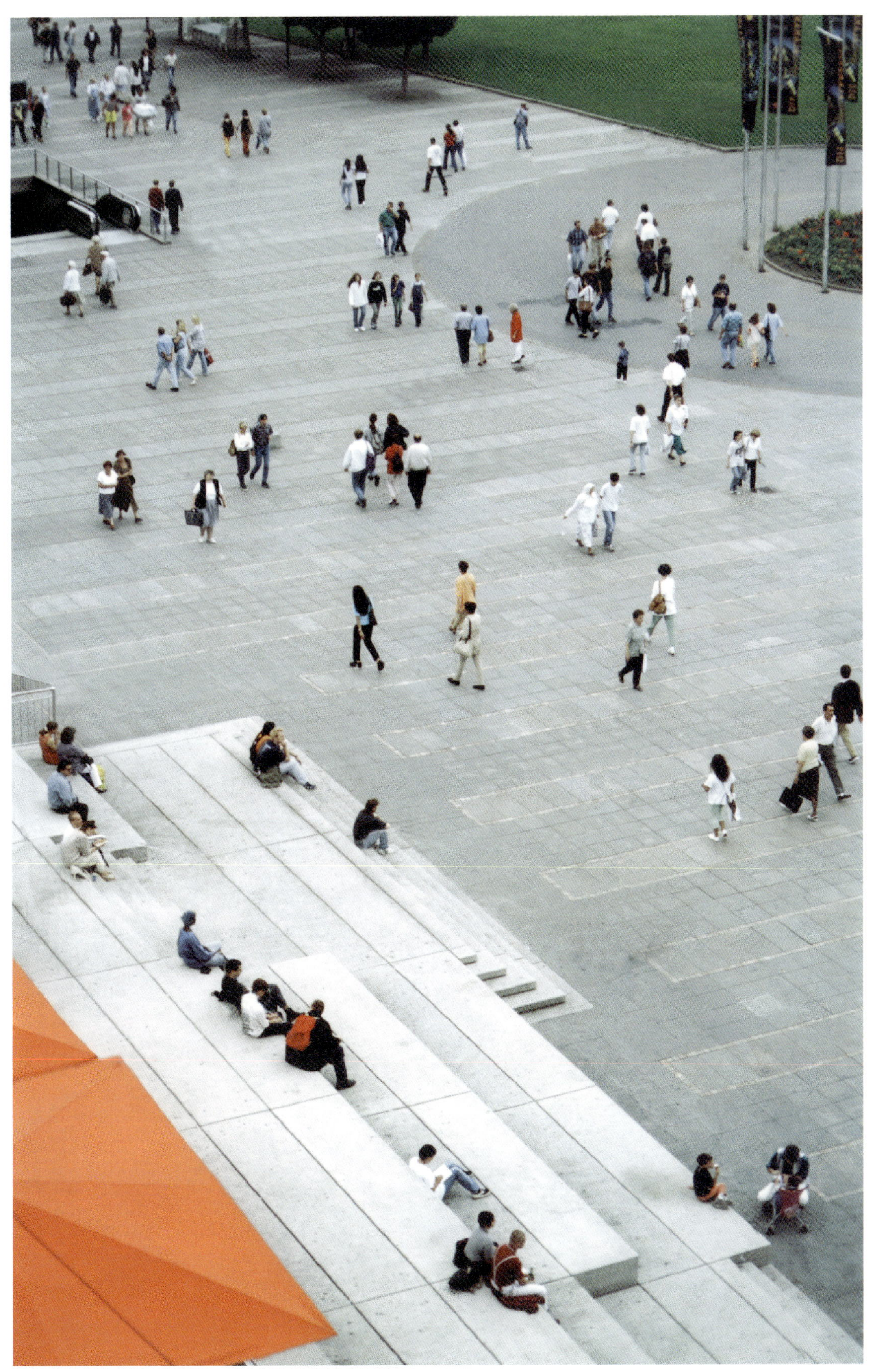

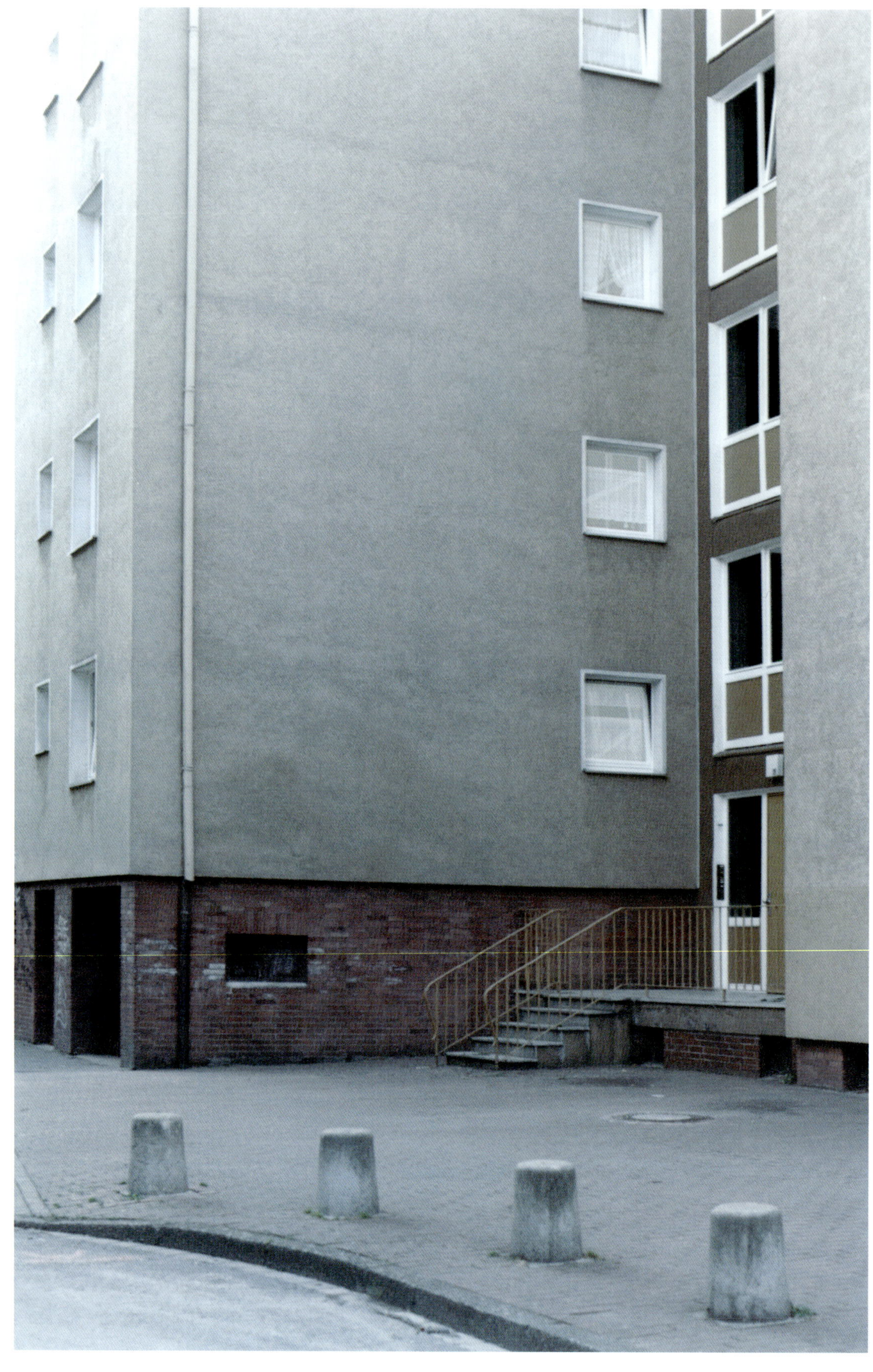

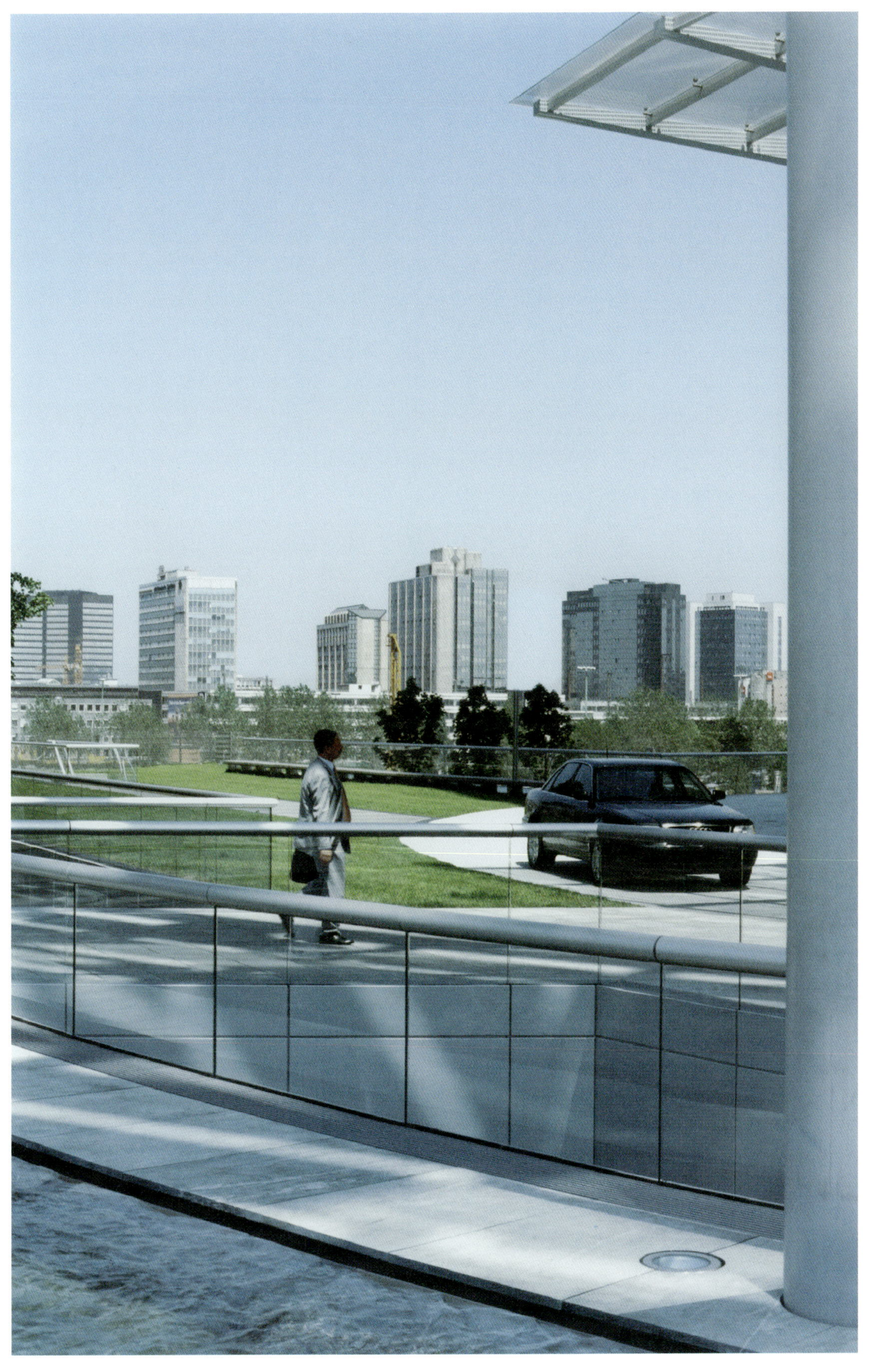

155 – 161 Die Zelle (The Cell), 1994

Gosbert Adler

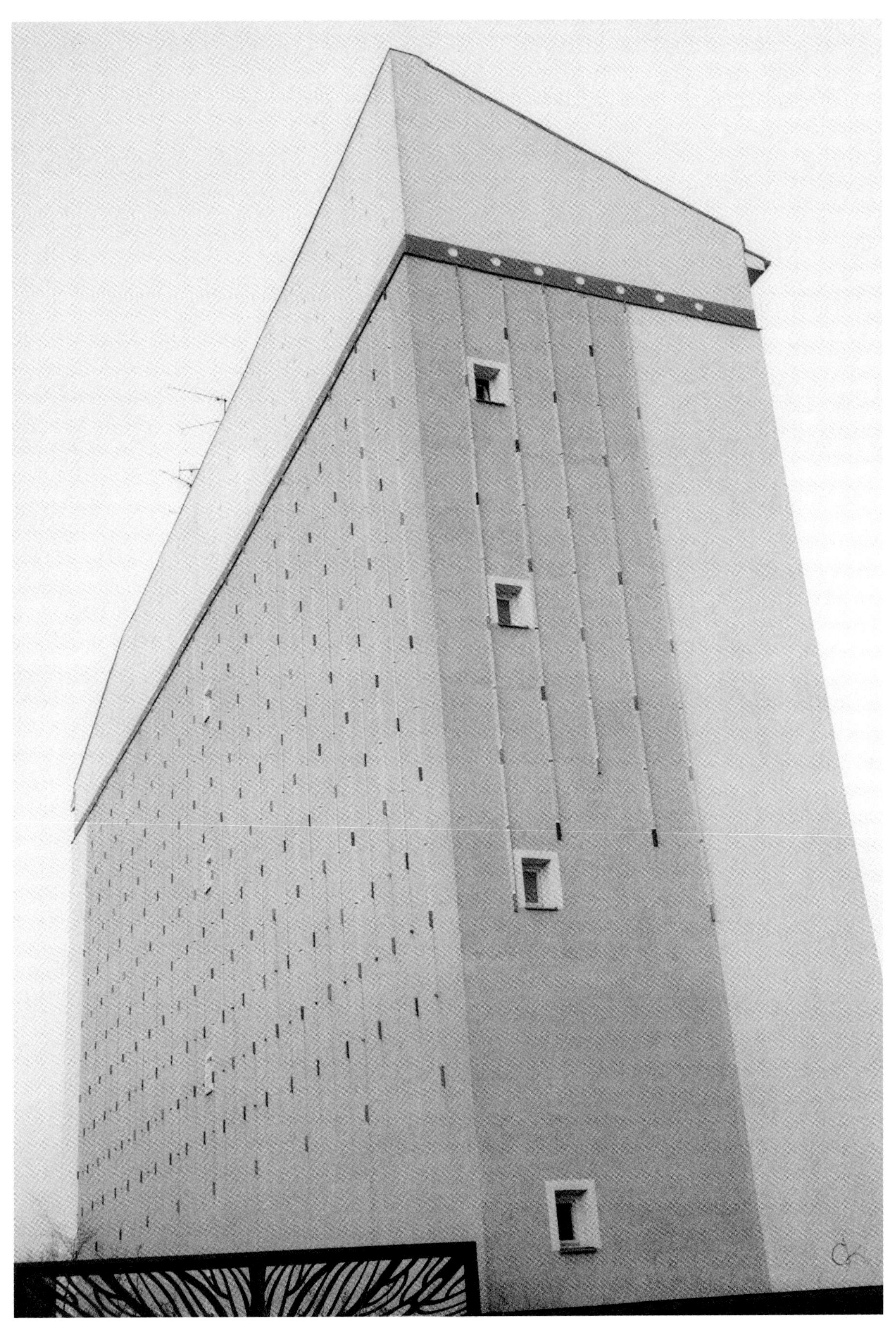

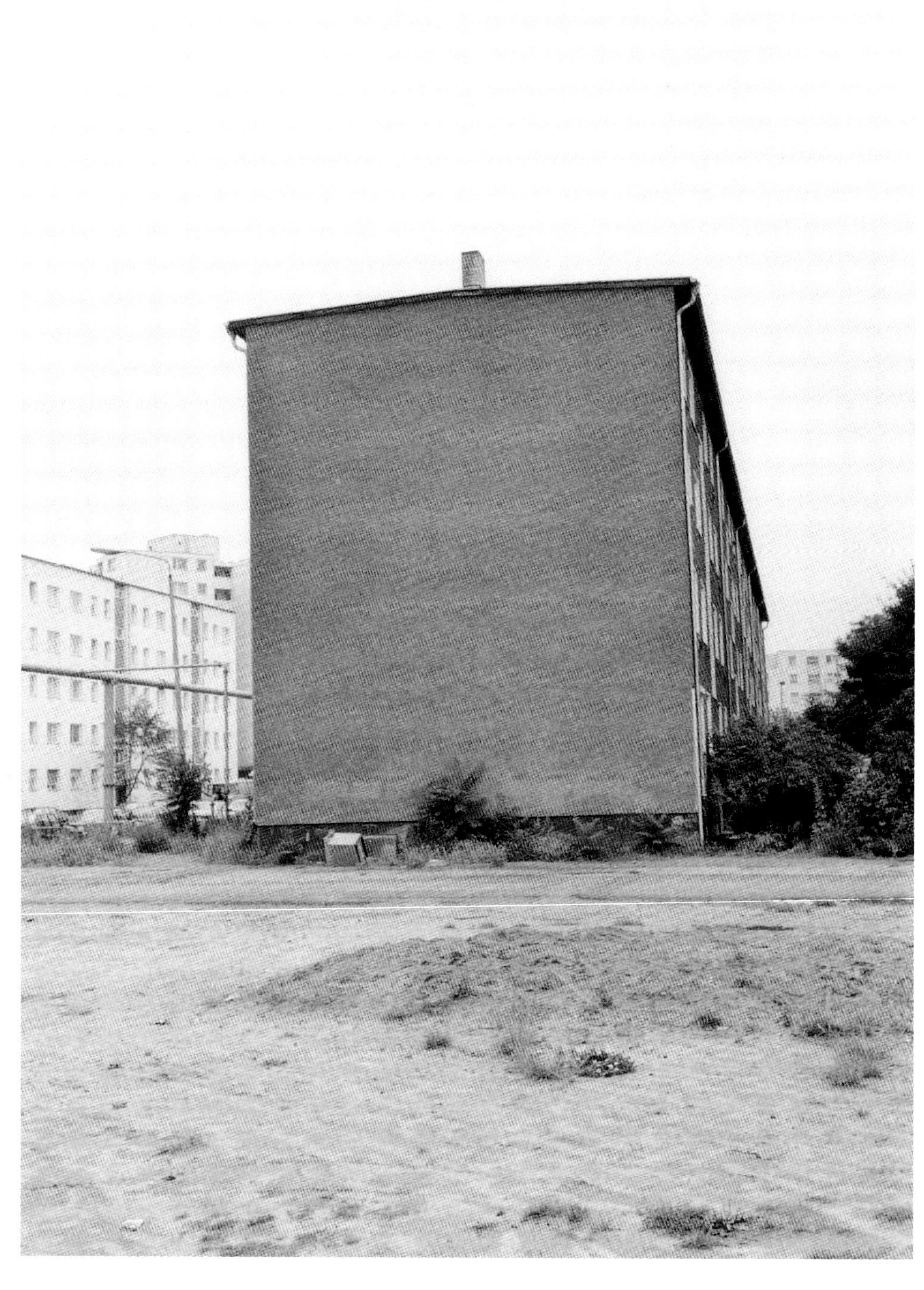

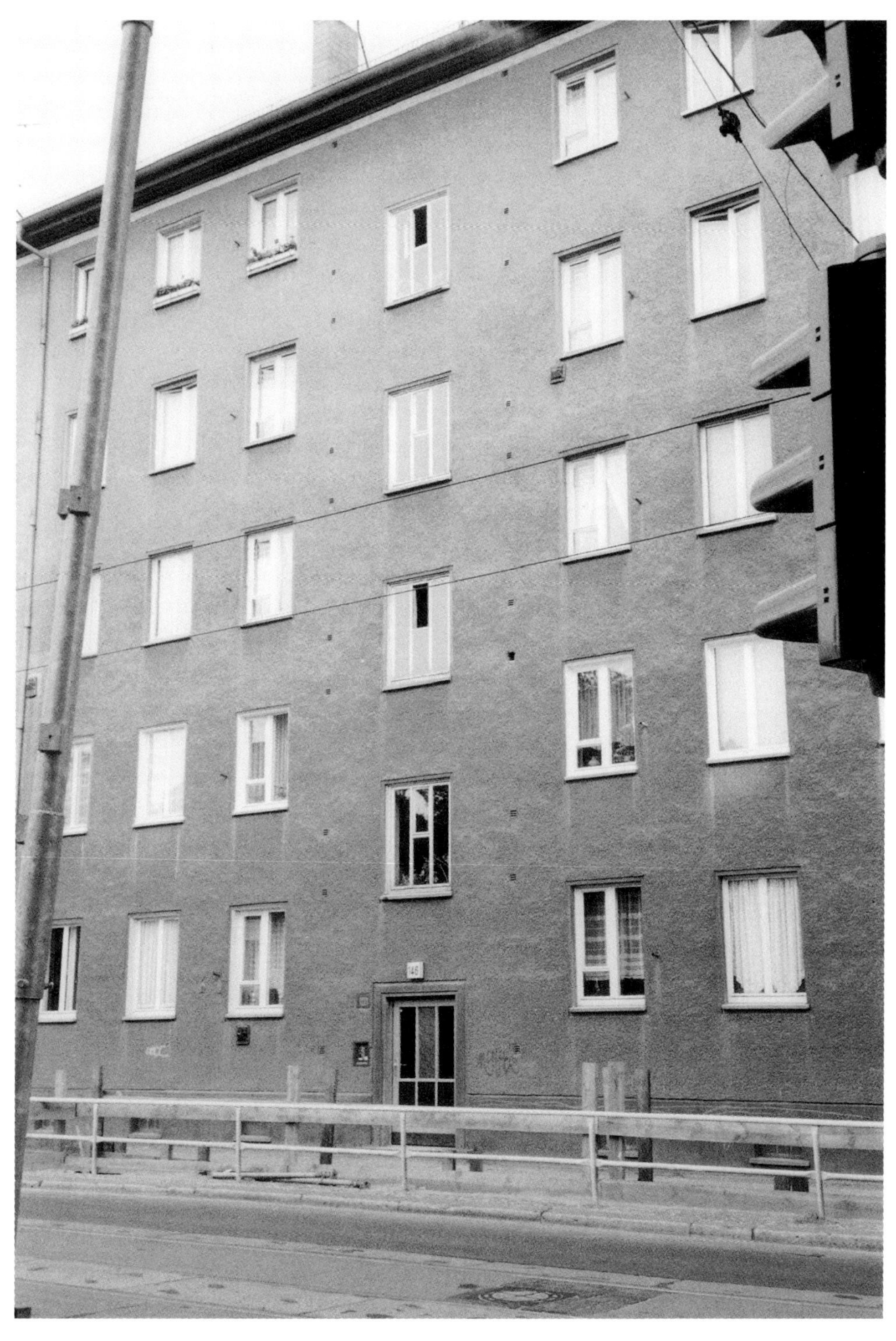

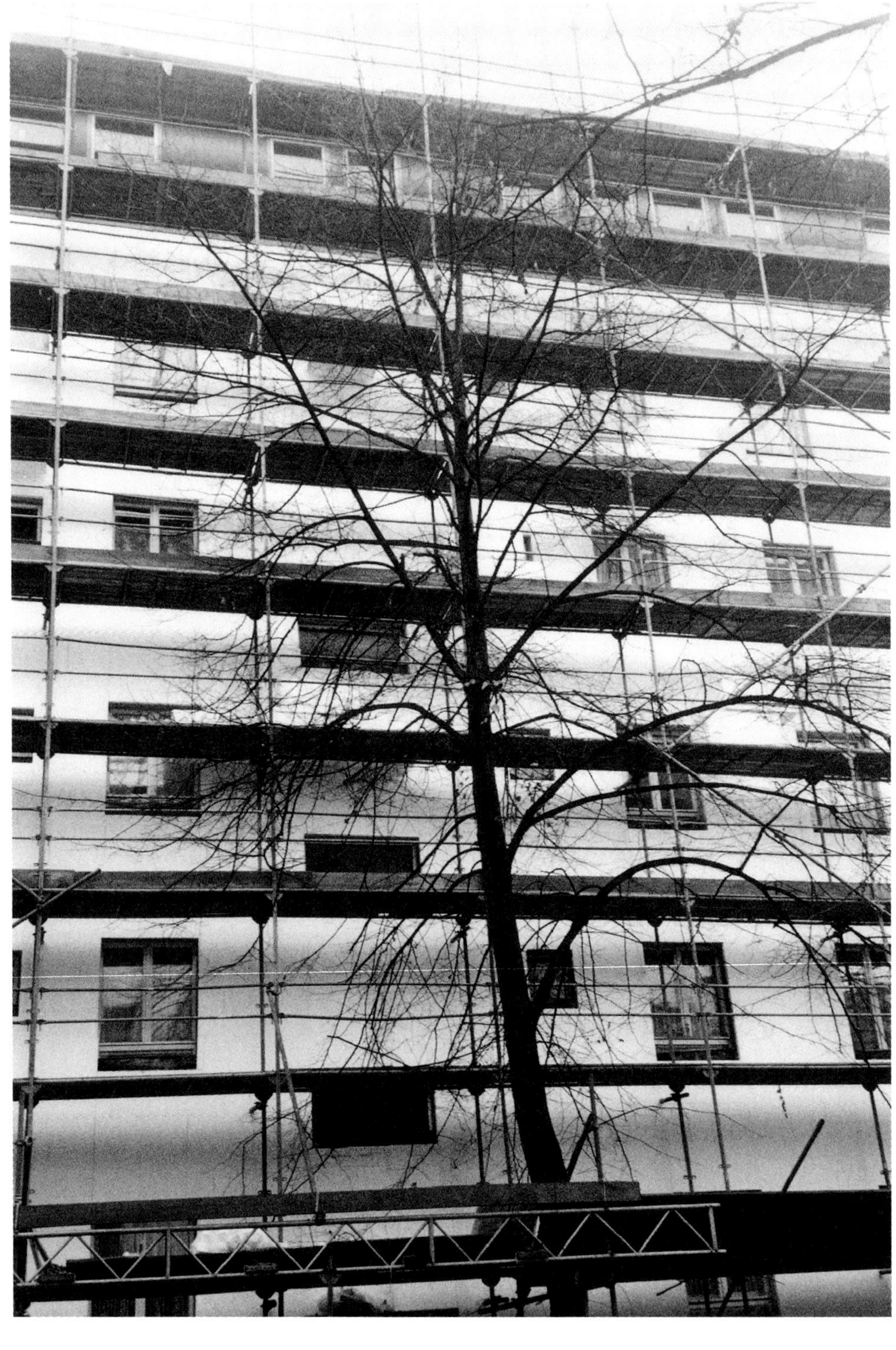

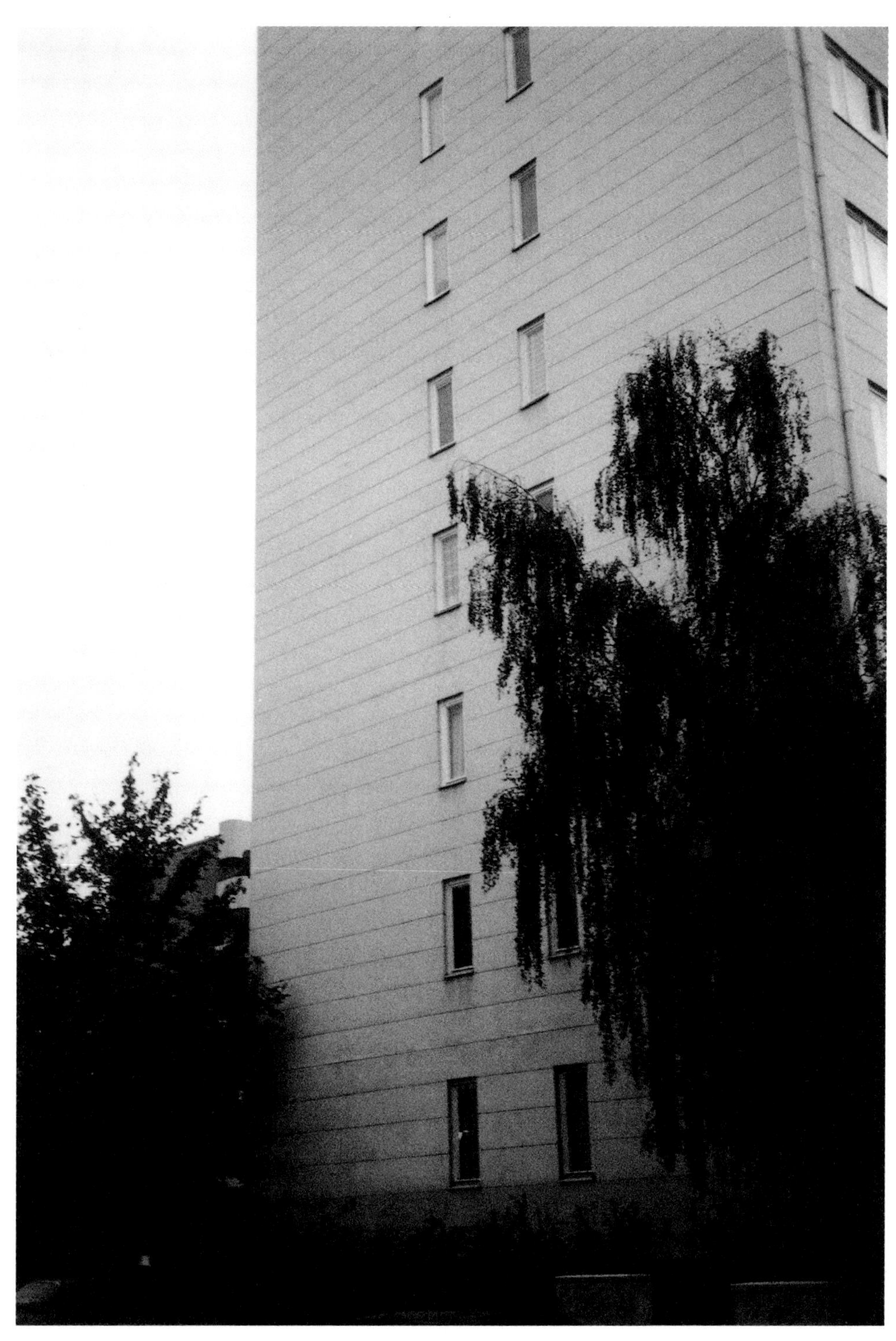

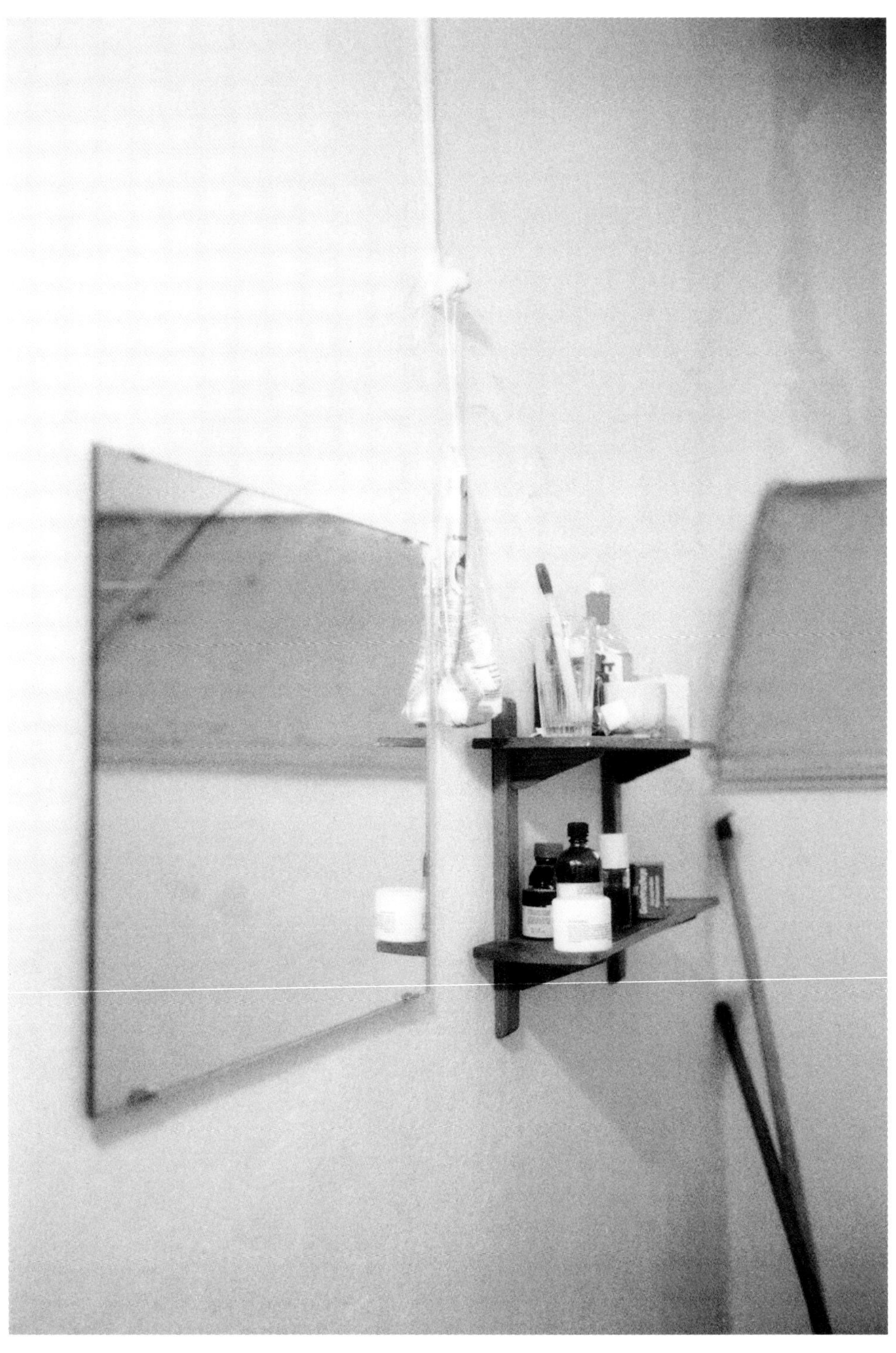

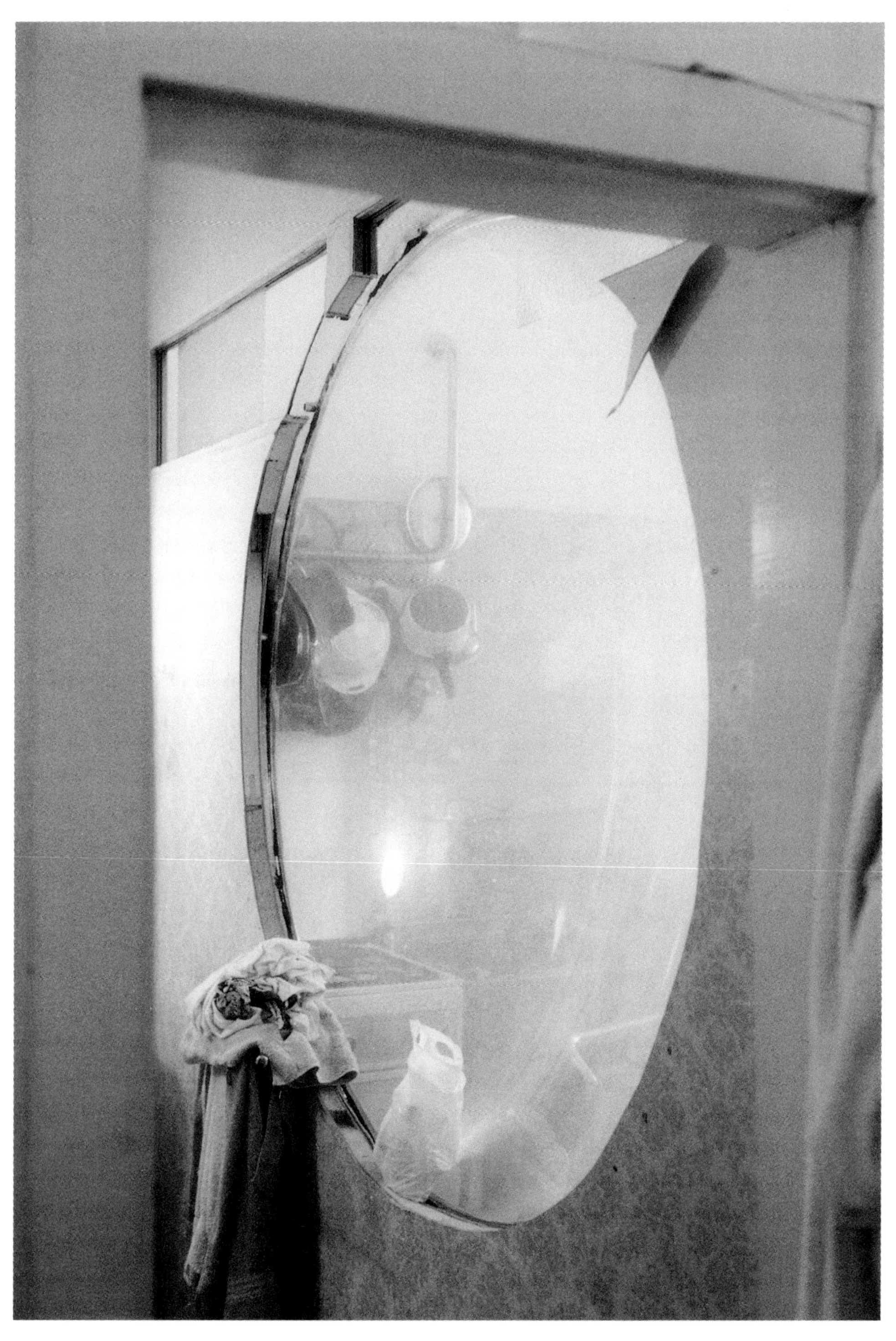

Candida Höfer

Candida Höfer's work has always been distinct from the Becher heritage from which it emerged. Her photography is not the application of a positivistic tool, and her practice has only recently accommodated a tripod and film format larger than 35 mm. Her work avoids the formality and certitude of a rigorously applied system, yet her highly deliberate views convey an expressive sense of the spaces photographed.

163 Volkswagenwerk Wolfsburg II, 1998

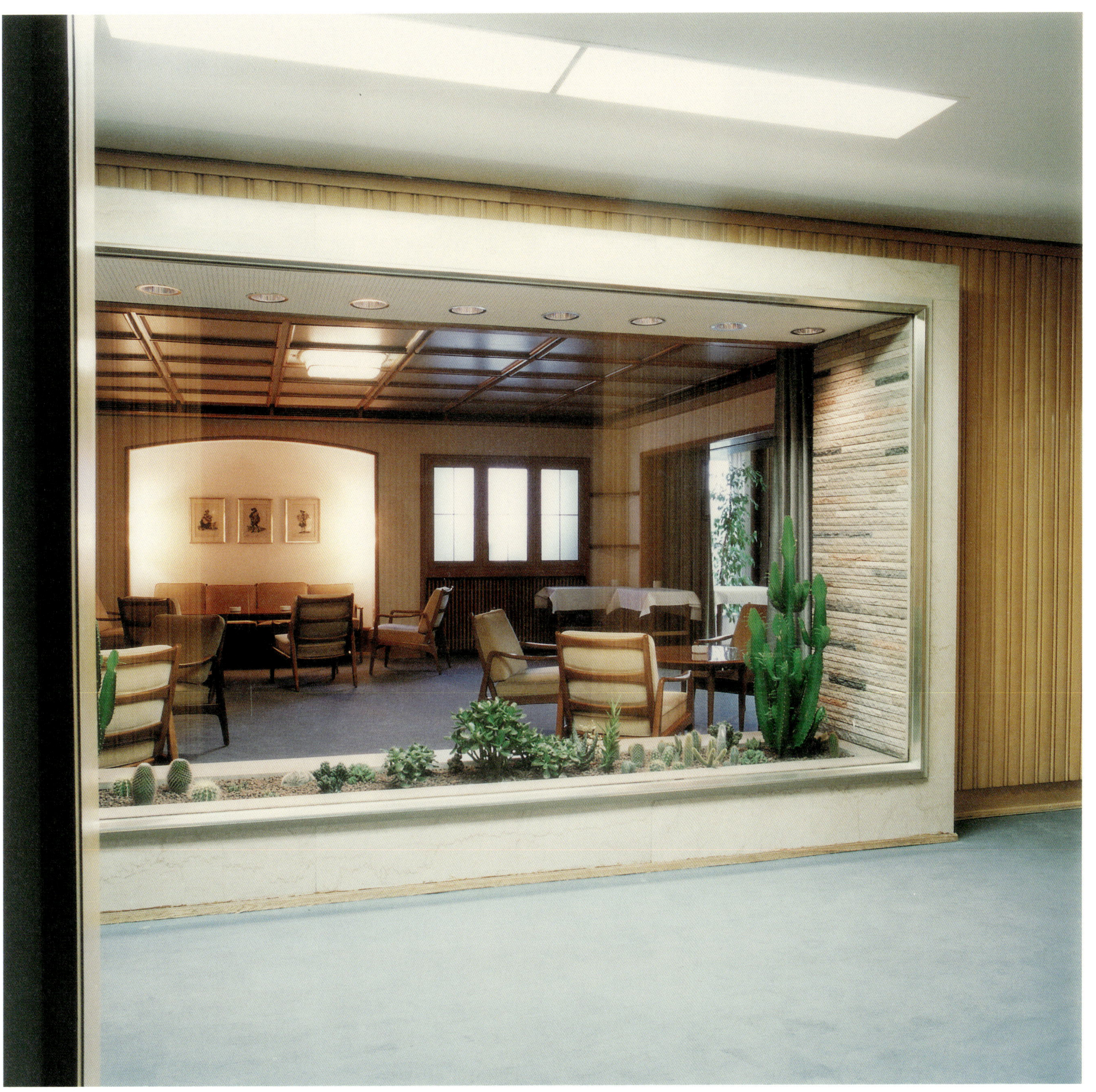

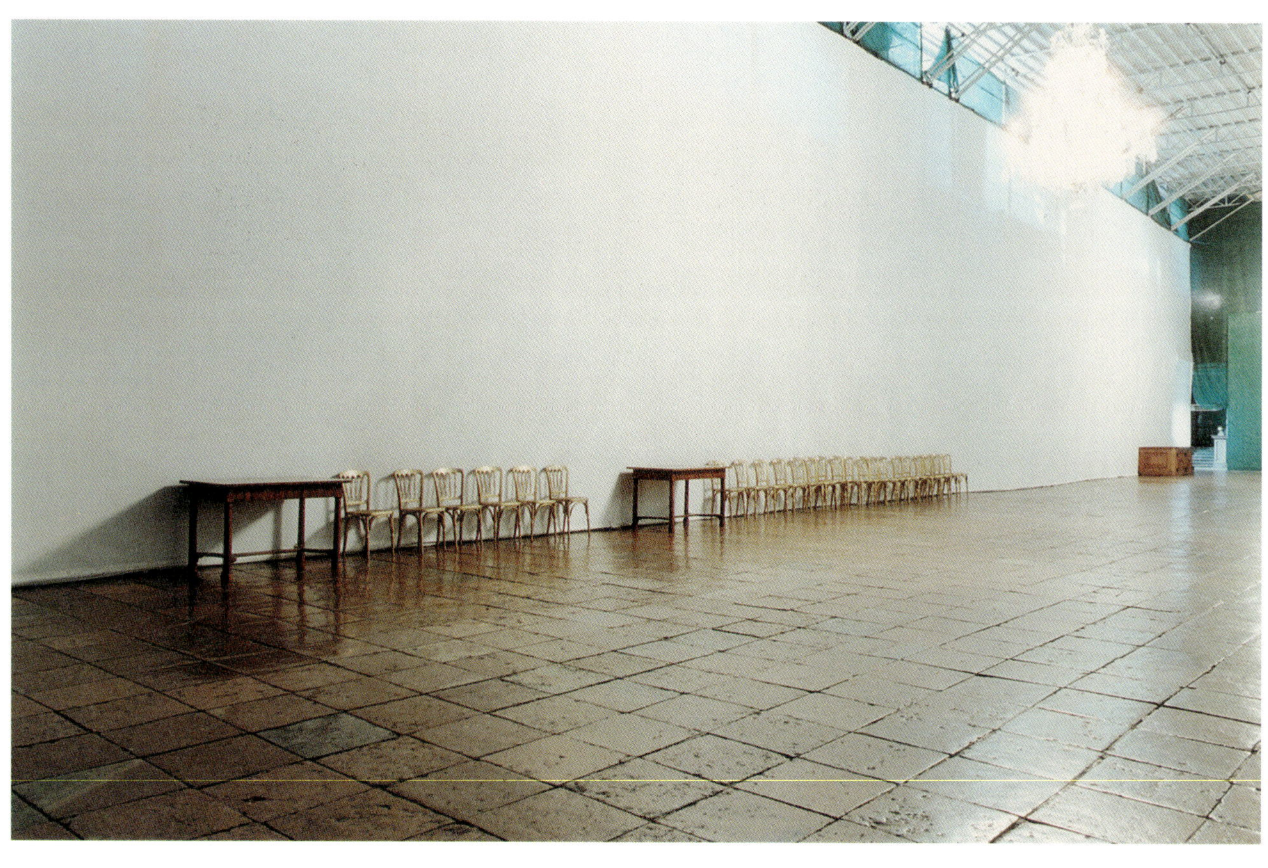

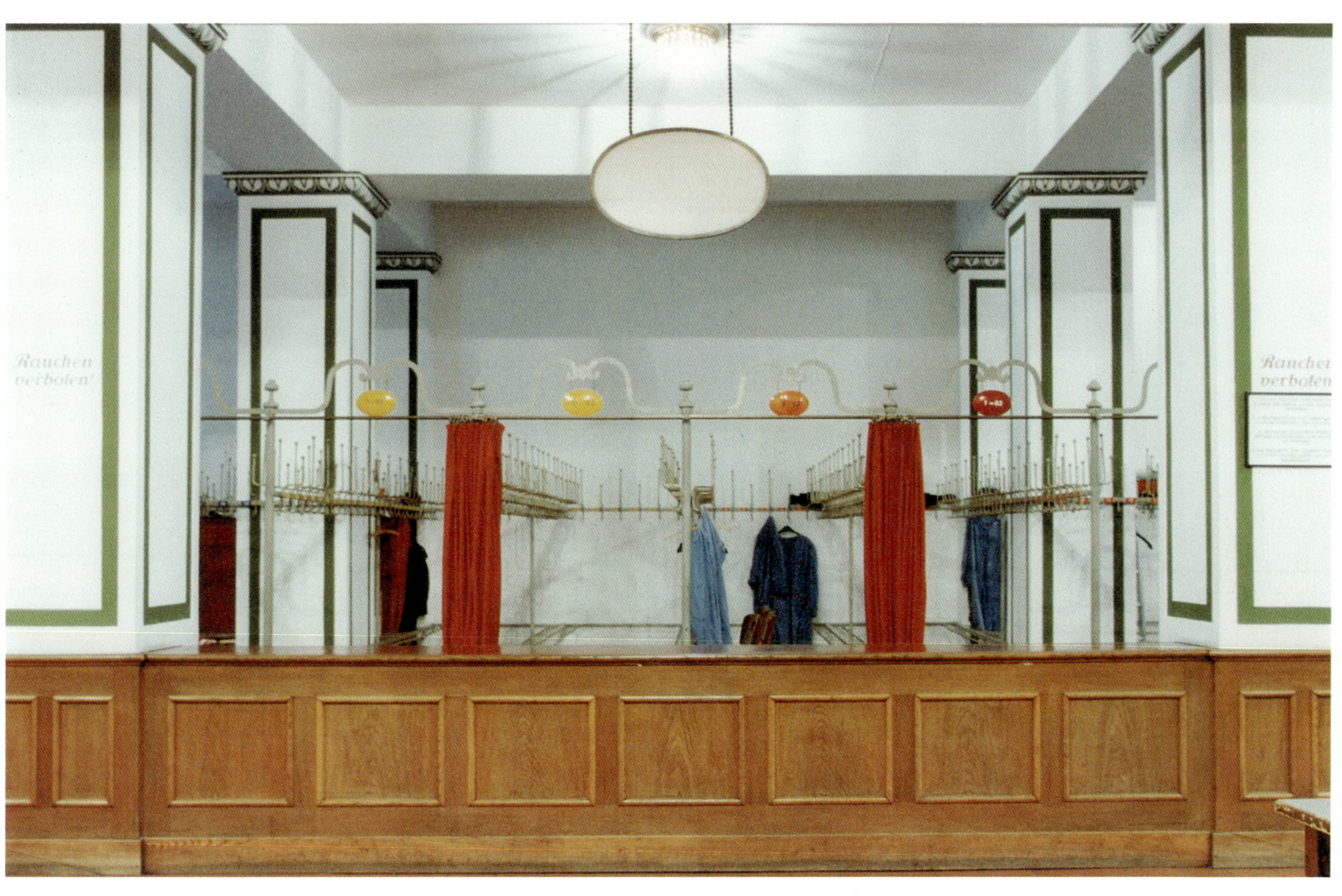

164 Residenz Salzburg II, 1996 165 Mozarteum Salzburg II, 1996

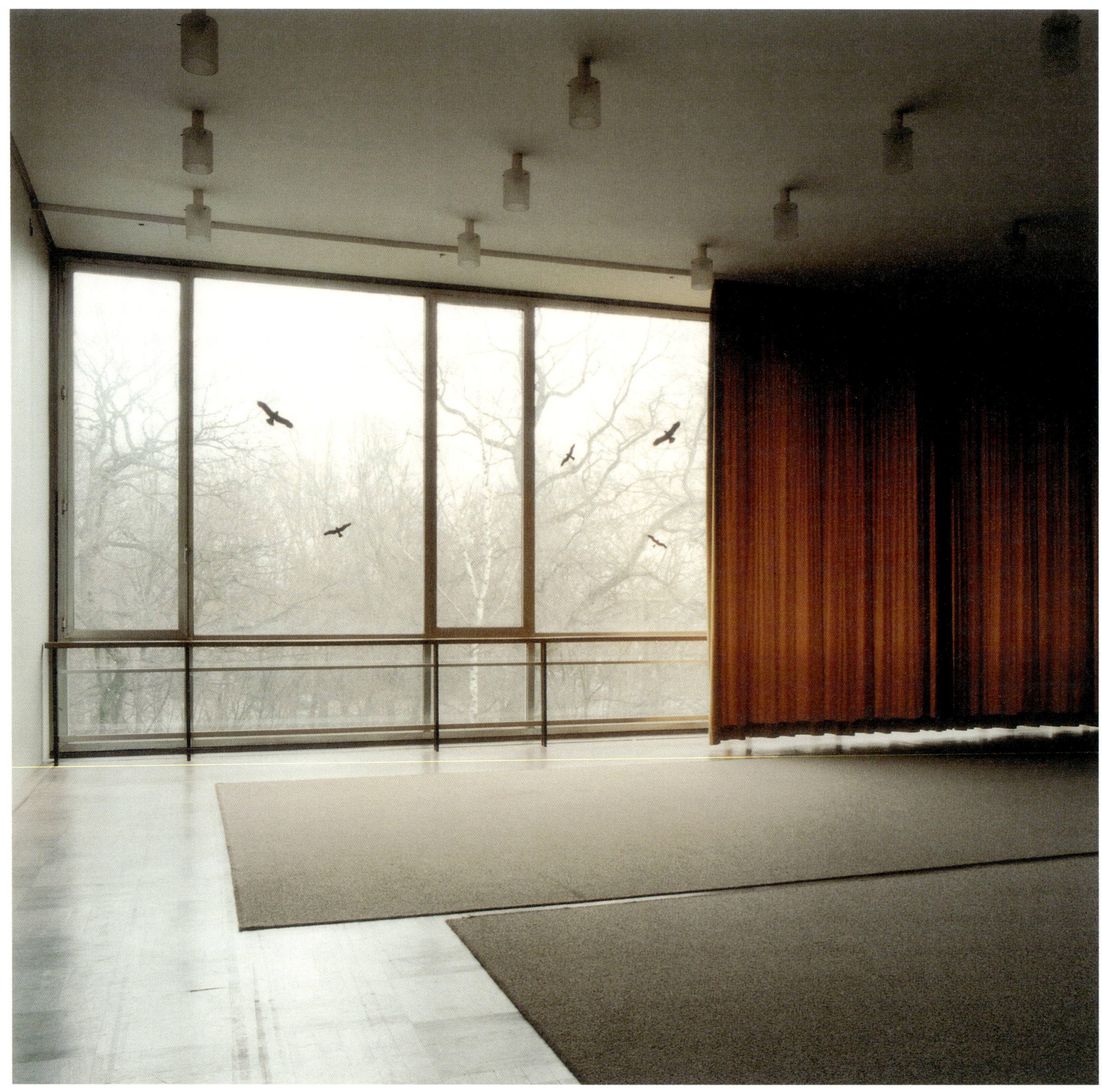

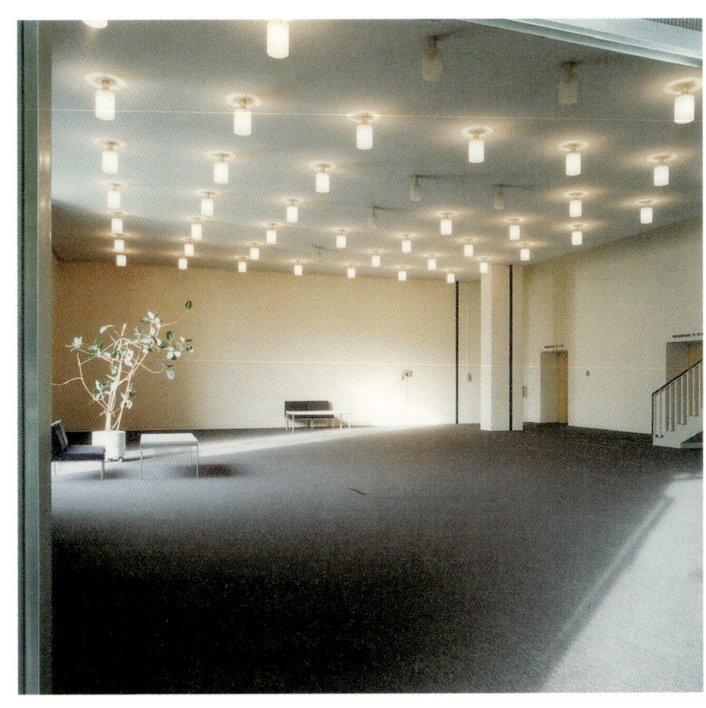

166 Festspielhaus Recklinghausen III, 1997 167 Festspielhaus Recklinghausen IV, 1997

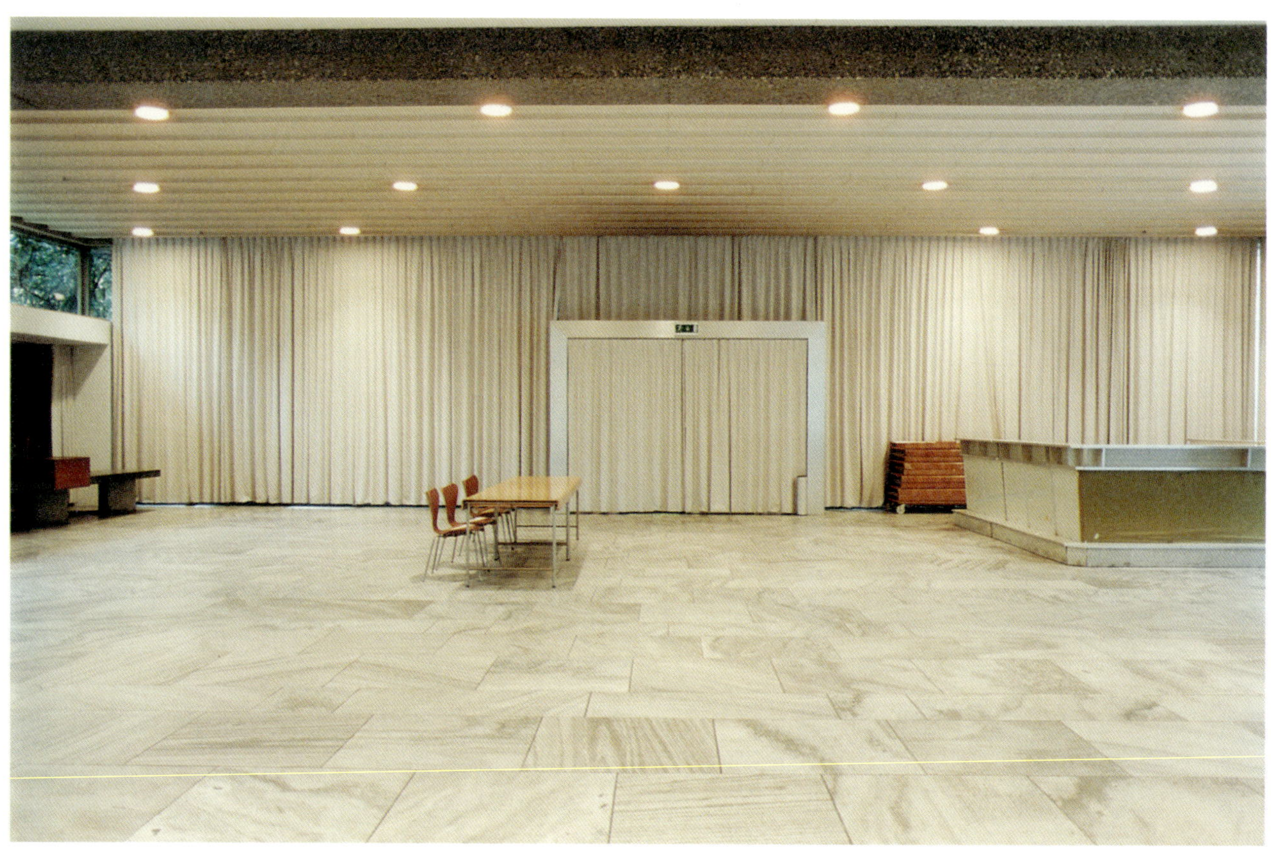

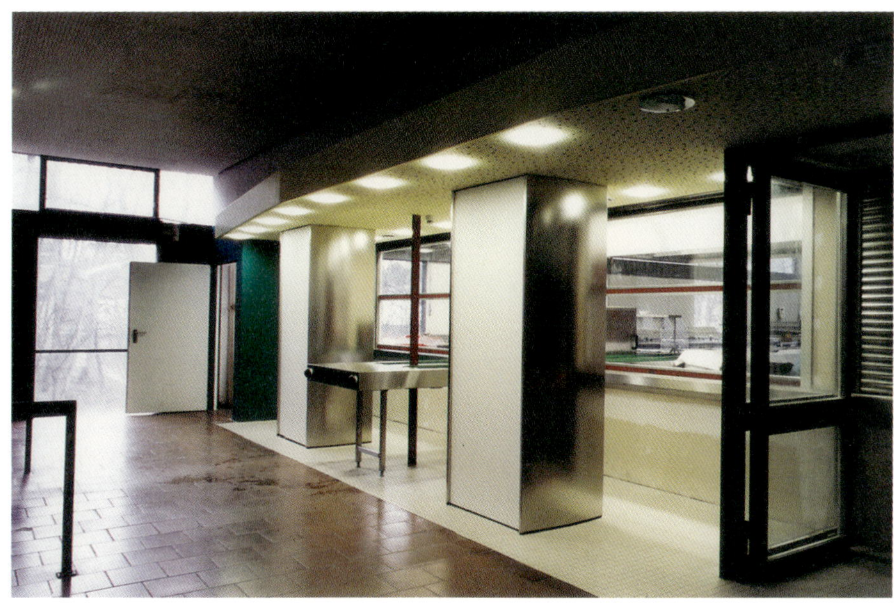

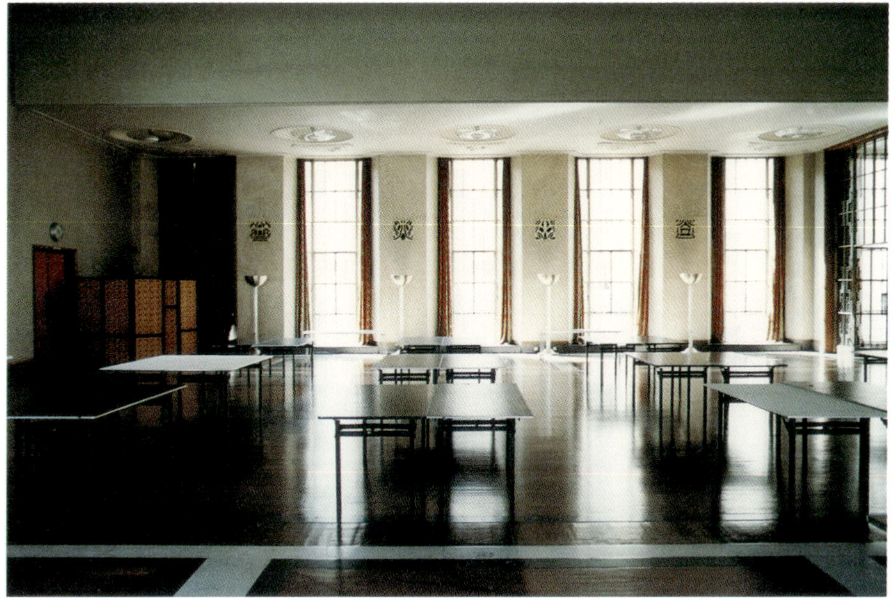

168 Kunsthaus, Zürich I, 1994 169 University Cafeteria, Karlsruhe 1998; RIBA London I, 1993

Heiner Schilling

Heiner Schilling's ongoing series, Entropic Forest, is a diary of his encounters with suburban Tokyo. His Becher-schooled visual perspicuity accompanies the hyper-surreal texts of urban designer and writer Hiroo Yamagata in monthly collaborative essays for the magazine *Space Design*.

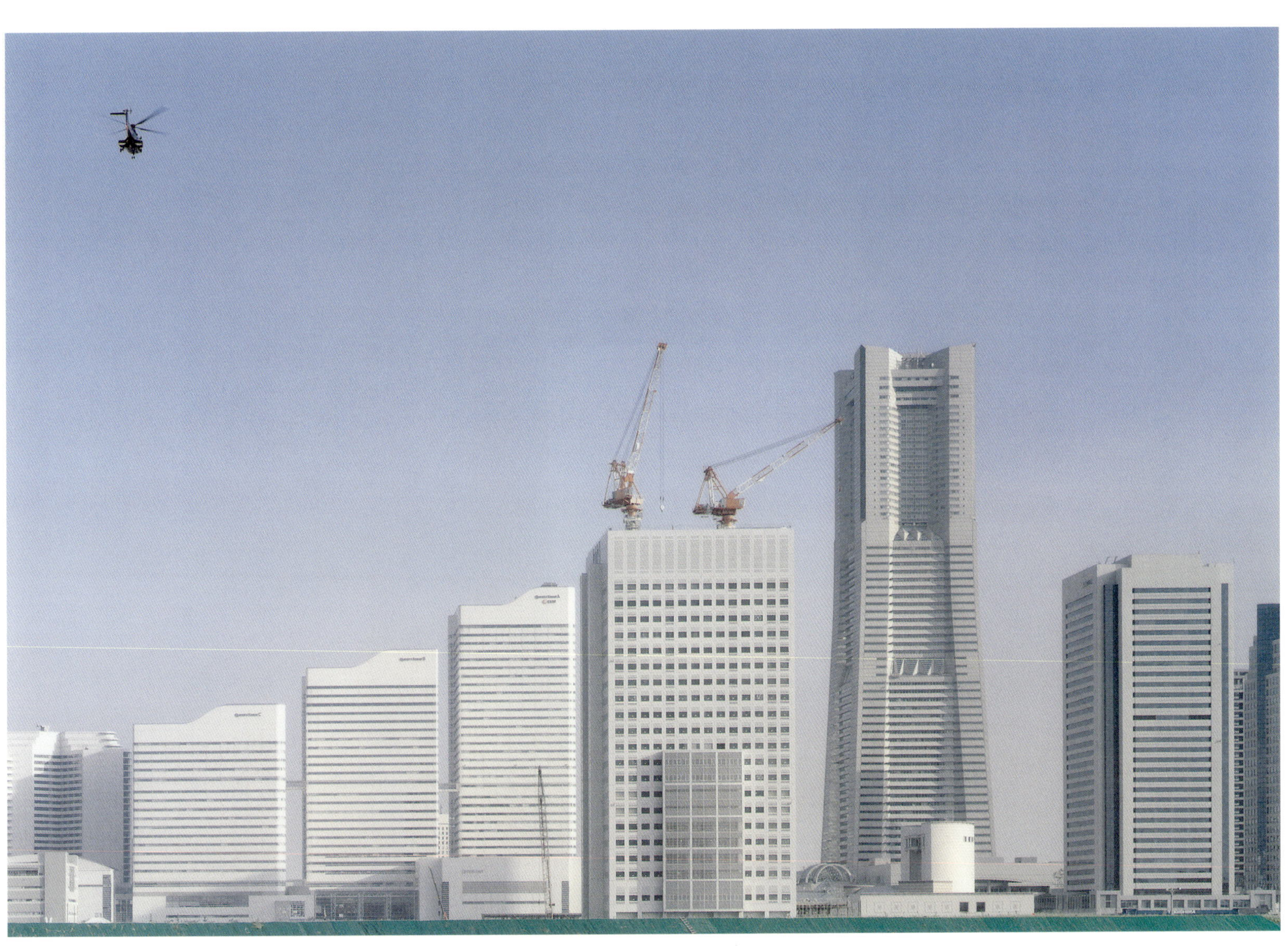

171 – 177 Entropic Forest

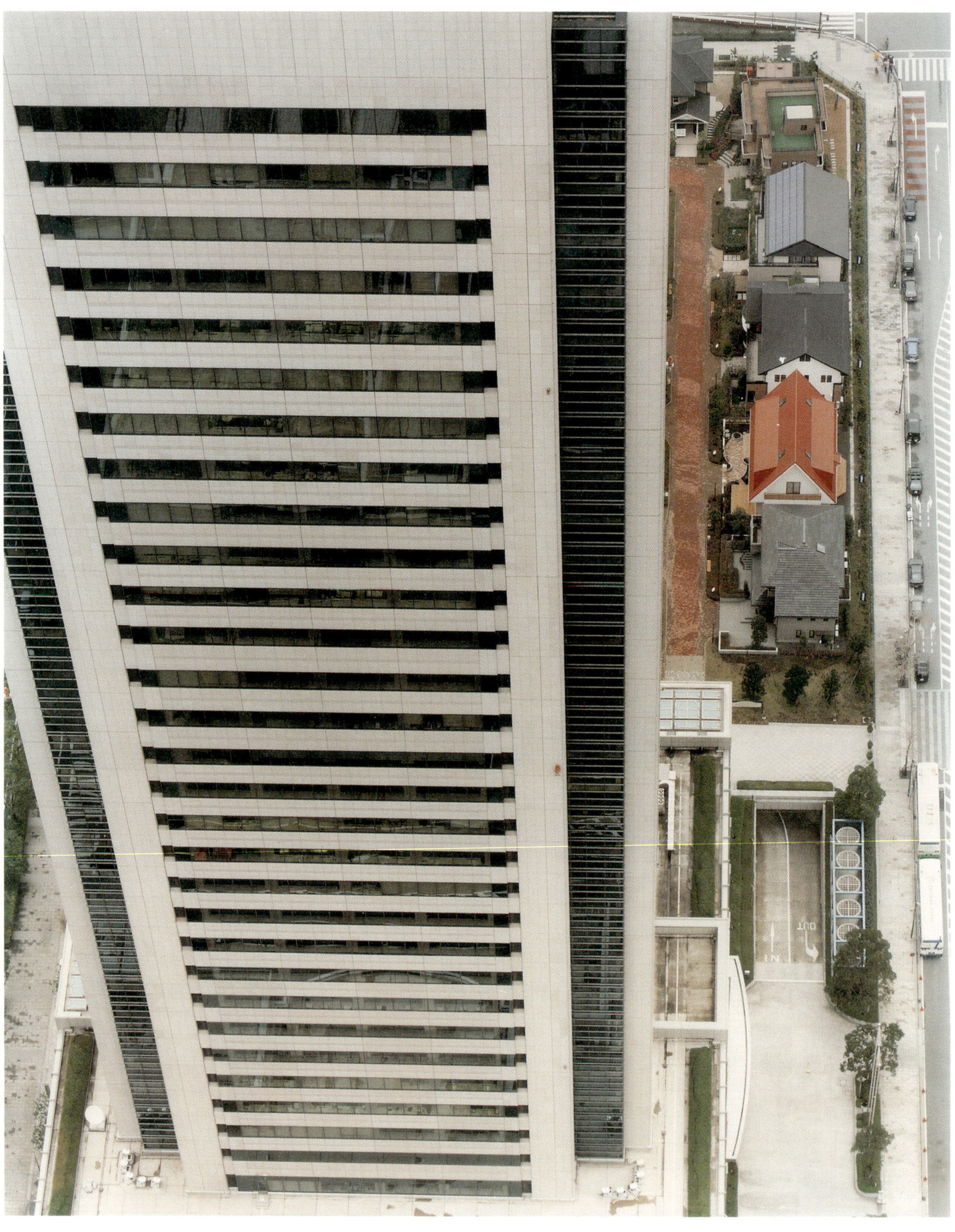

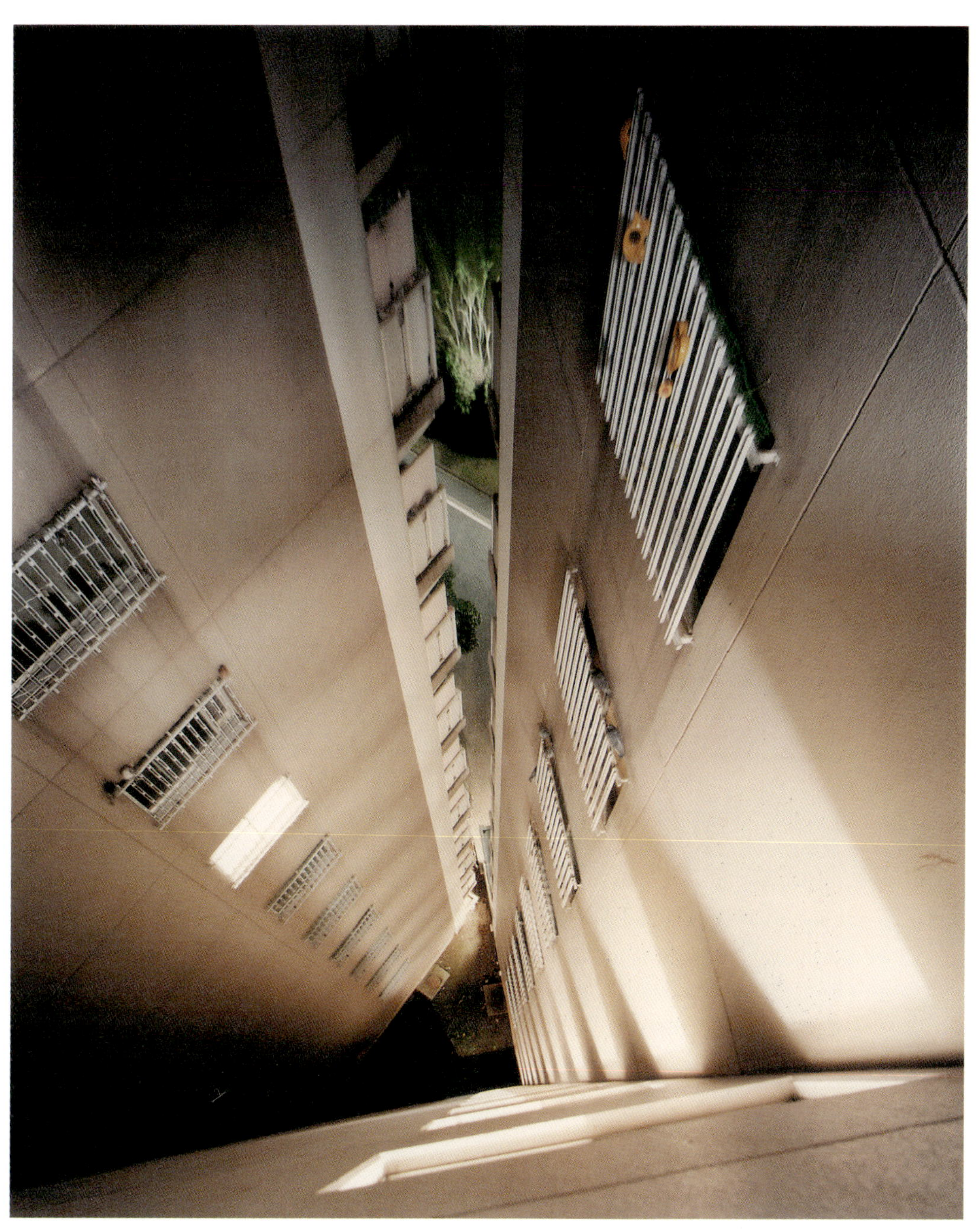

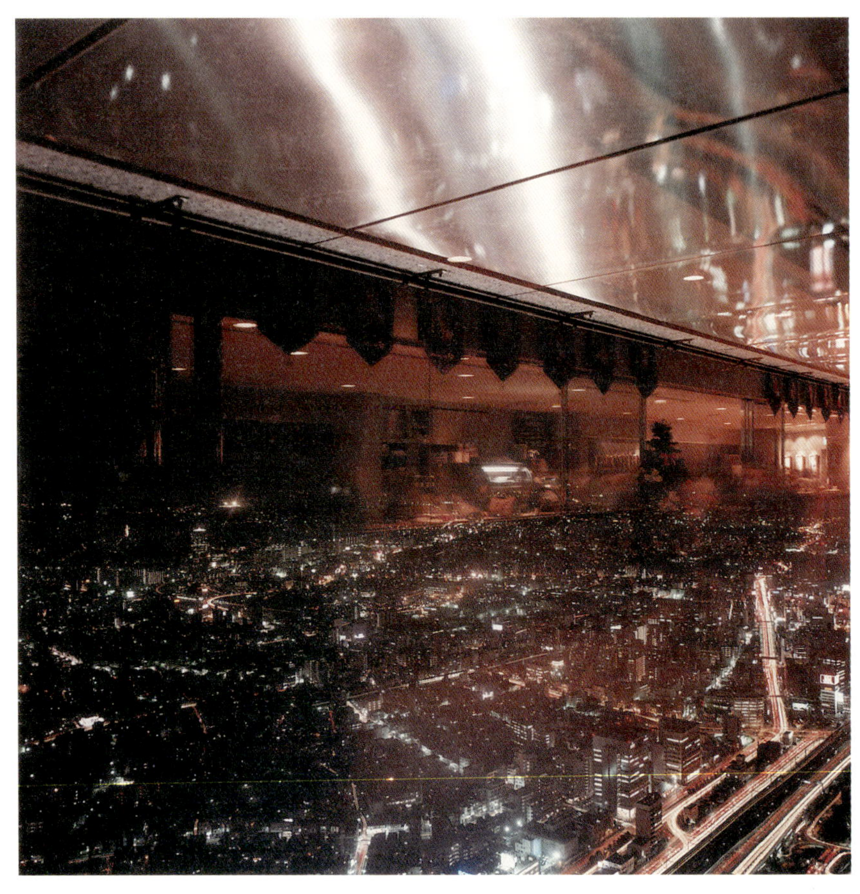

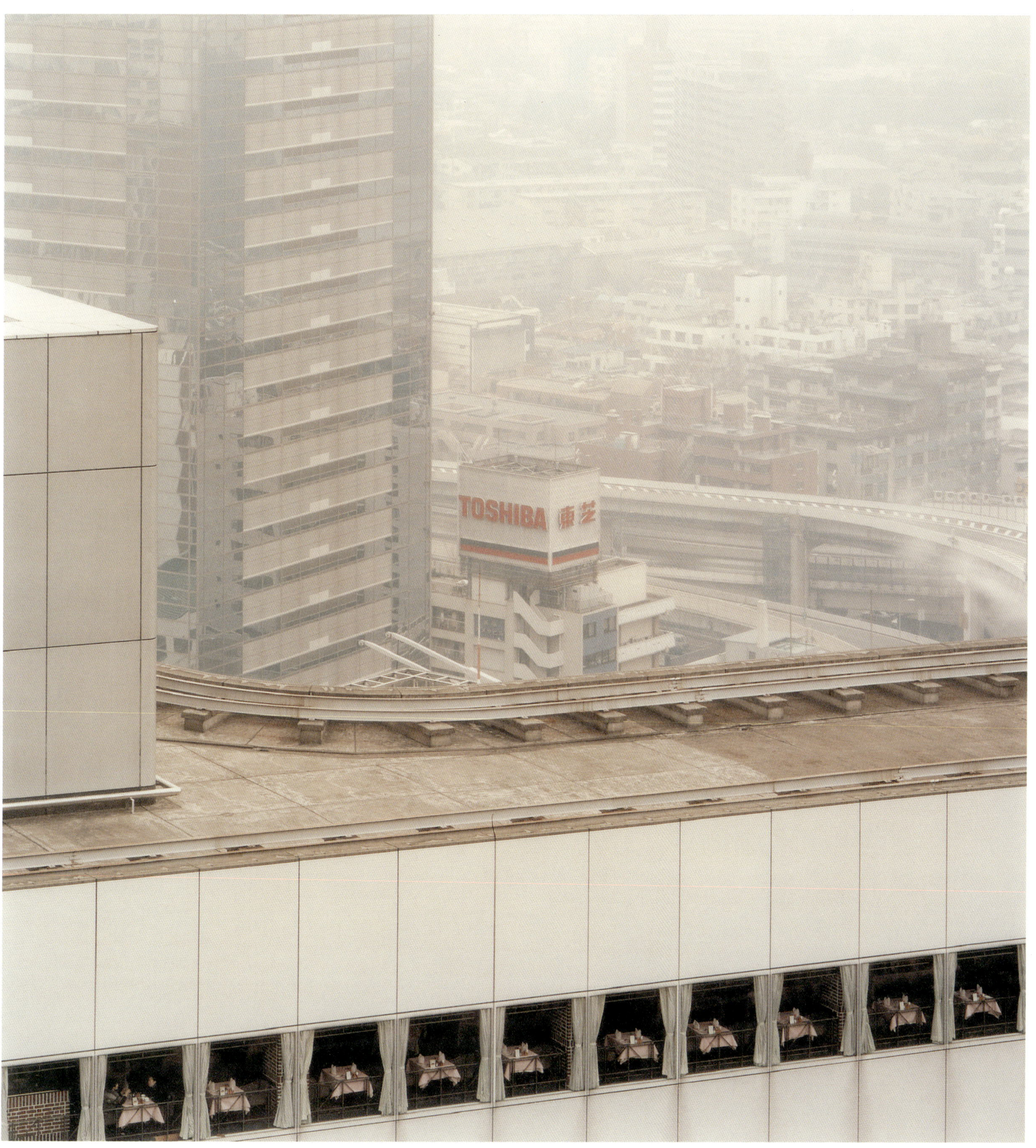
TOSHIBA 東芝

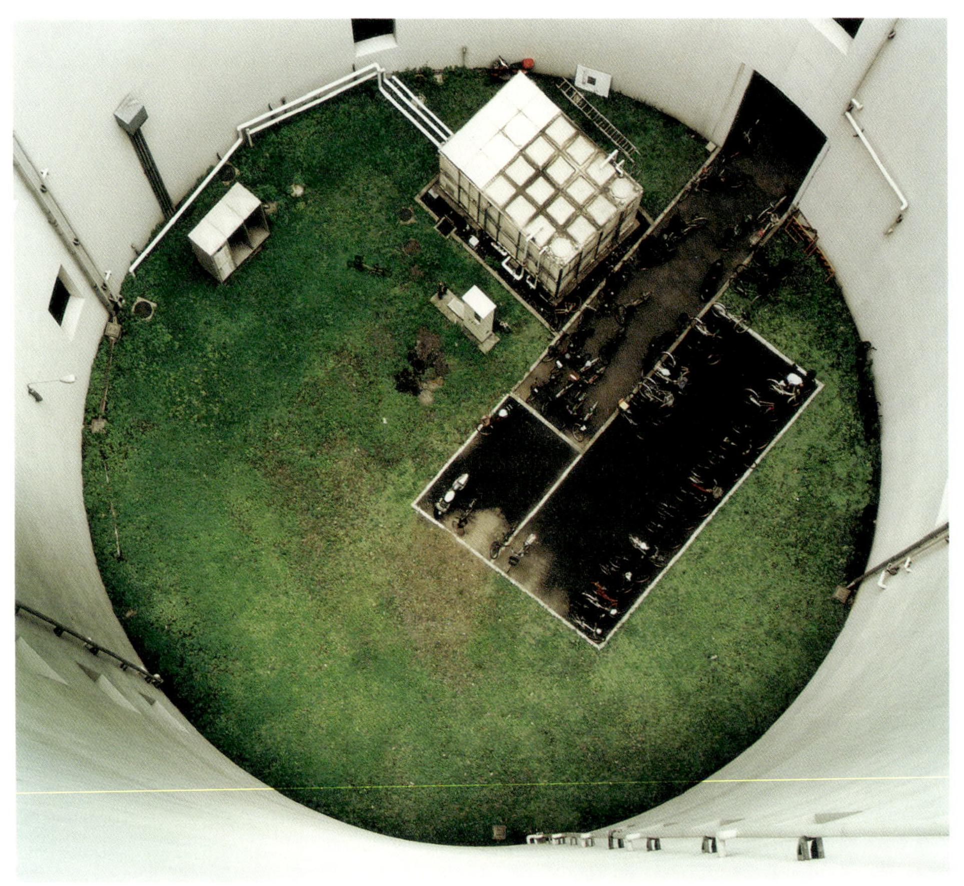

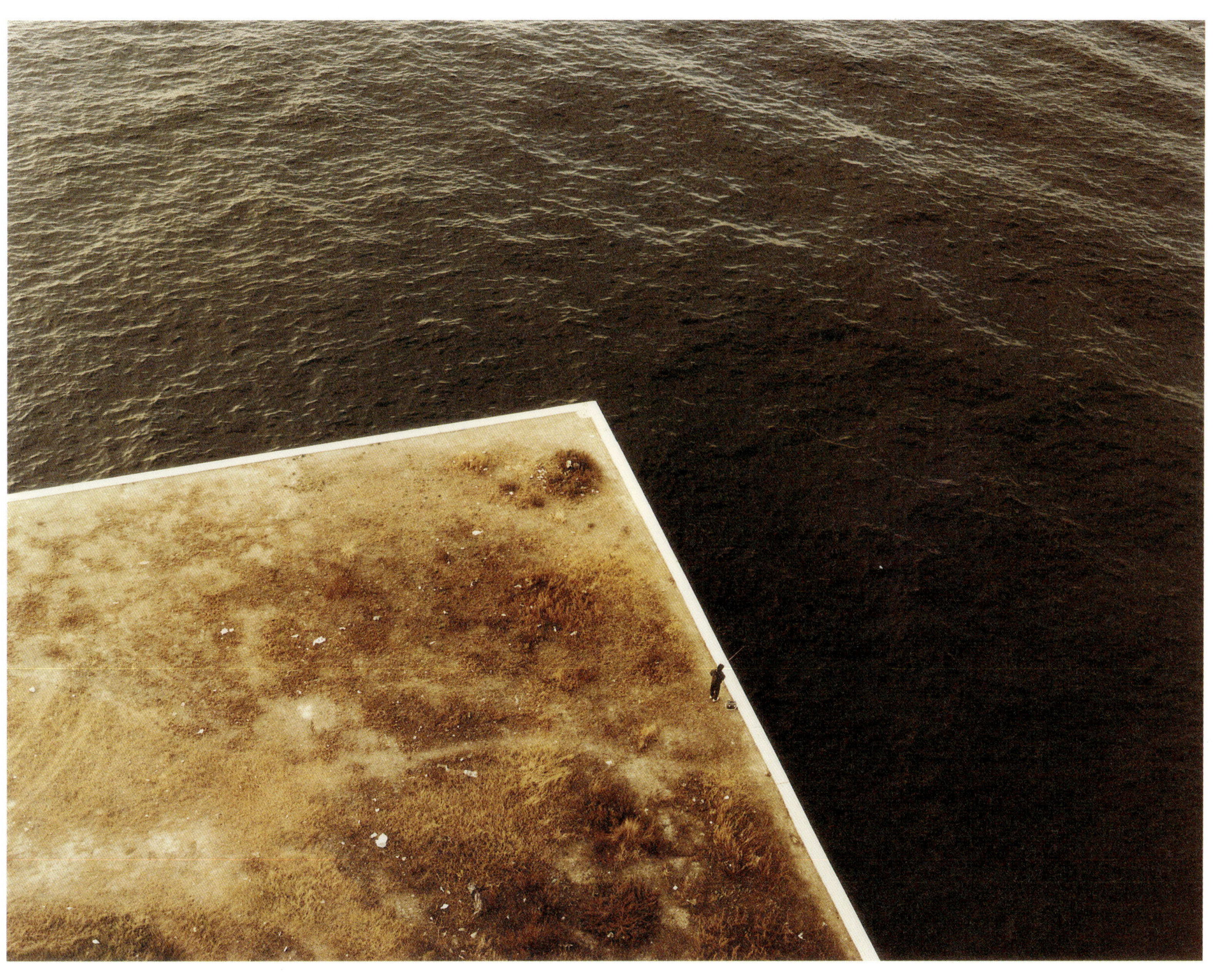

Petra Wunderlich has created a typology of the 'storefront' places of worship in New York's Manhattan and Brooklyn districts. The elevation perspective and absence of human figures establish a standardized context allowing the comparison of the architectural embodiment of each religion.

Petra Wunderlich

179 La Nouvelle Eglise H. Baptiser Bethlehem, Brooklyn, NY, 1998; The Gospel Tabernacle, Brooklyn, NY, 1998

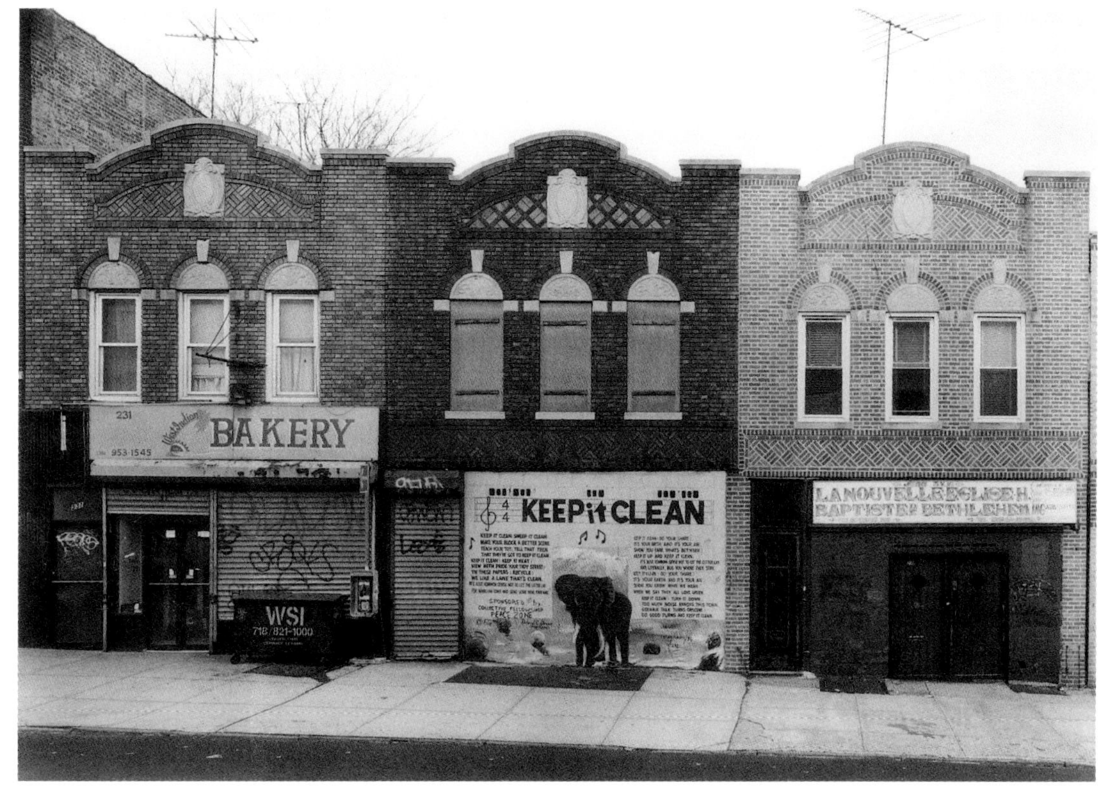

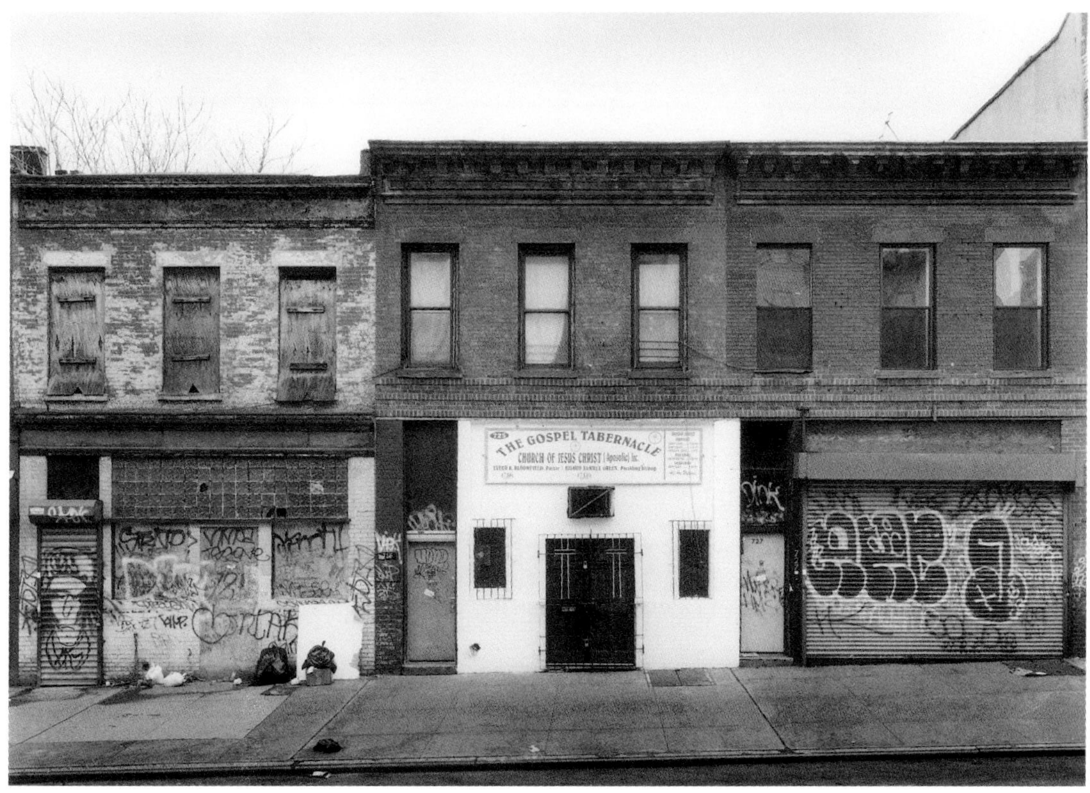

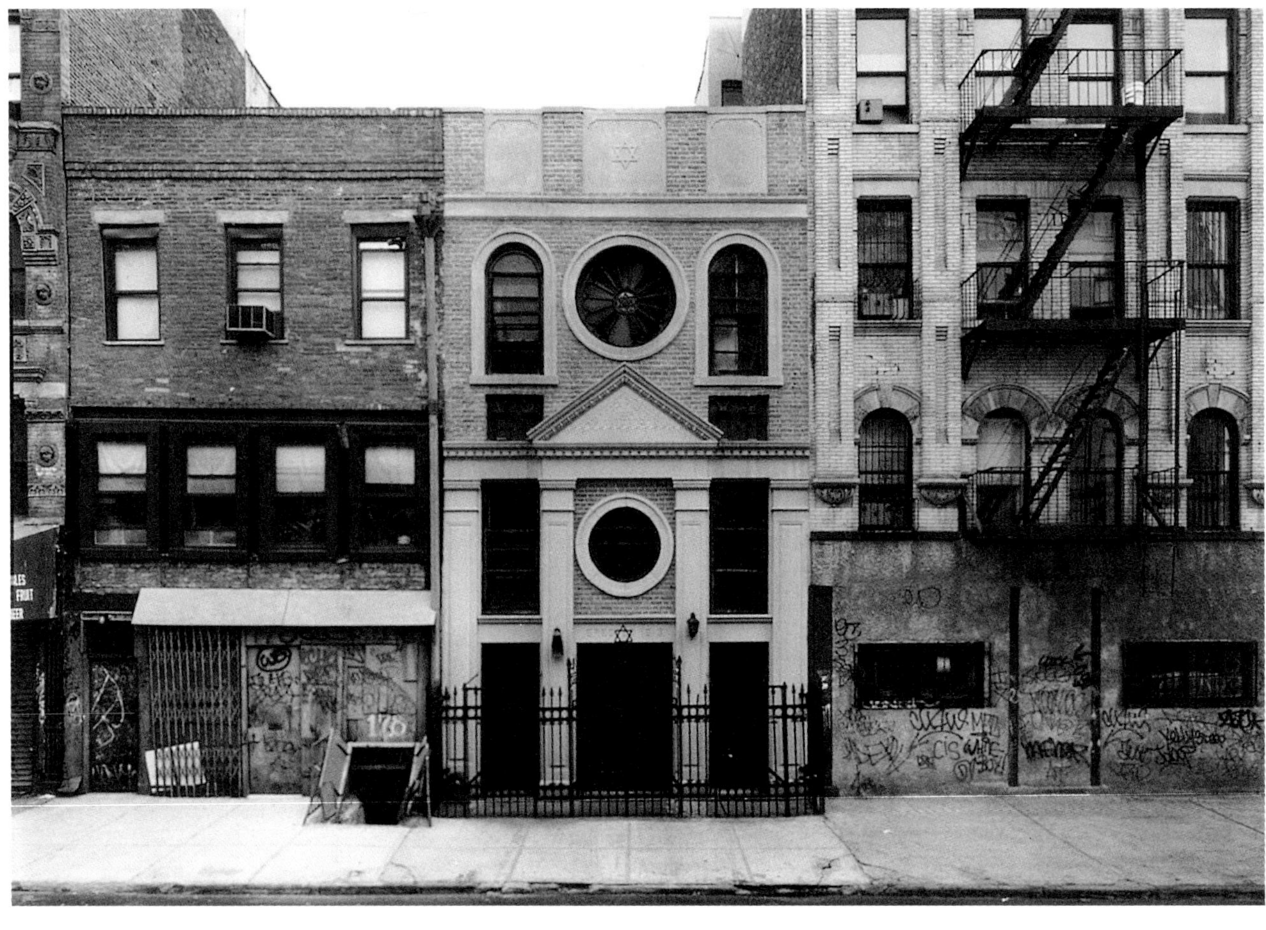

180 Cong. B'Nai Yaakov, NYC, 1995 181 Cong. Beth Hamedrash Hagodol, 1995

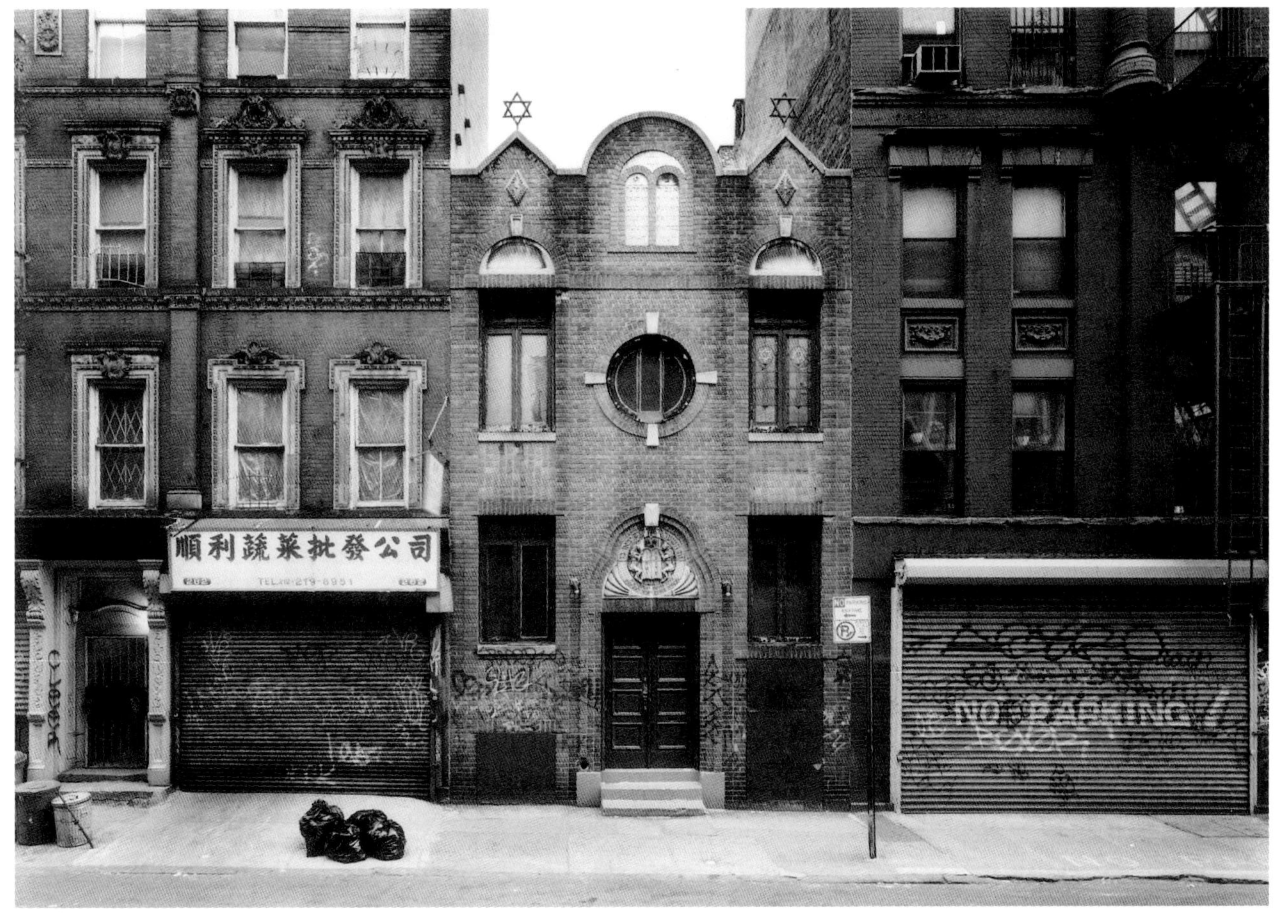

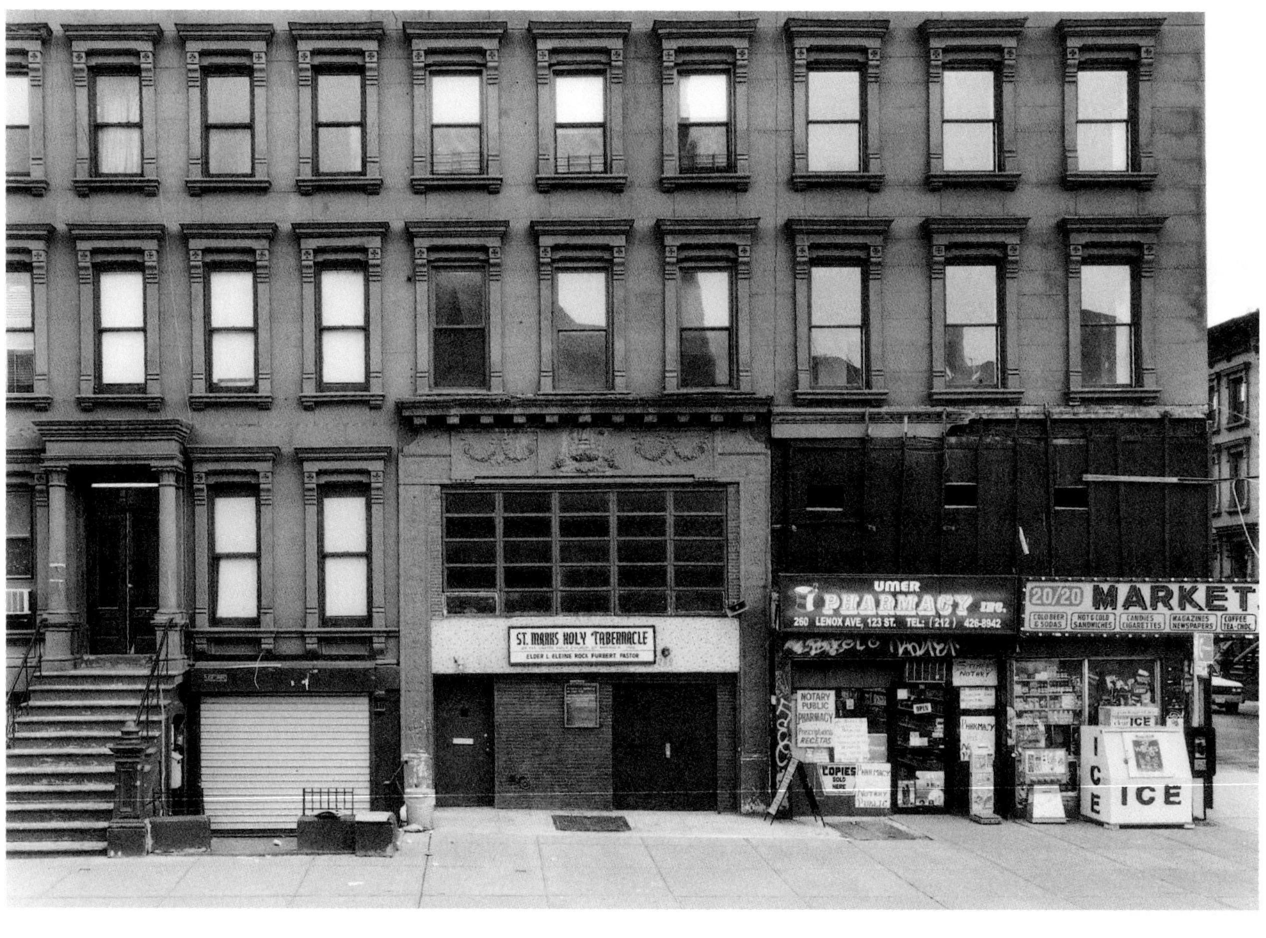
ST. MARKS HOLY TABERNACLE
ELDER L ELEINE ROCK FURBERT PASTOR
UMER
PHARMACY INC.
260 LENOX AVE, 123 ST. TEL: (212) 426-8942
20/20 MARKET
COLD BEER & SODAS
HOT & COLD SANDWICHES
CANDIES CIGARETTES
MAGAZINES NEWSPAPERS
COFFEE TEA-CHOC.
NOTARY PUBLIC
PHARMACY
RECETAS
COPIES SOLD HERE
ICE
ICE

182 St Mark's Holy Tabernacle, 1998 183 Greater Bibleway Temple, 1997

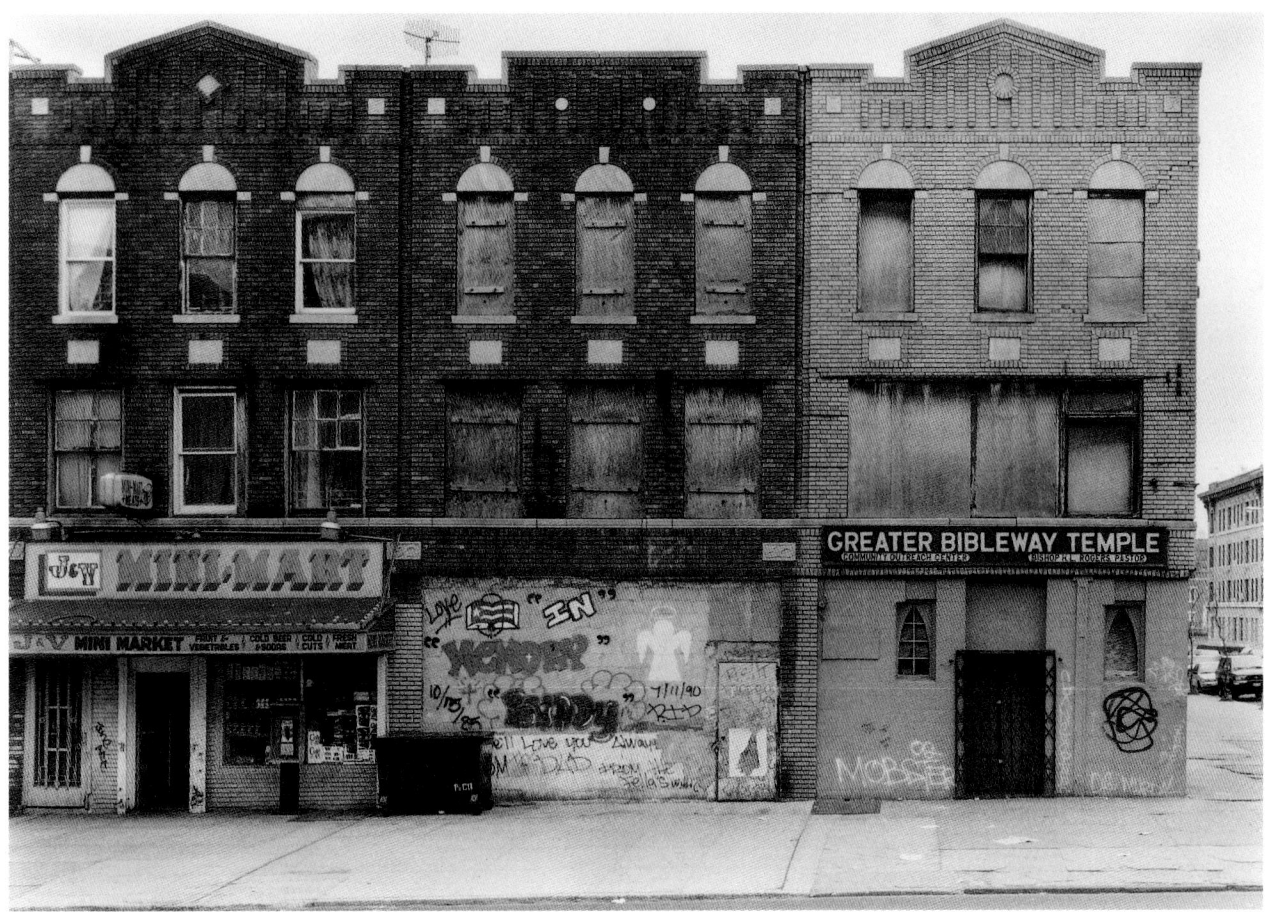

Thomas Ruff's early series of interiors were autobiographical in that they were photographs of his own locality. Like his early portrait series, they were an attempt to question the manner in which we perceive the people and objects around us. Since then his practice has included a range of mechanisms – including re-presenting newspaper images, digital manipulation, stereographic imagery and photomontage – which explore the nature of vision and the limitations of photography in mediating perception.

Thomas Ruff

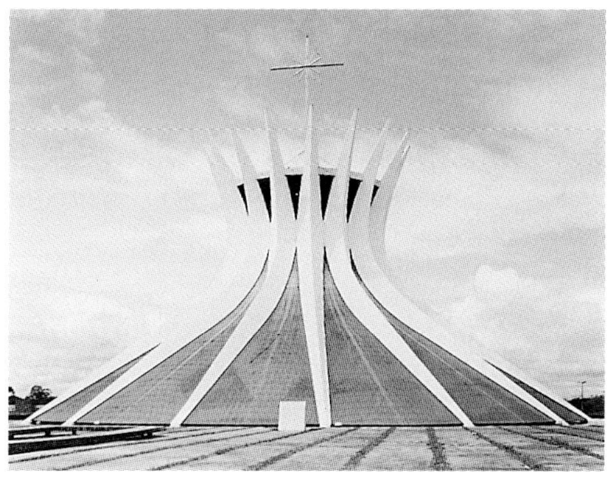

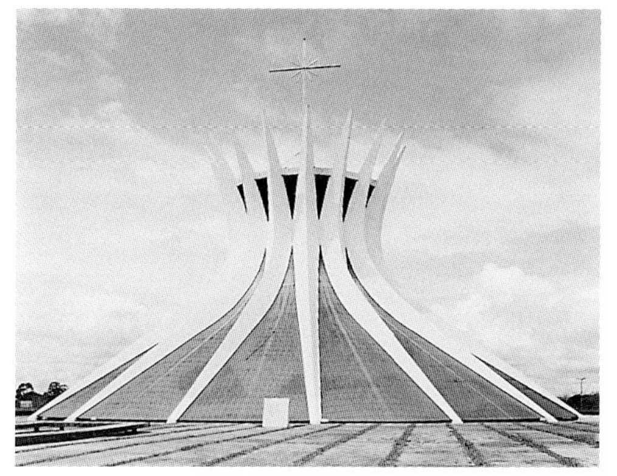

185 Church, Brasília, 1994

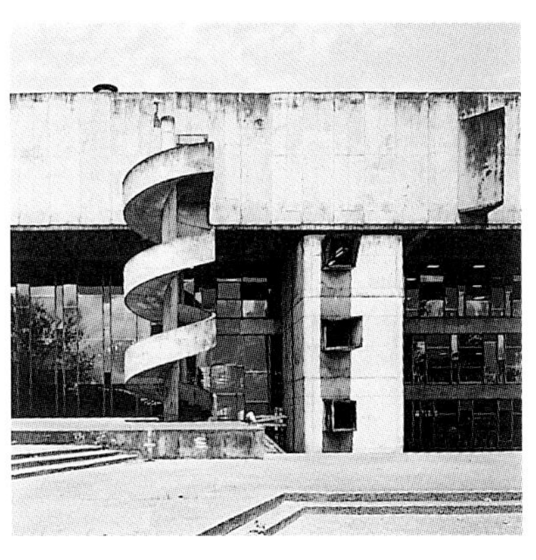

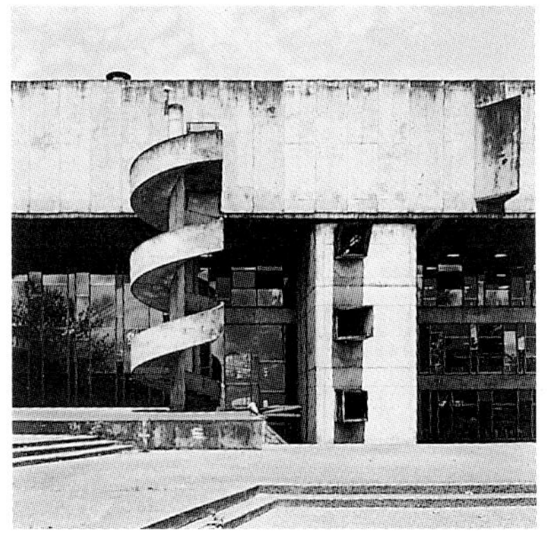

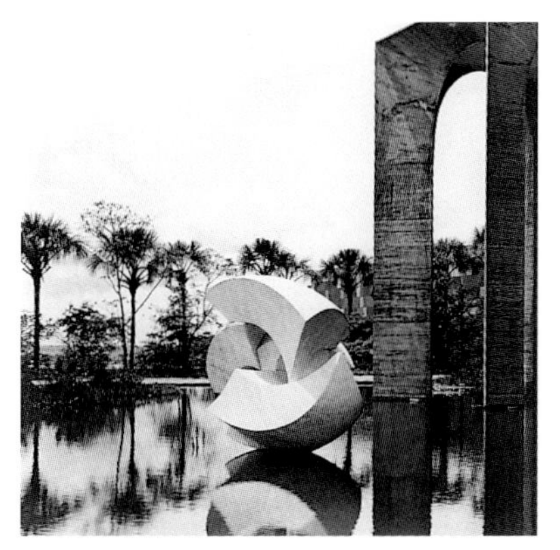

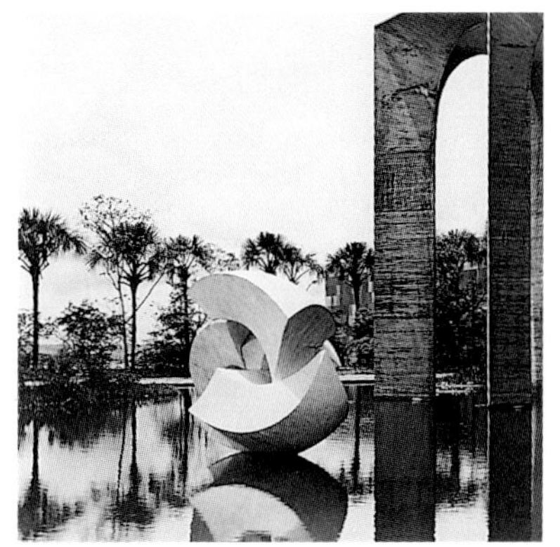

186 University, Brasília, 1994 187 Sculpture of the Five Continents, 1994

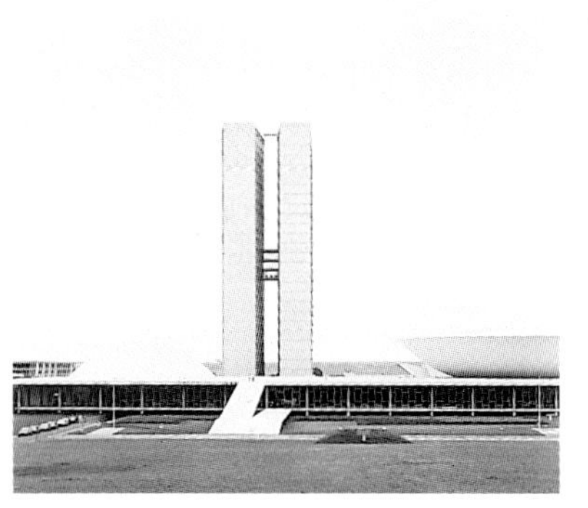

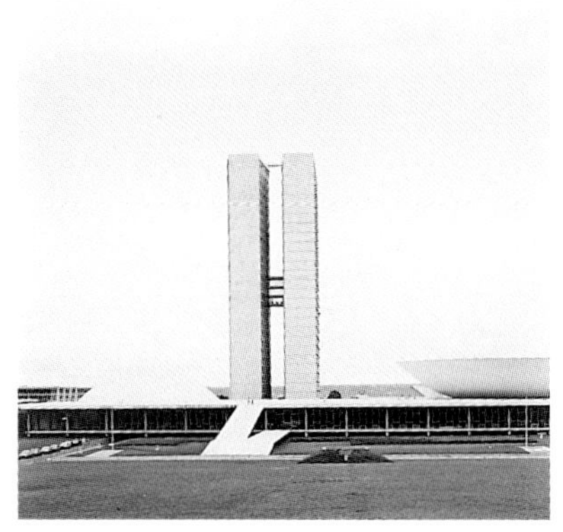

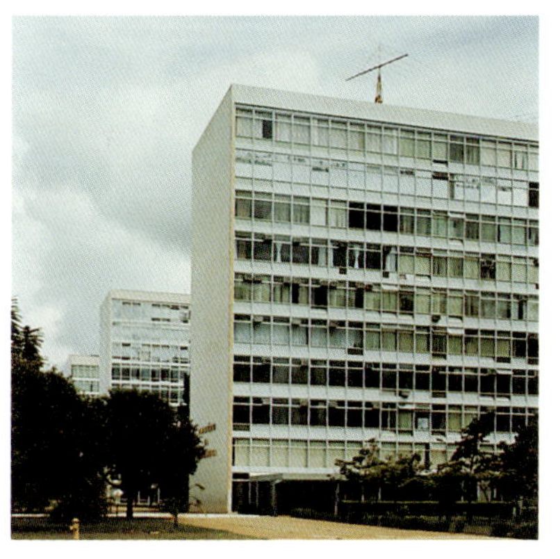

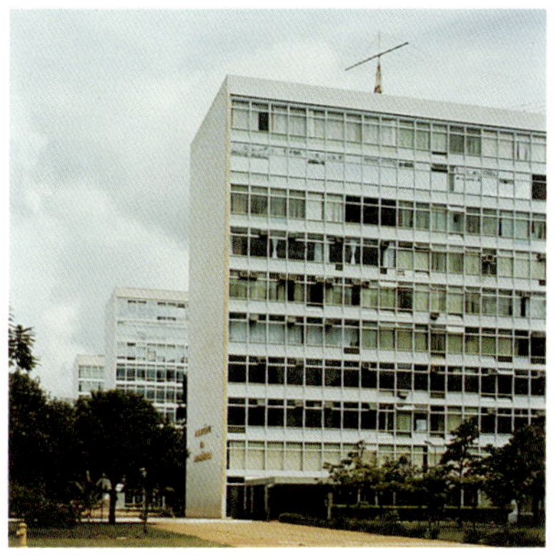

188 Congress I, Brasília, 1994 189 Ministry, Brasília, 1994

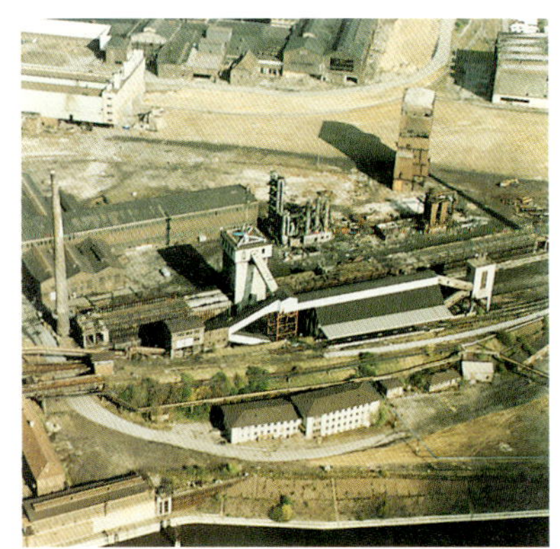

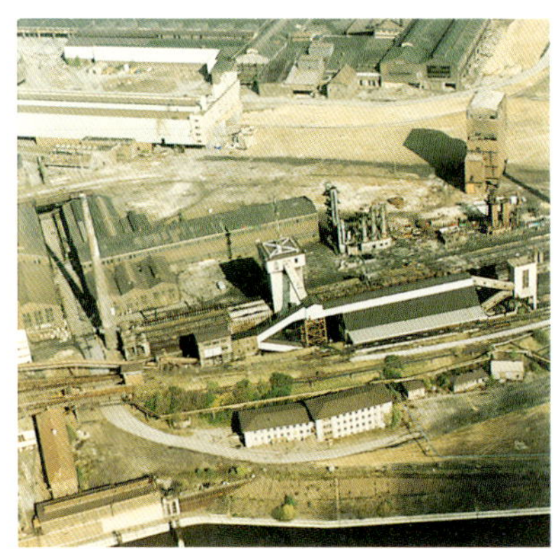

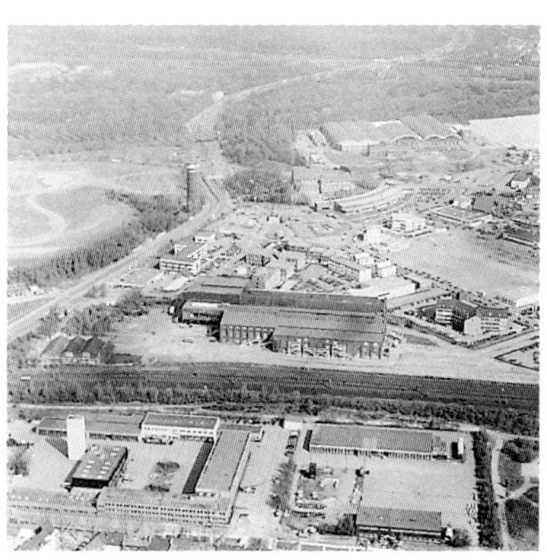
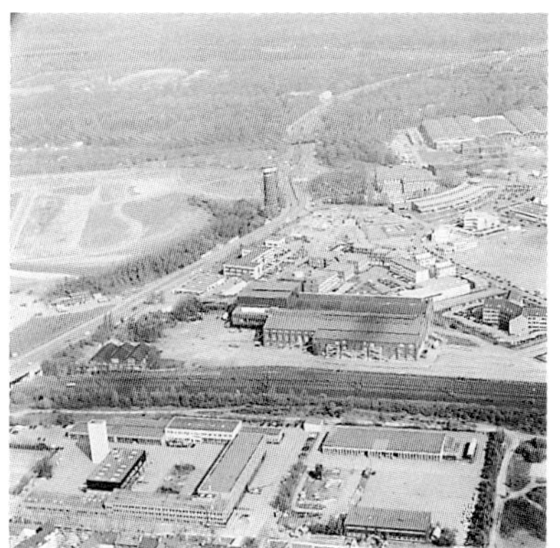

190 Ruhrgebiet I, 1996 191 Ruhrgebiet III, 1996

I am indebted to the artists who kindly allowed their work to be reproduced in this publication. Their involvement frequently went beyond supplying images and numerous conversations and exchanges added greatly to my research and facilitated an ever-broadening analysis of the ambit of this project. I could also not have completed this book without the assistance of numerous individuals who gave freely of their time and allowed me access to their wealth of material. In particular, conversations with Rolf Sachsse, Gerhard Stomberg, Alex de Rijke and Grainne Perkins were fundamental in the development of many of the ideas in this book. Thanks also to Antonio Homem, Barbara Honrath, James Lingwood, Gregorio Magnani, Bodo Niemann, Andrew Silewicz, Ronnie Simpson, Gerhard Steidl, Susan Stratton, Barbara Thumm and Anne Williams.

I am very grateful to Mohsen Mostafavi who supported this project from its inception. Thanks also to Andrew Mackenzie and Kate Jones in AA Exhibitions, and to everyone in the AA Print Studio, in particular Pamela Johnston, who bought to this book much needed patience and editorial insight.

Michael Mack

Bernd & Hilla Becher courtesy Sonnabend Gallery, New York.
Thomas Demand courtesy Victoria Miro Gallery, London.
Christine Erhard courtesy Galerie Bodo Niemann, Berlin.
Andreas Gursky courtesy Victoria Miro Gallery, London.
Candida Höfer courtesy Robert Prime Gallery, London.
Matthias Hoch courtesy Dogenhaus Galerie, Leipzig.
Gerhard Richter courtesy Städtische Galerie im Lenbachhaus, Münich.
Heidi Specker courtesy Galerie Barbara Thumm, Berlin.
Images on pages 28 and 31 courtesy Herzog & de Meuron, Basel.
Donald Judd image on page 23 courtesy Pace Wildenstein.